Alex Haley

THE PLAYBOY INTERVIEWS

EDITED WITH AN INTRODUCTION BY
MURRAY FISHER

ONE WORLD

Ballantine Books • New York

A One World Book published by Ballantine Books.

Copyright © 1962, 1963, 1964, 1965, 1966, 1967, 1968, 1976, 1977, 1979,
1990, 1992, 1993 by Playboy Enterprises, Inc.

Most of the contents of this work originally appeared
in *Playboy* Magazine, 1962–1992.

PLAYBOY is a mark of Playboy Enterprises, Inc. and is used with permission.

Excerpt from ROOTS by Alex Haley. Copyright © 1976 by Alex Haley. Published
by Doubleday, a division of Bantam Doubleday Dell Publishing Group, Inc.

Library of Congress Catalog Card Number: 92-93454

ISBN: 0-345-38300-1

Cover design by Kristine V. Mills
Cover photos: Malcolm X by Richard Saunders, Johnny Carson by
Jerry Yulsman, Miles Davis by Dennis Stock, Magnum Photos, Inc., Sammy
Davis, Jr. by George Rhodes, Martin Luther King, Jr. by Jay B. Leviton, Cassius Clay
by Jerry Yulsman, George Lincoln Rockwell by Vernon L. Smith
Manufactured in the United States of America

First Edition: July 1993

10 9 8 7 6 5 4 3 2 1

CONTENTS

INTRODUCTION BY MURRAY FISHER   vii

PLAYBOY INTERVIEW: MILES DAVIS (SEPTEMBER 1962)   3

PLAYBOY INTERVIEW: MALCOLM X (MAY 1963)   20

PLAYBOY INTERVIEW: CASSIUS CLAY (OCTOBER 1964)   46

PLAYBOY INTERVIEW: MARTIN LUTHER KING, JR.
(JANUARY 1965)   80

PLAYBOY INTERVIEW: MELVIN BELLI (JUNE 1965)   129

PLAYBOY INTERVIEW: GEORGE LINCOLN ROCKWELL
(APRIL 1966)   168

PLAYBOY INTERVIEW: SAMMY DAVIS, JR. (DECEMBER 1966)   212

PLAYBOY INTERVIEW: JOHNNY CARSON (DECEMBER 1967)   262

PLAYBOY INTERVIEW: JIM BROWN (FEBRUARY 1968)   304

ROOTS: THE MIXING OF THE BLOOD (OCTOBER 1976)   350

PLAYBOY INTERVIEW: ALEX HALEY (JANUARY 1977)   384

THERE ARE DAYS WHEN I WISH IT HADN'T HAPPENED
(MARCH 1979)   437

PLAYBOY INTERVIEW: QUINCY JONES (JULY 1990)   454

MALCOLM X REMEMBERED (JULY 1992)   489

INTRODUCTION

Had it only been fifteen years? The last time I'd sat here in a pew at the New Hope Church, early in 1977, the entire town of Henning, Tennessee, had turned out to honor its most celebrated citizen, who had just written a book called *Roots.* It seemed a lifetime ago, and now it was over. Along with all of those who knew and loved him best, I had returned to bury Alex Haley.

"He made history talk," said Jesse Jackson, sounding like the country preacher he liked to call himself. "He lit up the long night of slavery. He gave our grandparents personhood. He gave *Roots* to the rootless. He reconnected the human family." Alex's own family got up and spoke, too, each with their own very personal eulogy. But the most eloquent tribute came from Fred Montgomery, the elderly mayor of Henning and one of Alex's lifelong friends. Leaning unsteadily on his cane, Fred decided to *sing* his praises, and proceeded to pitch himself into a rafter-ringing spiritual so powerful and joyous that the entire congregation—including me—leaped up singing and clapping along with him. Alex would have loved it.

While George and Julius, his younger brothers, took

their turns in the pulpit, speaking of their pride in his accomplishments, I recalled Alex telling me that it hadn't always been that way. Their parents had been the first generation of Haleys to go to college, and they were determined that their children would grow up to amount to something. George had become a lawyer, Julius an architect, and Lois a music teacher but young Alex was a dreamer and a wanderer who wound up serving as a cook in the Coast Guard. To pass the time at sea, he read voraciously and earned pocket change writing love letters for his shipmates, like Cyrano. Inspired by the enthusiastic response they reported to him after returning from shore leave, he began submitting stories to true-confession magazines—but they were a harder sell. After four years and hundreds of mimeographed rejection slips, one of his manuscripts was finally returned with a handwritten note attached: "Nice try." Alex told me, "That was the most exciting day of my life. It was the only encouragement I'd ever received since the day I'd started writing four years before, but it was all I needed. I went back to work and four years later, I finally made a sale."

Mustering out after twenty years with the dream of becoming a professional writer, he moved to Greenwich Village, "prepared to starve." And he nearly did. Down to "eighteen cents and two cans of sardines," Alex received a small check from a magazine that enabled him to turn down a civil service job he'd just been offered. After serving his apprenticeship for men's adventure magazines, he soon graduated to *Reader's Digest, Saturday Evening Post* and finally, in 1962, to *Playboy,* which was already hitting its stride as an important national magazine.

Earlier that year, Hugh Hefner had told his editorial director, A. C. Spectorsky, that he'd like to launch a new monthly feature—the *Playboy Interview*—and asked him to have one of his editors rummage around for publishable material in the inventory of *Show Business Illustrated,* an ambitious but unsuccessful magazine he'd just been forced to fold. With the exception of the erudite dialogues that appeared regularly in *The Paris Review* and the "Impolite Interviews" of *The Realist,* an irreverent counterculture journal published by Paul Krassner, there was no Q&A of any consequence in American journalism at the time, certainly not in a mass-market magazine. And none as hot or hard-hitting as the unfinished transcript of a conversation I unearthed from the files and recommended to Spectorsky. It was an interview with Miles Davis, memorable less for his insights into jazz than for his scalding observations about white racism in America. It was explosive stuff, but I wanted more, so I called up the interviewer and asked him to go back for another session. Better him than me. In order to disarm his subject's notorious hostility to reporters, he volunteered as a sparring partner at Miles's gym and stepped into the ring with him for a couple of rounds. Two weeks later he walked into my office and emptied a half dozen audiocassettes from his briefcase. That was my introduction to Alex Haley. The resulting interview, published in September 1962, stirred a hornet's nest of controversy, and set the tone for those that followed.

After bagging a quarry as tough as Miles, I figured Alex might be ready to take on his next assignment: the fiery minister of the Nation of Islam, Malcolm X. True to his testy reputation, Malcolm ran Alex through a gauntlet of distrust—taunting him for being a lackey of "the white press," suspecting him of being wiretapped by the government—before surrendering reluctantly to what grew slowly into a warm rapport. Malcolm expressed amazement that *Playboy* dared to publish his interview in May 1963— and it *was* strong medicine, seething with rage at the "white devils"—but Hefner strongly supported the decision to run it without expurgation. The readers responded, for the most part, with shock and outrage, but the whole idea of the interview was to provoke debate by publishing even views we found abhorrent.

One of the readers who reacted most strongly to what Malcolm had to say was Ken McCormick, the editor-in-chief at Doubleday, who felt there was a book in it and asked Malcolm to tell his life story to Alex Haley. The rest is literary history, but for Grove Press, not Doubleday, whose owners got cold feet and backed out after reading the manuscript. I had volunteered to help Alex edit the book for publication, and when Malcolm had seen my handwriting in the margins, he demanded to know who I was and what I wanted. "How much are you paying him?" he asked Alex. "Not a penny," said Alex. "He's doing this as a friend." "A censor, you mean," said Malcolm. "Read it," said Alex, and Malcolm fell silent to read a few pages of my editing. "He's not trying to water it down. He's making it better." "That's right," said Alex. Malcolm thought about all this for a minute and said finally, "So where's his name going to appear, over yours and mine on the cover?" Alex said, "He doesn't want any billing either." That was the last thing either one said about it, but about a year later, while Malcolm was traveling in the Middle East during his period of spiritual rebirth, I received a postcard from him in Mecca: "The friendship of people like yourself gives me hope that black and white can learn to live in peace." Ten months later he was assassinated.

It was while Malcolm was still abroad, in the summer of 1964, that I assigned Alex to interview Cassius Clay for *Playboy*. Though he hadn't yet changed his name to Muhammad Ali, Clay had just defeated Sonny Liston for the heavyweight championship and the next day announced his conversion to the Black Muslim faith. Apparently undaunted by his friend's deepening rift with Muslim "Messenger" Elijah Muhammad, he had invited Malcolm and his wife Betty to Miami for the fight. Each man liked the other's style, and Alex had seen both in action—Malcolm in his second-hand sedan, Cassius in his chauffeur-driven limo—both princes of the city as they rode the streets of Harlem. Clay's interview, published in October 1964, provoked another storm of reader mail, some of it from racists who began to see *Playboy*'s interviews as part of an international conspiracy of pinkos against the white race.

Their suspicions must have been confirmed by my next assignment to Alex: Dr. Martin Luther King, Jr. Anticipating that Reverend King might have problems reconciling his Baptist faith with the nude photographs in *Playboy,* I armed Alex with the magazine's impressive sales figures—more than three million at that time—and he regaled King's advisors with a demographic breakdown of the readership: college-educated young men and women, "the very constituency that was most vital to King's interests, for anyone with a cause. Think what you will about the girls, but you can't ignore the audience." They were convinced.

But Alex's problems began after approval had been granted, because King's schedule made it next to impossible even for a conventional interview, let alone one like *Playboy*'s that would require many hours of taping. After a succession of frustrating cancellations, and three trips to Atlanta, he still hadn't met the man, and most interviewers would have given up. But Alex had taken pains to befriend King's secretary, and finally he threw himself on her mercy. He couldn't face his editor empty-handed again, he told her, and she sent him to a church barbecue King was attending. "Let him see you there, but don't press," she advised. He did as he was told, sitting there with a paper plate of chicken and potato salad until King finally took pity on him and came over to say hello, suggesting that they might talk for a few minutes over in his office.

Their little chat stretched late into the night, and then again for longer sessions over the next few weeks while Alex was working with Malcolm X correcting the manuscript for *The Autobiography*. Though they were bitter enemies in public, they were privately fascinated with one another, and even after the King interview was published in January 1965—the longest he ever granted—King kept asking Alex what "Brother Malcolm" was saying about him. Malcolm, in turn, used to say that it took somebody like him to make Martin sound moderate.

At the opposite end of the racial spectrum—the extreme right—was Alex's most bizarre experience as an interviewer: his April 1966 encounter with American Nazi *führer* George Lincoln Rockwell. By assigning Alex to the job, I had hoped to provoke the malicious Rockwell into a personal confrontation that would expose his lunatic racism for what it was. It exceeded even my wildest expectations. Alex called to request the interview, and was asked pointedly if he was Jewish. Alex said no—"but I didn't tell them I was black." When he stepped out of his cab at Nazi headquarters in Arlington, Virginia, Rockwell's "storm troopers" were stunned and outraged, but ushered him past Doberman watchdogs and swastika flags into the inner sanctum where Rockwell stood waiting dramatically beneath a portrait of Adolf Hitler. Greeting him without a smile or handshake, the "Commander" ushered him into a seat, placed a pearl-handled revolver pointedly on the armrest of his chair and began with the all-time classic opening to a *Playboy Interview*. Nothing personal, he said, but "I don't mix with your kind, and we call your race niggers." Said Alex amiably, without missing a beat, "I've been called nigger many times, Commander, but this is the first time I'm being paid for it. So you go right ahead." It was the beginning of a beautiful relationship. By the time they had finished sparring verbally throughout this astonishing interview, it was obvious that he had earned Rockwell's grudging respect, and the Nazi leader began corresponding with Alex—addressing him with letters inscribed "Alex Haley, VIN [Very Important Nigger]" and filled with open envy of his globe-trotting life-style as a *Playboy* interviewer. In a morbid footnote, one year after his interview was published, Rockwell became Alex's third *Playboy Interview* subject to become the victim of an assassin's bullet.

"When the word got around," said Alex wryly, "it became a bit difficult to line up new interviews." Not really. As a matter of fact, it became something of a coup among the celebrities we interviewed to draw Alex as their interviewer, not only because he was becoming something of a celebrity himself but because of the kind of interviews he did, and the kind of man he was. Stars are understandably wary with journalists, but without exception, Alex's subjects have called his interviews the best—the fullest, the fairest, the most revealing—that have ever been done with them. And many became lifelong friends. Melvin Belli (June 1965) still calls him "a very remarkable man, one of the gentlest, kindest, most decent guys I've ever met." He was so close to Sammy Davis Jr. (December 1966) that his widow Altovise and son Manny turned to Alex for company and comfort in the difficult months following Sammy's death in 1990. Even the press-shy Johnny Carson (December 1967) opened up to Alex's simple warmth, and many years later, on the night he appeared as Johnny's guest on the "Tonight" show after the publication of *Roots,* the unflappable host was moved to tears by Alex's surprise presentation of a genealogical chart of the Carson family all the way back to England in the 1700s. "I'll never forget it," Carson told me last fall. "It's still sitting behind me right here in my study." Alex's final assignment in the Sixties was his outspoken interview with football great and action hero Jim Brown (February 1968). Not easily impressed, Brown remembers Alex as a man worthy of his trust for the way in which he conducted the interview, and worthy of respect for his immortalization of Malcolm X in the *Autobiography,* which was already considered required reading among serious students of black history.

Alex was soon to make history himself. He had an idea for a second book and asked me to help him with it. As a little boy, he had sat behind his grandmother Cynthia's rocking chair on her front porch in Henning, Tennessee, while she and the other old ladies told stories about the family. They talked about Cynthia's grandfather, he told me, a colorful gamecock trainer known as "Chicken George," who returned home from his travels as a freedman after Emancipation with tales about Tennessee, a "promised land" with soil so rich that "if you planted a pig's tail, a hog'll grow." And the old ladies talked about Chicken George's son Tom Murray, who had led his wife and eight children to a new life in Henning from the plantation in Alamance County, North Carolina, where they'd lived as slaves. With the birth of each new child, Tom had recited the stories Chicken George had told him about his mother Kizzy, and *her* mother, a "big-house" cook named Bell. But for Alex, the most fascinating and mysterious character of all was Kizzy's father, a man they called "the African."

The "furthest-back person" in the entire family history, the African told Kizzy that he had been out in the forest one day, not far from his native village, chopping wood to make himself a drum, when he had been set upon by four men, beaten, chained and kidnapped into slavery. He said that he'd been brought across the ocean to a place called 'Naplis, that his foot had been cut off after a fourth attempt to run away from the plantation of his first owner, that he had rejected his slave name Toby and insisted on being called by his real name, which he pronounced "Kin-tay." When Kizzy was growing up, he had also taught her bits and pieces of his native language that she passed along to George, who passed them along to his son Tom, whose daughter Cynthia had passed them along to Alex.

That unbroken chain of memory was a priceless repository, and possibly also unique, Alex told me, because as far as he knew, there were no black families in America who could trace their lineage that far back. If he could find some way to decipher those scraps of words, he might be able to open the door to his own past by enabling him to trace "Kin-tay" back to Africa. If he was successful, he would also rediscover the past for 25 million other black Americans. He would be able to reclaim the rich cultural heritage that slavery took away from them, along with their names and their identities.

From that day on, Alex was a man possessed, embarked on a quest that took him hundreds of thousands of miles across three continents in an extraordinary search for his own origins. At the feet of a tribal griot—or oral historian—in a thatch-hut village four days upriver from the coast of Gambia, West Africa, he learned that a fifth-generation ancestor of the most distinguished family in that village, the Kinte clan, had been "out in the forest chopping wood one day—and was never seen again." From old shipping records and cargo manifests, Alex found out the name of the actual ship that carried that 17-year-old boy, Kunta Kinte, to America, and the very day it docked in Annapolis: September 15, 1767. And on the 200th anniversary of that date, Alex was standing on the pier gazing out to sea, trying to recapture the moment of Kunta's arrival in *toubabo-koumi*, the legendary land of white cannibals to which many of his terrified shipmates were sure they were being taken.

This was priceless material, but the research went on and on, for years on end. Alex felt he would never have enough to do the story justice, and he was tormented with a sense of inadequacy to the task he had set for himself. He even stripped down to his shorts and slept for several nights on the raw planks in the hold of a freighter on the high seas to immerse himself in the anguish his ancestor must have felt as he lay chained in the slave ship. He finally captured it with searing eloquence. But Kunta Kinte hadn't even reached America and the book was already five years late. Reassuring the publisher that it would take him only six more months to wrap it up, Alex pried loose enough expense money to keep going and plunged onward. On shipboard and planes, in hideaways from San Francisco to the West Indies, he led the publisher on a merry chase for the next three years—with the last 200 pages going directly from his desk to the typesetter after the book was already in galleys. From beginning to end, the entire project had taken twelve years of Alex's life. And no small portion of my own: I had left *Playboy* in 1974 to devote my full time to helping Alex finish. Alex's wife, My, and his lifelong friend and researcher, George Sims, were equally devoted.

Even then we knew that this book was special, that it would make a mark. But we weren't prepared for what happened from the day it appeared in the nation's bookstores. *Roots* shot straight to the top of the bestseller charts, and when the twelve-hour miniseries based on the book aired for eight nights in January of 1977, it became a national phenomenon. Theaters and restaurants that week stood empty while 130 million people stayed home to watch, and book sales escalated to more than 5.5 million copies in hardcover and paperback. Adulation poured in from critics all over the world—it was ultimately published in 37 languages—and at least one reviewer called it "among the most important books of the century." Another wrote: "It forever altered America's perceptions of itself and its past." *Playboy* published a riveting advance excerpt from the book (reproduced here as "The Mixing of the Blood") in October of 1976, and three months later, Alex became the only *Playboy* interviewer ever to become the subject of a *Playboy Interview*—with me as his interviewer. We knew the topic, and each other, so well by then that we could have done it in our sleep, and after years of working on the book around the clock, we almost did. But of all the interviews ever published, it became the magazine's sentimental favorite.

Alex won the Pulitzer Prize that year, the first among a list of honorary awards and academic degrees that filled the walls of his study and then began accumulating in closets. He was the most famous author in the world, adored and besieged every time he went out in public, embraced by strangers who wanted to thank him for what he'd done. Alex basked in all that warmth, but somewhere along the way he lost something more than his privacy. "I wish I could be famous one day a month," he told me. He was fond of saying in interviews that his family wasn't just his anymore: "They belong to everyone now." But from then on, so did Alex. To finance the writing of *Roots*, he had spent ten years talking about it on the lecture circuit, but his speaking schedule doubled and tripled in its wake. For years afterward he spoke to an average of 5000 people a day in cities around the world, sleeping mostly in catnaps en route, often being awakened in the middle of the night by well-wishers rapping at the door of his motel. Some of them wanted money. Others claimed to be long-lost relatives. And several people, authors of less successful books about slavery and plantation life, started suing him.

"There Are Days When I Wish It Hadn't Happened," Alex's mordant reflection on the high price of fame, published in March 1979, was the only piece he had time to write for *Playboy* for the next 11 years. In July of 1990, he came out of retirement as the magazine's premiere interviewer and reminded us how it was done in a richly textured conversation with his old friend Quincy Jones. And his final contribution to the magazine, in July of 1992, was "Malcolm X Remembered," a moving memoriam to the subject of his first book. It was also Alex's last piece of published writing, written during the production of Spike Lee's monumental epic of Malcolm's life, which was based on the *Autobiography*. In the wake of the hit movie, it seems a fitting tribute to both Malcolm and Alex that their collaboration is selling more copies now than it did when it was published 27 years ago—more than a million in 1992 alone.

Until the end, Alex kept taking long freighter cruises in search of the solitude and serenity to write. He would cart along two heavy satchels, one filled with research, the other with half-drafted book manuscripts he always planned to finish in "four to six months." But except for *A Different Kind of Christmas*, a short coda to *Roots* published in 1988, he never did. We had spent the last few months outlining a massive sequel to *Roots* called *The Merging*, a multigenerational saga about the white side of his family, traced all the way back to Ireland in the 1700s. He had worked with *Roots* producer David Wolper on *Queen*, a new six-hour miniseries based on the life of his paternal grandmother, scheduled to be telecast in the spring of 1993. And he was weeks away from the end of a book he had been writing for twelve years: *Henning*, a very personal memoir about his birthplace. A lyrical evocation of small-town America, it was the best work he'd ever done. A six-figure advance was only weeks away, promising relief from long-accumulating financial pressures that were hounding and haunting him. But he couldn't quite bring *Henning* home.

The manuscript was close enough to completion that it won't be lost to posterity, but Alex won't be here to see it happen, and I think he knew it at the end. As he lay dying from a heart attack in his apartment in Seattle on the night of February 9, 1992, the friend who was with him at the time said he began crying, seemingly not just from the pain, but from seeing all his hopes for a new beginning slip away just as they seemed to be within reach. But then, through the tears, he began to smile, perhaps in relief that he could finally put his burden down, but perhaps also because he was seeing "the promised land" at last.

Engulfed in memory and grief, I marched slowly with the other mourners behind the hearse that bore him from the New Hope Church in Henning to his burial plot two blocks away—in the front yard of his grandma Cynthia's white frame house, now an official State of Tennessee historic landmark. While six solemn Coast Guard pall-bearers carried his casket to the grave, a dashiki-clad musician blew plaintively on an African flute and beat a ceremonial *tan-tang* drum in cadence to their steps. A ten-gun salute sounded in the distance as the American flag atop his coffin was slowly furled and handed to his widow, My Haley. A bowl of Gambian dirt, mingled with the rich soil of Tennessee, was thrown into the grave. And while the casket was lowered, two black preachers led the crowd in a moving rendition of "Amazing Grace." It was Alex's favorite hymn, and I remembered something he had said to a white man standing next to him when it was being played on another occasion: "Makes you want to come home, doesn't it?" Now he had—and I felt that I had, too. As a white standing there among blacks, I had felt a little out of place. But as I sang "Amazing Grace" along with the others who were laying him to rest, I felt a benediction of embrace, not only by them but by Alex himself, and finally the tears came.

And so it ended where it all began, some seventy years ago, ten paces from that front porch where he had sat behind his grandma's rocking chair listening to all those tales about the family. But was it really over? At eight o'clock the next morning, the cars and buses started pulling into town, and those who hadn't been invited to the funeral began showing up to pay their last respects. There were hundreds of them, and they kept on coming, day after day, not just black people but people of every race and nation, men and women and children whose lives had been touched in some deep way by the man who was buried there and the story he had told. Looking down at the face of her husband in his coffin, his widow had put it best: "You have changed all of us forever, Alex. You have made us know who we truly are."

Alex's literary legacy is not a large one: two books and a sheaf of magazine articles. But what a legacy it is. The interviews he conducted for *Playboy* are among the finest ever published since he inaugurated that feature three decades ago; a few of them are historic. And his books are likely to endure among the most important ever published in America.

My friendship for Alex will endure as well. I still feel the way I did in my introduction to the interview I conducted with him for *Playboy*: "The following personal opinion may compromise my credibility as a journalist, but frankly I value more highly my credibility as a friend of Alex Haley. And the simple fact is that I consider him the finest and most decent man I've ever known." His death has left a void in my life, as it has for all of those who loved him best. But for more than thirty years, I got to know him and work with him, to share in his triumphs and his struggles. For that—and for the privilege of sharing them both in this collection of his work—I will be forever grateful.

Alex Haley

THE PLAYBOY
INTERVIEWS

MILES DAVIS

A Candid Conversation with the Jazz World's Premier Iconoclast

The technical and emotional brilliance of the trumpet played by Miles Davis has made him one of the most provocative influences in modern jazz. We spent two days with Miles not long ago in his rather unusual five-story home, a converted Russian Orthodox Church on West 77th Street near the Hudson River in New York City. Miles was between gigs at the time and we accompanied him on his restless daily home routine, asking questions at propitious moments while he worked out in his basement gymnasium, made veal chops Italian style for his family, took telephone calls from fellow musicians, his lawyer and stockbroker, gave boxing lessons

to his three sons, watched TV, plucked out beginner's chords on a guitar and, of course, blew one of his two Martin trumpets, running up and down the chromatic scale with searing speed. Spending time with Miles in the refuge of his own home, and seeing him surrounded by the activities and people he loves, it was hard to reconcile this reality with his sometimes flinty and truculent public posture. It was on this facet of his personality that we first queried him.

HALEY: Linked with your musical renown is your reputation for bad temper and rudeness to your audiences. Would you comment?

DAVIS: Why is it that people just have to have so much to say about me? It bugs me because I'm not that important. Some critic that didn't have nothing else to do started this crap about I don't announce numbers, I don't look at the audience, I don't bow or talk to people, I walk off the stage, and all that.

Look, man, all I am is a trumpet player. I only can do one thing—play my horn—and that's what's at the bottom of the whole mess. I ain't no entertainer, and ain't trying to be one. I am one thing, a musician. Most of what's said about me is lies in the first place. Everything I do, I got a reason.

The reason I don't announce numbers is because it's not until the last instant I decide what's maybe the best thing to play next. Besides, if people don't recognize a number when we play it, what difference does it make?

Why I sometimes walk off the stand is because when it's somebody else's turn to solo, I ain't going to just stand up there and be detracting from him. What am I going to stand up there *for*? I ain't no model, and I don't sing or dance, and I damn sure ain't no Uncle Tom just to be up there grinning. Sometimes I go over by the piano or the drums and listen to what they're doing. But if I don't want to do that, I go in the wings and listen to the whole band until it's the next turn for my horn.

Then they claim I ignore the audience while I'm playing. Man, when I'm working, I know the people are out there. But when I'm playing, I'm worrying about making my horn sound right.

And they bitch that I won't talk to people when we go off after a set. That's a damn lie. I talk plenty of times if everything's going like it ought to and I feel right. But if I got my mind on something about my band or something else, well, hell, no. I don't want to talk. When I'm working I'm concentrating. I bet you if I was a doctor sewing on some son of a bitch's heart, they wouldn't want me to talk.

Anybody wants to believe all this crap they hear about me, it's their problem, not mine. Because, look, man, I like people. I *love* people! I'm not going around telling everybody that. I try to say that my way—with my horn. Look, when I was a boy, 10 years old, I got a paper route and it got bigger than I could handle because my customers liked me so much. I just delivered papers the best I could and minded my business, the same way I play my horn now. But a lot of the people I meet now make me sick.

HALEY: What types of people do you find especially irritating?

DAVIS: Well, these people that's always coming up bugging me until they get me to act like this crap they heard. They ask you things, you say what you think, and if it ain't what they want to hear, then something's wrong with you and they go away mad and think you don't like them. I bet I have had that happen 500 times. In this last club I played, this newspaper reporter kept after me when I told him I didn't have no more to say. He wasn't satisfied with that. After the next set, he come up again, either drunk or playing drunk, and shoved into me. I told him to get the hell out of my way, and then he was fine—he went right out and wrote that. But he didn't tell how it happened.

And I'm mad every time I run into the Jim Crow scene. I don't care what form it takes. You can't hardly play anywhere you don't run into some of these cats full of prejudice. I don't know how many I've told, "Look, you want me to talk to you and you're prejudiced against me and all that. Why'n't you go on back where you're sitting and be prejudiced by yourself and leave me alone?" I have enough problems without trying to make them feel better. Then they go off and join the rest saying I'm such a big bastard.

I've got no plans of changing what I think. I don't dig people in clubs who don't pay the musicians respect. The average jazz musician today, if he's making it, is just as trained as classical musicians. You ever see anybody go up bugging the classical musicians when they are on the job and trying to work?

Even in jazz—you look at the white bandleaders—if they don't want anybody messing with them when they are working, you don't hear anybody squawking. It's just if a Negro is involved that there's something wrong with him. My troubles started when I learned to play the trumpet and hadn't learned to dance.

HALEY: You feel that the complaints about you are because of your race?

DAVIS: I know damn well a lot of it is race. White people have certain things they expect from Negro musicians— just like they've got labels for the whole Negro race. It goes clear back to the slavery days. That was when Uncle Tomming got started because white people demanded it. Every little black child grew up seeing that getting along with white people meant grinning and acting clowns. It helped white people to feel easy about what they had done, and were doing, to Negroes, and that's carried right on over to now. You bring it down to musicians, they want you to not only play your instrument, but to entertain them, too, with grinning and dancing.

HALEY: Generally speaking, what are your feelings with regard to race?

DAVIS: I hate to talk about what I think of the mess because my friends are all colors. When I say that some of my best friends are white, I sure ain't lying. The only white people I don't like are the prejudiced white people. Those the shoe don't fit, well, they don't wear it. I don't like the white people that show me they can't understand that not just the Negroes, but the Chinese and Puerto Ricans and any other races that ain't white, should be given dignity and respect like everybody else.

But let me straighten you—I ain't saying I think all Negroes are the salt of the earth. It's plenty of Negroes I can't stand, too. Especially those that act like they think white people want them to. They bug me worse than Uncle Toms.

But prejudiced white people can't see any of the other races as just individual people. If a white man robs a bank, it's just a man robbed a bank. But if a Negro or a Puerto Rican does it, it's them awful Negroes or Puerto Ricans. Hardly anybody not white hasn't suffered from some of white people's labels. It used to be said that all Negroes were shiftless and happy-go-lucky and lazy. But that's been proved a lie so much that now the label is that what Negroes want integration for is so they can sleep in the bed with white people. It's another damn lie. All Negroes want is to be free to do in this country just like anybody else. Prejudiced white people ask one another, "Would you want your sister to marry a Negro?" It's a jive question to ask in the first place—as if white women stand around helpless if some Negro wants to drag one off to a preacher. It makes me sick to hear that. A Negro just might not want your sister. The Negro is always to blame if some white woman decides she wants him. But it's all right that ever since slavery, white men been having Negro women. Every Negro you see that ain't black, that's what's happened somewhere in his background. The slaves they brought here were all black.

What makes me mad about these labels for Negroes is that very few white people really know what Negroes really feel like. A lot of white people have never even been in the company of an intelligent Negro. But you can hardly meet a white person, especially a white man, that don't think he's qualified to tell you all about Negroes.

You know the story the minute you meet some white cat and he comes off with a big show that he's with you. It's 10,000 things you can talk about, but the only thing he can think of is some other Negro he's such close friends with. Intelligent Negroes are sick of hearing this. I don't know how many times different whites have started talking, telling me they was raised up with a Negro boy. But I ain't found one yet that knows whatever happened to that boy after they grew up.

HALEY: Did you grow up with any white boys?

DAVIS: I didn't grow up with any, not as friends, to speak of. But I went to school with some. In high school, I was the best in the music class on the trumpet. I knew it and all the rest knew it—but all the contest first prizes went to the boys with blue eyes. It made me so mad I made up my mind to outdo anybody white on my horn. If I hadn't met that prejudice, I probably wouldn't have had as much drive in my work. I have thought about that a lot. I have thought that prejudice and curiosity have been responsible for what I have done in music.

HALEY: What was the role of the curiosity?

DAVIS: I mean I always had a curiosity about trying new things in music. A new sound, another way to do something—things like that. But man, look, you know one of the biggest things that needs straightening up? The whole communication system of this country! Take the movies and TV. How many times do you see anybody in the films but white people? You don't dig? Look, the next movie or

TV you see, you count how many Negroes or any other race but white that you see. But you walk around in any city, you see the other races—I mean, in life they are part of the scene. But in the films supposed to represent this country, they ain't there. You won't hardly even see any in the street crowd scenes—because the studios didn't bother to hire any as extras.

Negroes used to be servants and Uncle Toms in the movies. But so much stink was raised until they quit that. Now you do have some Negroes playing feature parts—maybe four or five a year. Most of the time, they have a role that's special so it won't *offend* nobody—then it's a big production made like that picture is going to prove our democracy. Look, I ain't saying that people making films are prejudiced. I can't say what I don't know. But I see the films they make, and I know they don't think about the trouble a lot of colored people find with the movies and TV.

A big TV network wanted to do a show featuring me. I said no, and they asked me to just look at a show featuring a big-name Negro singer. No, I ain't calling no names. Well, just like I knew, they had 18 girls dancing for the background—and every one of them was white. Later on, when I pointed this out to the TV people, they were shocked. They said they just hadn't *thought* about that. I said I knew they hadn't. Nobody seems to think much about the colored people and the Chinese and Puerto Ricans and Japanese that watch TV and buy the things they advertise. All these races want to see some of their own people represented in the shows—I mean, besides the big stars. I know I'd feel better to see some kids of all races dancing and acting on shows than I would feel about myself up there playing a horn. The only thing that makes me any different from them is I was lucky.

This black-white business is ticklish to try to explain. You don't want to see Negroes every time you click on your set. That would be just as bad as now when you don't see nobody but white people. But if movies and TV are supposed to reflect this country, and this country's supposed to be democratic, then why don't they do it? Let's see all kinds of people dancing and acting. I see all kinds of kids downtown at the schools of dancing and acting, but from what I see in the movies and TV, it's just the white ones that are getting any work.

Look, man, right in music you got the same thing happening. I got this album, *Someday My Prince Will Come,* and you know who's on the jacket cover? My wife— Frances. I just got to thinking that as many record albums as Negroes buy, I hadn't ever seen a Negro girl on a major album cover unless she was the artist. There wasn't any harm meant—they just automatically thought about a white model and ordered one. It was my album and I'm Frances' prince, so I suggested they use her for a model, and they did it.

But it ain't all cases where white people just didn't think about the other races. It's a lot of intended discrimination, right in music. You got plenty of places that either won't hire Negroes, or they hire just one that they point out. The network studios, the Broadway pit bands, the classical orchestras, the film studios, they all have color discrimination in hiring.

I tell you why I feel so strong about the communication system. I never have forgotten one time in Europe this nice old man told me how in World War II, the Europeans didn't know what to make of Negro troops. They had their picture of this country from our magazines and movies, and with a very few exceptions like Pops Armstrong and Joe Louis and Jesse Owens, they didn't know about any Negroes except servants and laborers.

HALEY: Do you feel that your views are shared by most Negroes? And Puerto Ricans? And Orientals?

DAVIS: I can't speak for them last two. I'm in no position.

I just know what I personally feel *for* them. But I know that pretty nearly *all* Negroes hardly have any other choice about how they feel. They ain't blind. They got to *see* what's happening. It's a thousand big and little ways that you run into the prejudices of white people. Just one thing—how long have Negroes been looking at immigrants coming into this country and can't even speak the language, and in the second generations, they are in places the Negroes haven't got to yet.

Look, not long ago this big magazine had this Southern truck driver saying he'd carry sandwiches if they let Negroes eat in them Maryland highway restaurants. But where he wants to eat ain't my point—I'm talking about what he said. He said, "You give them a finger, they take an arm" and a lot more. You dig? When it comes to human rights, these prejudiced white people keep on acting like they own the damn franchise! And, man, with the world in the mess it's in now, we trying to influence on our side all them Africans and Arabs and Indians and Chinese . . . You know two thirds of the people in the world ain't white? They see all this crap with Negroes and supposed to feel white people really think any different about them? Man, somebody better get straight!

Another thing—there was no upset about them restaurants not serving Negroes, until it was an African they turned away. You think every Negro in the country don't see what it says? It says that we been here 400 years, but it wasn't no mess until they put out an African that just flew over here on a jet.

HALEY: Do you, in your position as a famous Negro, meet prejudice?

DAVIS: I told you, someway or other, *every* Negro meets it, I don't care who he is! Look, man, I sent for an electrician to fix something in the house. When he rang the bell, I answered and he looked at me like I was dirt, and said, "I want to see the owner, Mr. Davis." When I said, "You

looking at him," the cat turned beet red. He had me figured
as the porter. Now he's mad and embarrassed. What had I
done to him but called to give him work?

That same week, I had seen a lot of them West Point
cadets, and in a bar I asked why there was so many of them
in town. Man, I just asked the cat a question and he moved
up the bar and didn't speak! But then somebody recognized
me and he got red as that electrician. He came trying to
apologize and saying he had my records. I told him I had
just paid enough taxes to cover his free ride at West Point,
and I walked out. I guess he's somewhere now with the
others saying I'm such a bastard. It bugged me so, man, I
wasn't worth a damn for two or three days. It wasn't just
him ignoring me I was thinking about, but in two or three
years, Gregory, my oldest boy, may be doing some Army
time. How am I supposed to feel about him maybe serving
under this cat?

Then take this tour I made—Frances and I had train
reservations to California. But this clerk I showed my
identification to, he took it and looked at me just like the
West Point cat. When he said he had to check with somebody else, I asked him what was the trouble. You know he
had the nerve to tell me I might have forged it! Ain't no
need of me telling you what I told him, nobody would print
it. But we went to the airport and took a plane. I'm spending my money, the railroads are broke, even this son of a
bitch's job's in trouble, but all he can see is I'm black, so
it's all right to insult me. Bad as I hate to fly, I ain't been
on a train since, because I haven't met Jim Crow on the
airlines.

HALEY: In your field, music, don't some Negro jazzmen
discriminate against white musicians?

DAVIS: Crow Jim is what they call that. Yeah. It's a lot of
the Negro musicians mad because most of the best-paying
jobs go to the white musicians playing what the Negroes
created. But I don't go for this, because I think prejudice

one way is just as bad as the other way. I wouldn't have no other arranger but Gil Evans—we couldn't be much closer if he was my brother. And I remember one time when I hired Lee Konitz, some colored cats bitched a lot about me hiring an ofay in my band when Negroes didn't have work. I said if a cat could play like Lee, I would hire him. I didn't give a damn if he was green and had red breath.

HALEY: Do you find that being the head of your band adds to your problems?

DAVIS: Fronting a band ain't no fun. A lot of people don't understand that music is business, it's hard work and a big responsibility. I hate to even think what all I've been through to play my horn, and still go through. I put everything I've got into it. Even after a good rehearsal, I feel empty. And you add to playing your instrument the running of a band and you got plenty of problems. I got my own family, and the guys that work for me and their families to think about. On one tour, I had this white woman in Kansas City meet me when I came off the stand and wanted me to come to her table with her and her husband for a drink. I told her I didn't like to do that, and she hollered, "They said you're like that!" I felt like throwing down my horn and kicking it. But I said to myself I was going to try and educate at least that one couple. So I went over and talked to them.

I told them an artist's first responsibility was to himself. I said if he kept getting upset with what other people think he ought to do, he never would get too far, or he sure wouldn't last. I tried to make them see how I had worked all my life to play myself and then to get a band worth people paying to hear. I said that a lot of times when people in a club wanted to talk to me, I needed to be worrying about something about my band. They said they understood. I hope they did.

HALEY: You have been quoted as not being in favor of jazz concerts. Why?

DAVIS: Nobody can relax at concerts, the musicians or the people, either. You can't do nothing but sit down, you can't move around, you can't have a drink. A musician has to be able to let loose everything in him to reach the people. If the musician can't relax, how's he going to make the people feel what he feels? The whole scene of jazz is feeling.

HALEY: Do you now ever indulge in jam sessions?

DAVIS: I wish there was some jam sessions to sit in. But there ain't none left—at least not in the big cities. I used to sit in some great ones around St. Louis and in Brooklyn, Illinois. We would blow sometimes clear up until the next afternoon. When I go back there now, I sit in with a little blues band. They have the feeling.

HALEY: You've won all the trumpet polls. After yourself, how would you rank others?

DAVIS: *After* me! Hell, it's plenty great trumpet players don't come *after* me, or *after* nobody else! That's what I hate so about critics—how they are always *comparing* artists . . . always writing that one's better than another one. Ten men can have spent all their lives learning technical expertness on their instruments, but just like in any art, one will play one style and the rest nine other ways. And if some critics just don't happen to like a man's style, they will knock the artist. That bugs the hell out of musicians. It's made some damn near mad enough to want to hang up their horns.

Trumpet players, like anybody else, are individualized by their different ideas and styles. The thing to judge in any jazz artist is does the man project, and does he have ideas. You take Dizzy—he does, all the time, every time he picks up his horn. Some more cats—Clark Terry, Ray Nance, Kenny Dorham, Roy Eldridge, Harold Baker, Freddie Hubbard, Lee Morgan, Bobby Hackett—a lot of them. Hell, that cat down in New Orleans, Al Hirt, he blows his ass off, too!

HALEY: Is there any special reason you didn't mention Louis Armstrong?

DAVIS: Oh, Pops? No, why I didn't mention him is because I was talking just about modern-jazz players. I love Pops, I love the way he sings, the way he plays—everything he does, except when he says something against modern-jazz music. He ought to realize that he was a pioneer, too. No, he wasn't an influence of mine, and I've had very little direct contact with Pops. A long time ago, I was at Bop City, and he came in and told me he liked my playing. I don't know if he would even remember it, but I remember how good I felt to have him say it. People really dig Pops like I do myself. He does a good job overseas with his personality. But they ought to send him down South for goodwill. They need goodwill worse in Georgia and Alabama and Mississippi than they do in Europe.

HALEY: To go back a moment, you expressed a sharp dislike of critics. Are there other reasons besides their comparing musicians?

DAVIS: Well, aside from that, I get sick of how a lot of them write whole columns and pages of big words and still ain't saying nothing. If you have spent your life getting to know your business and the other cats in it, and what they are doing, then you know if a critic knows what he's talking about. Most of the time they don't.

I don't pay no attention to what critics say about me, the good or the bad. The toughest critic I got, and the only one I worry about, is myself. My music has got to get past me and I'm too vain to play anything I think is bad.

No, I ain't going to name critics I don't like. But I will tell you some that I respect what they write—Nat Hentoff, Ralph Gleason and Leonard Feather. And some others, I can't right off think of their names. But it ain't a long list.

HALEY: Are there any particular places or clubs that you don't like to play?

DAVIS: There are plenty I *won't* play! I won't take a booking nowhere in the South. I told you I just can't stand Jim Crow, so I ain't going down there in it. There's enough of it here in the North, but at least you have the support of some laws.

I won't play nowhere I know has the kind of audiences that you waste your breath to play for. I'm talking about them expense-account ofays that use music as a background for getting high and trying to show off to the women they brought. They ain't come to hear good music. They don't even know how to enjoy themselves. They drink too much, they get loud, they got to be seen and heard. They'll jump up and dance jigs and sing. They ain't got no manners— don't pay their women no respect. What they really want is some Uncle Tom entertainment if it's a Negro group on the stand. These are the kind will holler, "Hey, boy, play *Sweet Georgia Brown!*" You supposed to grin and play that. I hate to play in a place full of those kind of squares so bad that if there wasn't nobody else to play to, I'd invest in some more property and just stay home and collect rents. I can't stand dumb-ass people not respecting the other customers that have come to hear the music. Sometimes one table like that has bugged me so that when I get home or to my hotel, I walk the floor because I can't sleep.

I told you I ain't going to play nowhere in the South that Negroes *can't* come. But I ain't going to play nowhere in the North that Negroes *don't* come. It's one of two reasons they won't, either because they know they ain't wanted, or because they don't like the joint's regular run of music. Negroes ain't got as much money to throw away in night clubs as white people. So a club that Negroes patronize, you can figure that everybody that goes there comes expecting to hear good music.

HALEY: What is your opinion of the jazz audiences in Europe?

DAVIS: European audiences are generally more hip about

the background of jazz than most of the fans here. Some cats hardly heard of here are big record sellers in Europe. In this country, it's more following of personalities. You want to hear something funny? One club-owner friend of mine said a lot of people pay their money to come where I'm playing just because they want to *see* me—they heard I'm so bad. Ain't that a bitch?

But this country has a lot of great fans. You know, they appreciate what you're trying to do, and that inspires a musician to give his best. I know some Americans that don't stop with just knowing jazz, but that even *think* just like musicians.

HALEY: Do you plan another European tour soon?

DAVIS: Maybe. I like to play in Europe every now and then, but I don't like to spend no more time out of this house than I can help. Jack Whittemore, my booking agent at Shaw Artists, schedules me so I don't stay long on the road. I like to have time at home to be with my kids and Frances, and to just think about things—like worrying about the people running this government maybe slipping and getting us into another war. But I like them Kennedy brothers—they're swinging people.

HALEY: Would it please you if the image of you changed, that people quit regarding you as a tough guy?

DAVIS: Well, nobody wants to be always accused of something he ain't done. But people that want to think that, it's their worry, it ain't mine. I'm like I am, and I ain't planning to change. I ain't scared of nothing or nobody. I already been through too much. I ought to be dead from just what I went through when I was on dope. I ain't going around anywhere trying to be tough and a racist. I just say what I think, and that bugs people, especially a lot of white people. When they look in my eyes and don't see no fear, they know it's a draw.

HALEY: Have you always been so sensitive about being a Negro?

DAVIS: About the first thing I can remember as a little boy was a white man running me down a street hollering "Nigger! Nigger!" My father went hunting him with a shotgun. Being sensitive and having race pride has been in my family since slave days. The slave Davises played classical string music on the plantations. My father, Miles the first, was born six years after the Emancipation. He wanted to play music, but my grandfather wanted him to be more than an entertainer for white folks. He made him go to Northwestern to be a dental surgeon. My father is worth more than I am. He's a high-priced dental surgeon with more practice than he can handle—because he's good at his business—and he raises hogs with pedigrees. It's a special breed of hogs with some funny name I would tell you, but I never can remember it.

HALEY: You're said to be one of the financially best-off popular musicians. Is this correct?

DAVIS: Well, I don't have any access to other musicians' bankbooks. But I never have been what you would call poor. I grew up with an allowance, and I had a big newspaper route. I saved most of what I made except for buying records. But when I first left home as a musician, I used to spend all I made, and when I went on dope, I got in debt. But after I got enough sense to kick the habit, I started to make more than I needed to spend unless I was crazy or something.

Now I got a pretty good portfolio of stock investments, and I got this house—it's worth into six figures, including everything in it. My four kids are coming up fine. When the boys get in from school, I want you to see them working out on the bags in our gym downstairs. I keep myself in shape and teach the kids how to box. They can handle themselves. Ain't nothing better that a father can pass along.

Then I got my music, I got Frances, and my Ferrari—and our friends. I got everything a man could want—if it just wasn't for this prejudice crap. It ain't that I'm mad at white people, I just see what I see and I know what's happening. I am going to speak my mind about anything that drags me about this Jim Crow scene. This whole prejudice mess is something you would feel so good if it could just be got rid of, like a big sore eating inside of your belly.

MALCOLM X

A Candid Conversation with the Militant Major-domo of the Black Muslims

RICHARD SAUNDERS

Within the past five years, the militant American Negro has
become an increasingly active combatant in the struggle for
civil rights. Espousing the goals of unqualified equality and
integration, many of these outspoken insurgents have participated in freedom rides and protest marches against their
segregationist foes. Today, they face opposition from not one,
but two inimical exponents of racism and segregation: the
white supremacists and the Black Muslims. A relatively
unknown and insignificant radical religious Negro cult until
a few years ago, the Muslims have grown into a dedicated,
disciplined nationwide movement which runs its own school,

publishes its own newspaper, owns stores and restaurants in four major cities, buys broadcast time on 50 radio stations throughout the country, stages mass rallies attended by partisan crowds of 10,000 and more, and maintains its own police force of judo-trained athletes called the Fruit of Islam.

Predicated on the proposition that the black man is morally, spiritually and intellectually superior to the white man, who is called a "devil," Muslim doctrine dooms him to extermination in an imminent Armageddon—along with Christianity itself, which is denounced as an opiate designed to lull Negroes—with the promise of heaven—into passive acceptance of inferior social status. Amalgamating elements of Christianity and Mohammedanism (both of which officially and unequivocally disown it) and spiked with a black-supremacy version of Hitler's Aryan racial theories, Muslimism was founded in 1931 by Elijah Poole, a Georgia-born ex-factory worker who today commands unquestioning obedience from thousands of followers as the Honorable Elijah Muhammad, Messenger of Allah. At the right hand of God's Messenger stands 36-year-old Malcolm Little, a lanky onetime dining-car steward, bootlegger, pimp and dope pusher who left prison in 1952 to heed Muhammad's message, abandoned his "slave name," Little, for the symbolic "X" (meaning identity unknown), and took an oath to abstain thereafter from smoking, drinking, gambling, cursing, dancing and sexual promiscuity—as required of every Muslim. The ambitious young man rose swiftly to become the Messenger's most ardent and erudite disciple, and today wields all but absolute authority over the movement and its membership as Muhammad's business manager, trouble shooter, prime minister and heir apparent.

In the belief that knowledge and awareness are necessary and effective antitoxins against the venom of hate, PLAYBOY *asked Malcolm X to submit to a cross-examination on the means and ends of his organization. The ensuing interview was conducted at a secluded table in a Harlem restaurant owned by the Muslims. Interrupting his replies occasionally with a sip of black African coffee and whispered asides to deferential aides, the dark-suited minister of Harlem's Muslim Temple Number Seven spoke with candor and—except for moments of impassioned execration of all whites—the impersonal tone of a self-assured corporation executive.*

Many will be shocked by what he has to say; others will be outraged. Our own view is that this interview is both an eloquent statement and a damning self-indictment of one noxious facet of rampant racism. As such, we believe it merits publication—and reading.

HALEY: What is the ambition of the Black Muslims?

MALCOLM X: Freedom, justice and equality are our principal ambitions. And to faithfully serve and follow the Honorable Elijah Muhammad is the guiding goal of every Muslim. Mr. Muhammad teaches us the knowledge of our own selves, and of our own people. He cleans us up— morally, mentally and spiritually—and he reforms us of the vices that have blinded us here in the Western society. He stops black men from getting drunk, stops their dope addiction if they had it, stops nicotine, gambling, stealing, lying, cheating, fornication, adultery, prostitution, juvenile delinquency. I think of this whenever somebody talks about someone investigating us. Why investigate the Honorable Elijah Muhammad? They should subsidize him. He's cleaning up the mess that white men have made. He's saving the government millions of dollars, taking black men off of welfare, showing them how to do something for themselves. And Mr. Muhammad teaches us love for our own kind. The white man has taught the black people in this country to hate themselves as inferior, to hate each other, to be divided against each other. Messenger Muhammad

restores our love for our own kind, which enables us to
work together in unity and harmony. He shows us how to
pool our financial resources and our talents, then to work
together toward a common objective. Among other things,
we have small businesses in most major cities in this country, and we want to create many more. We are taught by
Mr. Muhammad that it is very important to improve the
black man's economy, and his thrift. But to do this, we
must have land of our own. The brainwashed black man
can never learn to stand on his own two feet until he is on
his own. We must learn to become our own producers,
manufacturers and traders: we must have industry of our
own, to employ our own. The white man resists this because he wants to keep the black man under his thumb and
jurisdiction in white society. He wants to keep the black
man always dependent and begging—for jobs, food,
clothes, shelter, education. The white man doesn't want to
lose somebody to be supreme over. He wants to keep the
black man where he can be watched and retarded. Mr.
Muhammad teaches that as soon as we separate from the
white man, we will learn that we can do without the white
man just as he can do without us. The white man knows
that once black men get off to themselves and learn they
can do for themselves, the black man's full potential will
explode and he will *surpass* the white man.

HALEY: Do you feel that the Black Muslims' goal of ob-
taining "several states" is a practical vision?

MALCOLM X: Well, *you* might consider some things practical that are really impractical. Wasn't it impractical that
the Supreme Court could issue a desegregation order nine
years ago and there's still only eight percent compliance? Is
it practical that a hundred years after the Civil War there's
not freedom for black men yet? On the record for integration you've got the President, the Congress, the Supreme
Court—but show me your integration, where is it? That's

practical? Mr. Muhammad teaches us to be for what's *really*
practical—that's separation. It's more natural than integration.

HALEY: In the view of many, that is highly debatable.
However: In a recent interview, Negro author-lecturer
Louis Lomax said, "Eighty percent, if not more, of America's 20,000,000 Negroes vibrate sympathetically with the
Muslims' indictment of the white power structure. But this
does not mean we agree with them in their doctrines of
estrangement or with their proposed resolutions of the race
problem." Does this view represent a consensus of opinion
among Negroes? And if so, is it possible that your separa-
tionist and anti-Christian doctrine have the effect of alienating many of your race?

MALCOLM X: Sir, you make a mistake listening to people
who tell you how much our stand alienates black men in
this country. I'd guess actually we have the sympathy of 90
percent of the black people. There are 20,000,000 dormant
Muslims in America. A Muslim to us is somebody who is
for the black man; I don't care if he goes to the Baptist
Church seven days a week. The Honorable Elijah Muhammad says that a black man is born a Muslim by nature.
There are millions of Muslims not aware of it now. All of
them will be Muslims when they wake up; that's what's
meant by the Resurrection.

Sir, I'm going to tell you a secret: the black man is a
whole lot smarter than white people think he is. The black
man has survived in this country by fooling the white man.
He's been dancing and grinning and white men never
guessed what he was thinking. Now you'll hear the bourgeois Negroes pretending to be alienated, but they're just
making the white man *think* they don't go for what Mr.
Muhammad is saying. This Negro that will tell you he's so
against us, he's just protecting the crumbs he gets from the
white man's table. This kind of Negro is so busy trying to
be *like* the white man that he doesn't know what the real

masses of his own people are thinking. A fine car and house and clothes and liquor have made a lot think themselves different from their poor black brothers. But Mr. Muhammad says that Allah is going to wake up all black men to see the white man as he really is, and see what Christianity has done to them. The black masses that are waking up don't believe in Christianity anymore. All it's done for black men is help to keep them slaves. Mr. Muhammad is teaching that Christianity, as white people see it, means that whites can have their heaven here on earth, but the black man is supposed to catch his hell here. The black man is supposed to keep believing that when he dies, he'll float up to some city with golden streets and milk and honey on a cloud somewhere. Every black man in North America has heard black Christian preachers shouting about "tomorrow in good old Beulah's Land." But the thinking black masses today are interested in *Muhammad's* Land. The Promised Land that the Honorable Elijah Muhammad talks about is right here on this earth. Intelligent black men today are interested in a religious doctrine that offers a solution to their problems right now, right here on this earth, while they are alive.

You must understand that the Honorable Elijah Muhammad represents the fulfillment of Biblical prophecy to us. In the Old Testament, Moses lived to see his enemy, Pharaoh, drowned in the Red Sea—which in essence means that Mr. Muhammad will see the completion of his work in his lifetime, that he will live to see victory gained over his enemy.

HALEY: The Old Testament connection seems tenuous. Are you referring to the Muslim judgment day which your organization's newspaper, *Muhammad Speaks,* calls "Armageddon" and prophesies as imminent?

MALCOLM X: Armageddon deals with the final battle between God and the Devil. The Third World War is referred to as Armageddon by many white statesmen. There won't

be any more war after then because there won't be any
more warmongers. I don't know when Armageddon, whatever form it takes, is supposed to be. But I know the time
is near when the white man will be finished. The signs are
all around us. Ten years ago you couldn't have *paid* a
Southern Negro to defy local customs. The British Lion's
tail has been snatched off in black Africa. The Indonesians
have booted out such would-be imperialists as the Dutch.
The French, who felt for a century that Algeria was theirs,
have had to run for their lives back to France. Sir, the point
I make is that all over the world, the old day of standing
in fear and trembling before the almighty white man is
gone!

HALEY: You refer to whites as the guilty and the enemy;
you predict divine retribution against them; and you preach
absolute separation from the white community. Do not
these views substantiate that your movement is predicated
on race hatred?

MALCOLM X: Sir, it's from Mr. Muhammad that the black
masses are learning for the first time in 400 years the real
truth of how the white man brainwashed the black man,
kept him ignorant of his true history, robbed him of his
self-confidence. The black masses for the first time are
understanding that it's not a case of being anti-white or
anti-Christian, but it's a case of seeing the true nature of the
white man. We're anti-evil, anti-oppression, anti-lynching.
You can't be anti- those things unless you're also anti- the
oppressor and the lyncher. You can't be anti-slavery and
pro-slavemaster; you can't be anti-crime and pro-criminal.
In fact, Mr. Muhammad teaches that if the present generation of *whites* would study their own race in the light of
their true history, they would be anti-white themselves.

HALEY: Are you?

MALCOLM X: As soon as the white man hears a black man
say that he's through loving white people, then the white
man accuses the black man of hating him. The Honorable

Elijah Muhammad doesn't teach hate. The white man isn't *important* enough for the Honorable Elijah Muhammad and his followers to spend any time hating him. The white man has brainwashed himself into believing that all the black people in the world want to be cuddled up next to him. When he meets what we're talking about, he can't believe it, it takes all the wind out of him. When we tell him we don't want to be around him, we don't want to be like he is, he's staggered. It makes him re-evaluate his 300-year myth about the black man. What I want to know is how the white man, with the blood of black people dripping off his fingers, can have the audacity to be asking black people do they hate him. That takes a lot of nerve.

HALEY: How do you reconcile your disavowal of hatred with the announcement you made last year that Allah had brought you "the good news" that 120 white Atlantans had just been killed in an air crash en route to America from Paris?

MALCOLM X: Sir, as I see the law of justice, it says as you sow, so shall you reap. The white man has reveled as the rope snapped black men's necks. He has reveled around the lynching fire. It's only right for the black man's true God, Allah, to defend us—and for us to be joyous because our God manifests his ability to inflict pain on our enemy. We Muslims believe that the white race, which is guilty of having oppressed and exploited and enslaved our people here in America, should and will be the victims of God's divine wrath. All civilized societies in their courts of justice set a sentence of execution against those deemed to be enemies of society, such as murderers and kidnapers. The presence of 20,000,000 black people here in America is proof that Uncle Sam is guilty of kidnaping—because we didn't come here voluntarily on the Mayflower. And 400 years of lynchings condemn Uncle Sam as a murderer.

HALEY: We question that all-inclusive generalization. To return to your statement about the plane crash, when Dr.

Ralph Bunche heard about it, he called you "mentally depraved." What is your reaction?

MALCOLM X: I know all about what Dr. Bunche said. He's always got his international mouth open. He apologized in the UN when black people protested there. You'll notice that whenever the white man lets a black man get prominent, he has a job for him. Dr. Bunche serves the white man well—he represents, speaks for and defends the white man. He does none of this for the black man. Dr. Bunche has functioned as a white man's tool, designed to influence international opinion on the Negro. The white man has Negro local tools, national tools, and Dr. Bunche is an international tool.

HALEY: Dr. Bunche was only one of many prominent Negroes who deplored your statement in similar terms. What reply have you to make to these spokesmen for your own people?

MALCOLM X: Go ask their opinions and you'll be able to fill your notebook with what white people want to hear Negroes say. Let's take these so-called spokesmen for the black men by types. Start with the politicians. They never attack Mr. Muhammad personally. They realize he has the sympathy of the black masses. They know they would alienate the masses whose votes they need. But the black civic leaders, they do attack Mr. Muhammad. The reason is usually that they are appointed to their positions by the white man. The white man pays them to attack us. The ones who attack Mr. Muhammad the most are the ones who earn the most. Then take the black religious leaders, they also attack Mr. Muhammad. These preachers do it out of self-defense, because they know he's waking up Negroes. No one believes what the Negro preacher preaches except those who are mentally asleep, or in the darkness of ignorance about the true situation of the black man here today in this wilderness of North America. If you will take note, sir, many so-called Negro leaders who once attacked the

Honorable Elijah Muhammad don't do so anymore. And he never speaks against them in the personal sense except as a reaction if they speak against him. Islam is a religion that teaches us never to attack, never to be the aggressor— but you can waste somebody if he attacks you. These Negro leaders have become aware that whenever the Honorable Elijah Muhammad is caused by their attack to level his guns against them, they always come out on the losing end. Many have experienced this.

HALEY: Do you admire and respect any other American Negro leaders—Martin Luther King, for example?

MALCOLM X: I am a Muslim, sir. Muslims can see only one leader who has the qualifications necessary to unite all elements of black people in America. This is the Honorable Elijah Muhammad.

HALEY: Many white religious leaders have also gone on record against the Black Muslims. Writing in the official NAACP magazine, a Catholic priest described you as "a fascist-minded hate group," and B'nai B'rith has accused you of being not only anti-Christian but anti-Semitic. Do you consider this true?

MALCOLM X: Insofar as the Christian world is concerned, dictatorships have existed only in areas or countries where you have Roman Catholicism. Catholicism conditions your mind for dictators. Can you think of a single Protestant country that has ever produced a dictator?

HALEY: Germany was predominantly Protestant when Hitler—

MALCOLM X: Another thing to think of—in the 20th Century, the Christian Church has given us two heresies: fascism and communism.

HALEY: On what grounds do you attribute these "isms" to the Christian Church?

MALCOLM X: Where did fascism start? Where's the second-largest Communist party outside of Russia? The answer to both is Italy. Where is the Vatican? But let's not

forget the Jew. Anybody that gives even a just criticism of
the Jew is instantly labeled anti-Semite. The Jew cries
louder than anybody else if anybody criticizes him. You can
tell the truth about any minority in America, but make a
true observation about the Jew, and if it doesn't pat him on
the back, then he uses his grip on the news media to label
you anti-Semite. Let me say just a word about the Jew and
the black man. The Jew is always anxious to *advise* the
black man. But they never advise him how to solve his
problem the way the Jews solved their problem. The Jew
never went sitting-in and crawling-in and sliding-in and
freedom-riding, like he teaches and helps Negroes to do.
The Jews stood up, and stood together, and they used their
ultimate power, the economic weapon. That's exactly what
the Honorable Elijah Muhammad is trying to teach black
men to do. The Jews pooled their money and *bought* the
hotels that barred them. They bought Atlantic City and
Miami Beach and anything else they wanted. Who owns
Hollywood? Who runs the garment industry, the largest
industry in New York City? But the Jew that's advising the
Negro joins the NAACP, CORE, the Urban League, and
others. With money donations, the Jew gains control, then
he sends the black man doing all this wading-in, boring-in,
even burying-in—everything but buying-in. Never shows
him how to set up factories and hotels. Never advises him
how to own what he wants. No, when there's something
worth owning, the Jew's got it.

HALEY: Isn't it true that many Gentiles have also labored
with dedication to advance integration and economic improvement for the Negro, as volunteer workers for the
NAACP, CORE and many other interracial agencies?

MALCOLM X: A man who tosses worms in the river isn't
necessarily a friend of the fish. All the fish who take him
for a friend, who think the worm's got no hook in it,
usually end up in the frying pan. All these things dangled
before us by the white liberal posing as a friend and bene-

factor have turned out to be nothing but bait to make us think we're making progress. The Supreme Court decision has never been enforced. Desegregation has never taken place. The promises have never been fulfilled. We have received only tokens, substitutes, trickery and deceit.

HALEY: What motives do you impute to *Playboy* for providing you with this opportunity for the free discussion of your views?

MALCOLM X: I think you want to sell magazines. I've never seen a sincere white man, not when it comes to helping black people. Usually things like this are done by white people to benefit themselves. The white man's primary interest is not to elevate the thinking of black people, or to waken black people, or white people either. The white man is interested in the black man only to the extent that the black man is of use to him. The white man's interest is to make money, to exploit.

HALEY: Is there any white man on earth whom you would concede to have the Negro's welfare genuinely at heart?

MALCOLM X: I say, sir, that you can never make an intelligent judgment without evidence. If any man will study the entire history of the relationship between the white man and the black man, no evidence will be found that justifies any confidence or faith that the black man might have in the white man today.

HALEY: Then you consider it impossible for the white man to be anything but an exploiter and a hypocrite in his relations with the Negro?

MALCOLM X: Is it wrong to attribute a predisposition to wheat before it comes up out of the ground? Wheat's characteristics and nature make it wheat. It differs from barley because of its nature. Wheat perpetuates its own characteristics just as the white race does. White people are born devils by nature. They don't become so by deeds. If you never put popcorn in a skillet, it would still be popcorn. Put the heat to it, it will pop.

HALEY: You say that white men are devils by nature. Was Christ a devil?

MALCOLM X: Christ wasn't white. Christ was a black man.

HALEY: On what Scripture do you base this assertion?

MALCOLM X: Sir, Billy Graham has made the same statement in public. Why not ask *him* what Scripture he found it in? When Pope Pius XII died, *Life* magazine carried a picture of him in his private study kneeling before a black Christ.

HALEY: Those are hardly quotations from Scripture. Was He not reviled as "King of the Jews"—a people the Black Muslims attack?

MALCOLM X: Only the poor, brainwashed American Negro has been made to believe that Christ was white, to maneuver him into worshiping the white man. After becoming a Muslim in prison, I read almost everything I could put my hands on in the prison library. I began to think back on everything I had read and especially with the histories, I realized that nearly all of them read by the general public have been made into white histories. I found out that the history-whitening process either had left out great things that black men had done, or some of the great black men had gotten whitened.

HALEY: Would you list a few of these men?

MALCOLM X: Well, Hannibal, the most successful general that ever lived, was a black man. So was Beethoven; Beethoven's father was one of the blackamoors that hired themselves out in Europe as professional soldiers. Haydn, Beethoven's teacher, was of African descent. Columbus, the discoverer of America, was a half-black man.

HALEY: According to biographies considered definitive, Beethoven's father, Johann, was a court tenor in Cologne; Haydn's parents were Croatian; Columbus' parents were Italian—

MALCOLM X: Whole black empires, like the Moorish,

have been whitened to hide the fact that a great black empire had conquered a white empire even before America was discovered. The Moorish civilization—black Africans—conquered and ruled Spain; they kept the light burning in Southern Europe. The word "Moor" means "black," by the way. Egyptian civilization is a classic example of how the white man stole great African cultures and makes them appear today as white European. The black nation of Egypt is the only country that has a science named after its culture: Egyptology. The ancient Sumerians, a black-skinned people, occupied the Middle Eastern areas and were contemporary with the Egyptian civilization. The Incas, the Aztecs, the Mayans, all dark-skinned Indian people, had a highly developed culture here in America, in what is now Mexico and northern South America. These people had mastered agriculture at the time when European white people were still living in mud huts and eating weeds. But white children, or black children, or grownups here today in America don't get to read this in the average books they are exposed to.

HALEY: Can you cite any authoritative historical documents for these observations?

MALCOLM X: I can cite a great many, sir. You could start with Herodotus, the Greek historian. He outright described the Egyptians as "black, with woolly hair." And the American archaeologist and Egyptologist James Henry Breasted did the same thing.

HALEY: You seem to have based your thesis on the premise that all nonwhite races are necessarily black.

MALCOLM X: Mr. Muhammad says that the red, the brown and the yellow are indeed all part of the black nation. Which means that black, brown, red, yellow, all are brothers, all are one family. The white one is a stranger. He's the odd fellow.

HALEY: Since your classification of black peoples apparently includes the light-skinned Oriental, Middle Eastern and possibly even Latin races as well as the darker Indian and Negroid strains, just how do you decide how light-skinned it's permissible to be before being condemned as white? And if Caucasian whites are devils by nature, do you classify people by degrees of devilishness according to the lightness of their skin?

MALCOLM X: I don't worry about these little technicalities. But I know that white society has always considered that one drop of black blood makes you black. To me, if one drop can do this, it only shows the power of one drop of black blood. And I know another thing—that Negroes who used to be light enough to pass for white have seen the handwriting on the wall and are beginning to come back and identify with their own kind. And white people who also are seeing the pendulum of time catching up with them are now trying to join with blacks, or even find traces of black blood in their own veins, hoping that it will save them from the catastrophe they see ahead. But no devil can fool God. Muslims have a little poem about them. It goes, "One drop will make you black, and will also in days to come save your soul."

HALEY: As one of this vast elite, do you hold the familiar majority attitude toward minority groups—regarding the white race, in this case, as inferior in quality as well as quantity to what you call the "black nation"?

MALCOLM X: Thoughtful white people *know* they are inferior to black people. Even Eastland knows it. Anyone who has studied the genetic phase of biology knows that white is considered recessive and black is considered dominant. When you want strong coffee, you ask for black coffee. If you want it light, you want it weak, integrated with white milk. Just like these Negroes who weaken themselves and their race by this integrating and intermixing with whites. If you want bread with no nutritional value, you ask for white bread. All the good that was in it has been bleached out of it, and it will constipate you. If you want pure flour, you ask for dark flour, whole-wheat flour. If you want pure sugar, you want dark sugar.

HALEY: If all whites are devilish by nature, as you have alleged, and if black and white are essentially opposite, as you have just stated, do you view all black men—with the exception of their non-Muslim leaders—as fundamentally angelic?

MALCOLM X: No, there is plenty wrong with Negroes. They have no society. They're robots, automatons. No minds of their own. I hate to say that about us, but it's the truth. They are a black body with a white brain. Like the monster Frankenstein. The top part is your bourgeois Negro. He's your integrator. He's not interested in his poor black brothers. He's usually so deep in debt from trying to copy the white man's social habits that he doesn't have time to worry about nothing else. They buy the most expensive clothes and cars and eat the cheapest food. They act more like the white man than the white man does himself. These are the ones that hide their sympathy for Mr. Muhammad's teachings. It conflicts with the sources from which they get their white-man's crumbs. This class to us are the fence-sitters. They have one eye on the white man and the other eye on the Muslims. They'll jump whichever way they see the wind blowing. Then there's the middle class of the Negro masses, the ones not in the ghetto, who realize that life is a struggle, who are conscious of all the injustices being done and of the constant state of insecurity in which they live. They're ready to take some stand against everything that's against them. Now, when this group hears Mr. Muhammad's teachings, they are the ones who come forth faster and identify themselves, and take immediate steps toward trying to bring into existence what Mr. Muhammad advocates. At the bottom of the social heap is the black man in the big-city ghetto. He lives night and day with the rats and cockroaches and drowns himself with alcohol and anesthetizes himself with dope, to try and forget where and what he is. That Negro has given up all hope. He's the hardest one for us to reach, because he's the deepest in the mud. But when you get him, you've got the best kind of Muslim. Because he makes the most drastic change. He's the most fearless. He will stand the longest. He has nothing to lose, even his life, because he didn't have that in the first place. I look upon myself, sir, as a prime example of this category—and as graphic an example as you could find of the salvation of the black man.

HALEY: Could you give us a brief review of the early life that led to your own "salvation"?

MALCOLM X: Gladly. I was born in Omaha on May 19, 1925. My light color is the result of my mother's mother having been raped by a white man. I hate every drop of white blood in me. Before I am indicted for hate again, sir—is it wrong to hate the blood of a rapist? But to continue: My father was a militant follower of Marcus Garvey's "Back to Africa" movement. The Lansing, Michigan, equivalent of the Ku Klux Klan warned him to stop preaching Garvey's message, but he kept on and one of my earliest memories is of being snatched awake one night with a lot of screaming going on because our home was afire. But my father got louder about Garvey, and the next time he was found bludgeoned in the head, lying across streetcar tracks. He died soon and our family was in a bad way. We were so hungry we were dizzy and we had nowhere to turn. Finally the authorities came in and we children were scattered about in different places as public wards. I happened to become the ward of a white couple who ran a correctional school for white boys. This family liked me in the way they liked their house pets. They got me enrolled in an all-white school. I was popular, I played sports and everything, and studied hard, and I stayed at the head of my class through the eighth grade. That summer I was 14, but I was big enough and looked old enough to get away with telling a lie that I was 21, so I got a job working in the dining car of a train that ran between Boston and New York City.

On my layovers in New York, I'd go to Harlem. That's where I saw in the bars all these men and women with what looked like the easiest life in the world. Plenty of money, big cars, all of it. I could tell they were in the rackets and vice. I hung around those bars whenever I came in town, and I kept my ears and eyes open and my mouth shut. And they kept their eyes on me, too. Finally, one day a numbers man told me that he needed a runner, and I never caught the night train back to Boston. Right there was when I started my life in crime. I was in all of it that the white police and the gangsters left open to the black criminal, sir. I was in numbers, bootleg liquor, "hot" goods, women. I sold the bodies of black women to white men, and white women to black men. I was in dope, I was in everything evil you could name. The only thing I could say good for myself, sir, was that I did not indulge in hitting anybody over the head.

HALEY: By the time you were 16, according to the record, you had several men working for you in these various enterprises. Right?

MALCOLM X: Yes, sir. I turned the things I mentioned to you over to them. And I had a good working system of paying off policemen. It was here that I learned that vice and crime can only exist, at least the kind and level that I was in, to the degree that the police cooperate with it. I had several men working and I was a steerer myself. I steered white people with money from downtown to whatever kind of sin they wanted in Harlem. I didn't care what they wanted, I knew where to take them to it. And I tell you what I noticed here—that my best customers always were the officials, the top police people, businessmen, politicians and clergymen. I never forgot that. I met all levels of these white people, supplied them with everything they wanted, and I saw that they were just a filthy race of devils. But despite the fact that my own father was murdered by whites, and I had seen my people all my life brutalized by whites, I was still blind enough to mix with them and socialize with them. I thought they were gods and goddesses—until Mr. Muhammad's powerful spiritual message opened my eyes and enabled me to see them as a race of devils. Nothing had made me see the white man as he is until one word from the Honorable Elijah Muhammad opened my eyes overnight.

HALEY: When did this happen?

MALCOLM X: In prison. I was finally caught and spent 77 months in three different prisons. But it was the greatest thing that ever happened to me, because it was in prison that I first heard the teachings of the Honorable Elijah Muhammad. His teachings were what turned me around. The first time I heard the Honorable Elijah Muhammad's statement, "The white man is the devil," it just clicked. I am a good example of why Islam is spreading so rapidly across the land. I was nothing but another convict, a semi-illiterate criminal. Mr. Muhammad's teachings were able to reach into prison, which is the level where people are considered to have fallen as low as they can go. His teachings brought me from behind prison walls and placed me on the podiums of some of the leading colleges and universities in the country. I often think, sir, that in 1946, I was sentenced to 8 to 10 years in Cambridge, Massachusetts, as a common thief who had never passed the eighth grade. And the next time I went back to Cambridge was in March 1961, as a guest speaker at the Harvard Law School Forum. This is the best example of Mr. Muhammad's ability to take nothing and make something, to take nobody and make somebody.

HALEY: Your rise to prominence in the Muslim organization has been so swift that a number of your own membership have hailed you as their articulate exemplar, and many anti-Muslims regard you as the real brains and power of the movement. What is your reaction to this sudden eminence?

MALCOLM X: Sir, it's heresy to imply that I am in any way whatever even equal to Mr. Muhammad. No man on earth today is his equal. Whatever I am that is good, it is through what I have been taught by Mr. Muhammad.

HALEY: Be that as it may, the time is near when your leader, who is 65, will have to retire from leadership of the Muslim movement. Many observers predict that when this day comes, the new Messenger of Allah in America—a role which you have called the most powerful of any black man in the world—will be Malcolm X. How do you feel about this prospect?

MALCOLM X: Sir, I can only say that God chose Mr. Muhammad as his Messenger, and Mr. Muhammad chose me and many others to help him. Only God has the say-so. But I will tell you one thing. I frankly don't believe that I or anyone else am worthy to succeed Mr. Muhammad. No one preceded him. I don't think I could make the sacrifice he has made, or set his good example. He has done more than lay down his life. But his work is already done with the seed he has planted among black people. If Mr. Muhammad and every identifiable follower he has, certainly including myself, were tomorrow removed from the scene by more of the white man's brutality, there is one thing to be sure of: Mr. Muhammad's teachings of the naked truth have fallen upon fertile soil among 20,000,000 black men here in this wilderness of North America.

HALEY: Has the soil, in your opinion, been as fertile for Mr. Muhammad's teachings elsewhere in the world— among the emerging nations of black Africa, for instance?

MALCOLM X: I think not only that his teachings have had considerable impact even in Africa but that the Honorable Elijah Muhammad has had a greater impact on the world than the rise of the African nations. I say this as objectively as I can, being a Muslim. Even the Christian missionaries are conceding that in black Africa, for every Christian conversion, there are two Muslim conversions.

HALEY: Might conversions be even more numerous if it weren't for the somewhat strained relations which are said by several Negro writers to exist between the black people of Africa and America?

MALCOLM X: Perhaps. You see, the American black man sees the African come here and live where the American black man can't. The Negro sees the African come here with a sheet on and go places where the Negro—dressed like a white man, talking like a white man, sometimes as wealthy as the white man—can't go. When I'm traveling around the country, I use my real Muslim name, Malik Shabazz. I make my hotel reservations under that name, and I always see the same thing I've just been telling you. I come to the desk and always see that "here-comes-a-Negro" look. It's kind of a reserved, coldly tolerant cordiality. But when I say "Malik Shabazz," their whole attitude changes: they snap to respect. They think I'm an African. People say what's in a name? There's a whole lot in a name. The American black man is seeing the African respected as a human being. The African gets respect because he has an identity and cultural roots. But most of all because the African owns some land. For these reasons he has his human rights recognized, and that makes his civil rights automatic.

HALEY: Do you feel this is true of Negro civil and human rights in South Africa, where the doctrine of apartheid is enforced by the government of Prime Minister Verwoerd?

MALCOLM X: They don't stand for anything different in South Africa than America stands for. The only difference is over there they *preach* as well as practice apartheid. America preaches freedom and practices slavery. America preaches integration and practices segregation. Verwoerd is an honest white man. So are the Barnetts, Faubuses, Eastlands and Rockwells. They want to keep all white people white. And we want to keep all black people black. As between the racists and the integrationists, I highly prefer the racists. I'd rather walk among rattlesnakes, whose constant rattle warns me where they are, than among those Northern snakes who grin and make you forget you're still in a snake pit. Any white man is against blacks. The entire American economy is based on white supremacy. Even the religious philosophy is, in essence, white supremacy. A white Jesus. A white Virgin. White angels. White everything. But a black Devil, of course. The "Uncle Sam" political foundation is based on white supremacy, relegating nonwhites to second-class citizenship. It goes without saying that the social philosophy is strictly white supremacist. And the educational system perpetuates white supremacy.

HALEY: Are you contradicting yourself by denouncing white supremacy while praising its practitioners, since you admit that you share their goal of separation?

MALCOLM X: The fact that I prefer the candor of the Southern segregationist to the hypocrisy of the Northern integrationist doesn't alter the basic immorality of white supremacy. A devil is still a devil whether he wears a bed sheet or a Brooks Brothers suit. The Honorable Elijah Muhammad teaches separation simply because any forcible attempt to integrate America completely would result in another Civil War, a catastrophic explosion among whites which would destroy America—and still not solve the problem. But Mr. Muhammad's solution of separate black and white would solve the problem neatly for both the white and black man, and America would be saved. Then the whole world would give Uncle Sam credit for being something other than a hypocrite.

HALEY: Do you feel that the Administration's successful stand on the integration of James Meredith into the University of Mississippi has demonstrated that the Government—far from being hypocritical—is sympathetic with the Negro's aspirations for equality?

MALCOLM X: What was accomplished? It took 15,000

troops to put Meredith in the University of Mississippi. Those troops and $3,000,000—that's what was spent—to get one Negro in. That $3,000,000 could have been used much more wisely by the Federal government to elevate the living standards of all the Negroes in Mississippi.

HALEY: Then in your view, the principle involved was not worth the expense. Yet it is a matter of record that President Kennedy, in the face of Southern opposition, championed the appointment of Dr. Robert Weaver as the first Negro Cabinet member. Doesn't this indicate to you, as it does to many Negro leaders, that the Administration is determined to combat white supremacy?

MALCOLM X: Kennedy doesn't *have* to fight; he's the President. He didn't have any fight replacing Ribicoff with Celebrezze. He didn't have any trouble putting Goldberg on the Supreme Court. He hasn't had any trouble getting anybody in but Weaver and Thurgood Marshall. He wasn't worried about Congressional objection when he challenged U.S. Steel. He wasn't worried about either Congressional reaction or Russian reaction or even world reaction when he blockaded Cuba. But when it comes to the rights of the Negro, who helped to put him in office, then he's afraid of little pockets of white resistance.

HALEY: Has *any* American President, in your opinion— Lincoln, FDR, Truman, Eisenhower, Kennedy—accomplished anything for the Negro?

MALCOLM X: None of them have ever done anything for Negroes. All of them have tricked the Negro, and made false promises to him at election times which they never fulfilled. Lincoln's concern wasn't freedom for the blacks but to save the Union.

HALEY: Wasn't the Civil War fought to decide whether this nation could, in the words of Lincoln, "endure permanently half slave and half free"?

MALCOLM X: Sir, many, many people are completely misinformed about Lincoln and the Negro. That war involved two thieves, the North and the South, fighting over the spoils. The further we get away from the actual incident, the more they are trying to make it sound as though the battle was over the black man. Lincoln said that if he could save the Union without freeing the slaves, he would. But after two years of killing and carnage he found out he would *have* to free the slaves. He wasn't interested in the slaves but in the Union. As for the Emancipation Proclamation, sir, it was an empty document. If it freed the slaves, why, a century later, are we still battling for civil rights?

HALEY: Despite the fact that the goal of racial equality is not yet realized, many sociologists—and many Negro commentators—agree that no minority group on earth has made as much social, civil and economic progress as the American Negro in the past 100 years. What is your reaction to this view?

MALCOLM X: Sir, I hear that everywhere almost exactly as you state it. This is one of the biggest myths that the American black man himself believes in. Every immigrant ethnic group that has come to this country is now a genuinely first-class citizen group—every one of them but the black man, who was here when they came. While everybody else is sharing the fruit, the black man is just now starting to be thrown some seeds. It is our hope that through the Honorable Elijah Muhammad, we will at last get the soil to plant the seeds in. You talk about the progress of the Negro—I'll tell you, mister, it's just because the Negro has been in America while *America* has gone forward that the Negro appears to have gone forward. The Negro is like a man on a luxury commuter train doing 90 miles an hour. He looks out of the window, along with all the white passengers in their Pullman chairs, and he thinks *he's* doing 90, too. Then he gets to the men's room and looks in the mirror—and he sees he's not really getting anywhere at all. His reflection shows a black man standing there in the white uniform of a dining-car steward. He may

get on the 5:10, all right, but he sure won't be getting off
at Westport.

HALEY: Is there anything then, in your opinion, that
could be done—by either whites or blacks—to expedite
the social and economic progress of the Negro in America?

MALCOLM X: First of all, the white man must finally
realize that *he's* the one who has committed the crimes that
have produced the miserable condition that our people are
in. He can't hide this guilt by reviling us today because we
answer his criminal acts—past and present—with extreme
and uncompromising resentment. He cannot hide his guilt
by accusing us, his victims, of being racists, extremists and
black supremacists. The white man must realize that the
sins of the fathers are about to be visited upon the heads
of the children who have continued those sins, only in more
sophisticated ways. Mr. Elijah Muhammad is warning this
generation of white people that they, too, are also facing a
time of harvest in which they will have to pay for the crime
committed when their grandfathers made slaves out of us.

But there *is* something the white man can do to avert this
fate. He must atone—and this can only be done by allowing black men, those who choose, to leave this land of
bondage and go to a land of our own. But if he doesn't want
a mass movement of our people away from this house of
bondage, then he should separate this country. He should
give us several states here on American soil, where those of
us who wish to can go and set up our own government, our
own economic system, our own civilization. Since we have
given over 300 years of our slave labor to the white man's
America, helped to build it up for him, it's only right that
white America should give us everything *we* need in finance
and materials for the next 25 years, until our own nation
is able to stand on its feet. Then, if the Western Hemisphere
is attacked by outside enemies, we would have both the
capability and the motivation to join in defending the
hemisphere, in which we would then have a sovereign stake.

The Honorable Elijah Muhammad says that the black man has served under the rule of all the other peoples of the earth at one time or another in the past. He teaches that it is now God's intention to put the black man back at the top of civilization, where he was in the beginning—before Adam, the white man, was created. The world since Adam has been white—and corrupt. The world of tomorrow will be black—and righteous. In the white world there has been nothing but slavery, suffering, death and colonialism. In the black world of tomorrow, there will be *true* freedom, justice and equality for all. And that day is coming—sooner than you think.

HALEY: If Muslims ultimately gain control as you predict, do you plan to bestow "*true* freedom" on white people?

MALCOLM X: It's not a case of what would we do, it's a case of what would God do with whites. What does a judge do with the guilty? Either the guilty atone, or God executes judgment.

CASSIUS CLAY

A Candid Conversation with the Flamboyantly Fast-talking, Hard-hitting Heavyweight Champ

It wasn't until 9:55 on a night last February that anyone
began to take seriously the extravagant boasts of Cassius
Marcellus Clay: That was the moment when the redoubtable
Sonny Liston, sitting dazed and disbelieving on a stool in
Miami Beach's Convention Hall, resignedly spat out his
mouthpiece—and relinquished the world's heavyweight
boxing championship to the brash young braggart whom he,
along with the nation's sportswriters and nearly everyone
else, had dismissed as a loudmouthed pushover.

Leaping around the ring in a frenzy of glee, Clay

screamed, "I am the greatest! I am the king!"—the strident rallying cry of a campaign of self-celebration, punctuated with rhyming couplets predicting victory, which had rocketed him from relative obscurity as a 1960 Olympic Gold Medal winner to dubious renown as the "villain" of a title match with the least lovable heavyweight champion in boxing history. Undefeated in 100 amateur fights and all 18 professional bouts, the cocky 22-year-old had become, if not another Joe Louis, at least the world's wealthiest poet (with a purse of $600,000), and one of its most flamboyant public figures.

Within 24 hours of his victory, he also became sports' most controversial cause célèbre when he announced at a press conference that he was henceforth to be billed on fight programs only as Muhammad Ali, his new name as a full-fledged member of the Black Muslims, the militant nationwide Negro religious cult that preaches racial segregation, black supremacy and unconcealed hostility toward whites.

Amidst the brouhaha that ensued—besieged by the world press, berated by more temperate Negro leaders, threatened with the revocation of his title—Cassius preened and prated in the limelight, using his world-wide platform as a pulpit for hymns of self-adulation and sermons on the virtues of Islam. Still full of surprises, he then proceeded to appoint himself as an international goodwill ambassador and departed with an entourage of six cronies on an 8000-mile tour of Africa and the Middle East, where he was received by several heads of state (including Ghana's Nkrumah and Egypt's Nasser), and was accorded, said observers, the warmest reception ever given an American visitor.

We approached the mercurial Muslim with our request for a searching interview about his fame, his heavyweight crown and his faith. Readily consenting, he invited us to join him on his peripatetic social rounds of New York's Harlem, where he rents a three-room suite at the Hotel Theresa (in which another celebrated guest, Fidel Castro, hung his hat and plucked his chickens during a memorable visit to the UN).

For the next two weeks, we walked with him on brisk morning constitutionals, ate with him at immaculate Muslim restaurants (no pork served), sat with him during his daily shoeshine, rode with him in his chauffeured, air-conditioned Cadillac limousine on leisurely drives through Harlem. We interjected our questions as the opportunities presented themselves—between waves and shouts exchanged by the champion and ogling pedestrians, and usually over the din of the limousine's dashboard phonograph, blaring Clay's recording of "I Am the Greatest." We began the conversation on our own blaring note.

HALEY: Are you really the loudmouthed exhibitionist you seem to be, or is it all for the sake of publicity?

CLAY: I been attracting attention ever since I been able to walk and talk. When I was just a little boy in school, I caught onto how nearly everybody likes to watch somebody that acts different. Like, I wouldn't ride the school bus. I would *run* to school alongside it, and all the kids would be waving and hollering at me and calling me nuts. It made me somebody special. Or at recess time, I'd start a fight with somebody to draw a crowd. I always liked drawing crowds. When I started fighting serious, I found out that grown people, the fight fans, acted just like those school kids. Almost from my first fights, I'd bigmouth to anybody who would listen about what I was going to do to whoever I was going to fight, and people would go out of their way to come and see, hoping I would get beat. When I wasn't no more than a kid fighter, they would put me on bills because I was a drawing card, because I run my mouth so much. Other kids could battle and get all bloody and lose or win and didn't hardly nobody care, it seemed like, except maybe their families and their buddies. But the minute I would come in sight, the people would start to hollering "Bash in his nose!" or "Button his fat lip!" or something like that. You would have thought I was some well-known pro 10 years older than I was. But I didn't care what they said, long as they kept coming to see me fight. They paid their money, they was entitled to a little fun.

HALEY: How did your first fight come about?

CLAY: Well, on my twelfth birthday, I got a new bicycle as a present from my folks, and I rode it to a fair that was being held at the Columbia Gymnasium, and when I come out, my bike was gone. I was so mad I was crying, and a policeman, Joe Martin, come up and I told him I was going to whip whoever took my bike. He said I ought to take some boxing lessons to learn how to whip the thief better, and I did. That's when I started fighting. Six weeks later, I won my first fight over another boy twelve years old, a white boy. And in a year I was fighting on TV. Joe Martin advised me against trying to just fight my way up in clubs and preliminaries, which could take years and maybe get me all beat up. He said I ought to try the Olympics, and if I won, that would give me automatically a number-ten pro rating. And that's just what I did.

HALEY: When did you hit upon the gimmick of reciting poetry?

CLAY: Somewhere away back in them early fights in Louisville, even before I went to the Olympics, I started thinking about the poetry. I told a newspaperman before a fight, "This guy must be done/I'll stop him in one." It got in the newspaper, but it didn't catch on then. Poetry didn't even catch on with *me* until a lot later, when I was getting ready to fight Archie Moore. I think the reason then was that *he* talked so much, I had to figure up something new to use on him. That was when I told different reporters, "Moore will go in four." When he *did* go down in four, just like I said, and the papers made so much of it, I knew I had stumbled on something good. And something else I found out was how it had bugged Archie Moore. Before the fight, some people got it to me that he was walking around and around in the Alexandria Hotel in Los Angeles, saying over and over, "He's not going to get me in no four, he's not going to get me in no four"—and the next thing he knew, he was getting up off the floor. I been making up things that rhyme for every fight since.

HALEY: Your poetry has been described by many critics as "horrible." Do you think it is?

CLAY: I bet my poetry gets printed and quoted more than any that's turned out by the poem writers that them critics like. I don't pay no attention to no kind of critics about nothing. If they knew as much as they claim to about what they're criticizing, they ought to be doing that instead of just standing on the side lines using their mouth.

HALEY: As your own best critic, what do you consider your finest poem?

CLAY: I don't know. The one the newspapers used the most, though, was the time I covered the water front with a poem I wrote before my fight with Doug Jones. I said, "Jones likes to mix / So I'll let it go six. / If he talks jive / I'll cut it to five. / And if he talks some more / I'll cut it to four. / And if he talks about me / I'll cut it to three. / And if that don't do / I'll cut it to two. / And if you want some fun / I'll cut it to one. / And if he don't want to fight / He can stay home that night."

HALEY: How often have you been right in predicting the round of a knockout?

CLAY: I ain't missed but twice. If you figure out the man you're up against, and you know what you can do, then you can pretty much do it whenever you get ready. Once I call the round, I plan what I'm going to do in the fight. Like, you take Archie Moore. He's a better fighter than Sonny Liston. He's harder to hit, the way he bobs and weaves, and he's smart. You get careless and he'll drop you. I guess he knows more tricks in the ring than anybody but Sugar Ray. But he was fat and 45, and he had to be looking for a lucky punch before he got tired. I just had to pace myself so as to tire him. I hooked and jabbed him silly the first round, then I coasted the second. Right at the end of the second, he caught me with a good right on the jaw, but it didn't do me no harm. Then I started out the third throwing leather on him, and when I could feel him wearing down, I slowed up, looking for my spots to hit him. And then in the fourth round, when I had said he was going down, I poured it on him again. And he did go down; he was nearly out. But he got up at eight. A few combinations sent him back down, and then the referee stopped it. It was just like I planned.

HALEY: In that fight, you were 20 and Moore was 45. It's often been said that you got to the top by beating a succession of carefully picked setups. What's your response?

CLAY: I didn't beat nobody that wasn't trying to beat me. I don't care who I fought fair and beat, but they said something was wrong. Archie Moore, yeah, they said he was an old man. Doug Jones, he was one of the toughest fights I ever had. He was one of them what-round calls that I missed. I had said just before the fight, "I'll shut the door on Jones in four," but it went the limit, ten rounds. When the judges and referee gave me the decision, everybody was calling it a fix. Then Henry Cooper in London, after he caught me in the fourth with a right that sent me through the ropes, I took him out in the fifth just like I had said I would; I had said, "It ain't no jive/Henry Cooper will go in five." But sure enough, people said that Cooper hadn't been in shape. I'm surprised they haven't been saying Liston was underage, or something, since I whipped *him* good.

HALEY: To get back to Archie Moore for a moment: Do you give him any credit, as a master of self-promotion, for helping you develop your own bally-hoo technique?

CLAY: I learned a lot from the old man, yeah. He showed me some proof of what I had already figured out myself, that talking is a whole lot easier than fighting, and it was a way to get up fast. It's a shame he wasn't fighting big time when he was in his prime. It would have been like a young Satchel Paige in the big leagues. I picked up quick how the old man would talk up a fight to make a gate, how he'd talk it up that the guy he wanted next didn't want no part of him. But the big difference between the old man and me is I'm bigger and louder and better. He believed in whispering something to reporters for them to print—but I believe in yelling.

HALEY: At what point in your career did you first put this yelling technique into practice?

CLAY: Right after I had won the Olympic Gold Medal. One day, back home in Louisville, I was riding on a bus. I was reading a paper about Patterson and Ingemar Johansson. I didn't have no doubt I could beat either one of them, if I had a chance to fight them. But Machen, Folley, Jones and all of them other bums were standing in the way, and I decided I wasn't just about to stand around like them. I'd won the Olympic title, that was all in the papers, but hadn't nobody really heard of me though, and they never would as long as I just sat thinking about it. Right there on that bus is where I figured I'd just open up my big mouth and start people listening and paying attention to me. Not just talking, but really screaming, and acting like some kind of a nut. That day was when I started out after getting in the ring with the champion.

HALEY: Even though you never fought him officially, you did have a run-in of sorts with Ingemar Johansson, didn't you?

CLAY: Yeah. Boy, I sure made him mad! He hired me as his sparring partner in Miami, and by the end of the first round I had him pinned against the ropes, all shook up and very mad. And he hadn't put a glove on me at the end of the second round. You talk about somebody upset! He was so mad he wanted me to go to Palm Beach, where we could spar in private. Not me! I wanted the newspapermen to see me if I did anything great and sensational.

HALEY: Do you feel that you could have beaten Johansson?

CLAY: I just finished telling you I did beat him. The only difference between that and a regular fight was that we had on headgear and we didn't have no big fight crowd, and I didn't have no contract.

HALEY: After you had scored victories over Archie Moore, Charley Powell, Doug Jones and Henry Cooper, how did you go about your campaign to get a match with Liston?

CLAY: Well, the big thing I did is that until then, I had just been loudmouthing mostly for the *public* to hear me, to build up gates for my fights. I hadn't never been messing personally with whoever I was going to fight—and that's what I started when it was time to go after Liston. I had been studying Liston careful, all along, ever since he had come up in the rankings, and Patterson was trying to duck him. You know what Patterson was saying—that Liston had such a bad police record, and prison record and all that. He wouldn't be a good example for boxing like Patterson would—the pure, clean-cut American boy.

HALEY: You were saying you had been studying Liston . . .

CLAY: Yeah. His fighting style. His strength. His punch. Like that—but that was just part of what I was looking at. Any fighter will study them things about somebody he wants to fight. The big thing for me was observing how Liston acted *out* of the ring. I read everything I could where he had been interviewed. I talked with people who had been around him, or had talked with him. I would lay in bed and put all of the things together and think about them, to try to get a good picture of how his mind worked. And that's how I first got the idea that if I would handle the thing right, I could use psychology on him—you know, needle him and work on his nerves so bad that I would have him beat before he ever got in the ring with me. And that's just what I did!

HALEY: How?

CLAY: I mean I set out to make him think what I wanted him thinking; that all I was was some clown, and that he never would have to give a second thought to me being able to put up any real fight when we got to the ring. The more out of shape and overconfident I could get him to be, the better. The press, everybody—I didn't want nobody thinking nothing except that I was a joke. Listen here, do you realize that of all them ring "experts" on the newspapers, wasn't hardly one that wasn't as carried away with Liston's reputation as Liston was himself? You know what everybody was writing? Saying I had been winning my fights, calling the rounds, because I was fighting "nothing" fighters. Like I told you already, even with people like Moore and Powell and Jones and Cooper, the papers found some excuse; it never was that maybe I could fight. And when it come to Liston, they was all saying it was the end of the line for me. I might even get killed in there; he was going to put his big fist in my big mouth so far they was going to have to get doctors to pull it out, stuff like that. You couldn't read nothing else. That's how come, later on, I made them reporters tell me I was the greatest. They had been so busy looking at Liston's record with Patterson that didn't nobody stop to think about how it was making Liston just about a setup for me.

HALEY: Would you elaborate?

CLAY: I told you. Overconfidence. When Liston finally got to Patterson, he beat him so bad, plus that Patterson *looked* so bad, that Liston quit thinking about keeping himself trained. I don't care who a fighter is, he has got to stay in shape. While I was fighting Jones and Cooper, Liston was up to his neck in all of that rich, fat ritual of the champion. I'd nearly clap my hands every time I read or heard about him at some big function or ceremony, up half the night and drinking and all that. I was looking at Liston's age, too. Wasn't nothing about him helping him to be sharp for me, whenever I got to him. I ain't understood it yet that didn't none of them "experts" ever realize these things.

What made it even better for me was when Liston just half-trained for the Patterson rematch, and Patterson looked worse yet—and Liston signed to fight me, not rating me even as good as he did Patterson. He felt like he was getting ready to start off on some bum-of-the-month club like Joe Louis did. He couldn't see nothing at all to me but mouth. And you know I didn't make no sound that wasn't planned to keep him thinking in that rut. He spent more time at them Las Vegas gambling tables than he did at the punching bag. He was getting fatter and flabbier every day, and I was steady hollering louder to keep him that way: "I'm going to skin the big bear!" . . . "I'm the greatest!" . . . "I'm so pretty I can't hardly stand to look at myself!" Like that. People can't stand a blowhard, but they'll always listen to him. Even people in Europe and Africa and Asia was hearing my big mouth. I didn't miss no radio or television show or newspaper I could get in. And in between them, on the street, I'd walk up to people and they'd tell one another about what "that crazy Cassius Clay" said. And then, on top of this, what the public didn't know was that every chance I got, I was needling Liston *direct.*

HALEY: How?

CLAY: I don't see no harm in telling it now. The first time, it was right after Liston had bought his new home in Denver, and my buddies and me was driving from Los Angeles to New York in my bus. This was Archie Robinson, who takes care of business for me, and Howard Bingham, the photographer, and some more buddies. I had bought this used 30-passenger bus, a 1953 Flexible—you know, the kind you see around airports. We had painted it red and white with WORLD'S MOST COLORFUL FIGHTER across the top. Then I had LISTON MUST GO IN EIGHT painted across the side right after Liston took the title. We had been driving around Los Angeles, and up and down the freeways in the bus, blowing the horn, "Oink! Oink! Oink!" drawing people's attention to me. When I say I'm colorful, I believe in *being* colorful. Anyway, this time, when we started out for New York, we decided it would be a good time to pay Liston a visit at his new house.

We had the address from the newspapers, and we pulled up in his front yard in the bus about three o'clock in the morning and started blowing: *"Oink! Oink! Oink! Oink!"* In other houses, lights went on and windows went up. You know how them white people felt about that black man just moved in there anyway, and we sure wasn't helping it none. People was hollering things, and we got out with the headlights blazing and went up to Liston's door, just about as Liston got there. He had on nylon shorty pajamas. And he was mad. He first recognized Howard Bingham, the photographer, whom he had seen in Los Angeles. "What you want, black mother?" he said to Howard. I was standing right behind Howard, flinging my cane back and forth in the headlights, hollering loud enough for everybody in a mile to hear me, "Come on out of there! I'm going to whip you right now! Come on out of there and protect your home! If you don't come out of that door, I'm going to break it down!"

You know that look of Liston's you hear so much about? Well, he sure had it on standing in that door that night. Man, he was tore up! He didn't know what to do. He wanted to come out there after me, but he was already in enough troubles with the police and everything. And you know, if a man figures you're crazy, he'll think twice before he acts, because he figures you're liable to do *anything.* But before he could make up his mind, the police came rushing in with all their sirens going, and they broke it up, telling us we would be arrested for disturbing the peace if we didn't get out of there. So we left. You can bet we laughed all the way to New York.

HALEY: You said this was your first direct needling of Liston. What came next?

CLAY: Every time I got anywhere near him, I'd needle him. Sometimes it was just little things. I had to keep right on him, because I knew he was confused. He had told different people, who got it to me, that he was just going along with my clowning because it would help to build up a gate that would make money for him. So at first I couldn't get him really mad, because he had this idea fixed in his mind. But I kept right on working on him. A man with Liston's kind of mind is very funny. He ain't what you would call a fast thinker. Like I am.

HALEY: What do you mean by the "kind of mind" Liston has?

CLAY: He's got one of them bulldog kind of minds. You understand what I mean. Once he ever starts to thinking something, he won't let hold of it quick.

HALEY: And you feel that your mind is faster?

CLAY: I know it is. What I did to Liston proves it. I'll tell you another way I know. Nobody ever could have conned me the way I did him. If I know a man is going to get in the ring and try to beat me, and take the title, then anything he does outside of regular training, I figure he's got some good reason, and I'd sit down and give his actions careful examination. Liston didn't never even *think* about doing that. Neither did nobody around him, all of his advisors and trainers—didn't even none of them think about it. Even if they had, they sure couldn't have never told him that I represented danger. He was too fixed in his thinking. That's what I mean by his kind of mind.

HALEY: What other direct confrontations did you have with Liston before the fight?

CLAY: Well, another time was just before we signed to fight. It was in Las Vegas. I was there to be on *David*

Brinkley's Journal, and it didn't take me no time to find Liston at a gambling table. People was standing around watching him. He was shooting craps, and I walked up behind him and reached and took some of his chips. He turned around, and I said, "Man, you can't shoot dice!" But he was good-humored. Maybe it was because the people were watching, and maybe he was seeing me helping build up a gate for the fight we were about to sign for—or maybe he was *winning* something for a change. I don't know *what* it was that put him in good spirits, but I just kept right on him. I'd snatch up the dice from him. I could see I was beginning to get to him a little, but not enough. Finally, I had to shoot a loaded water pistol on him. That did it. But he still played it cool, trying to show the people he was trying to humor me. Naturally, the word had spread and people were piling around us. But then very suddenly, Liston *froze* me with that look of his. He said real quiet, "Let's go on over here," and he led the way to a table, and the people hung back. I ain't going to lie. This was the only time since I have known Sonny Liston that he really scared me. I just felt the power and the meanness of the man I was messing with. Anybody tell me about how he has fought cops and beat up tough thugs and all of that, I believe it. I saw that streak in him. He told me, "Get the hell out of here or I'll wipe you out."

HALEY: What did you do?

CLAY: I got the hell out of there. I told you, he had really scared me.

HALEY: Did you consider giving up your campaign to rattle him?

CLAY: Oh, no, I never did think about that. Soon as I got time to think about how he had reacted, I saw I had started for the first time to really get under his skin, and I made up my mind right then that by the time we got to Miami in training, I was going to have him so mad that he would forget everything he knew about fighting, just trying to kill me.

HALEY: Was the scene you made at the airport, when Liston arrived in Miami, part of the plan?

CLAY: You know it. They were making such a big thing of his arriving, you would have thought the Cubans was landing. Well, I wasn't just about to miss *that*! Liston came down off the plane, all cool, and the press was ganged around waiting for an interview. That was when I rushed in the scene, hollering, "Chump! Big ugly bear! I'm going to whip you right now!" Stuff like that. Police were grabbing for me and holding me and I was trying to break loose, and finally I did. I could see I was really turning Liston on. I got up close enough to him and he gave me that evil look again, but I wasn't even thinking about him. "Look, this clowning, it's not cute, and I'm not joking," he said. And I nearly threw a fit. "Joking? Why, you big chump, I'll whip you right here!" And people were grabbing me again, and somebody had rushed up one of them little VIP cars they have at airports. They got Liston, his wife and his bodyguard in it. Joe Louis and Jack Nilon were trying to calm things down. I saw the little car taking off down the tunnel. So I broke loose and took out after it. I was waving my cane, and hollering at Liston. In the tunnel, I guess he told the driver to stop, and he hopped off. Was he *mad*! He hollered, "Listen, you little punk, I'll punch you in the mouth—this has gone too far!" Then people was rushing in and hollering at both of us, and I was throwing off my coat and shouting, "Come on chump, right here!" Finally Liston swung at me, and I ducked. He didn't know he'd had his preview of the fight right then.

HALEY: Who won?

CLAY: I bet you it went on two hours before it really got settled. There weren't no more swings, but Joe Louis and Jack Nilon and the cops and bodyguards got Liston in the airport lounge, and they were guarding the doors to keep me out. I was banging my cane on the door, hollering, "Free! I'll fight you free!" I knew everybody inside could hear me. They couldn't hear nothing else *but* me. "Free! You think I'm jiving, chump? I'll fight you free, right here!"

HALEY: And, of course, it was all an act?

CLAY: Completely—and it was also building the gate. At least, if it hadn't been for the reporters, it would have been a better gate. But right then I didn't want nobody in Miami, except at my camp, thinking I wasn't crazy. I didn't want nobody never thinking nothing about I had any fighting ability.

HALEY: Why do you say that if it hadn't been for the reporters, the gate would have been better?

CLAY: They made people think that Liston was so mean and I was so nothing that they would be throwing away money to buy a ticket. There was over 16,000 seats in that Convention Hall, and it was only about half full. I read where the promoter, Bill MacDonald, lost something like $300,000. But he sure can't blame *me* for it. I was the one that let him get seat prices up as high as $250. I was the first fighter who ever talked a fight into being bounced off Telstar to fifty nations. I got more publicity than any fight ever had. I'm colorful when I rumble. But the people listened to the so-called "experts." If they had listened to me, that Convention Hall would have been overflowing even if they had charged twice the prices.

HALEY: But the reporters' attitudes, you have said, were in the best interests of your strategy.

CLAY: It's six of one and half a dozen of the other. They still made me mad. But, lookahere, I wasn't nearly about done with Liston yet. I mean, right up to the fight I was messing with him. Everybody in my camp carried canes and wore jackets with BEAR-HUNTING across the back. Guys from my camp went into Liston's camp, standing around, watching him training, until Liston quit to personally order them out. We put out the word that we was going to raid Liston's camp. He got so jumpy and under strain that every day, different reporters would come telling me, serious, "Stop angering that man—he will literally kill you!" It was music to my ears. It meant if he was that mad, he had lost all sense of reasoning. If he wasn't thinking nothing but killing me, he wasn't thinking fighting. And you got to think to fight.

HALEY: The press was generally unimpressed with your workouts, and the Liston camp knew it. Was that part of your plan, too?

CLAY: You ain't so stupid. I made sure nobody but my people saw me *really* working out. If anybody else was around, I didn't do no more than go through motions. But look, I'm going to tell you where Liston really lost the fight. Or *when* he lost it. Every day we had been leaking word over there that we were going to pull our raid that day. The Liston people got to the mayor and the police, and we got cautioned that we'd be arrested if we did it. So we made a court case out of it. We requested legal permission to picket Liston's camp, but we were told that a city ordinance prevented carrying signs. We had paid, I remember, $325 for signs like BIG UGLY BEAR, BEAR-HUNTING SEASON, TOO PRETTY TO BE A FIGHTER, BEAR MUST FALL, and like that. So we taped the signs all over my bus. It wasn't no ordinance against signs on a bus. And we loaded the bus up with people from my camp, and screaming teenage girls, and we drove over there and caused such a commotion that people left off from watching Liston train, and we heard he nearly had a fit. One of his men—I know his name, but I guess I better not call it—even pulled a knife on Howard Bingham. Joe Louis run and asked the guy what in the world was the matter with him. But that's the day Liston lost. We heard he went to pieces. It wasn't long before the weigh-in, where they said *I* was the one went to pieces.

HALEY: One doctor described your conduct at the weigh-in as "dangerously disturbed." Another said you acted "scared to death." And seasoned sportswriters used such terms as "hysterical" and "schizophrenic" in reporting your tantrum, for which you were fined $2500. What was the real story?

CLAY: I would just say that it sounds like them doctors and sportswriters had been listening to each other. You know what they said and wrote them things for—to match in what they expected was about to happen. That's what I keep on telling you. If all of them had had their way, I wouldn't have been allowed in the ring.

HALEY: Had you worked out a fight plan by this time?

CLAY: I figured out my strategy and announced it *months* before the fight: "Float like a butterfly, sting like a bee," is what I said.

HALEY: We read that. But what specifically did you mean?

CLAY: To start with, I knew that Liston, overconfident as he was, and helped by reading what all of the newspapers were saying, he never was going to train to fight more than two rounds. I don't know if you happened to read it later that some of his handlers admitted, after the fight, that this was exactly what he did. So that was my guide how to train, to pace myself. You know, a fighter can condition his body to go hard certain rounds, then to coast certain rounds. Nobody can *fight* fifteen rounds. So I trained to fight the first two rounds, and to protect myself from getting hit by Liston. I knew that with the third, he'd start tiring, then he'd get worse every round. So I trained to coast the third, fourth and fifth rounds. I had two reasons for that. One was that I wanted to prove I had the ability to stand up to Liston. The second reason was that I wanted him to wear himself out and get desperate. He would be throwing wild punches, and missing. If I just did that as long as he lasted on his feet, I couldn't miss winning the fight on points. And so I conditioned myself to fight full steam from the sixth through the ninth round, if it lasted that long. I never did think it would go past nine rounds. That's why I announced

I'd take him in eight. I figured I'd be in command by the sixth. I'd be careful—not get hit—and I'd cut him up and shake him up until he would be like a bull, just blind, and missing punches until he was nearly crazy. And I planned that sometime in the eighth, when he had thrown some punch and left himself just right, I'd be all set, and I'd drop him.

Listen here, man, I *knew* I was going to upset the world! You know the only thing I was scared of? I was scared that some of them newspaper "experts" was going to quit praising Liston's big fists long enough to wake up and see what was just as clear as day to me and my camp; and if they printed it, that Liston's camp people might be able to get it into his skull. But I was lucky; that didn't happen. Them newspaper people couldn't have been working no better for me if I had been paying them.

HALEY: Then the fight went about as you had planned?

CLAY: Almost. He came in there at 220 pounds, and untrained to go more than two rounds, and as old as he is—too old—against a kid, and I didn't have an ounce of fat on me. And he didn't have *no* respect for me as a fighter. He was figuring on killing me inside of two rounds. He was a perfect setup. If you remember, I didn't throw many punches, but when I did, they made their mark. I have vicious combinations, and just like I had planned, I hurt his body and I closed his eyes.

HALEY: But Liston did do you some damage, too.

CLAY: You don't expect to fight no fighter without getting hit sometime. But you don't want to get hurt bad, and knocked out—that's the point. Yeah, he hit me some damaging punches. With all the talking I been doing, ain't nobody never heard me say Liston can't hit. He got me in the first with a right to the stomach. In the second, I made the mistake of getting maneuvered on the ropes, and he got in some good shots. And in the last of that second round, after I had cut his eye, he really staggered me there for a minute with a long, hard left. In fact, he did me more damage with that than any other punch. In the fifth, when that stuff—rosin, I guess it was—was in my eyes, and I couldn't see, he hit me with a good left hook to the head.

HALEY: Would you be able to give us a round-by-round account of the fight from your viewpoint?

CLAY: Yeah, I guess I could. The first round, I beat him out, dancing, to keep from getting hit. He was shuffling that way he does, giving me that evil eye. Man, he meant to *kill* me, I ain't kidding! He was jabbing his left—but missing. And I was backpedaling, bobbing, weaving, ducking. He missed with a right hook that would have hurt me. I got away from that, but that was when he got me with that right to my stomach. I just kept running, watching his eyes. Liston's eyes tip you when he's about to throw a heavy punch. Some kind of way, they just flicker. He didn't dream that I'd suddenly stop running when I did, if you remember—and I hit him with a good left and then a flurry of lefts and rights. That was good for points, you know. He nearly flipped, and came after me like a bull. I was hitting and ducking at the same time: that's how neither one of us heard the bell, and was still fighting after it. I remember I got to my corner thinking, "He was supposed to kill me. Well, I'm still alive." Angelo Dundee was working over me, talking a mile a minute. I just watched Liston, so mad he didn't even sit down. I thought to myself, "You gonna wish you had rested all you could when we get past this next round." I could hear some radio or television expert, all excited, you know the way they chatter. The big news was that I hadn't been counted out yet.

Then, at the second-round bell, just like I knew he would, Liston come at me throwing everything. He was going to make up for looking so bad that I had lasted *one* round. This was when he got me on the ropes, where everybody had said he was supposed to kill me. He hit me some, but I weaved and ducked away from most of his shots. I remember one time feeling his arm grazing the back of my neck and thinking—it was like I shouted to myself—"All I got to do is keep this up." And I got out from under and I caught him with some lefts and rights. Then I saw that first cut, high up on his cheekbone. When a man's first cut, it usually looks a bright pink. Then I saw the blood, and I knew that eye was my target from then on. It was my concentrating on that cut that let me get caught with the hardest punch I took, that long left. It rocked me back. But he either didn't realize how good I was hit or he was already getting tired, and he didn't press his chance. I sure heard the bell *that* time. I needed to get to my corner to get my head clear.

Starting in the third round, I saw his expression, how shook he was that we were still out there and *he* was the one cut and bleeding. He didn't know what to do. But I wasn't about to get careless, like Conn did that time against Joe Louis. This was supposed to be one of my coasting, resting rounds, but I couldn't waste no time. I needed one more good shot, for some more insurance with that eye. So when the bell rang, I just tested him to see was he tiring, and he was; and then I got him into the ropes. It didn't take but one good combination. My left was square on his right eye, and a right under his left eye opened a deep gash. I knew it was deep, the way the blood spurted right out. I saw his face up close when he wiped his glove at that cut and saw the blood. At that moment, let me tell you, he looked like he's going to look 20 years from now. Liston was tiring fast in the fourth, and I was coasting. We didn't neither one do very much. But you can bet it wasn't nobody in there complaining they wasn't getting their money's worth.

Then, in the fifth, all of a sudden, after one exchange of shots, there was a feeling in my eyes like some acid was in them. I could see just blurry. When the bell sounded, it felt like fire, and I could just make it back to my corner, telling

Angelo, "I can't see!" And he was swabbing at my eyes. I could hear that excited announcer; he was having a fit. "Something seems to be wrong with Clay!" It sure was something wrong. I didn't care if it was a heavyweight title fight I had worked so long for, I wasn't going out there and get murdered because I couldn't see. Every time I blinked it hurt so bad I said, "Cut off my gloves, Angelo—leave me out of here." Then I heard the bell, and the referee, Barney Felix, yelled to me to get out there, and at the same time Angelo was pushing me up, shouting, "This is the big one, daddy. We aren't going to quit now!" And I was out there again, blinking. Angelo was shouting, "Stay away from him! Stay away!" I got my left in Liston's face and kept it there, kind of staving him off, and at the same time I knew where he was. I was praying he wouldn't guess what was the matter. But he had to see me blinking, and then he shook me with that left to the head and a lot of shots to the body. Now, I ain't too sorry it happened, because it proved I could take Liston's punching. He had found some respect for me, see? He wasn't going so much for the knockout; he was trying to hurt my body, then try for a kill. Man, in that round, my plans were *gone*. I was just trying to keep alive, hoping the tears would wash out my eyes. I could open them just enough to get a good glimpse of Liston, and then it hurt so bad I blinked them closed again. Liston was snorting like a horse. He was trying to hit me square, and I was just moving every which way, because I knew if he connected right, it could be all over right there.

But in the corner after that fifth round, the stuff pretty well washed out of my eyes. I could see again, and I was ready to carry the fight to Liston. And I was gaining my second wind now, as I had conditioned myself, to pace the fight, like I was telling you. My corner people knew it, and they were calling to me, "Get mad, baby!" They knew I was ready to go the next three rounds at top steam, and I knew I was going to make Liston look terrible. I hit him with eight punches in a row, until he doubled up. I remember thinking something like, "Yeah, you old sucker! You try to be so big and bad!" He was gone. He knew he couldn't last. It was the first time in the fight that I set myself flat-footed. I missed a right that might have dropped him. But I jabbed and jabbed at that cut under his eye, until it was wide open and bleeding worse than before. I knew he wasn't due to last much longer. Then, right at the end of the round, I rocked back his head with two left hooks.

I got back to my stool, and under me I could hear the press like they was gone wild. I twisted around and hollered down at the reporters right under me, "I'm gonna upset the world!" I never will forget how their faces was looking up at me like they couldn't believe it. I happened to be looking right at Liston when that warning buzzer sounded, and I didn't believe it when he spat out his mouthpiece. I just couldn't believe it—but there it was laying there. And then something just told me he wasn't coming out! I give a whoop and come off that stool like it was red hot. It's a funny thing, but I wasn't even thinking about Liston—I was thinking about nothing but that hypocrite press. All of them down there had wrote so much about me bound to get killed by the big fists. It was even rumors that right after the weigh-in I had been taken to the asylum somewhere, and another rumor that I had caught a plane and run off. I couldn't think about nothing but all that. I went dancing around the ring, hollering down at them reporters, "Eat your words! Eat! Eat!" And I hollered at the people, "I am the *king*!"

HALEY: Despite your victory, the fight ended under a cloud of doubt about the genuineness of Liston's arm injury. What's your own opinion?

CLAY: Eight doctors said his arm was hurt. I ain't going to argue with no eight doctors' opinion. And I don't mean that I think nothing different at all. You take a man punching with the strength and force Liston has in a punch; if all he connects with is air—because wherever he hit, I wasn't there—then, yeah, I think it explains how he could have torn a muscle.

HALEY: There was another controversy about the honesty of your failure to pass the three Army preinduction qualification tests that you took shortly after the fight. Any comment?

CLAY: The truth don't hurt nobody. The fact is I never was too bright in school. I just barely graduated. I had a D-minus average. I ain't ashamed of it, though. I mean, how much do school principals make a month? But when I looked at a lot of the questions they had on them Army tests, I just didn't know the answers. I didn't even know how to *start* after finding the answers. That's all. So I didn't pass. It was the Army's decision that they didn't want me to go in the service. They're the boss. I don't want to say no whole lot about it.

HALEY: Was it embarrassing to be declared mentally unfit?

CLAY: I have said I am the greatest. Ain't nobody ever heard me say I was the smartest.

HALEY: What is your feeling about the fact that your purse was withheld after the fight?

CLAY: I don't understand it. I'm not involved in any tax problems. How can they justify holding up my money? But let me tell you something: Money and riches don't mean nothing to me. I don't care nothing about being no rich individual. I'm not living for glory or for fame; all this is doomed for destruction. You got it today, tomorrow it's gone. I got bigger things on my mind than that. I got Islam on my mind.

HALEY: Speaking of Islam, the National Boxing Association announced that it was considering the revocation of your heavyweight title because of your membership in the Black Muslims, which you announced just after the fight. Have you heard any official word on their decision?

CLAY: It just fizzled out. But until it did, the N.B.A. was going to condemn me, try me, sentence me and execute me, all by themselves. Ain't this country supposed to be where every man can have the religion he wants, even *no* religion if that's what he wants? It ain't a court in America that would take a man's job, or his title, because of his religious convictions. The Constitution forbids Congress from making any laws involving a man's religion. But the N.B.A. would take it on itself to take away my title—for what? What have I done to hurt boxing? I've *helped* boxing. I don't smoke, I don't drink, I don't bother with nobody. Ain't it funny they never said nothing about Liston? He's been arrested for armed robbery, beating up cops, carrying concealed weapons, and I don't know *what* all. And how come they didn't lift Gene Fullmer's title? He was a Mormon. His religion believes Negroes are inferior; they ban Negroes from membership. But I guess that's all right. The N.B.A. don't have no power noway. They can't stop nobody from fighting. And even if they could, it wouldn't matter, because I don't put that much value on no heavyweight crown anyway. Time was when I did, but that was before I found the religious convictions that I have. When I started getting attacked so bad because I am a Muslim, I had to decide, if it would come to me having to give up one or the other, what was most important to me, my religion or my fighting. I made up my mind that I could give up fighting and never look back. Because it's a whole pile of other ways I could make a living. Me being the world heavyweight champion feels very small and cheap to me when I put that alongside of how millions of my poor black brothers and sisters are having to struggle just to get their human rights here in America. Maybe God got me here for a sacrifice. I don't know. But I do know that God don't want me to go down for standing up.

HALEY: What or who made you decide to join the Muslims?

CLAY: Nobody or nothing *made* me decide. I make up my mind for myself. In 1960, in Miami, I was training for a fight. It wasn't long after I had won the 1960 Olympic Gold Medal over there in Rome. Herb Liler was the fellow I was going to fight, I remember. I put him on the floor in four. Anyway, one day this Muslim minister came to meet me and he asked me wouldn't I like to come to his mosque and hear about the history of my forefathers. I never had heard no black man talking about no forefathers, except that they were slaves, so I went to a meeting. And this minister started teaching, and the things he said really shook me up. Things like that we 20,000,000 black people in America didn't know our true identities, or even our true family names. And we were the direct descendants of black men and women stolen from a rich black continent and brought here and stripped of all knowledge of themselves and taught to hate themselves and their kind. And that's how us so-called "Negroes" had come to be the only race among mankind that loved its enemies. Now, I'm the kind that catches on quick. I said to myself, listen here, this man's *saying* something! I hope don't nobody never hit me in the ring hard as it did when that brother minister said the Chinese are named after China, Russians after Russia, Cubans after Cuba, Italians after Italy, the English after England, and clear on down the line everybody was named for somewhere he could call home, except us. He said, "What country are we so-called 'Negroes' named for? *No* country! We are just a lost race." Well, *boom!* That really shook me up.

HALEY: Was that when you joined the Muslims?

CLAY: Not right then, no. Before I joined, I attended a lot of mosque meetings in different places I went. I never did come out of a meeting not understanding something I hadn't known or even thought about before. Everywhere I looked, I started seeing things in a new light. Like, I remember right in our house back in Louisville, all the pictures on

the walls were white people. Nothing about us black people. A picture of a white Jesus Christ. Now, what painter
ever *saw* Jesus? So who says Jesus was white? And all my
life, I had been seeing the black man getting his head
whipped by the white man, and stuck in the white man's
jails, and things like that. And myself, I had to admit that
up to then, I had always hated being black, just like other
Negroes, hating our kind, instead of loving one another.
The more I saw and thought, the more the truth made sense
to me. Whatever I'm for, I always have believed in talking
it up, and the first thing you know, I was in Muslim
meetings calling out just like the rest, "Right, brother! Tell
it, brother! Keep it coming!" And today my religion is
Islam, and I'm proud of it.

HALEY: How has it changed your life?

CLAY: In every way. It's pulled me up and cleaned me up
as a human being.

HALEY: Can you be more explicit?

CLAY: Well, before I became a Muslim, I used to drink.
Yes, I did. The truth is the truth. And after I had fought and
beat somebody, I didn't hardly go nowhere without two
big, pretty women beside me. But my change is one of the
things that will mark me as a great man in history. When
you can live righteous in the hell of North America—
when a man can control his life, his physical needs, his
lower self, he elevates himself. The downfall of so many
great men is that they haven't been able to control their
appetite for women.

HALEY: But you have?

CLAY: We Muslims don't touch a woman unless we're
married to her.

HALEY: Are you saying that you don't have affairs with
women?

CLAY: I don't even kiss a woman. I'm ashamed of myself,
but sometimes I've caught myself wishing I had found
Islam about five years from now, maybe—with all the

temptations I have to resist. But I don't even kiss none, because you get too close, it's almost impossible to stop. I'm a young man, you know, in the prime of life.

HALEY: You mention temptations. What are they?

CLAY: All types of women—white women, too—make passes at me. Girls find out where I live and knock at the door at one and two in the morning. They send me their pictures and phone numbers, saying please just telephone them, they would like to meet me, do I need a secretary? I've even had girls come up here wearing scarves on their heads, with no make-up and all that, trying to act like young Muslim sisters. But the only catch is a Muslim sister never would do that.

HALEY: Did you have any other religious affiliation before Islam?

CLAY: When I was twelve years old, and didn't know what I was doing, I was baptized in the Centennial Baptist Church in Louisville.

HALEY: Have you given up Christianity, then?

CLAY: The Christian religion has just been used to brainwash the black man here in America. It has just taught him to look for his heaven in the sky, in the hereafter, while the white man enjoys his heaven here on earth.

HALEY: As the owner of four Cadillacs and the recipient of a $600,000 purse earned largely from white patronage of your fight with Liston, do you think that assertion is entirely true in your own case?

CLAY: Have you heard anybody complaining he didn't get his money's worth? No! All of the noise is about my religion, something that has nothing to do with fighting. They didn't mind my being champion until they found out I was a Muslim. Then they didn't want nothing to do with me. White people, they worry more about Islam than they do about the championship.

HALEY: Don't you feel that whites have some reason for

concern that the heavyweight champion belongs to an organization that is alleged to teach hatred of whites?

CLAY: Look, the black man that's trying to integrate, he's getting beat up and bombed and shot. But the black man that says he don't want to integrate, he gets called a "hate teacher." Lookahere, now Chubby Checker is catching hell with a white woman. And I'm catching hell for *not* wanting a white woman. The followers of Mr. Elijah Muhammad, we're not trying to marry no white man's sisters and daughters. We're not trying to force our way into no white neighborhoods. It look like to me that the white people who are so against integrated schools and restaurants and hotels ought to be *glad* about what Mr. Muhammad is teaching his followers. The only way for peace between the races is a separation of the races.

HALEY: Are you against the Civil Rights Act, then?

CLAY: I think that the Civil Rights Act will lead to bloodshed. It already has. It won't change people's hearts. But I don't call it hate. I call it human nature. I don't think that white people hate colored people. You just don't never see a rabbit eating with a lion. I think that all of this "integration" started backfiring when it put the white man on the spot. It ain't going to go on much further. I think that the black man needs to get together with his own kind. He needs to say, "Let's don't go where we're not wanted." You take Sonny Liston. He was the champion of the world, and that's supposed to include America. But when he tried to buy a house in a segregated neighborhood in Miami, he was turned down. The white people don't want integration: I don't believe in forcing it and the Muslims don't either.

HALEY: Is that why you've chosen to live in Harlem?

CLAY: Right. I could be living all exclusive, downtown, in some skyscraper hotel. I could be living right up in the hotel's penthouse, with my friends in rooms all around me. But I don't want none of that. I stay right in the heart of

Harlem, in a place that a workingman with a good job could afford. I'm just used to being around my own people. I like being around my own people. It's just human nature to enjoy being around your own kind. I don't want no trouble. I am up here in the heart of blacktown. I can't find nothing wrong with that, but it seems to bother everybody else, it looks like. I been around my own people all of my life. Why would I want to try to leave them now? You have to be all the time putting on an act when you're trying to live and hang around somewhere you're not wanted, or they just put up with you for your money. I'm at ease living among my people. I'm never all tensed up; I don't have to be a side show all the time. I'm around unity, rhythm and soul. Our people are warm people. I don't like to be around cold people. I go out every morning early and walk up and down in the streets, and I talk to winos and the working people and everybody. I stand where they go down to the subway, and I say hello. I'm different from when Patterson was the champ. He wasn't anywhere near as popular as I am—not among our people, anyway.

HALEY: What do you have to say about the fact that many Negroes, including several Negro leaders, have said that they have no desire to be identified with a heavyweight champion who is a Black Muslim?

CLAY: It's ridiculous for Negroes to be attacking somebody trying to stand up for their own race. People are always telling me "what a good example I could set for my people" if I just wasn't a Muslim. I've heard over and over how come I couldn't have been like Joe Louis and Sugar Ray. Well, they're gone now, and the black man's condition is just the same, ain't it? We're still catching hell. The fact is that my being a Muslim moved me from the sports pages to the front pages. I'm a whole lot bigger man than I would be if I was just a champion prizefighter. Twenty-four hours a day I get offers—to tour somewhere overseas, to visit colleges, to make speeches. Places like Harvard and Tuskegee, television shows, interviews, recordings. I get letters from all over. They are addressed to me in ways like "The Greatest Boxer in the World, U.S.A." and they come straight to me wherever they're mailed from. People want to write books about me. And I ought to have stock in Western Union and cable companies, I get so many of them. I'm trying to show you how I been elevated from the normal stature of fighters to being a world figure, a leader, a statesman.

HALEY: Statesman?

CLAY: That's what I said. Listen, after I beat Liston, some African diplomats invited me to the United Nations. And because I'm a Muslim, I was welcomed like a king on my tour of Africa and the Middle East. I'm the first world champion that ever toured the world that he is champion of.

HALEY: Is it true that you incensed Nigerians during your tour, by reneging on a promise to fight an exhibition match there, and by making the remark, on departing for Egypt, that "Cairo is more important than Nigeria"?

CLAY: It was a whole lot of confusion going on. We had planned a week in Nigeria, then a week in Ghana. But when we got over there, somehow with all kinds of this and that functions calling for me, our whole schedule got messed up. One Sunday I come back from Ghana to Nigeria to fight that exhibition. It was arranged for us to get to Cairo that Wednesday. Then my exhibition fight date got put forward. I figured it would make us disappoint the Cairo government that had bumped people off planes for us, things like that. So I said how important it was to get to Cairo on time. But when somebody got done quoting it, it wasn't told like I had said it. Any time you hear about me insulting black people, it's a lie. Anyway, wasn't nobody over there mad at me because of my *religion.* Somebody told me over there that I got the biggest welcome ever given to any American.

HALEY: You met both Prime Minister Nkrumah of

Ghana and Egypt's President Nasser on the trip. What was your impression of them?

CLAY: Well, I looked at Prime Minister Nkrumah, and it come to me that he looked just like so many Negroes in America—except there he was, the head of a country. And President Nasser, one of the six most powerful men in the world, he welcomed me as a Black Muslim, just as friendly as if he had been knowing me all my life.

HALEY: Apart from influential friends, what do you feel you got out of the trip?

CLAY: Well, it showed me what Mr. Elijah Muhammad's teachings had taught me: that Africa is the home of Original Man, the black man, and that Africa, where the slaves was stolen from, has all kinds of rich history. And it is the richest continent on earth. Everybody knows that the biggest diamond ever found was found in black Africa. And let me tell you something—it wasn't just seeing the new buildings and cars and stuff; it's what you *feel* in Africa. Black people that's free and proud—they don't *feel* like that over here. I never have felt it here except among my Muslim brothers and sisters.

HALEY: Your Muslim activities will soon have to be interrupted long enough to defend your title against Sonny Liston in your upcoming rematch. Now that he's familiar with your strategy and skills, do you think he'll be a tougher opponent?

CLAY: I know one thing: He would have to think he could put up a better fight than he did the last time. Liston has been through quite a bit.

HALEY: Do *you* think he'll put up a better fight?

CLAY: Maybe, but I'll have the edge again. Liston will be fighting a comeback. He'll be in the position of having to *prove* he can beat me. So he'll come in that ring scared he's going to lose. A lot of people still refuse to accept it, but Liston *knows* he was whipped by a better boxer. Another thing, don't never forget that boxing is for young men. How old is Liston?

HALEY: According to published reports, around 32.

CLAY: Well, I hear he's pushing forty. He ain't physically *capable* of forcing a body that old through four and a half months of the strong training a fighter would need to meet a young, strong fighter like me.

HALEY: Doug Jones has been touted as another possible contender for your title. What's your appraisal of him?

CLAY: He's a good, strong man, a good boxer. He's fast, and he's got determination. He's the possible champ after I quit.

HALEY: How about Patterson? Do you think he has a chance to regain his title a second time?

CLAY: Patterson! Don't make me laugh. I'm a natural heavyweight, and he was never anything but a blown-up light-heavy. He could never take my punches. I could play with him, cut him up and take him out whenever I got ready. And he knows it. That's why he always ducked me when he was champ. He ain't no fool. You know, at the Olympic games in Rome, I told Patterson, "Two, three years from now, I'm going to take your title." He said, "You're a good kid, keep trying, kid." Well, I bet you he has since thought that over many a day.

HALEY: If he knows he couldn't beat you, how do you explain his recent campaign to meet you in a title match?

CLAY: Only reason he's decided to come out of his shell now is to try and make himself a big hero to the white man by saving the heavyweight title from being held by a Muslim. I wish you would print for Patterson to read that if he ever convinces my managers to let him in the same ring with me, it's going to be the first time I ever trained to develop in myself a brutal killer instinct. I've never felt that way about nobody else. Fighting is just a sport, a game, to me. But Patterson I would want to beat to the floor for the way he rushed out of hiding after his last whipping, announcing that he wanted to fight me because no Muslim deserved to be the champ. I never had no concern about his having the Catholic religion. But he was going to jump up to fight me to be the white man's champion. And I don't know no sadder example of nobody making a bigger fool of himself. I don't think three more weeks had passed before it was in the papers about him trying to sell his big, fine home in a so-called "integrated" neighborhood because his white neighbors wouldn't speak to his family, and white children were calling his children "nigger" and a white man next door even had put up a fence to keep from having to even *see* Patterson. I ain't never read nothing no more pitiful than how Patterson told the newspapers, "I tried to integrate—it just didn't work." It's like when he was the champion, the only time he would be caught in Harlem was when he was in the back of a car, waving, in some parade. The big shot didn't have no time for his own kind, he was so busy "integrating." And now he wants to fight me because I stick up for black people. I'll tell him again, he sure better think five or six times before he gets into any ring with me.

HALEY: Are there any other active heavyweights, apart from Doug Jones, whom you rate as title contenders?

CLAY: Not in my class, of course. But below that, after Jones—and Liston—there's Ernie Terrell. He's a tall boy, a good left jab. He moves good, but he tires easy. He doesn't have enough experience to take me on yet. But he's a good kid. And Cleveland Williams. If he even *dreamed* he fought me, he'd apologize. He needs a *lot* more experience. Liston knocked him out twice. Williams, if he's pressured, will quit in a minute. I can't see any more after these. I don't really even watch fighting much, except films of the greatest.

HALEY: Just you?

CLAY: Just me.

HALEY: Are you the greatest now fighting, or the greatest in boxing history?

CLAY: Now, a whole lot of people ain't going to like this. But I'm going to tell you the truth—you asked me. It's too many great old champions to go listing them one by one. But ain't no need to. I think that Joe Louis, in his prime, could have whipped them all—I mean anyone you want to name. And I would have beat Louis. Now, look—people don't like to face the facts. All they can think about is Joe Louis' punch. Well, he did have a deadly punch, just like Liston has a deadly punch. But if Louis didn't hit nothing but air, like Liston didn't with me, then we got to look at other things. Even if Louis did hit me a few times, remember they all said Liston was a tougher one-punch man than even Joe Louis. And I took some of Liston's best shots. Remember that. Then, too, I'm taller than Louis. But I tell you what would decide the fight: I'm *faster* than Louis was. No, Louis and none of the rest of them couldn't whip me. Look—it ain't *never* been another fighter like me. Ain't never been no *nothing* like me.

MARTIN LUTHER KING, JR.

A Candid Conversation with the Nobel Prize—winning Leader of the Civil Rights Movement

JAY B. LEVITON

On December 5, 1955, to the amused annoyance of the white citizens of Montgomery, Alabama, an obscure young Baptist minister named Martin Luther King, Jr., called a city-wide Negro boycott of its segregated bus system. To their consternation, however, it was almost 100 percent successful; it lasted for 381 days and nearly bankrupted the bus line. When King's home was bombed during the siege, thousands of enraged Negroes were ready to riot, but the soft-spoken clergyman prevailed on them to channel their anger into nonviolent protest—and became world-renowned as a champion of Gandhi's philosophy of passive resistance.

*Within a year the Supreme Court had ruled Jim Crow
seating unlawful on Montgomery's buses, and King found
himself, at 27, on the front lines of a nonviolent Negro
revolution against racial injustice.*

*Moving to Atlanta, he formed the Southern Christian
Leadership Conference, an alliance of church-affiliated civil
rights organizations which joined such activist groups as
CORE and SNCC in a widening campaign of sit-in demonstrations and freedom rides throughout the South. Dissatis-
fied with the slow pace of the protest movement, King
decided to create a crisis in 1963 that would "dramatize the
Negro plight and galvanize the national conscience." He
was abundantly successful, for his mass nonviolent demonstration in arch-segregationist Birmingham resulted in the
arrest of more than 3300 Negroes, including King himself;
and millions were outraged by front-page pictures of Negro
demonstrators being brutalized by the billy sticks, police
dogs and fire hoses of police chief Bull Connor.*

*In the months that followed, mass sit-ins and demonstra-
tions erupted in 800 Southern cities; President Kennedy
proposed a Civil Rights Bill aimed at the enforcement of
voting rights, equal employment opportunities, and the
desegregation of public facilities; and the now-famous march
on Washington, 200,000 strong, was eloquently addressed
by King on the steps of the Lincoln Memorial. By the end of
that "long hot summer," America's Negroes had won more
tangible gains than in any year since 1865—and Martin
Luther King had become their acknowledged leader and
most respected spokesman.*

*He earned it the hard way: In the course of his civil rights
work he has been jailed 14 times and stabbed once in the
chest; his home has been bombed three times; and his daily
mail brings a steady flow of death threats and obscenities.
Undeterred, he works 20 hours a day, travels 325,000 miles
and makes 450 speeches a year throughout the country on
behalf of the Negro cause. Inundated by calls, callers and*

correspondence at his S.C.L.C. office in Atlanta, he also finds time somehow to preach, visit the sick and help the poor among his congregation at the city's Ebenezer Baptist Church, of which he and his father are the pastors.

So heavy, in fact, were his commitments when we called him last summer for an interview, that two months elapsed before he was able to accept our request for an appointment. We kept it—only to spend a week in Atlanta waiting vainly for him to find a moment for more than an apology and a hurried handshake. A bit less pressed when we returned for a second visit, King was finally able to sandwich in a series of hour and half-hour conversations with us among the other demands of a grueling week. The resultant interview is the longest he has ever granted to any publication.

Though he spoke with heartfelt and often eloquent sincerity, his tone was one of businesslike detachment. And his mood, except for one or two flickering smiles of irony, was gravely serious—never more so than the moment, during a rare evening with his family on our first night in town, when his four children chided him affectionately for "not being home enough." After dinner, we began the interview on this personal note.

HALEY: Dr. King, are your children old enough to be aware of the issues at stake in the civil rights movement, and of your role in it?

KING: Yes, they are—especially my oldest child, Yolanda. Two years ago, I remember, I returned home after serving one of my terms in the Albany, Georgia, jail, and she asked me, "Daddy, why do you have to go to jail so much?" I told her that I was involved in a struggle to make conditions better for the colored people, and thus for *all* people. I explained that because things are as they are, someone has to take a stand, that it is necessary for someone to go to jail because many Southern officials seek to maintain the barriers that have historically been erected to exclude the colored people. I tried to make her understand that someone had to do this to make the world better— for *all* children. She was only six at that time, but she was already aware of segregation because of an experience that we had had.

HALEY: Would you mind telling us about it?

KING: Not at all. The family often used to ride with me to the Atlanta airport, and on our way, we always passed Funtown, a sort of miniature Disneyland with mechanical rides and that sort of thing. Yolanda would inevitably say, "I want to go to Funtown," and I would always evade a direct reply. I really didn't know how to explain to her why she couldn't go. Then one day at home, she ran downstairs exclaiming that a TV commercial was urging people to come to Funtown. Then my wife and I had to sit down with her between us and try to explain it. I have won some applause as a speaker, but my tongue twisted and my speech stammered seeking to explain to my six-year-old daughter why the public invitation on television didn't include her, and others like her. One of the most painful experiences I have ever faced was to see her tears when I told her that Funtown was *closed* to colored children, for I realized that at that moment the first dark cloud of inferiority had floated into her little mental sky, that at that moment her personality had begun to warp with that first unconscious bitterness toward white people. It was the first time that prejudice based upon skin color had been explained to her. But it was of paramount importance to me that she not grow up bitter. So I told her that although many white people were against her going to Funtown, there were many others who *did* want colored children to go. It helped somewhat. Pleasantly, word came to me later that Funtown had quietly desegregated, so I took Yolanda.

A number of white persons there asked, "Aren't you Dr. King, and isn't this your daughter?" I said we were, and she heard them say how glad they were to see us there.

HALEY: As one who grew up in the economically comfortable, socially insulated environment of a middle-income home in Atlanta, can you recall when it was that you yourself first became painfully and personally aware of racial prejudice?

KING: Very clearly. When I was 14, I had traveled from Atlanta to Dublin, Georgia, with a dear teacher of mine, Mrs. Bradley; she's dead now. I had participated there in an oratorical contest sponsored by the Negro Elks. It turned out to be a memorable day, for I had succeeded in winning the contest. My subject, I recall, ironically enough, was "The Negro and the Constitution." Anyway, that night, Mrs. Bradley and I were on a bus returning to Atlanta, and at a small town along the way, some white passengers boarded the bus, and the white driver ordered us to get up and give the whites our seats. We didn't move quickly enough to suit him, so he began cursing us, calling us "black sons of bitches." I intended to stay right in that seat, but Mrs. Bradley finally urged me up, saying we had to obey the law. And so we stood up in the aisle for the 90 miles to Atlanta. That night will never leave my memory. It was the angriest I have ever been in my life.

HALEY: Wasn't it another such incident on a bus, years later, that thrust you into your present role as a civil rights leader?

KING: Yes, it was—in Montgomery, Alabama, in 1955. E. D. Nixon, a Pullman porter long identified with the NAACP, telephoned me late one night to tell me that Mrs. Rosa Parks had been arrested around seven-thirty that evening when a bus driver demanded that she give up her seat, and she refused—because her feet hurt. Nixon had already bonded Mrs. Parks out of prison. He said, "It's time this stops; we ought to boycott the buses." I agreed and said,

"Now." The next night we called a meeting of Negro community leaders to discuss it, and on Saturday and Sunday we appealed to the Negro community, with leaflets and from the pulpits, to boycott the buses on Monday. We had in mind a one-day boycott, and we were banking on 60-percent success. But the boycott saw instantaneous 99-percent success. We were so pleasantly surprised and impressed that we continued, and for the next 381 days the boycott of Montgomery's buses by Negroes was 99%⁄10 successful.

HALEY: Were you sure you'd win?

KING: There was one dark moment when we doubted it. We had been struggling to make the boycott a success when the city of Montgomery successfully obtained an injunction from the court to stop our car pool. I didn't know what to say to our people. They had backed us up, and we had let them down. It was a desolate moment. I saw, all of us saw, that the court was leaning against us. I remember telling a group of those working closest with me to spread in the Negro community the message, "We must have the faith that things will work out somehow, that God will make a way for us when there seems no way." It was about noontime, I remember, when Rex Thomas of the Associated Press rushed over to where I was sitting and told me of the news flash that the U.S. Supreme Court had declared that bus segregation in Montgomery was unconstitutional. It had literally been the darkest hour before the dawn.

HALEY: You and your followers were criticized, after your arrest for participating in the boycott, for accepting bail and leaving jail. Do you feel, in retrospect, that you did the right thing?

KING: No; I think it was a mistake, a tactical error for me to have left jail, by accepting bail, after being indicted along with 125 others, mainly drivers of our car pool, under an old law of doubtful constitutionality, an "antiboycott" ordinance. I should have stayed in prison. It would have nationally dramatized and deepened our movement even earlier, and it would have more quickly aroused and keened America's conscience.

HALEY: Do you feel you've been guilty of any comparable errors in judgment since then?

KING: Yes, I do—in Albany, Georgia, in 1962. If I had that to do again, I would guide that community's Negro leadership differently than I did. The mistake I made there was to protest against segregation generally rather than against a single and distinct facet of it. Our protest was so vague that we got nothing, and the people were left very depressed and in despair. It would have been much better to have concentrated upon integrating the buses or the lunch counters. One victory of this kind would have been symbolic, would have galvanized support and boosted morale. But I don't mean that our work in Albany ended in failure. The Negro people there straightened up their bent backs; you can't ride a man's back unless it's bent. Also, thousands of Negroes registered to vote who never had voted before, and because of the expanded Negro vote in the next election for governor of Georgia—which pitted a moderate candidate against a rabid segregationist— Georgia elected its first governor who had pledged to respect and enforce the law impartially. And what we learned from our mistakes in Albany helped our later campaigns in other cities to be more effective. We have never since scattered our efforts in a general attack on segregation, but have focused upon specific, symbolic objectives.

HALEY: Can you recall any other mistakes you've made in leading the movement?

KING: Well, the most pervasive mistake I have made was in believing that because our cause was just, we could be sure that the white ministers of the South, once their Christian consciences were challenged, would rise to our aid. I felt that white ministers would take our cause to the white power structures. I ended up, of course, chastened and disillusioned. As our movement unfolded, and direct appeals were made to white ministers, most folded their hands—and some even took stands *against* us.

HALEY: Their stated reason for refusing to help was that it was not the proper role of the church to "intervene in secular affairs." Do you disagree with this view?

KING: Most emphatically. The essence of the Epistles of Paul is that Christians should *rejoice* at being deemed worthy to suffer for what they believe. The projection of a social gospel, in my opinion, is the true witness of a Christian life. This is the meaning of the true *ekklēsia*—the inner, spiritual church. The church once changed society. It was then a thermostat of society. But today I feel that too much of the church is merely a thermometer, which measures rather than molds popular opinion.

HALEY: Are you speaking of the church in general—or the white church in particular?

KING: The white church, I'm sorry to say. Its leadership has greatly disappointed me. Let me hasten to say there are some outstanding exceptions. As one whose Christian roots go back through three generations of ministers—my father, grandfather and great-grandfather—I will remain true to the church as long as I live. But the laxity of the white church collectively has caused me to weep tears of love. There cannot be deep disappointment without deep love. Time and again in my travels, as I have seen the outward beauty of white churches, I have had to ask myself, "What kind of people worship there? Who is their God? Is their God the God of Abraham, Isaac and Jacob, and is their Savior the Savior who hung on the cross at Golgótha? Where were their voices when a black race took upon itself the cross of protest against man's injustice to man? Where were their voices when defiance and hatred were called for by white men who sat in these very churches?"

As the Negro struggles against grave injustice, most white churchmen offer pious irrelevancies and sanctimonious trivialities. As you say, they claim that the gospel of Christ should have no concern with social issues. Yet white churchgoers, who insist that they are Christians, practice segregation as rigidly in the house of God as they do in movie-houses. Too much of the white church is timid and ineffectual, and some of it is shrill in its defense of bigotry and prejudice. In most communities, the spirit of *status quo* is endorsed by the churches.

My personal disillusionment with the church began when I was thrust into the leadership of the bus protest in Montgomery. I was confident that the white ministers, priests and rabbis of the South would prove strong allies in our just cause. But some became open adversaries, some cautiously shrank from the issue, and others hid behind silence. My optimism about help from the white church was shattered; and on too many occasions since, my hopes for the white church have been dashed. There are many signs that the judgment of God is upon the church as never before. Unless the early sacrificial spirit is recaptured, I am very much afraid that today's Christian church will lose its authenticity, forfeit the loyalty of millions, and we will see the Christian church dismissed as a social club with no meaning or effectiveness for our time, as a form without substance, as salt without savor. The real tragedy, though, is not Martin Luther King's disillusionment with the church—for I am sustained by its spiritual blessings as a minister of the gospel with a lifelong commitment; the tragedy is that in my travels, I meet young people of all races whose disenchantment with the church has soured into outright disgust.

HALEY: Do you feel that the Negro church has come any closer to "the projection of a social gospel" in its commitment to the cause?

KING: I must say that when my Southern Christian Leadership Conference began its work in Birmingham, we encountered numerous Negro church reactions that had to be overcome. Negro ministers were among other Negro leaders who felt they were being pulled into something that they had not helped to organize. This is almost always a problem. Negro community unity was the first requisite if our goals were to be realized. I talked with many groups, including one group of 200 ministers, my theme to them being that a minister cannot preach the glories of heaven while ignoring social conditions in his own community that cause men an earthly hell. I stressed that the Negro minister had particular freedom and independence to provide strong, firm leadership, and I asked how the Negro would ever gain freedom without his minister's guidance, support and inspiration. These ministers finally decided to entrust our movement with their support, and as a result, the role of the Negro church today, by and large, is a glorious example in the history of Christendom. For never in Christian history, within a Christian country, have Christian churches been on the receiving end of such naked brutality and violence as we are witnessing here in America today. Not since the days of the Christians in the catacombs has God's house, as a symbol, weathered such attack as the Negro churches.

I shall never forget the grief and bitterness I felt on that terrible September morning when a bomb blew out the lives of those four little, innocent girls sitting in their Sunday-school class in the 16th Street Baptist Church in Birmingham. I think of how a woman cried out, crunching through broken glass, "My God, we're not even safe in church!" I think of how that explosion blew the face of Jesus Christ from a stained-glass window. It was symbolic of how sin and evil had blotted out the life of Christ. I can remember thinking that if men were this bestial, was it all worth it? Was there any hope? Was there any way out?

HALEY: Do you still feel this way?

KING: No, time has healed the wounds—and buoyed me with the inspiration of another moment which I shall never forget: when I saw with my own eyes over 3000 young Negro boys and girls, totally unarmed, leave Birmingham's 16th Street Baptist Church to march to a prayer meeting— ready to pit nothing but the power of their bodies and souls against Bull Connor's police dogs, clubs and fire hoses. When they refused Connor's bellowed order to turn back, he whirled and shouted to his men to turn on the hoses. It was one of the most fantastic events of the Birmingham story that these Negroes, many of them on their knees, stared, unafraid and unmoving, at Connor's men with the hose nozzles in their hands. Then, slowly the Negroes stood up and advanced, and Connor's men fell back as though hypnotized, as the Negroes marched on past to hold their prayer meeting. I saw there, I felt there, for the first time, the pride and the *power* of nonviolence.

Another time I will never forget was one Saturday night, late, when my brother telephoned me in Atlanta from Birmingham—that city which some call "Bombing-ham"—which I had just left. He told me that a bomb had wrecked his home, and that another bomb, positioned to exert its maximum force upon the motel room in which I had been staying, had injured several people. My brother described the terror in the streets as Negroes, furious at the bombings, fought whites. Then, behind his voice, I heard a rising chorus of beautiful singing: "We shall overcome." Tears came into my eyes that at such a tragic moment, my race still could sing its hope and faith.

HALEY: *We Shall Overcome* has become the unofficial song and slogan of the civil rights movement. Do you consider such inspirational anthems important to morale?

KING: In a sense, songs are the *soul* of a movement. Consider, in World War Two, *Praise the Lord and Pass the Ammunition,* and in World War One, *Over There* and *Tipperary,* and during the Civil War, *Battle Hymn of the Republic* and *John Brown's Body.* A Negro song anthology would include sorrow songs, shouts for joy, battle hymns, anthems. Since slavery, the Negro has sung throughout his struggle in America. *Steal Away* and *Go Down, Moses* were the songs of faith and inspiration which were sung on the plantations. For the same reasons the slaves sang, Negroes today sing freedom songs, for we, too, are in bondage. We sing out our determination that "We shall overcome, black and white together, we shall overcome someday." I should also mention a song parody that I enjoyed very much which the Negroes sang during our campaign in Albany, Georgia. It goes: "I'm comin', I'm comin' / And my head *ain't* bendin' low / I'm walkin' tall, I'm talkin' strong / I'm America's *New* Black Joe."

HALEY: Your detractors in the Negro community often refer to you snidely as "De Lawd" and "Booker T. King." What's your reaction to this sort of Uncle Tom label?

KING: I hear some of those names, but my reaction to them is never emotional. I don't think you can be in public life without being called bad names. As Lincoln said, "If I answered all criticism, I'd have time for nothing else." But with regard to both of the names you mentioned, I've always tried to be what I call militantly nonviolent. I don't believe that anyone could seriously accuse me of not being totally committed to the breakdown of segregation.

HALEY: What do you mean by "militantly nonviolent"?

KING: I mean to say that a strong man must be militant as well as moderate. He must be a realist as well as an idealist. If I am to merit the trust invested in me by some of my race, I must be both of these things. This is why nonviolence is a powerful as well as a *just* weapon. If you confront a man who has long been cruelly misusing you, and say, "Punish me, if you will; I do not deserve it, but I will accept it, so that the world will know I am right and you are wrong," then you wield a powerful and a just weapon. This man, your oppressor, is automatically morally defeated, and if he has any conscience, he is ashamed. Wherever this weapon is used in a manner that stirs a community's, or a nation's, anguished conscience, then the pressure of public opinion becomes an ally in your just cause.

Another of the major strengths of the nonviolent weapon is its strange power to transform and transmute the individuals who subordinate themselves to its disciplines, investing them with a cause that is larger than themselves. They become, for the first time, *somebody,* and they have, for the first time, the courage to be free. When the Negro finds the courage to be free, he faces dogs and guns and clubs and fire hoses totally unafraid, and the white men with those dogs, guns, clubs and fire hoses see that the Negro they have traditionally called "boy" has become a man.

We should not forget that, although nonviolent direct action did not originate in America, it found a natural home where it has been a revered tradition to rebel against injustice. This great weapon, which we first tried out in Montgomery during the bus boycott, has been further developed throughout the South over the past decade, until by today it has become instrumental in the greatest mass-action crusade for freedom that has occurred in America since the Revolutionary War. The effectiveness of this weapon's ability to dramatize, in the world's eyes, an oppressed people's struggle for justice is evident in the fact that of 1963's top ten news stories after the assassination of President Kennedy and the events immediately connected with it, nine stories dealt with one aspect or another of the Negro struggle.

HALEY: Several of those stories dealt with your own nonviolent campaigns against segregation in various Southern cities, where you and your followers have been branded "rabble-rousers" and "outside agitators." Do you feel you've earned these labels?

KING: Wherever the early Christians appeared, spreading Christ's doctrine of love, the resident power structure accused them of being "disturbers of the peace" and "outside agitators." But the small Christian band continued to teach and exemplify love, convinced that they were "a colony of heaven" on this earth who were missioned to obey not man but God. If those of us who employ nonviolent direct action today are dismissed by our white brothers as "rabble-rousers" and "outside agitators," if they refuse to support our nonviolent efforts and goals, we can be assured that the summer of 1965 will be no less long and hot than the summer of 1964.

Our white brothers must be made to understand that nonviolence is a weapon fabricated of love. It is a sword that heals. Our nonviolent, direct-action program has as its objective not the creation of tensions, but the *surfacing* of tensions already present. We set out to precipitate a crisis situation that must open the door to negotiation. I am not afraid of the words "crisis" and "tension." I deeply oppose violence, but constructive crisis and tension are necessary for growth. Innate in all life, and all growth, is tension. Only in death is there an absence of tension. To cure injustices, you must expose them before the light of human conscience and the bar of public opinion, regardless of whatever tensions that exposure generates. Injustices to the Negro must be brought out into the open where they cannot be evaded.

HALEY: Is this the sole aim of your Southern Christian Leadership Conference?

KING: We have five aims: first, to stimulate nonviolent, direct, mass action to expose and remove the barriers of segregation and discrimination; second, to disseminate the creative philosophy and techniques of nonviolence through local and area workshops; third, to secure the right and unhampered use of the ballot for every citizen; fourth, to achieve full citizenship rights, and the total integration of the Negro into American life; and fifth, to reduce the cultural lag through our citizenship training program.

HALEY: How does S.C.L.C. select the cities where nonviolent campaigns and demonstrations are to be staged?

KING: The operational area of S.C.L.C. is the entire South, where we have affiliated organizations in some 85 cities. Our major campaigns have been conducted only in cities where a request for our help comes from one of these affiliate organizations, and only when we feel that intolerable conditions in that community might be ameliorated with our help. I will give you an example. In Birmingham, one of our affiliate organizations is the Alabama Christian Movement for Human Rights, which was organized by the Reverend Fred Shuttlesworth, a most energetic and indomitable man. It was he who set out to end Birmingham's racism, challenging the terrorist reign of Bull Connor. S.C.L.C. watched admiringly as the small Shuttlesworth-led organization fought in the Birmingham courts and with boycotts. Shuttlesworth was jailed several times, his home and church were bombed, and still he did not back down. His defiance of Birmingham's racism inspired and encouraged Negroes throughout the South. Then, at a May 1962 board meeting of the S.C.L.C. in Chattanooga, the first discussions began that later led to our joining Shuttlesworth's organization in a massive direct-action campaign to attack Birmingham's segregation.

HALEY: One of the highlights of that campaign was your celebrated "Letter from a Birmingham Jail"—written during one of your jail terms for civil disobedience—an eloquent reply to eight Protestant, Catholic and Jewish clergymen who had criticized your activities in Birmingham. Do you feel that subsequent events have justified the sentiments expressed in your letter?

KING: I would say yes. Two or three important and constructive things have happened which can be at least partially attributed to that letter. By now, nearly a million copies of the letter have been widely circulated in churches of most of the major denominations. It helped to focus

MARTIN LUTHER KING, JR.

greater international attention upon what was happening in
Birmingham. And I am sure that without Birmingham, the
march on Washington wouldn't have been called—which
in my mind was one of the most creative steps the Negro
struggle has taken. The march on Washington spurred and
galvanized the consciences of millions. It gave the American
Negro a new national and international stature. The press
of the world recorded the story as nearly a quarter of a
million Americans, white and black, assembled in grandeur
as a testimonial to the Negro's determination to achieve
freedom in this generation.

It was also the image of Birmingham which, to a great
extent, helped to bring the Civil Rights Bill into being in
1963. Previously, President Kennedy had decided not to
propose it that year, feeling that it would so arouse the
South that it would meet a bottleneck. But Birmingham,
and subsequent developments, caused him to reorder his
legislative priorities.

One of these decisive developments was our last major
campaign before the enactment of the Civil Rights Act—
in St. Augustine, Florida. We received a plea for help from
Dr. Robert Hayling, the leader of the St. Augustine movement. St. Augustine, America's oldest city, and one of the
most segregated cities in America, was a stronghold of the
Ku Klux Klan and the John Birch Society. Such things had
happened as Klansmen abducting four Negroes and beating
them unconscious with clubs, brass knuckles, ax handles
and pistol butts. Dr. Hayling's home had been shot up with
buckshot, three Negro homes had been bombed and several
Negro night clubs shotgunned. A Negro's car had been
destroyed by fire because his child was one of the six Negro
children permitted to attend white schools. And the homes
of two of the Negro children in the white schools had been
burned down. Many Negroes had been fired from jobs that
some had worked on for 28 years because they were somehow connected with the demonstrations. Police had beaten

and arrested Negroes for picketing, marching and singing freedom songs. Many Negroes had served up to 90 days in jail for demonstrating against segregation, and four teenagers had spent six months in jail for picketing. Then, on February seventh of last year, Dr. Hayling's home was shotgunned a second time, with his pregnant wife and two children barely escaping death; the family dog was killed while standing behind the living-room door. So S.C.L.C. decided to join in last year's celebration of St. Augustine's gala 400th birthday as America's oldest city—by converting it into a nonviolent battleground. This is just what we did.

HALEY: But isn't it true, Dr. King, that during this and other "nonviolent" demonstrations, violence has occurred—sometimes resulting in hundreds of casualties on both sides?

KING: Yes, in part that is true. But what is always overlooked is how few people, in ratio to the numbers involved, have been casualties. An army on maneuvers, against no enemy, suffers casualties, even fatalities. A minimum of whites have been casualties in demonstrations solely because our teaching of nonviolence disciplines our followers not to fight even if attacked. A minimum of Negroes are casualties for two reasons: Their white oppressors know that the world watches their actions, and for the first time they are being faced by Negroes who display no fear.

HALEY: It was shortly after your St. Augustine campaign last summer, as you mentioned, that the Civil Rights Bill was passed—outlawing many of the injustices against which you had been demonstrating. Throughout the South, predictably, it was promptly anathematized as unconstitutional and excessive in its concessions to Negro demands. How do you feel about it?

KING: I don't feel that the Civil Rights Act has gone far *enough* in some of its coverage. In the first place, it needs a stronger voting section. You will never have a true democracy until you can eliminate *all* restrictions. We need to do away with restrictive literacy tests. I've seen too much of native intelligence to accept the validity of these tests as a criterion for voting qualifications. Our nation needs a universal method of voter registration—one man, one vote, literally. Second, there is a pressing, urgent need to give the attorney general the right to initiate Federal suits in any area of civil rights denial. Third, we need a strong and strongly enforced fair-housing section such as many states already have. President Kennedy initiated the present housing law, but it is not broad enough. Fourth, we need an extension of FEPC to grapple more effectively with the problems of poverty. Not only are millions of Negroes caught in the clutches of poverty, but millions of poor whites as well. And fifth, conclusive and effective measures must be taken immediately at the Federal level to curb the worsening reign of terror in the South—which is aided and abetted, as everyone knows, by state and local law-enforcement agencies. It's getting so that anybody can kill a Negro and get away with it in the South, as long as they go through the motions of a jury trial. There is very little chance of conviction from lily-white Southern jurors. It must be fixed so that in the case of interracial murder, the Federal government can prosecute.

HALEY: Your dissatisfaction with the Civil Rights Act reflects that of most other Negro spokesmen. According to recent polls, however, many whites resent this attitude, calling the Negro "ungrateful" and "unrealistic" to press his demands for more.

KING: This is a litany to those of us in this field. "What more will the Negro want?" "What will it take to make these demonstrations end?" Well, I would like to reply with another rhetorical question: Why do white people seem to find it so difficult to understand that the Negro is sick and tired of having reluctantly parceled out to him those rights and privileges which all others receive upon birth or entry in America? I never cease to wonder at the amazing presumption of much of white society, assuming that they have the right to bargain with the Negro for his freedom. This continued arrogant ladling out of pieces of the rights of citizenship has begun to generate a *fury* in the Negro. Even so, he is not pressing for revenge, or for conquest, or to gain spoils, or to enslave, or even to marry the sisters of those who have injured him. What the Negro wants—and will not stop until he gets—is absolute and unqualified freedom and equality here in this land of his birth, and not in Africa or in some imaginary state. The Negro no longer will be tolerant of anything less than his due right and heritage. He is pursuing only that which he knows is honorably his. He knows that he is right.

But every Negro leader since the turn of the century has been saying this in one form or another. It is because we have been so long and so conscientiously ignored by the dominant white society that the situation has now reached such crisis proportions. Few white people, even today, will face the clear fact that the very future and destiny of this country are tied up in what answer will be given to the Negro. And that answer must be given soon.

HALEY: Relatively few dispute the justness of the struggle to eradicate racial injustice, but many whites feel that the Negro should be more patient, that only the passage of time—perhaps generations—will bring about the sweeping changes he demands in traditional attitudes and customs. Do you think this is true?

KING: No, I do not. I feel that the time is always right to do what is right. Where progress for the Negro in America is concerned, there is a tragic misconception of time among whites. They seem to cherish a strange, irrational notion that something in the very flow of time will cure all ills. In truth, time itself is only neutral. Increasingly, I feel that time has been used destructively by people of ill will much more than it has been used constructively by those of *good* will.

If I were to select a timetable for the equalization of human rights, it would be the *intent* of the "all deliberate speed" specified in the historic 1954 Supreme Court decision. But what has happened? A Supreme Court decision was met, and balked, with utter defiance. Ten years later, in most areas of the South, less than one percent of the Negro children have been integrated in schools, and in some of the deepest South, not even one tenth of one percent. Approximately 25 percent of employable Negro youth, for another example, are presently unemployed. Though many would prefer not to, we must face the fact that progress for the Negro—to which white "moderates" like to point in justifying gradualism—has been relatively insignificant, particularly in terms of the Negro masses. What little progress has been made—and that includes the Civil Rights Act—has applied primarily to the middle-class Negro. Among the masses, especially in the Northern ghettos, the situation remains about the same, and for some it is worse.

HALEY: It would seem that much could be done at the local, state and Federal levels to remedy these inequities. In your own contact with them, have you found government officials—in the North, if not in the South—to be generally sympathetic, understanding, and receptive to appeals for reform?

KING: On the contrary, I have been dismayed at the degree to which abysmal ignorance seems to prevail among many state, city and even Federal officials on the whole question of racial justice and injustice. Particularly, I have found that these men seriously—and dangerously—underestimate the explosive mood of the Negro and the gravity of the crisis. Even among those whom I would consider to be both sympathetic and sincerely intellectually committed, there is a lamentable lack of understanding. But this white failure to comprehend the depth and dimension of the Negro problem is far from being peculiar to government officials. Apart from bigots and backlashers, it seems to be a malady even among those whites who like to regard themselves as "enlightened." I would especially refer to those who counsel, "Wait!" and to those who say that they sympathize with our goals but cannot condone our methods of direct-action pursuit of those goals. I wonder at men who dare to feel that they have some paternalistic right to set the timetable for another man's liberation. Over the past several years, I must say, I have been gravely disappointed with such white "moderates." I am often inclined to think that they are more of a stumbling block to the Negro's progress than the White Citizen's Councilor or the Ku Klux Klanner.

HALEY: Haven't both of these segregationist societies been implicated in connection with plots against your life?

KING: It's difficult to trace the authorship of these death threats. I seldom go through a day without one. Some are telephoned anonymously to my office; others are sent— unsigned, of course—through the mails. Drew Pearson wrote not long ago about one group of unknown affiliation that was committed to assassinate not only me but also Chief Justice Warren and President Johnson. And not long ago, when I was about to visit in Mississippi, I received some very urgent calls from Negro leaders in Mobile, who had been told by a very reliable source that a sort of guerrilla group led by a retired major in the area of Lucyville, Mississippi, was plotting to take my life during the visit. I was strongly urged to cancel the trip, but when I thought about it, I decided that I had no alternative but to go on into Mississippi.

HALEY: Why?

KING: Because I have a job to do. If I were constantly worried about death, I couldn't function. After a while, if your life is more or less constantly in peril, you come to a point where you accept the possibility philosophically. I must face the fact, as all others in positions of leadership must do, that America today is an extremely sick nation, and that something could well happen to me at any time. I feel, though, that my cause is so right, so moral, that if I should lose my life, in some way it would aid the cause.

HALEY: That statement exemplifies the total dedication to the civil rights movement for which you are so widely admired—but also denounced as an "extremist" by such segregationist spokesmen as Alabama's Governor Wallace. Do you accept this identification?

KING: It disturbed me when I first heard it. But when I began to consider the true meaning of the word, I decided that perhaps I would *like* to think of myself as an extremist—in the light of the spirit which made Jesus an extremist for love. If it sounds as though I am comparing myself to the Savior, let me remind you that all who honor themselves with the claim of being "Christians" *should* compare themselves to Jesus. Thus I consider myself an extremist for that brotherhood of man which Paul so nobly expressed: "There is neither Jew nor Greek, there is neither bond nor free, there is neither male nor female: for ye are all one in Christ Jesus." Love is the only force on earth that can be dispensed or received in an extreme manner, without any qualifications, without any harm to the giver or to the receiver.

HALEY: Perhaps. But the kind of extremism for which you've been criticized has to do not with love, but with your advocacy of willful disobedience of what you consider to be "unjust laws." Do you feel you have the right to pass judgment on and defy the law—nonviolently or otherwise?

KING: Yes—morally, if not legally. For there are two kinds of laws: man's and God's. A man-made code that squares with the moral law, or the law of God, is a just law. But a man-made code that is inharmonious with the moral law is an unjust law. And an unjust law, as St. Augustine said, is no law at all. Thus a law that is unjust is morally null and void, and must be defied until it is legally null and void as well. Let us not forget, in the memories of 6,000,000 who died, that everything Adolf Hitler did in Germany was "legal," and that everything the Freedom Fighters in Hungary did was "illegal." In spite of that, I am sure that I would have aided and comforted my Jewish brothers if I had lived in Germany during Hitler's reign, as some Christian priests and ministers did do, often at the cost of their lives. And if I lived now in a Communist country where principles dear to the Christian's faith are suppressed, I know that I would openly advocate defiance of that country's anti-religious laws—again, just as some Christian priests and ministers are doing today behind the Iron Curtain. Right here in America today there are white ministers, priests and rabbis who have shed blood in the support of our struggle against a web of human injustice, much of which is supported by immoral man-made laws.

HALEY: Segregation laws?

KING: Specifically, court injunctions. Though the rights of the First Amendment guarantee that any citizen or group of citizens may engage in peaceable assembly, the South has seized upon the device of invoking injunctions to block our direct-action civil rights demonstrations. When you get set to stage a nonviolent demonstration, the city simply secures an injunction to cease and desist. Southern courts are well known for "sitting on" this type of case; conceivably a two- or three-year delay could be incurred. At first we found this to be a highly effective subterfuge against us. We first experienced it in Montgomery when, during the bus boycott, our car pool was outlawed by an injunction. An injunction also destroyed the protest movement in Talladega, Alabama. Another injunction outlawed the oldest civil rights organization, the NAACP, from the whole state of Alabama. Still another injunction thwarted our organization's efforts in Albany, Georgia. Then in Birmingham, we felt that we had to take a stand and disobey a court injunction against demonstrations, knowing the consequences and being prepared to meet them—or the unjust law would break our movement.

We did not take this step hastily or rashly. We gave the matter intense thought and prayer before deciding that the right thing was being done. And when we made our decision, I announced our plan to the press, making it clear that we were not anarchists advocating lawlessness, but that in good conscience we could not comply with a misuse of the judicial process in order to perpetuate injustice and segregation. When our plan was made known, it bewildered and immobilized our segregationist opponents. We felt that our decision had been morally as well as tactically right—in keeping with God's law as well as with the spirit of our nonviolent direct-action program.

HALEY: If it's morally right for supporters of civil rights to violate segregation laws which they consider unjust, why is it wrong for segregationists to resist the enforcement of integration laws which *they* consider unjust?

KING: Because segregation, as even the segregationists know in their hearts, is morally wrong and sinful. If it weren't, the white South would not be haunted as it is by a deep sense of guilt for what it has done to the Negro— guilt for patronizing him, degrading him, brutalizing him, depersonalizing him, thingifying him; guilt for lying to itself. This is the source of the schizophrenia that the South will suffer until it goes through its crisis of conscience.

HALEY: Is this crisis imminent?

KING: It may not come next week or next year, but it is certainly more imminent in the South than in the North. If the South is honest with itself, it may well outdistance the North in the improvement of race relations.

HALEY: Why?

KING: Well, the Northern white, having had little actual contact with the Negro, is devoted to an abstract principle of cordial interracial relations. The North has long considered, in a theoretical way, that it supported brotherhood and the equality of man, but the truth is that deep prejudices and discriminations exist in hidden and subtle and covert disguises. The South's prejudice and discrimination, on the other hand, has been applied against the Negro in obvious, open, overt and glaring forms—which make the problem easier to get at. The Southern white man has the advantage of far more actual contact with Negroes than the Northerner. A major problem is that this contact has been paternalistic and poisoned by the myth of racial superiority.

HALEY: Many Southern whites, supported by the "research" of several Southern anthropologists, vow that white racial superiority—and Negro inferiority—are a biological fact.

KING: You may remember that during the rise of Nazi Germany, a rash of books by respected German scientists appeared, supporting the master-race theory. This utterly ignorant fallacy has been so thoroughly refuted by the social scientists, as well as by medical science, that any individual who goes on believing it is standing in an absolutely misguided and diminishing circle. The American Anthropological Association has unanimously adopted a resolution repudiating statements that Negroes are biologically, in innate mental ability or in any other way inferior to whites. The collective weight and authority of world scientists are embodied in a Unesco report on races which flatly refutes the theory of innate superiority among *any* ethnic group. And as far as Negro "blood" is concerned, medical science finds the same four blood types in all race groups.

When the Southern white finally accepts this simple fact—as he eventually must—beautiful results will follow, for we will have come a long way toward transforming his master-servant perspective into a person-to-person perspective. The Southern white man, discovering the "nonmyth" Negro, exhibits all the passion of the new convert, seeing the black man as a man among men for the first time. The South, if it is to survive economically, must make dramatic changes, and these must include the Negro. People of good will in the South, who are the vast majority, have the challenge to be open and honest, and to turn a deaf ear to the shrill cries of the irresponsible few on the lunatic fringe. I think and pray they will.

HALEY: Whom do you include among "the irresponsible few"?

KING: I include those who preach racism and commit violence; and those who, in various cities where we have sought to peacefully demonstrate, have sought to goad *Negroes* into violence as an excuse for violent mass reprisal. In Birmingham, for example, on the day it was flashed about the world that a "peace pact" had been signed between the moderate whites and the Negroes, Birmingham's segregationist forces reacted with fury, swearing vengeance against the white businessmen who had "betrayed" them by negotiating with Negroes. On Saturday night, just outside of Birmingham, a Ku Klux Klan meeting was held, and that same night, as I mentioned earlier, a bomb ripped the home of my brother, the Reverend A. D. King, and another bomb was planted where it would have killed or seriously wounded anyone in the motel room which I had been occupying. Both bombings had been timed just as Birmingham's bars closed on Saturday midnight, as the streets filled with thousands of Negroes who were not trained in nonviolence, and who had been drinking. Just as whoever planted the bombs had *wanted* to happen, fighting began, policemen were stoned by Negroes, cars were overturned and fires started.

HALEY: Were none of your S.C.L.C. workers involved?

KING: If they had been, there would have been no riot, for we believe that only just means may be used in seeking a just end. We believe that lasting gains can be made—and they *have* been made—only by practicing what we preach: a policy of nonviolent, peaceful protest. The riots, North and South, have involved mobs—not the disciplined, nonviolent, direct-action demonstrators with whom I identify. We do not condone lawlessness, looting and violence committed by the racist or the reckless of *any* color.

I must say, however, that riots such as have occurred do achieve at least one partially positive effect: They dramatically focus national attention upon the Negro's discontent. Unfortunately, they also give the white majority an excuse, a provocation, to look away from the cause of the riots— the poverty and the deprivation and the degradation of the Negro, especially in the slums and ghettos where the riots occur—and to talk instead of looting, and of the breakdown of law and order. It is never circulated that some of the looters have been white people, similarly motivated by their own poverty. In one riot in a Northern city, aside from the Negroes and Puerto Ricans who were arrested, there were also 158 white people—including mothers stealing food, children's shoes and other necessity items. The poor, white and black, were rebelling together against the establishment.

HALEY: Whom do you mean by "the establishment"?

KING: I mean the white leadership—which I hold as responsible as anyone for the riots, for not removing the conditions that cause them. The deep frustration, the seething desperation of the Negro today is a product of slum housing, chronic poverty, woefully inadequate education and substandard schools. The Negro is trapped in a long and desolate corridor with no exit sign, caught in a vicious socioeconomic vise. And he is ostracized as is no other minority group in America by the evil of oppressive and constricting prejudice based solely upon his color. A righteous man has no alternative but to resist such an evil system. If he does not have the courage to resist nonviolently, then he runs the risk of a violent emotional explosion. As much as I deplore violence, there is one evil that is *worse* than violence, and that's cowardice. It is still my basic article of faith that social justice can be achieved and democracy advanced only to the degree that there is firm adherence to *nonviolent* action and resistance in the pursuit of social justice. But America will be faced with the ever-present threat of violence, rioting and senseless crime as long as Negroes by the hundreds of thousands are packed into malodorous, rat-plagued ghettos; as long as Negroes remain smothered by poverty in the midst of an affluent society; as long as Negroes are made to feel like exiles in their own land; as long as Negroes continue to be dehumanized; as long as Negroes see their freedom endlessly delayed and diminished by the head winds of tokenism and small handouts from the white power structure. No nation can suffer any greater tragedy than to cause millions of its citizens to feel that they have no stake in their own society.

Understand that I am trying only to explain the *reasons* for violence and the threat of violence. Let me say again that by no means and under no circumstance do I condone outbreaks of looting and lawlessness. I feel that every responsible Negro leader must point out, with all possible vigor, that anyone who perpetrates and participates in a riot is immoral as well as impractical—that the use of immoral means will not achieve the moral end of racial justice.

HALEY: Whom do you consider the most responsible Negro leaders?

KING: Well, I would say that Roy Wilkins of the NAACP has proved time and again to be a very articulate spokesman for the rights of Negroes. He is a most able administrator and a dedicated organization man with personal resources that have helped the whole struggle. Another outstanding man is Whitney Young Jr. of the National Urban League, an extremely able social scientist. He has developed a meaningful balance between militancy and moderation. James Farmer of CORE is another courageous, dedicated and thoughtful civil rights spokesman. I have always been impressed by how he maintains a freshness in his awareness of the meaning of the whole quest for freedom. And John Lewis of SNCC symbolizes the kind of strong militancy, courage and creativity that our youth have brought to the civil rights struggle. But I feel that the greatest leader of these times that the Negro has produced is A. Philip Randolph, president of the Brotherhood of Sleeping Car Porters, whose total integrity, depth of dedication and caliber of statesmanship set an example for us all.

HALEY: Many whites feel that last summer's riots occurred because leadership is no longer being offered by the men you named.

KING: The riots we have had are *minute* compared to what would have happened *without* their effective and restraining leadership. I am convinced that unless the nonviolent philosophy had emerged and taken hold among Negroes, North and South, by today the streets of dozens of American communities would have flowed with blood. Hundreds of cities might now be mourning countless dead, of both races, were it not for the nonviolent influence which has given political surgeons the time and opportunity to boldly and safely excise some aspects of the peril of violence that faced this nation in the summers of 1963 and 1964. The whole world has seen what happened in communities such as Harlem, Brooklyn, Rochester, Philadelphia, Newark, St. Petersburg and Birmingham, where this emergency operation was either botched or not performed at all.

HALEY: Still, doesn't the very fact that riots have occurred tend to indicate that many Negroes are no longer heeding the counsels of nonviolence?

KING: Not the majority, by any means. But it *is* true that some Negroes subscribe to a deep feeling that the tactic of nonviolence is not producing enough concrete victories.

We have seen, in our experience, that nonviolence thrives best in a climate of justice. Violence grows to the degree that injustice prevails; the more injustice in a given community, the more violence, or potential violence, smolders in that community. I can give you a clear example. If you will notice, there have been fewer riots in the South. The reason for this is that the Negro in the South can see some visible, concrete victories in civil rights. Last year, the police would have been called if he sat down at a community lunch counter. This year, if he chooses to sit at that counter, he is served. More riots have occurred in the North because the fellow in Harlem, to name one Northern ghetto, can't see any victories. He remains throttled, as he has always been, by vague, intangible economic and social deprivations. Until the concerned power structures begin to grapple creatively with these fundamental inequities, it will be difficult for violence to be eliminated. The longer our people see no progress, or halting progress, the easier it will be for them to yield to the counsels of hatred and demagoguery.

HALEY: The literature of the John Birch Society, accusing you of just such counsels, has branded you "a conscious agent of the Communist conspiracy."

KING: As you know, they have sought to link many people with communism, including the Chief Justice of the Supreme Court and a former President of the United States. So I'm in good company, at least. The Birchers thrive on sneer and smear, on the dissemination of half-truths and outright lies. It would be comfortable to dismiss them as the lunatic fringe—which, by and large, they are; but some priests and ministers have also shown themselves to be among them. They are a very dangerous group—and they could become even more dangerous if the public doesn't reject the un-American travesty of patriotism that they espouse.

HALEY: Was there any basis in fact for the rumors, still circulating in some quarters, that last summer's riots were fomented and stage-directed by Communist agitators?

KING: I'm getting sick and tired of people saying that this movement has been infiltrated by Communists. There are as many Communists in this freedom movement as there are Eskimos in Florida. The FBI provided the best answer to this absurd rumor in its report to the President after a special investigation which he had requested. It stated that the riots were not caused or directed by any such groups, although they did try to capitalize upon and prolong the riots. All Negro leaders, including myself, were most happy with the publication of these findings, for the public whisperings had troubled us. We knew that it could prove vitally harmful to the Negro struggle if the riots had been catalyzed or manipulated by the Communists or some other extremist group. It would have sown the seed of doubt in the public's mind that the Negro revolution is a genuine revolution, born from the same womb that produces all massive social upheavals—the womb of intolerable conditions and unendurable situations.

HALEY: Is it destined to be a violent revolution?

KING: God willing, no. But white Americans must be made to understand the basic motives underlying Negro demonstrations. Many pent-up resentments and latent frustrations are boiling inside the Negro, and he must release them. It is not a threat but a fact of history that if an oppressed people's pent-up emotions are not nonviolently released, they will be violently released. So let the Negro march. Let him make pilgrimages to city hall. Let him go on freedom rides. And above all, make an effort to understand why he must do this. For if his frustration and despair are allowed to continue piling up, millions of Negroes will seek solace and security in black-nationalist ideologies. And this, inevitably, would lead to a frightening racial nightmare.

HALEY: Among whites, the best-known and most feared of these militantly racist Negro sects is the Black Muslims. What is your estimation of its power and influence among the Negro masses?

KING: Except in a few metropolitan ghettos, my experience has been that few Negroes have any interest at all in this organization, much less give any allegiance to its pessimistic doctrines. The Black Muslims are a quasi-religious, sociopolitical movement that has appealed to some Negroes who formerly were Christians. For the first time, the Negro was presented with a choice of a religion other than Christianity. What this appeal actually represented was an indictment of Christian failures to live up to Christianity's precepts; for there is nothing in Christianity, nor in the Bible, that justifies racial segregation. But when the Negroes' genuine fighting spirit rose during 1963, the appeal of the Muslims began to diminish.

HALEY: One of the basic precepts of black nationalism has been the attempt to engender a sense of communion between the American Negro and his African "brother," a sense of identity between the emergence of black Africa and the Negro's struggle for freedom in America. Do you feel that this is a constructive effort?

KING: Yes, I do, in many ways. There is a distinct, significant and inevitable correlation. The Negro across America, looking at his television set, sees black statesmen voting in the United Nations on vital world issues, knowing that in many of America's cities, he himself is not yet permitted to place his ballot. The Negro hears of black kings and potentates ruling in palaces, while he remains ghettoized in urban slums. It is only natural that Negroes would react to this extreme irony. Consciously or unconsciously, the American Negro has been caught up by the black *Zeitgeist*. He feels a deepening sense of identification with his black African brothers, and with his brown and yellow brothers of Asia, South America and the Caribbean. With them he is moving with a sense of increasing urgency toward the promised land of racial justice.

HALEY: Do you feel that the African nations, in turn, should involve themselves more actively in American Negro affairs?

KING: I do indeed. The world is now so small in terms of geographic proximity and mutual problems that no nation should stand idly by and watch another's plight. I think that in every possible instance Africans should use the influence of their governments to make it clear that the struggle of their brothers in the U.S. is part of a world-wide struggle. In short, injustice anywhere is a threat to justice everywhere, for we are tied together in a garment of mutuality. What happens in Johannesburg affects Birmingham, however indirectly. We are descendants of the Africans. Our heritage is Africa. We should never seek to break the ties, nor should the Africans.

HALEY: One of the most articulate champions of black Afro-American brotherhood has been Malcolm X, the former Black Muslim leader who recently renounced his racist past, and converted to orthodox Mohammedanism. What is your opinion of him and his career?

KING: I met Malcolm X once in Washington, but circumstances didn't enable me to talk with him for more than a minute. He is very articulate, as you say, but I totally disagree with many of his political and philosophical views—at least insofar as I understand where he now stands. I don't want to seem to sound self-righteous, or absolutist, or that I think I have the only truth, the only way. Maybe he *does* have some of the answer. I don't know how he feels now, but I know that I have often wished that he would talk less of violence, because violence is not going to solve our problem. And in his litany of articulating the despair of the Negro without offering any positive, creative alternative, I feel that Malcolm has done himself and our people a great disservice. Fiery, demagogic oratory in the black ghettos, urging Negroes to arm themselves and prepare to engage in violence, as he has done, can reap nothing but grief.

HALEY: For them or for whites?

KING: For everyone, but mostly for them. Even the extremist leaders who preach revolution are invariably unwilling to lead what they know would certainly end in bloody, chaotic and total defeat; for in the event of a violent revolution, we would be sorely outnumbered. And when it was all over, the Negro would face the same unchanged conditions, the same squalor and deprivation—the only difference being that his bitterness would be even more intense, his disenchantment even more abject. Thus, in purely practical as well as moral terms, the American Negro has no rational alternative to nonviolence.

HALEY: You categorically reject violence as a tactical technique for social change. Can it not be argued, however, that violence, historically, has effected massive and sometimes constructive social change in some countries?

KING: I'd be the first to say that some historical victories have been won by violence; the U.S. Revolution is certainly one of the foremost. But the Negro revolution is seeking integration, not independence. Those fighting for independence have the purpose to *drive out* the oppressors. But here in America, we've got to live together. We've got to find a way to reconcile ourselves to living in community, one group with the other. The struggle of the Negro in America, to be successful, must be waged with resolute efforts, but efforts that are kept strictly within the framework of our democratic society. This means reaching, educating and moving large enough groups of people of both races to stir the conscience of the nation.

HALEY: How do you propose to go about it?

KING: Before we can make any progress, we must avoid retrogression—by doing everything in our power to avert further racial violence. To this end, there are three immediate steps that I would recommend. Firstly, it is mandatory that people of good will across America, particularly those who are in positions to wield influence and power, conduct honest, soul-searching analyses and evaluations of the environmental causes that spawn riots. All major industrial and ghetto areas should establish serious biracial discussions of community problems, and of ways to begin solving them. Instead of ambulance service, municipal leaders need to provide preventive medicine. Secondly, these communities should make serious efforts to provide work and training for unemployed youth, through job-and-training programs such as the HarYouAct program in New York City. Thirdly, all cities concerned should make first-priority efforts to provide immediate quality education for Negro youth—instead of conducting studies for the next five years. Young boys and girls now in the ghettos must be enabled to feel that they count, that somebody cares about them; they must be able to feel *hope*. And on a longer-range basis, the physical ghetto itself must be eliminated, because these are the environmental conditions that germinate riots. It is both socially and morally suicidal to continue a pattern of deploring effects while failing to come to grips with the *causes*. Ultimately, law and order will be maintained only when justice and dignity are accorded impartially to all.

HALEY: Along with the other civil rights leaders, you have often proposed a massive program of economic aid, financed by the Federal government, to improve the lot of the nation's 20,000,000 Negroes. Just one of the projects you've mentioned, however—the HarYouAct program to provide jobs for Negro youths—is expected to cost $141,000,000 over the next ten years, and that includes only Harlem. A nationwide program such as you propose would undoubtedly run into the billions.

KING: About 50 billion, actually—which is less than one year of our present defense spending. It is my belief that with the expenditure of this amount, over a 10-year period, a genuine and dramatic transformation could be achieved in the conditions of Negro life in America. I am positive, moreover, that the money spent would be more than amply justified by the benefits that would accrue to the nation through a spectacular decline in school dropouts, family breakups, crime rates, illegitimacy, swollen relief rolls, rioting and other social evils.

HALEY: Do you think it's realistic to hope that the government would consider an appropriation of such magnitude other than for national defense?

KING: I certainly do. This country has the resources to solve *any* problem once that problem is accepted as national policy. An example is aid to Appalachia, which has been made a policy of the Federal government's much-touted war on poverty; one billion was proposed for its relief—without making the slightest dent in the defense budget. Another example is the fact that after World War Two, during the years when it became policy to build and maintain the largest military machine the world has ever known, America also took upon itself, through the Marshall Plan and other measures, the financial relief and rehabilitation of millions of European people. If America can afford to underwrite its allies and ex-enemies, it can certainly afford—and has a much greater obligation, as I see it—to do at least as well by its own no-less-needy countrymen.

HALEY: Do you feel it's fair to request a multibillion-dollar program of preferential treatment for the Negro, or for any other minority group?

KING: I do indeed. Can any fair-minded citizen deny that the Negro has been deprived? Few people reflect that for two centuries the Negro was enslaved, and robbed of *any* wages—potential accrued wealth which would have been the legacy of his descendants. *All* of America's wealth today could not adequately compensate its Negroes for his centuries of exploitation and humiliation. It is an economic fact that a program such as I propose would certainly cost far less than any computation of two centuries of unpaid wages plus accumulated interest. In any case, I do not intend that this program of economic aid should apply only to the Negro; it should benefit the disadvantaged of *all* races.

Within common law, we have ample precedents for special compensatory programs, which are regarded as settlements. American Indians are still being paid for land in a settlement manner. Is not two centuries of labor, which helped to build this country, as real a commodity? Many other easily applicable precedents are readily at hand: our child labor laws, social security, unemployment compensation, man-power retraining programs. And you will remember that America adopted a policy of special treatment for her millions of veterans after the War—a program which cost far more than a policy of preferential treatment to rehabilitate the traditionally disadvantaged Negro would cost today.

The closest analogy is the GI Bill of Rights. Negro rehabilitation in America would require approximately the same breadth of program—which would not place an undue burden on our economy. Just as was the case with the returning soldier, such a bill for the disadvantaged and impoverished could enable them to buy homes without cash, at lower and easier repayment terms. They could negotiate loans from banks to launch businesses. They could receive, as did ex-GIs, special points to place them ahead in competition for civil service jobs. Under certain circumstances of physical disability, medical care and long-term financial grants could be made available. And together with these rights, a favorable social climate could be created to encourage the preferential *employment* of the disadvantaged, as was the case for so many years with veterans. During those years, it might be noted, there was no appreciable resentment of the preferential treatment being given to the special group. America was only compensating her veterans for their time lost from school or from business.

HALEY: If a nationwide program of preferential employment for Negroes were to be adopted, how would you propose to assuage the resentment of whites who already feel that their jobs are being jeopardized by the influx of Negroes resulting from desegregation?

KING: We must develop a Federal program of public works, retraining and jobs for all—so that none, white or black, will have cause to feel threatened. At the present time, thousands of jobs a week are disappearing in the wake of automation and other production efficiency techniques. Black and white, we will *all* be harmed unless something grand and imaginative is done. The unemployed, poverty-stricken white man must be made to realize that he is in the very same boat with the Negro. Together, they could exert massive pressure on the government to get jobs for all. Together, they could form a grand alliance. Together, they could merge all people for the good of all.

HALEY: If Negroes are also granted preferential treatment in housing, as you propose, how would you allay the alarm with which many white homeowners, fearing property devaluation, greet the arrival of Negroes in hitherto all-white neighborhoods?

KING: We must expunge from our society the myths and half-truths that engender such groundless fears as these. In the first place, there is no truth to the myth that Negroes depreciate property. The fact is that most Negroes are kept out of residential neighborhoods so long that when one of us is finally sold a home, it's *already* depreciated. In the second place, we must dispel the negative and harmful atmosphere that has been created by avaricious and unprincipled realtors who engage in "blockbusting." If we had in America really serious efforts to break down discrimination in housing, and at the same time a concerted program of Government aid to improve housing for Negroes, I think that many white people would be surprised at how many Negroes would choose to live among themselves, exactly as Poles and Jews and other ethnic groups do.

HALEY: The B'nai B'rith, a prominent social-action organization which undertakes on behalf of the Jewish people many of the activities that you ask the Government to perform for Negroes, is generously financed by Jewish charities and private donations. All of the Negro civil rights groups, on the other hand—including your own—are perennially in financial straits and must rely heavily on white philanthropy in order to remain solvent. Why do they receive so little support from Negroes?

KING: We have to face and live with the fact that the Negro has not developed a sense of stewardship. Slavery was so divisive and brutal, so molded to break up unity, that we never developed a sense of oneness, as in Judaism. Starting with the individual family unit, the Jewish people are closely knit into what is, in effect, one big family. But with the Negro, slavery separated families from families, and the pattern of disunity that we see among Negroes today derives directly from this cruel fact of history. It is also a cruel fact that the Negro, generally speaking, has not developed a responsible sense of financial values. The best economists say that your automobile shouldn't cost more than half of your annual income, but we see many Negroes earning $7000 a year paying $5000 for a car. The home, it is said, should not cost more than twice the annual income, but we see many Negroes earning, say, $8000 a year living in a $30,000 home. Negroes, who amount to about 11 percent of the American population, are reported to consume over 40 percent of the Scotch whiskey imported into the U.S., and to spend over $72,000,000 a year in jewelry stores. So when we come asking for civil rights donations, or help for the United Negro College Fund, most Negroes are trying to make ends meet.

HALEY: The widespread looting that took place during

last summer's riots would seem to prove your point. Do you agree with those who feel that this looting—much of which was directed against Jewish-owned stores—was anti-Semitic in motivation?

KING: No, I do not believe that the riots could in any way be considered expressions of anti-Semitism. It's true, as I was particularly pained to learn, that a large percentage of the looted stores were owned by our Jewish friends, but I do not feel that anti-Semitism was involved. A high percentage of the merchants serving most Negro communities simply happen to be Jewish. How could there be anti-Semitism among Negroes when our Jewish friends have demonstrated their commitment to the principle of tolerance and brotherhood not only in the form of sizable contributions, but in many other tangible ways, and often at great personal sacrifice? Can we ever express our appreciation to the rabbis who chose to give moral witness with us in St. Augustine during our recent protest against segregation in that unhappy city? Need I remind anyone of the awful beating suffered by Rabbi Arthur Lelyveld of Cleveland when he joined the civil rights workers there in Hattiesburg, Mississippi? And who can ever forget the sacrifice of two Jewish lives, Andrew Goodman and Michael Schwerner, in the swamps of Mississippi? It would be impossible to record the contribution that the Jewish people have made toward the Negro's struggle for freedom—it has been so great.

HALEY: In conspicuous contrast, according to a recent poll conducted by *Ebony*, only one Negro in ten has ever participated physically in any form of social protest. Why?

KING: It is not always sheer numbers that are the measure of public support. As I see it, every Negro who does participate represents the sympathy and the moral backing of thousands of others. Let us never forget how one photograph, of those Birmingham policemen with their knees on that Negro woman on the ground, touched something emotionally deep in most Negroes in America, no matter who they were. In city after city, where S.C.L.C. has helped to achieve sweeping social changes, it has been not only because of the quality of its members' dedication and discipline, but because of the moral support of many Negroes who never took an active part. It's significant, I think, that during each of our city struggles, the usual average of crimes committed by Negroes has dropped to almost nothing.

But it is true, undeniably, that there are many Negroes who will *never* fight for freedom—yet who will be eager enough to accept it when it comes. And there are millions of Negroes who have never known anything but oppression, who are so devoid of pride and self-respect that they have resigned themselves to segregation. Other Negroes, comfortable and complacent, consider that they are *above* the struggle of the masses. And still others seek personal profit from segregation.

HALEY: Many Southern whites have accused *you* of being among those who exploit the race problem for private gain. You are widely believed throughout the South, in fact, to have amassed a vast personal fortune in the course of your civil rights activities.

KING: *Me* wealthy? This is so utterly fallacious and erroneous that I often wonder where it got started. For the sixth straight year since I have been S.C.L.C.'s president, I have rejected our board's insistent recommendation that I accept some salary beyond the one dollar a year which I receive, which entitles me to participate in our employees' group insurance plan. I have rejected also our board's offer of financial gifts as a measure and expression of appreciation. My only salary is from my church, $4000 a year, plus $2000 more a year for what is known as "pastoral care." To earn a grand total of about $10,000 a year, I keep about $4000 to $5000 a year for myself from the honorariums that

I receive from various speaking engagements. About 90 percent of my speaking is for S.C.L.C., and it brings into our treasury something around $200,000 a year. Additionally, I get a fairly sizable but fluctuating income in the form of royalties from my writings. But all of this, too, I give to my church, or to my alma mater, Morehouse College, here in Atlanta.

I believe as sincerely as I believe anything that the struggle for freedom in which S.C.L.C. is engaged is not one that should reward any participant with individual wealth and gain. I think I'd rise up in my grave if I died leaving two or three hundred thousand dollars. But people just don't seem to believe that this is the way I feel about it. If I have any weaknesses, they are not in the area of coveting wealth. My wife knows this well; in fact, she feels that I overdo it. But the Internal Revenue people, they stay on me; they feel sure that one day they are going to find a fortune stashed in a mattress. To give you some idea of my reputed affluence, just last week I came in from a trip and learned that a television program had announced I was going to purchase an expensive home in an all-white neighborhood here in Atlanta. It was news to me!

HALEY: Your schedule of speaking engagements and civil rights commitments throughout the country is a punishing one—often 20 hours a day, seven days a week, according to reports. How much time do you get to spend at home?

KING: Very little, indeed. I've averaged not more than two days a week at home here in Atlanta over the past year—or since Birmingham, actually. I'm away two and three weeks at a time, mostly working in communities across the South. Wherever I am, I try to be in a pulpit as many Sundays as possible. But every day when I'm at home, I break from the office for dinner and try to spend a few hours with the children before I return to the office for some night work. And on Tuesdays when I'm not out of town, I don't go to the office. I keep this for my quiet day of reading and silence and meditation, and an entire evening with Mrs. King and the children.

HALEY: If you could have a week's uninterrupted rest, with no commitments whatever, how would you spend it?

KING: It's difficult to imagine such a thing, but if I had the luxury of an entire week, I would spend it meditating and reading, refreshing myself spiritually and intellectually. I have a deep nostalgia for the periods in the past that I was able to devote in this manner. Amidst the struggle, amidst the frustrations, amidst the endless work, I often reflect that I am forever *giving*—never pausing to take in. I feel urgently the need for even an hour of time to get away, to withdraw, to refuel. I need more time to think through what is being done, to take time out from the mechanics of the movement, to reflect on the *meaning* of the movement.

HALEY: If you were marooned on the proverbial desert island, and could have with you only one book—apart from the Bible—what would it be?

KING: That's tough. Let me think about it—one book, not the Bible. Well, I think I would have to pick Plato's *Republic.* I feel that it brings together more of the insights of history than any other book. There is not a creative idea extant that is not discussed, in some way, in this work. Whatever realm of theology or philosophy is one's interest—and I am deeply interested in both—somewhere along the way, in this book, you will find the matter explored.

HALEY: If you could send someone—anyone—to that desert island in your stead, who would it be?

KING: That's another tough one. Let me see, I guess I wouldn't mind seeing Mr. Goldwater dispatched to a desert island. I hope they'd *feed* him and everything, of course. I *am* nonviolent, you know. Politically, though, he's already on a desert island, so it may be unnecessary to send him there.

HALEY: We take it you weren't overly distressed by his defeat in the Presidential race.

KING: Until that defeat, Goldwater was the most dangerous man in America. He talked soft and nice, but he gave aid and comfort to the most vicious racists and the most extreme rightists in America. He gave respectability to views totally alien to the democratic process. Had he won, he would have led us down a fantastic path that would have totally destroyed America as we know it.

HALEY: Until his withdrawal from the race following Goldwater's nomination, Alabama's Governor Wallace was another candidate for the Presidency. What's your opinion of *his* qualifications for that office?

KING: Governor Wallace is a demagog with a capital D. He symbolizes in this country many of the evils that were alive in Hitler's Germany. He is a merchant of racism, peddling hate under the guise of States' rights. He wants to turn back the clock, for his own personal aggrandizement, and he will do literally *anything* to accomplish this. He represents the misuse, the corruption, the destruction of leadership. I am not sure that he believes all the poison that he preaches, but he is artful enough to convince others that he does. Instead of guiding people to new peaks of reasonableness, he intensifies misunderstanding, deepens suspicion and prejudice. He is perhaps the most dangerous racist in America today.

HALEY: One of the most controversial issues of the past year, apart from civil rights, was the question of school prayer, which has been ruled unlawful by the Supreme Court. Governor Wallace, among others, has denounced the decision. How do you feel about it?

KING: I endorse it. I think it was correct. Contrary to what many have said, it sought to outlaw neither prayer nor belief in God. In a pluralistic society such as ours, who is to determine what prayer shall be spoken, and by whom? Legally, constitutionally or otherwise, the state certainly has no such right. I am strongly opposed to the efforts that have been made to nullify the decision. They have been motivated, I think, by little more than the wish to embarrass the Supreme Court. When I saw Brother Wallace going up to Washington to testify against the decision at the Congressional hearings, it only strengthened my conviction that the decision was right.

HALEY: Governor Wallace has intimated that President Johnson, in championing the cause of civil rights only since he became vice-president, may be guilty of "insincerity."

KING: How President Johnson may or may not have felt about or voted on civil rights during his years in Congress is less relevant, at this point, than what he has said and done about it during his tenure as President of the United States. In my opinion, he has done a good job up to now. He is an extremely keen political man, and he has demonstrated his wisdom and his commitment in forthrightly coming to grips with the problem. He does not tire of reminding the nation of the moral issues involved. My impression is that he will remain a strong President for civil rights.

HALEY: Late in 1963, you wrote, "As I look toward 1964, one fact is unmistakably clear: The thrust of the Negro toward full emancipation will *increase* rather than decrease." As last summer's riots testified, these words were unhappily prophetic. Do you foresee more violence in the year ahead?

KING: To the degree that the Negro is not thwarted in his thrust forward, I believe that one can predict *less* violence. I am not saying that there will be no demonstrations. There assuredly will, for the Negro in America has not made one civil rights gain without tense legal and extralegal pressure. If the Constitution were today applied equally and impartially to all of America's citizens, in every section of the country, in every court and code of law, there would be no need for any group of citizens to seek extralegal redress.

Our task has been a difficult one, and will continue to

be, for privileged groups, historically, have not volunteered to give up their privileges. As Reinhold Niebuhr has written, individuals may see the moral light and voluntarily abandon their unjust posture, but groups tend to be more immoral, and more intransigent, than individuals. Our nonviolent direct-action program, therefore—which has proved its strength and effectiveness in more than a thousand American cities where some baptism of fire has taken place—will continue to dramatize and demonstrate against local injustices to the Negro until the last of those who impose those injustices are forced to negotiate; until, finally, the Negro wins the protections of the Constitution that have been denied to him; until society, at long last, is stricken gloriously and incurably color-blind.

HALEY: In well-earned recognition of your dedication to and leadership of the struggle to achieve these goals, you became, in October of last year, the youngest man ever to receive the Nobel Peace Prize. What was your reaction to the news?

KING: It made me feel very humble indeed. But I would like to think that the award is not a personal tribute, but a tribute to the entire freedom movement, and to the gallant people of both races who surround me in the drive for civil rights which will make the American dream a reality. I think that this internationally known award will call even more attention to our struggle, gain even greater sympathy and understanding for our cause, from people all over the world. I like to think that the award recognizes symbolically the gallantry, the courage and the amazing discipline of the Negro in America, for these things are to his eternal credit. Though we have had riots, the bloodshed that we would have known without the discipline of nonviolence would have been truly frightening. I know that many whites feel the civil rights movement is getting out of hand; this may reassure them. It may let them see that basically this is a disciplined struggle, let them appreciate the *meaning* of our struggle, let them see that a great struggle for human freedom can occur within the framework of a democratic society.

HALEY: Do you feel that this goal will be achieved within your lifetime?

KING: I confess that I do not believe this day is around the corner. The concept of supremacy is so imbedded in the white society that it will take many years for color to cease to be a judgmental factor. But it is certainly my hope and dream. Indeed, it is the keystone of my faith in the future that we will someday achieve a thoroughly integrated society. I believe that before the turn of the century, if trends continue to move and develop as presently, we will have moved a long, long way toward such a society.

HALEY: Do you intend to dedicate the rest of your life, then, to the Negro cause?

KING: If need be, yes. But I dream of the day when the demands presently cast upon me will be greatly diminished. I would say that in the next five years, though, I can't hope for much letup—either in the South or in the North. After that time, it is my hope that things will taper off a bit.

HALEY: If they do, what are your plans?

KING: Well, at one time I dreamed of pastoring for a few years, and then of going to a university to teach theology. But I gave that up when I became deeply involved in the civil rights struggle. Perhaps, in five years or so, if the demands on me have lightened, I will have the chance to make that dream come true.

HALEY: In the meanwhile, you are now the universally acknowledged leader of the American civil rights movement, and chief spokesman for the nation's 20,000,000 Negroes. Are there ever moments when you feel awed by this burden of responsibility, or inadequate to its demands?

KING: One cannot be in my position, looked to by some for guidance, without being constantly reminded of the awesomeness of its responsibility. I live with one deep concern: Am I making the right decisions? Sometimes I am uncertain, and I must look to God for guidance. There was one morning I recall, when I was in the Birmingham jail, in solitary, with not even my lawyers permitted to visit, and I was in a nightmare of despair. The very future of our movement hung in the balance, depending upon capricious turns of events over which I could have no control there, incommunicado, in an utterly dark dungeon. This was about 10 days after our Birmingham demonstrations began. Over 400 of our followers had gone to jail; some had been bailed out, but we had used up all of our money for bail, and about 300 remained in jail, and I felt personally responsible. It was then that President Kennedy telephoned my wife, Coretta. After that, my jail conditions were relaxed, and the following Sunday afternoon—it was Easter Sunday—two S.C.L.C. attorneys were permitted to visit me. The next day, word came to me from New York that Harry Belafonte had raised $50,000 that was available immediately for bail bonds, and if more was needed, he would raise that. I cannot express what I felt, but I knew at that moment that God's presence had never left me, that He had been with me there in solitary.

I subject myself to self-purification and to endless self-analysis; I question and soul-search constantly into myself to be as certain as I can that I am fulfilling the true meaning of my work, that I am maintaining my sense of purpose, that I am holding fast to my ideals, that I am guiding my people in the right direction. But whatever my doubts, however heavy the burden, I feel that I must accept the task of helping to make this nation and this world a better place to live in—for *all* men, black and white alike.

I never will forget a moment in Birmingham when a white policeman accosted a little Negro girl, seven or eight years old, who was walking in a demonstration with her mother. "What do you want?" the policeman asked her gruffly, and the little girl looked him straight in the eye and answered, "Fee-dom." She couldn't even pronounce it, but she knew. It was beautiful! Many times when I have been in sorely trying situations, the memory of that little one has come into my mind, and has buoyed me.

Similarly, not long ago, I toured in eight communities of the state of Mississippi. And I have carried with me ever since a visual image of the penniless and the unlettered, and of the expressions on their faces—of deep and courageous determination to cast off the imprint of the past and become free people. I welcome the opportunity to be a part of this great drama, for it is a drama that will determine America's destiny. If the problem is not solved, America will be on the road to its self-destruction. But if it *is* solved, America will just as surely be on the high road to the fulfillment of the founding fathers' dream, when they wrote: "We hold these truths to be self-evident . . ."

MELVIN BELLI

*A Candid Conversation
with the Embattled, Outspoken Attorney
who Defended Jack Ruby*

J. BARRY O'ROURKE

*"The mad genius of the San Francisco bar" . . . "a court
jester" . . . "a publicity-mad pettifogger" . . . "the S. Hurok
of the legal profession"—these are among the kinder things
said about San Francisco attorney Melvin Mouron Belli
(pronounced "bell-eye"). That he is unquestionably among
the greatest living trial lawyers, however, is conceded even
by Belli's legion of enemies, including no few as formidable
in stature as the American Bar Association, the American
Medical Association, most major insurance firms, J. Edgar
Hoover, Robert Kennedy, Richard Nixon and, perhaps most
recently, the city of Dallas, Texas, ever since Jack Ruby—*

with Belli as his counsel—was sentenced to death there for the murder of Lee Harvey Oswald.

An eminent attorney long before the Ruby trial, "Belli has had more effect on the law in the past 10 years than any 50 lawyers in the last century," in the possibly overenthusiastic opinion of a colleague. Indeed, many of his cases have established, or carried forward, major precedents in America's civil and criminal law. Defending those accused of rape, robbery, assault, arson, murder, fraud, pimping, income-tax evasion, forgery and even overtime parking, he has won literally hundreds of criminal cases. But he is best known as "The King of Torts"—a title he cordially dislikes—for his victories in more than 100 personal-injury and medical-malpractice suits, in which he has earned for clients awards ranging from $100,000 to a record-setting $675,000. He has also pioneered the use of "demonstrative evidence" before juries—graphic, and sometimes grisly, courtroom displays of artificial limbs, autopsy photographs, skeletons, mannequins, X rays, witnesses on stretchers—inspiring William Prosser, former dean of the University of California Law School, to call him "a Hollywood producer," and his trials "epics of the supercolossal." So potent is the Belli image, however, that defendant insurance companies have sometimes made substantial settlements when mere mention was made that Belli might be hired.

An international law practice, plus a prodigious schedule of writing, lecturing and teaching, takes Belli around the world, usually followed by a wake of controversy. But no case has earned him as many headlines as the one he lost 15 months ago in Dallas, where he caused a courtroom sensation by leaping up after the announcement of the verdict, tears in his eyes, to denounce the death sentence for Jack Ruby as "the shotgun justice of a kangaroo court."

It was to explore the issues and the aftermath of this historic trial, as well as the other unpopular causes he has espoused during his 32-year career, that we went to San

Francisco early this spring for an exclusive interview with the embattled 57-year-old attorney. He greeted us in the three-story Belli Building, which he had bought from 10 Chinese owners and spent $450,000 restoring to such turn-of-the-century elegance that it has been formally designated State Landmark Number 40S by the California Historical Association. The local San Francisco Gray Line tours include a glimpse from the street through the picture window of his ornate office, where Belli himself may be seen at his vintage desk consulting with clients and colleagues amid a spectacular Victorian mélange of heavy crystal chandeliers, velvet chairs, leather couches, antimacassars, quill pens, oil paintings, awards for Belli's forensic triumphs, thousands of legal and medical books, an array of apothecary jars, several human skeletons and a 25-foot-long bar. With a small communications network of telephones and speaker systems, Belli maintains touch with 18 lawyers on the premises, their secretaries, private investigators and sundry other specialists attending the cases of clients by the dozens who have been lured by Belli's magic name and lofty courtroom batting average.

In a casual display of expansive graciousness, millionaire Belli flipped to us the keys to his Rolls-Royce Silver Cloud for our use during the visit; and he wined and dined us regally in his $280,000 Twin Peaks home. During our week-long series of conversations, we accompanied him to speaking engagements and joined him at his tailor's for the fitting of three new suits. And on our first morning in town, we even helped him transplant geraniums in his office window box as his fire-engine-red slacks and shirt wowed the ogling tourists in the street outside. In this bizarre setting, we began by posing a hypothetical question.

HALEY: You said once that "any lawyer worthy of the name has a commitment to defend the pariahed, unpopular

defendant." You proved your point when you defended
Jack Ruby. Would you have been as willing to defend Lee
Oswald if he had lived?

BELLI: I would have hated to, for I loved Jack Kennedy
very much. But as a lawyer, I must acknowledge that any
man charged with any crime, however heinous, is entitled
to competent representation. So if Oswald had lived, and he
hadn't been able to obtain other competent counsel, and I
had been asked to take his case—yes, I would have represented him. If I had refused, I feel I would have had to turn
in my shingle. I like to think that the American Bar hasn't
sunk so low that there are not other defense attorneys in
this country who would have done the same thing.

HALEY: Do you think Oswald's rights as an accused were
adequately protected by the Dallas authorities?

BELLI: Oswald's treatment by the law was the biggest
scandal in the history of American justice. The world saw
the horrendous spectacle of Oswald, *without* legal counsel,
interrogated for hours and thrust into that Friday-night
mob-scene "press conference" and shouted questions in
police headquarters corridors. He had no counsel to object
as dozens of self-seeking, self-serving "authorities" volunteered to the press their prejudicial, incriminating and otherwise unwarranted statements regarding Oswald's guilt.
He went a full day without counsel. In my belief, the
public's mounting outcry shamed the city into sending the
president of the Dallas Bar Association, H. Louis Nichols,
to visit him in his cell. As far as I know, Nichols has never
been inside a trial courtroom except for official inductions
to office, eulogies and ceremonial purposes: this legal para-
gon then did what strikes me as unthinkable and unforgiv-
able by giving an interview to the press that probably
destroyed Oswald's obvious and valid defense, that he was
mentally deranged. Nichols told the press that "he looked
perfectly all right to me," which gratuitously and automatically helped the Dallas establishment condition public

opinion against any insanity defense by Oswald. Where was an Oswald defense counsel to scream in protest when Dallas' prosecutor told millions watching on television, "Oswald is the guilty man. There is no doubt about it, and we're going to *fry* him!" What kind of defense counsel would have consented to the Dallas police department's utterly unbelievably stupid act of marching Oswald right out into the open—for television? An expert defense counsel for Oswald should have been of urgent priority for the American Bar Association—while he was *alive.* But not until Oswald was safely dead did he get a counsel. When his lawyer couldn't be embarrassed by being seen sitting next to an assassin, an unpopular defendant, then national A.B.A. president Walter E. Craig was appointed to represent Oswald at the Warren Commission hearing.

HALEY: Despite the *Warren Report,* the belief persists in some circles, especially abroad, that Oswald and Ruby were parties to a right-wing plot against the President's life—a plot in which the FBI, the Secret Service and even the Warren Commission conspired to conceal "the truth." Do you feel that these suspicions have any substance?

BELLI: They're hallucinatory and utterly preposterous. Do you want to know who I believe is solely responsible for starting these rumors? The Dallas police department and the Dallas district attorney's office. Their ominous insinuations that Oswald and Ruby knew each other started during the trial. In the judge's chambers I tried to persuade the D.A. to announce in court that there was no truth to those rumors—which could have been quashed right there—but it appeared to me that the D.A. *encouraged* them, so as to make Jack Ruby seem some kind of conspiratorial monster. So the rumor that he had killed Oswald to "silence" him got cabled abroad, and it steadily mushroomed, besmirching the image not only of our law-enforcement agencies, but of our nation. It has been made to appear that our FBI either could not or would not report the full story of the "plot." There was even an outrageous rumor that our own President Lyndon Johnson conspired in the assassination, to succeed to the Presidency. Now, I know as much about the assassination as any man alive, and I can tell you flatly that it was the barren, solitary act of Lee Oswald. He was a crazy man. And he and Ruby were strangers. Those are facts. The most incredible thing to me is why the FBI didn't pass along to the Secret Service the lengthy file it had on Oswald. But as much as I detest the type of man that J. Edgar Hoover is, I can't make myself believe that the FBI or the CIA or anyone else suppressed knowledge of any plot. On the Warren Commission, we had seven wise and honorable men, some of the best. If they couldn't come up with the truth, then God pity us all!

HALEY: What significance do you attach to Warren's statement, during the Commission's deliberations, that the full story of the assassination "won't come out in our lifetimes"?

BELLI: None. That was a horse's-ass thing for Justice Warren to say. I don't know what he meant, but I don't think he meant anything ominous by it. If you're looking for untold facts, though, I can tell you something most people never knew. The night before Oswald was shot, I learned, a Dallas policeman and his girlfriend talked with Jack Ruby, trying to get him to approve of the idea of having Oswald lynched. Their reason was that they knew what a weak-minded guy Jack Ruby was. At the trial, I never mentioned the cop and his girl, because I never could locate them again; they just disappeared.

HALEY: Why did you take on the Ruby case? Some say it was for the publicity.

BELLI: Look, I'm for hire. I will defend *anyone* who comes to me—even the president of the Bar Association suing a guy for defamation, for accusing him of being a liberal, in favor of civil rights, due process of law, and against wire tapping. My service to the community as a trial lawyer is that I am for hire by either side. As far as publicity is concerned, I'd had my fill of that long before that travesty of a trial ever came along. My motive in taking the case was that I hoped I might be able to do something for that sick man, Jack Ruby, for psychiatry, for law, and for tolerance. But I didn't volunteer for the job. Jack's brother Earl asked me if I would take the case, and he offered me a defense fee of $100,000.

HALEY: Did that sum play any part in your decision?

BELLI: I agreed to take the case for the reasons I've just stated. But since you've brought up the money, it might interest you to know that I never got anything like $100,000 for the case. What I got was debts—bills, expenses for our defense team, for the medical experts who flew to Dallas to testify for Ruby, and other costs. I did get about $12,000 from the Rubys, but I paid for every other cent of the costs out of my own pocket—about $15,000. It might also interest you to know that I was offered $100,000 from another source *not* to defend Jack Ruby. I'm not saying what source.

HALEY: There has been some speculation that the offer came from a well-known right-wing Dallas oil millionaire.

BELLI: If that's what you heard, that's what you heard.

HALEY: That's all you want to say about it?

BELLI: No more—*now.*

HALEY: All right. Once you accepted the case, what made you decide on a plea of temporary insanity?

BELLI: The incontrovertible evidence of psychiatric examinations. Jack Ruby was and is a very sick man who belongs in a mental hospital. We owed to our national image a dramatic example of how the American legal system pursues and protects a defendant's rights. We owed to our own law an exposure of the incongruities in our law's understanding of mental illness. Indeed, for the world to see and appreciate the modern medical specialty of psychotherapy at work was one of the great promises of that trial. And those brilliant clinical experts—psychologists and neurologists—who examined Jack Ruby put together an unmistakably clear picture of a mentally unstable man whom the assassination had stunned and shocked and impelled into frantic, attention-seeking compulsions beyond his power to control. Nothing I've ever sensed in advance about the line of defense for a client has ever been more graphically justified by the evidence—or more ignored by a jury.

I never dreamed what a kangaroo court of mockery and errors and prejudice in law and decency we were going to face in that city. There isn't one fair-minded lawyer who won't appreciate what I'm saying when the transcript can be read. I've disagreed with jury verdicts before; every lawyer has. But I've never felt that the jurors weren't honestly trying to do their very best—except on that black day there in Dallas.

HALEY: Bitter criticism and even American Bar Association censure have been leveled at you for shouting after the verdict, "May I thank the jury for a victory of bigotry and injustice!" How do you feel about it now?

BELLI: As outraged as I did then. It was a spontaneous outburst of horror at the callous death sentence from a jury that had taken actually less than one hour to consider all of the complex scientific testimony about that pitiful, afflicted little man. I shouted long, vituperatively, and in tears, that a kangaroo court and a bigoted jury had railroaded Jack Ruby to purge their collective conscience in a rape of American justice that made Dallas a city of shame forevermore. Too often have our courts of law shown us that vindictive streak, that drive to heap society's sins upon an individual, that hypocritical refusal to face facts inherent in which are unpleasant truths about ourselves. The watching, listening world needed to hear a voice from among those Americans who recognized what had happened, and who were sickened by Dallas' cruelty, the smugness, the community defensiveness and the blind determination to crucify one man for everyone's sins.

HALEY: Do you think that's any more true of Dallas than it would have been of any other city where the President might have been murdered?

BELLI: It's *uniquely* true of Dallas. Dallas is unlike any other city in America; even the rest of Texas, thank God, is different from Dallas. Federal Judge Sarah Hughes called Dallas "the only American city in which the President could have been shot." Every major publication had veteran writers there who appraised and reported Dallas in such terms as "murder capital of the world," "a sick city," "a festering sore," "a city of shame and hate." Here is a city where a minister told his flock, "If any of you vote for this Catholic Kennedy, don't you ever come to my church again." Here is a city where I took my wife and son to a beautiful Baptist church and on the Sunday program an usher gave me, the Lord's message was squeezed down in a corner under the church's impressive balance sheet full of dollar signs. Here is a city where I entered a barbershop, unrecognized, and someone discussing the trial said, "I hear they got those Jew psychiatrists out from Maryland," and someone replied, "Yeah, with their slick Jew lawyers." I swept the towel from around my neck, stood straight up, gave the Nazi salute, yelled *"Achtung! Heil Hitler!"* and goose-stepped outside. Here is a city whose prosecutor said of a St. Patrick's Day parade, "Maybe we're pressing our luck too far to allow another parade so soon for another Irishman!" And the same prosecutor said, "Well, if they want to look inside of Jack Ruby's brain, we'll give it to them after we fry him!"

Dallas is where Adlai Stevenson was spat upon and hit upon the head with a picket sign, and where the American flag was hung upside down by General Edwin Walker, an ardent advocate of the philosophy of the John Birch Society. In Dallas in 1960 even Lyndon Johnson and his lady had been insulted. Dallas is a city where the "Minute-women" get on telephones and call all over with such messages as "Mental health is Communistic" and "Fluoridation of water is Communistic."

HALEY: Aren't you describing the activities of a lunatic fringe?

BELLI: Look, I'm not talking about *all* the citizens of Dallas. I'm talking about the oligarchy that *rules* and *runs* the city. I'd be the first to admit that some of America's truly fine people live there. In Dallas I met two of the greatest stand-up guys I ever knew: Stanley Marcus of Neiman-Marcus—it took visceral courage to speak out as he did; and Rabbi Silverman—he was one of the bravest men there. No, my contempt is reserved solely for the city's archreactionary oligarchy. You know what made them madder at me than anything else? It was when I said what *symbolized* Dallas for me: a gold-plated bidet I'd seen with a philodendron growing out of it. They were enraged at the implication that they hadn't known what to do with it. Well, I take that back. They *do* know what they can do with it.

I'll never forget how Sheriff Bill Decker said he was going to see to the "safety" of Joe Tonahill, my trial assistant, and me: He was going to have a police car deliver us to court "because there's so much high feeling around here." I told him, "Look, I appreciate your concern, but we're going to walk down goddamn Main Street to the courthouse. Whenever it gets to the point here in America, in my own country, that I can't walk down any main street as a trial lawyer, then I'll have to take down my shingle." And I would. I'd go to Congress and walk outside wearing a sandwich board. I'd howl to the heavens. I might have to do some flamboyant things to get my story heard, but you know I know just how to do it. In any case, we *did* walk down that Main Street in Dallas to the trial, but I'm going to tell you the truth. I was scared shitless. I used to say, despite all my enemies, that no one would ever actually want to shoot me. But now, after walking down that street and seeing the hate in the eyes of everyone who watched, I never would say that again.

HALEY: Was your outburst in court the reason for your being dismissed as Ruby's lawyer after the trial?

BELLI: I was not fired. I bowed out of my own accord. I lost my objectivity that day in Dallas. Once I lose my objectivity, I've lost my value in our adversary system of justice. So I got out of the case. It's as simple as that.

HALEY: What do you think will result from the appeal of Ruby's conviction which is now pending?

BELLI: I think that everyone in law knows what will almost automatically happen when an appellate court reviews that trial transcript away from that emotionally charged Dallas courtroom. I pray to God that the terrible miscarriages of American justice that trial transcript contains will cause the case to be reversed. And I pray, for the sake of that sick, pathetic little man, Jack Ruby—whose already paranoid-schizophrenic condition has deteriorated shockingly during his long imprisonment without psychiatric care, and who has tried several times to commit suicide in his cell, once by butting his head against the wall—that his cruel death sentence will be commuted to life imprisonment in a mental hospital, where he has belonged since the day they put him in Dallas' city jail a year and a half ago.

HALEY: Do you favor capital punishment in murder cases where the assailant is adjudged mentally sound?

BELLI: I don't favor institutional vengeance under *any* circumstances. Who in God's name has the right to pass judgment on the life of another human being? Who's to usurp this divine prerogative? Only a primitive mind sanctions this kind of barbarity. Just look at the creeps who are in favor of it; you get the feeling they want to be the ones to pull the switch. Dick Nixon is all out for capital punishment; I can't think of a better argument for its abolition. I only wish I could take him, and all the rest of them who believe in gassing and "frying" felons, through the agonizing ordeal of the last days of waiting in the death house to be hanged or electrocuted, through the gut-wrenching last meal, through the writing of the last heartbreaking letter to one's wife or daughter. Let me do just this, nothing more— and I'd be able to defeat capital punishment singlehandedly.

HALEY: Do you disagree with the view that the death penalty deters crime?

BELLI: Naturally, punishment does deter *some* crime. A lot of crime hasn't happened because whoever considered it simply feared he'd wind up in the clink. But you've got a different breed of motivation in murder—because of its irrationality. Most murderers just don't *think* in terms of consequences; they don't think at all, as a matter of fact. Thus, the death penalty does very little, if anything, to deter murder. I've seen prisoners join a jailbreak, going right past condemned row, doing exactly what they knew could put *them* in the death house, and it didn't deter them a bit.

HALEY: Examining another aspect of American justice in a recent book called *Innocence,* author Edward D. Radin estimated that some 14,000 people each year are convicted, imprisoned and in some cases executed for crimes they didn't commit. Are those figures accurate, in your opinion?

BELLI: We can't have any way of knowing for sure unless their convictions are reversed—and nothing like that number are. Circumstantial evidence can often be loaded or misleading, and eyewitnesses can be mistaken or untruthful, but I'm still not among those who feel that a great number of innocent people are convicted because of either. I have too much respect for our system of law to believe that justice could miscarry so often and on such a scale. Over and above that, I've had the practical experience to deny the allegation. But, of course, miscarriages do occur, and probably always will, for man-made law will always be fallible; but even if it happens only once in a million cases, we must rectify it and look for means to improve our system of justice so that the same mistake isn't made again.

If by protecting the rights of an accused, providing him as we do with recourse to appeal for a reversed decision on the basis of irregularities in the conduct of his trial, we enable ten guilty men to go free because their lawyers get them off on a "legal technicality," it would still be better than for one innocent man to be convicted and imprisoned, or even executed, because he had no such recourse.

HALEY: A moment ago you brought up the fallibility of eyewitness testimony. Would you regard policemen, who frequently testify in criminal cases on behalf of the prosecution, as more reliable witnesses than the average man in the street?

BELLI: I'm glad you asked that question. It happens to be one of the axes I grind in my book *Dallas Justice.* In it, I said I was convinced that the testimonial credibility of policemen on the witness stand is often highly suspect, for it stems from the belief, deep in their law-abiding hearts, that they are serving a higher truth than justice when they testify for the prosecution. They often know a lot about the case in which they are testifying that might be helpful to the defendant—but they sometimes neither make it available to his attorney nor mention it in court. They are convinced—it's part of being a cop—that the reason the defendant is sitting there is that the law, their part of the law, has done its job and that the job of judge and jury is to provide a quick, questionless conviction and a stiff sentence. The presumption of innocence until guilt is proven is for lawyers, not for cops. The man *must* be guilty, they think, or else why has he been arrested, arraigned and brought to trial? So they sometimes convince themselves that a modicum of truth stretching or truth omission on their part could achieve the desirable end that strict adherence to the rule of evidence could not.

Perhaps, of all people, from what you've read of me, and because of what I've just said, you wouldn't expect me to say this, but I think the average American policeman not only is a good guy, but he's underpaid, overworked, and a pretty damned good human being. He goes out of his way to help kids, and to help people in trouble. It's only the black sheep, the errant cop, who gets into the newspapers. And thank God there aren't many of them.

HALEY: The U.S. crime rate is steadily rising, and many law-enforcement officers are convinced that part of the cause lies in the courts' insistence on strict rules of evidence that provide lawyers, as you mentioned a moment ago, with "legal loopholes" to spring their clients. How do you feel about it?

BELLI: What the police mentality seems unable to comprehend is that these "loopholes," these technicalities of the law, are among the inalienable protections against the violation and usurpation of human rights. I admit that I've seen a few flagrantly guilty men slip through legal loopholes and go scot-free in my time; but far more often I've seen these same loopholes used to save innocent men and women who would otherwise have perished or been sent to prison for the best years of their lives. No, that's not the reason for the rising crime rate. And it's certainly not because people are growing more lawless and depraved, as some have darkly hinted. As a matter of fact, I think we're slowly growing better. More likely it's because of the catapulting rate of population growth among the poor, the uneducated and the underprivileged in our squalid, sprawling city slums: because of the struggle to retain our individual identities in an increasingly anonymous mass society; because of our liberation from Victorian sexual strictures, which has set many young people morally adrift; because we find ourselves burdened with more leisure time than ever before, and the Devil is finding work for idle hands; and maybe partly because we have too many laws telling us what not to do—some of them damned silly laws. Instead of trying to legislate morality for adults, why don't we try teaching it to children? The better, the more tolerantly, the more sympathetically we educate our children, the less crime we'll have when they grow up.

HALEY: Another "legal technicality" decried, and occasionally defied, by law-enforcement officials is the Constitutional amendment that safeguards the public from "unreasonable searches and seizures," thus prohibiting police, say on a gambling or vice raid, from entering a private residence without knocking, or from searching a premises without a warrant. Do they have a valid complaint?

BELLI: In a word, no. I'm still Victorian enough to feel that my home is my castle. Damn it, if I were growing marijuana in my back yard, I'd still insist that J. Edgar get a search warrant before I'd let him wipe his feet on my door mat. Once the uninvited have the carte-blanche right to prowl my home and search my person, next they'll be trespassing in my *mind*, as they're already trying to do with truth serum and lie detectors. Such Gestapo information procedures are not only unnecessary but unendurable in a democracy.

Except perhaps to our God, we all have a façade, even to our closest friends; some of us even to ourselves, and to our spouses—our spouses in particular, for that matter. It may not be good that we have it, but I don't believe the state or anyone else has a right to pierce that façade without the individual's consent—even though it might be good therapy for us to have the veil drawn aside. But that's the psychotherapists' realm, not the cops'.

HALEY: How do you feel about legalized wire tapping? Is it morally or legally defensible?

BELLI: Wire tapping, like lie detectors and truth serum, isn't only impolite, it's morally, legally, innately wrong; it stinks of spying. We can't let Big Brother get away with it. He's already got his long arm up to the elbow into our pocketbooks, our offices and our daily life.

HALEY: Doesn't your own firm employ wire tapping in its investigative work?

BELLI: Yes, I'm afraid we do. I don't have to *like* it to be forced to appreciate the fact of its widespread use, which makes its counteruse unavoidable. If I'm a layman, I can turn away from an ugly wound, but not if I'm a surgeon— and as a lawyer, I *am* a surgeon of sorts: I have to use every means at my command to represent my client, just as a surgeon has to use every instrument or drug at his command to save his patient. It's simply that bugging is now so commonplace that no conscientious and realistic lawyer, however much he deplores it, has any choice but to use it.

HALEY: Among the staunchest supporters of legalized electronic surveillance is the FBI. What do you think of its vaunted reputation for scientific crime detection?

BELLI: Their technical expertise is more impressive than their reputation. Sure, it's a patriotic institution, as sacrosanct as motherhood—but both can get a bit sickening when overportrayed, which they are. While it spends its time and the taxpayers' money chasing two-bit car thieves and looking for Communist spies in Greyhound bus stations, organized crime continues to get fat off of prostitution, dope, gambling, "juice" and murder for hire; it's the nation's biggest business. With its resources and its power, there's no reason in God's world why the FBI couldn't have broken up the syndicate long ago if Hoover really wanted to. The reason he hasn't is simply that syndicate bigwigs are so good at covering up their tracks that it's hellishly difficult to get a conviction, and he wants to keep his precious FBI's gleaming escutcheon unbesmirched by failure.

HALEY: We take it you're not one of his greatest admirers.

BELLI: You might say that. If you want a good scare, get a copy of Fred Cook's book, *The FBI Nobody Knows,* and read it some dark night. It tells the cold, hard facts about Hoover. As the FBI's revered director, he's done a great job—of making his position more secure than that of most crowned heads in this troubled world. Hoover's dictatorial ideas and ideology have no place in a position of such power in a democracy.

HALEY: What *is* his ideology?

BELLI: The ideology of fascism, of rightism. Look at how many ex–FBI men are members of the John Birch Society; I wonder where they picked it up. Hoover is an archreactionary autocrat who deprecates the concept that "we the people" are fit to govern ourselves. He's a dangerous, dangerous man whom we should have gotten rid of a long time ago. Given full rein, he'd legalize not only wire tapping but search-without-warrant and no-knock-and-enter; in the name of law and order, he would completely abandon due process and the constitutional protections guaranteed to every citizen.

HALEY: Aren't you going a bit far?

BELLI: I probably am—because I'm telling the truth. When this appears in print, I fully expect a knock at the door from Mr. Hoover's gray-flannel minions. They've already tried to tap my phones and monkey with my mail. But I've had uninvited nocturnal visitors before. I'm ready for them. The question is: Are they ready for me?

HALEY: Speaking of violating individual rights, do you feel, as some have charged, that Robert Kennedy, as Attorney General, unduly and extralegally harassed Teamster boss Jimmy Hoffa?

BELLI: God pity Hoffa. Any individual is in trouble today if he gets the eagle after him. One vicious man, Bobby Kennedy, subverting the powers of government, made it a mission to "get" Hoffa. Now, Hoffa's done a lot I don't like—but I think some of his convictions will be reversed. If Hoffa has done wrong—and maybe he has—the law will take care of him. He should be prosecuted, not *persecuted.*

HALEY: *Fact* magazine recently attributed to you the following remarks about Robert Kennedy: "He's the most

vicious, evil son of a bitch in American politics today. . . .
Sure, he wants to be President, but what he *really* wants
is to become head of the universe. . . . The *Pope* isn't safe
with that little bastard around. . . . He's arrogant, rude, and
even ignorant of the law. . . . He's the monied Little Lord
Fauntleroy of government. . . . Every newspaperman knows
what he is, and even Johnson can't stand him, but everybody is too scared of the son of a bitch." Are these accurate
quotes?

BELLI: That's what I said. But I certainly didn't expect to
see it on the cover of a magazine; indeed, I didn't expect to
be directly quoted. But I've since had hundreds of both
lawyers and laymen write and telephone me to say, "I wish
to hell I'd had the guts to say the same thing." Kennedy as
Attorney General had absolutely no experience for the job
as top lawyer of the United States. Who is this man, who
has never been in a courtroom, to tell me how to act, or to
tell my colleague trial lawyers how to act? Which he did.
But quite apart from that, and his vendetta against Hoffa,
I know of nothing Bobby Kennedy as Attorney General did
that he could point to with pride.

HALEY: How about his department's dedication to the
enforcement of civil rights legislation?

BELLI: His office did a tremendous and good job on civil
rights; but in *Jack* Kennedy's Administration, could *any*
Attorney General's office have done less?

HALEY: What do you feel can be done to rectify the
mockery of justice in Southern courts, which perennially
exonerate whites charged with murdering Negroes?

BELLI: These segregationist barbarians—the ones who
pull the trigger and the ones who let them off—affront not
only the law of man but the law of God; they disgrace
themselves and our country before the world. But this
conspiracy of hate and bigotry won't last; its days are
numbered. In practical terms, however, we can't change the
state laws or the inbred prejudices that keep them in force.

I'm afraid we must resign ourselves to the fact that these atrocities, and these travesties of justice, will continue until the white South learns to understand and respect the spirit as well as the letter of due process and equality before the law. It just takes time. Pretty soon all the subterfuges, tricks and deceits designed to circumvent the civil rights laws will have been tried by the die-hards and eliminated by the Supreme Court. Then, and only then, will Negroes in the South begin to enjoy the fruits of true freedom.

HALEY: Do you share the conservative view that the present Supreme Court, because of its trail-blazing decisions in civil rights, censorship, school prayer and the like, is "too liberal"? And do you agree with those who feel that it has begun to unrightfully usurp legislative authority?"

BELLI: What do you mean by "liberal" and "conservative"? If you mean that "liberals" are more concerned with human rights, and "conservatives" with property rights, I think that's as good a definition as any. According to that definition, the present Supreme Court is the most liberal we've ever had. But *too* liberal? No. As for assuming legislative authority, of course it has. But *unrightfully?* No. For good or for bad, our Supreme Court has without question become the second legislature in Washington. I say that not in criticism, only as something in the nature of things. I happen to think we have a *great* Supreme Court, the greatest decision-making Court we've ever had, the most humanitarian in our history. Earl Warren is a great administrator; he has integrity, ability. The individual justices are sincere and hard working; they try hard to be objective, to put country above personality; they're the best we've ever had. The Court has done the American people great justice in rendering the law consonant with the changing needs and increasing complexities of the contemporary world.

HALEY: Since the turn of the century, many attempts at censorship of sexually explicit books and films have been made by the U.S. Post Office, the U.S. Customs Bureau, various state governments and scores of religious and citizens' censor boards. Almost all of these bans have been judicially overruled, some of them in historic decisions by the Supreme Court. With whom do you feel should ultimate authority rest for passing on the "redeeming social merit" of allegedly obscene creative works?

BELLI: With the public, through the courts. If I were defending a so-called "dirty" book, I'd feel a jury of my peers fully qualified to judge its redeeming merits. Juries do a damned good soul-searching job that speaks for their community's collective morality. Let literary men, ministers, professors, the tolerant, the bigoted, the broad-minded and the narrow-minded all have at it in a jury room. The sparks of conflict will shed the light by which justice may be illuminated. Only a jury will arrive at a judgment that is the wish, the temper of the community—which I think should be the ultimate criterion of judgment.

HALEY: How do you feel in general about the much-discussed revolution in sexual attitudes and practices that's taking place in America today?

BELLI: I believe in the Constitution, the Bill of Rights, and sex, and not necessarily in that order. But sex has been here since the Garden of Eden and no overnight revolution in the sex relationship is going to accomplish anything good. Greater candor, yes; greater permissiveness, no. I can't believe that premarital and extramarital relations per se can lead to a fuller life or more enduring happiness. I'm certainly not Victorian, except in my office decor, and I've certainly seen enough of life as an able-bodied seaman, knocking around the world with Errol Flynn, and trying cases in every state; but I do not believe, in this particular area of human relationship, that lack of will power will achieve any greater degree of happiness. I will say, however, that I don't think we're more meretricious sexually than lecherous old grandpa. We've just brought sex a little more into the open. And that's all to the good.

HALEY: You and Errol Flynn were close friends, weren't you?

BELLI: Yes, we were. We met when I was retained to represent a sailor who had been accidentally harpooned in the foot by a guest on Errol's yacht, the *Zaca.* When I went down to Hollywood to question Errol and walked in wearing a white suit and a black Homburg, his eyes lit up. He had always been impressed with the histrionics of trial law, and I've always felt that I might have been an actor. After I'd taken his deposition, we had a most enjoyable legal tussle, and a friendship began. He was great company. He lived life to the fullest: he was up at all hours; he drank vodka before he got out of bed in the morning. And he had the Devil in him. He loved pixy tricks, and played more than his share of them. In a dresser drawer, I remember, Errol kept about 30 emerald-looking rings, which he'd give to girls, telling them with great feeling, "This belonged to my mother."

He and I also played great jokes on each other. One hot afternoon in Paris, Errol took off all his clothes to be cool and lay down on his bed for a nap. I left him sleeping soundly and went downstairs to the hotel bar and sold tickets for five dollars apiece to about 20 women—Frenchwomen and tourists—whom I brought upstairs for a guided tour of Errol in the altogether. Well, we were all tiptoeing through the bedroom when some silly Frenchwoman began giggling and yelled "Fleen! Fleen!" and woke him up. Did he get sore!

This was in 1949. I had been in Rome on a business trip, and was about to leave for Tokyo when Errol called from Paris. He said, "Dear boy, you've got to come to Paris. They've got me over a barrel." I went, intending to stay two days, and stayed months. Errol was making a movie partially financed by the French government and there were plenty of complications on which he needed my help. We stayed about half the time on the *Zaca*, anchored off Nice.

Errol would go down to the bilge, where he kept some gold ingots hidden, bring one back, row to shore with it, turn it in for currency—and we'd be off for a night at the casino.

In Paris, at the Belle Aurora, an exquisite little French restaurant, after we'd gotten up at noon, we'd sit from about one to four and have imaginary trials, drinking bottles of calvados. That's applejack made in Normandy country; it would chase white lightning out of business. We'd drink and invent legal cases, usually murders, which we tried on the spot. People would crowd outside in the street until they blocked it. I'd accuse Errol and examine him, then he would accuse me and examine me. We'd get almost to the point of blows.

In later years, back in this country, my family came to know Errol well. He sometimes stayed with us. But he wasn't well. My little son, Caesar, called him "a sick man"—the perception of children. My wife would plead with him to take it easier. He told her, "Look, I've done everything twice, why should I bother? If I had an attack, there wouldn't be anyone to give a damn." Right at the end, he was planning to play me in a film. It was about this time that he sent me galleys of *My Wicked, Wicked Ways*. I wasn't home when he telephoned, on his way to Vancouver to sell the *Zaca*; it was like selling his life. He told my wife, "Tell the guy I love him; just tell him that for me." Then, later—it was midnight—I was in bed at our Los Angeles home when Errol's valet telephoned and said, "He's gone."

HALEY: You talk about him like a brother.

BELLI: I guess we *were* brothers, in a way—though I was an only child. Like him, I'm wild, enthusiastic; I love people. I'm a Leo, you see, born July 29, 1907.

HALEY: In Sonora, California, according to your biography. Is that where you grew up?

BELLI: Until I reached college age, when I went off to the University of California in Berkeley. But I almost didn't make it. I was the valedictorian of my high school graduating class, but I had to sue the principal to get my diploma.

HALEY: How did that happen?

BELLI: Well, I was brutally attacked the evening before graduation—by a huge bottle of whiskey. I was so sick the next day that I couldn't get to school to make my speech, and when the principal found out why, he withheld my diploma. He was adamant, so my father took me to see an old family friend, a judge. When the judge heard the story, he said, "My boy, you've been wronged!" And he hauled out of his desk a couple of writs, a replevin, a bench warrant, a couple of *subpoena duces tecums,* a habeas corpus, a *habeas diploma,* a handful of old bail bonds, and he stuck all of them together with notary public seals and red ribbon and he marched over to the school and served all of it on the principal. I got my diploma on the spot. Up to that day I had been thinking about being a doctor, but right then I knew the law was for me.

My father lost his money in the crash, so I had to work my way through college as a soda jerk, a summer farm hand and things like that. I even wrote off for free samples of things like soap and shaving cream and sold them to my fraternity brothers. After I graduated, I spent a year traveling around the world on merchant ships as an able-bodied seaman. Then I entered the University of California Boalt Hall Law School. I stood a lucky 13th in a class of 150.

In 1933, when I got my degree, I was lucky enough to get a job as a Government investigator, posing as an itinerant bum, moving around with the Okies. My name was supposed to be "Joe Bacigalupi." I was supposed to submit reports on what the Okies were talking about and what they wanted. I had a card with a special Los Angeles telephone number to call if I ever got in really bad trouble— not for just getting arrested or beaten up; it had to be really important. I never had to use it. One of my first deep impressions was watching Los Angeles deputy cops standing on the city line clubbing back poor Okies trying desperately to get into the city to get on relief rolls, or at least to get a meal. Eventually, I wrote a report that was used as the basis for migratory-worker relief in that area.

Moving out and about then, riding in and on and underneath freight cars, "bumming," standing in soup lines, sleeping in skid-row "jungles," I don't know how many times I got thrown out of different towns about the Southwest—but I know that's when I developed my deep, strong sympathy for the underdog and the outcast, and it's where I learned about the kangaroo courts in this country. Well, after that migratory hobo investigation job ended— Say, I seem to be telling my life story. Do you really want to hear it?

HALEY: Certainly.

BELLI: All right, you asked for it. Well, I got desk space in a small San Francisco law firm. But nothing happened. I just sat there. Finally, in 1934, a well-known defense lawyer took me on for the lordly wage of $25 a month. But nothing happened there either, so I managed to save $20 and went down to Los Angeles looking for a better job. One big lawyer there who turned me down I later opposed in a case; I won my client a $187,500 settlement. The guy could have hired me in 1935 and sent me to Palm Springs for the rest of my life at $100 a week and still saved his client money. Now he tells people, "I recognized Belli as a comer the first time I saw him." Sure he did! I know ever since then, I've never refused to see a guy fresh from law school. You never can tell.

I finally learned to quit waiting for business to find me. If I was going to get any clients, I decided people would have to know I was around. I got the idea of spreading it around that I'd take, free of charge, any cases of criminals in lots of trouble. One of the first clients I found was Avilez, "the Black-Gloved Rapist." He had been tried, convicted and sentenced to a total of 400 years. For whatever it was worth, I got 200 years knocked off his sentence. He wrote me a thank-you note. After that, I got a number of other hopeless cases—one of them a convicted counterfeiter who had resumed printing the stuff right in San Quentin's print shop.

Although I didn't realize it at the time, the case that first showed me the thing that would later get me on my way was that of a young Negro convict named Ernie Smith. He had been indicted for murder for killing another convict, in a fight in the San Quentin prison yard. Smith told me he had done it in self-defense, that the other man was about to throw a knife at him. I couldn't believe it, but the captain of the guard confirmed for me that most of the convicts carried knives. He showed me a desk drawer full of over a hundred lethal-looking pigstickers, explaining, "We take away the big ones." Before the trial, I served a subpoena on the captain of the guard, ordering him to come to court with his drawer full of knives to be admitted into the evidence. Walking past the jury box with it, I was struck by a hell of a thought. My whole case, every argument to determine if Ernie Smith would live or die, was *in that drawer!* So I "accidentally" stumbled and dropped it; a hundred wicked-looking knives spilled all over the floor in front of the shocked jury—broken saw blades, sharpened files with tire-tape handles, the works. The jurors took one look and they *knew* it had been self-defense. You realize what I had hit upon by accident? The effect of *demonstrative* evidence in trials. I might never have talked those jurors into seeing self-defense, but I had *proved* it when I dropped that drawer.

Well, that's background. I had a lot of different cases after that, all kinds. And I gradually built up a pretty good practice, at least enough to live on.

HALEY: How did you come to specialize in personal-injury suits?

BELLI: Mainly because when I entered practice, the average individual who had suffered a personal injury faced a pretty dismal financial-award prospect if he went to court. Well up into the 1900s, settlements were in the neighborhood of $1100 for the loss of a leg, $5500 for the loss of a male organ. Sometimes people who were even paralyzed with permanent spinal injuries would get simply *nothing*, perhaps on the basis of a "contributory negligence" claim by the defense. Some states had laws making $10,000 the maximum allowable death award.

The average suffering, scared, inexperienced plaintiff had usually been rendered penniless by medical costs and the loss of habitual income. If he did get an attorney to go to court, a fee of one third of the average award wouldn't permit the attorney to present a really persuasive case. And when 12 well-meaning but confused jurors sat hearing a jumble of legal terminology they couldn't understand, if the plaintiff got anything, it was the usual, totally inadequate award.

Well, I began to make a practice of showing demonstrative evidence to juries: human skeletons, moving pictures, enlarged X rays, still pictures in color, infrared pictures, wooden scale models. When the jurors graphically *saw* the nature and extent of injuries, my clients began getting substantially increased awards. And when other personal-injury attorneys around San Francisco, then around California, caught on and began doing the same thing, the whole picture of awards began improving.

It was about then that the defendant insurance companies began campaigning against us. Awards were getting "too high." "Ambulance chasers!" they called us. "Shysters!" Since personal-injury law is 75 percent of all trial work, their implication was that only 25 percent of lawyers in America were respectable—a thought to conjure with.

HALEY: Still, any business—including the insurance companies—must make a profit to survive. Isn't it reasonable that they would resist personal-injury awards of often hundreds of thousands of dollars?

BELLI: Tell me: Who is the victim—the poor injury-bankrupt plaintiff trying to collect adequate damages from a rich insurance company; or the rich insurance company trying to whittle down or avoid payment of an adequate award for a personal injury inflicted through the fault of the defendant whose paid-up insurance premium that company has regularly collected? Which is the greater perfidy? You talk about insurance-company profits—well, let me tell you something: The insurance companies are among the world's biggest businesses, and they got that way by taking in unbelievable amounts of the public's money in premiums—billions of dollars a year. The public is buying protection. But the insurance-company executives seem to forget that they are holding the public's money in *trust.* They come to regard that money as *theirs,* and they'll be damned if they'll give it up without a struggle. They accept your money readily enough, but did you ever try to *collect* any money from a big insurance company? Nine times out of ten, when the time comes to pay off, they fight tooth and nail to get out of their obligation.

Their cries that adequate awards threaten to bankrupt them are *nothing* alongside their shrill cries whenever someone suggests now and then that the state take over their business. Isn't it odd for someone claiming to be losing so much to scream so loudly against losing the opportunity to keep on losing money? No, the six-figure adequate awards I've pioneered are equitable, just and necessary. These awards are here to stay, and I think the trend is *further* upward. But I will guarantee you that awards to the personal-injury plaintiffs will never keep pace with the insurance companies' fantastic and mounting profits.

Let me ask you something: Except an adequate award, what else can be offered to the personal-injury victim? We have nothing that will make the permanently injured victim whole again, nothing that will let him walk without a limp, nothing but drugs to let him sleep without pain. For many, one day not even morphine any longer eases their frightful suffering, and the only alternative left is a cordotomy—the severing of the spinal cord to halt the dreadful journey of the pain impulses to the brain. Think about that the next time you see one of these propaganda pieces about the "high awards" that are "ruining" the country's insurance companies. Think about those pitiful personal-injury victims who tempt one to say "They'd be better off dead." But the law forbids them to choose death; they have no legal choice but to go on living—and suffering. Think about the double amputees, the "basket cases," the traumatic psychotics, the paraplegics, the spinal-injury invalids, the blinded, the grotesquely burned and scarred. Think about the permanently immobilized cases, the people who were once just like you and me but who are doomed for their lives to a wheelchair or a brace, or to the indignities of bowel and bladder incontinence.

Let me give you an example of a typical case of mine and let *you* decide whether the award I won for my client was "too high" or not. He was a happy, redheaded kid, just back from the War. He had a wife, a child, a job, and then his life was ruined in an accident caused by the negligence of the San Francisco municipal railway. He suffered a crushed pelvis, and a rupture of the urethra at the juncture of the prostate gland. He will be impotent for the rest of his life. And every tenth day for the rest of his life he must endure a painful urethra catheterization, or his urethra will close, whereupon his bladder would burst. His hospital and doctor bills were over $25,000 at the time of trial, and they will be at least $2000 a year as long as he lives. Two years afterward, I saw that boy again, and what I had feared within myself had happened—his wife had divorced him, his home was gone; he had nothing left but the remainder of his award money. Would you swap places with that boy for the $125,000 he was awarded? Or for a million dollars? Two million? Ten million? I think not.

Yet according to them, the noble, stalwart simon-pure insurance companies are being "victimized by fakers" for $50,000 and $100,000—just for having lost a lousy arm or leg! When I started winning this kind of award, they began sending out letters and buying expensive ads aimed at potential jurors in personal-injury cases: "Keep those awards low, or you'll force your automobile insurance to go up." Bushwa! Today, with personal-injury awards higher than ever before, insurance-company stocks are among the best market buys.

Anyway, when I won three verdicts for more than $100,000 apiece in 1949 and 1950, I really began to draw fire from the insurance companies. "Belli is a Barnum!" they screamed. "The courtrooms are being turned into horror chambers!" But headway was being made everywhere. Asking not a cent of fee, I began lecturing all over the country—to law students, to bar associations, to groups of plaintiff lawyers. Sometimes my speaking in a state would start an immediate rise in personal-injury awards. An example of that is Mississippi, which was for many years one of this country's lowest-verdict states; soon after I addressed its State Bar Association in 1951, Mississippi awards rose sharply—to at least an equitable level.

Finally I decided that I would write a book of all that I thought was modern and just in trial procedures, in both criminal and civil law. It took me two years to write it: in those two years, I averaged about two hours of sleep on week nights and one hour a night on weekends, but finally I turned out the three volumes that were published in 1955, called *Modern Trials*. I'm happy to say that it's becoming something of a standard textbook in the field.

HALEY: What about your Belli Seminars? Will you describe what they are and what they do?

BELLI: For the past 13 consecutive years, I and my associates have held these Belli Seminars in almost every state and major city in America, and they have been widely and enthusiastically attended and accepted by trial lawyers, law students and even some laymen. In them we teach in all phases of modern trial law, on civil and criminal, substantive and procedural law. These seminars have done a lot for the law, but not one has failed to draw criticism from some local member of the American Bar Association, some insurance lawyer, or some large law firm with a "business practice." They raise their old cry: My lectures are "illegal" or "unethical."

HALEY: On what grounds?

BELLI: I'm teaching lawyers how to raise awards to injured people. I'm teaching them how to sue malpracticing doctors who refuse to testify and who condone the American Medical Association's conspiracy of silence. I'm teaching lawyers how to sue the reluctant insurance company and how to serve the process evader. Among the politicians and the fat cats of the A.B.A. hierarchy, needless to say, none of this law for the benefit of the little man is particularly popular—though social-circuiting A.B.A. presidents are constantly trumpeting on the majestic subject "The Defense of Unpopular Causes," and proclaiming that it's every lawyer's duty to give a courageous representation of his unfortunate brother, however unpopular he is, however heinous his crime. These are the same great vocal defenders who whimper, from behind their corporate desks, when some poor unfortunate's unpopular case has to be tried, "Sure, he's entitled to the best defense, but *you* defend him, I can't afford to!" Even worse, these preachers of lofty sentiments are the quickest to impose guilt by association on the lawyer of the heinous-crime client. And these same A.B.A. presidents are approving the abolition of law-school courses that would teach the student lawyer how to *try* an unpopular case! If we continue diminishing the hours devoted to criminal law in our law schools and increasing those devoted to taxation, accounting and the like, we may as well move over into the business-administration schools. Then the few of us remaining criminal lawyers and general trial men may as well be displayed at the monkey house where the public can stare at our odd and nearly extinct species—attracted to the zoo by the A.B.A. presidents' public barking against us.

HALEY: For a member of a nearly extinct species, you seem to be making a pretty good living. It's been reported that you earn more than $300,000 a year from the "adequate awards" you win for your clients.

BELLI: Every *penny* I get, I earn! Do you think all a lawyer has to do is pick up a phone and get an insurance company to settle for $100,000 and then bite off a third of it? To start with, I'm gambling when I take a case. Especially when it's a large award to be sought, the layman has no dream of the amounts of time and talent and money that the plaintiff's lawyer must invest in preparing the best presentation possible. If we get to court and a jury votes against my client, I've lost all I advanced—in cash as well as effort. I don't just sit in my office and work my cases. Our firm here, we aren't just some fat-ass corporation of lawyers sitting around thinking about new ways to screw the Government out of taxes; we are a firm of concerned and committed people representing men and women who need help. We care. It's the most precious thing we've got here, our *feeling* for the people who come here wanting help. I'm working my cases in the shower, when I'm trying to sleep and can't, when I'm on the john, when I'm driving my car, when I'm sitting in those late-night planes. If I win the adequate award for my client, I feel I *deserve* the one third I take for the work that got the award. Most personal-injury lawyers take a bigger cut than I do—many of them 40 and 50 percent.

HALEY: Still, you've managed to amass a sizable fortune from the proceeds of such cases. How much would you say you're worth today?

BELLI: I could cash out today with—well, look, let's put it this way: I feel that after he makes a million dollars a guy should start counting his blessings instead of money. I'm counting my blessings.

HALEY: Your remarkable success in winning six-figure awards, and earning five-figure fees, in medical-malpractice cases has made your name a red flag to the American Medical Association as well as to the nation's insurance companies. What's your brief against the medical profession?

BELLI: George Bernard Shaw wrote it better than I could say it, in *The Doctor's Dilemma*: "We're a conspiracy, not a profession. . . . Every doctor will allow a colleague to decimate a whole countryside sooner than violate the bond of professional etiquette by giving him away." The same as with chicken-hearted, fat-cat lawyers, my complaint isn't against the individual doctors; 99 percent of them are great guys, doing their best and working hard. But here again, the *individual* doctor has a far higher code of ethics than when he acts in convention, through his association. With lawyers *and* doctors, it seems there's some sort of collective amorality, a callous mob psychology, that takes over the individual practitioner's ethics and honesty. Doctors as a group condone malpractice acts that individually they wouldn't dream of sanctioning. The individual doctor is so busy treating the sick and performing operations that he's forfeited the administration of his national organization to a bunch of dirty sons of bitches who try, because of their own shortcomings in their profession, to make him conform to what *they* think medicine should be. They tell him not to publicly criticize his fellow practitioners; they have usurped his conscience.

HALEY: Do you think it's reasonable to expect a doctor to jeopardize his professional standing by testifying against a colleague?

BELLI: Look, every doctor is licensed by us, the public, to practice. His training, his talent, his title, is given to him in trust, by society. To whom, morally, does he owe more— to mankind, or to the A.M.A. and the insurance companies who underwrite his practice? Think of yourself as a victim of some doctor who was simply careless. Think of your being maimed, maybe irreparably, because of his bungling and of your being unable to get another doctor to testify against a wrong that he can plainly see.

My first malpractice case was my eye opener to this incredible conspiracy. I was retained to sue a doctor who had prescribed enemas and cathartics for a young man who was suffering classic *appendicitis* symptoms. The boy's cramping worsened, the doctor sent him to a hospital where he let him wait; the appendix burst and the boy died. Not only was the treatment patently wrong, but later I had good reason to believe that the doctor was intoxicated when he made the house call. Are you ready? I *lost* that case! Not one of this drunken doctor's colleagues would testify in court to what he had obviously done. Worse, five doctors testified in his *behalf,* including the head of one of our largest university hospitals. Five years later, that defendant doctor killed himself; he had become a dope addict and a habitual drunkard.

Twenty-five years have passed since then, but it's *still* next to impossible to get one doctor to testify against another, and it doesn't matter *how* flagrant the case is. Good old Doc Frebish may have come into the operating room dead drunk, carrying a rusty knife and wearing an old pair of overalls, but as long as he's a member in good standing of the A.M.A., not one doctor in 10,000 will testify against him. You can *force* a doctor to take the stand as a witness, but all you can get out of him is a grudging acknowledgment that good old Doc Frebish may have forgotten to wash his hands before taking out Mrs. Smith's uterus instead of her tonsils, and that he may have absent-mindedly left a sponge in her abdomen, but that this "could happen to any of us," and certainly couldn't be considered negligent.

HALEY: Aren't you exaggerating a bit?

BELLI: You think so? Listen, an entire *book* has been written about things left in patients—not just sponges and forceps, but rings, wrist watches, even eyeglasses, for God's sake. Imagine: "What time is it, nurse? I've lost my watch." "Just a minute, doctor, I'll put on my glasses. Oops! Where *are* my glasses?"

Now I have personal knowledge that most doctors privately *do* deplore this sort of thing. A number have told me privately of incompetent colleagues generally regarded as disgraces to their profession. "But Mel," they say, "don't ask me to testify against him. My insurance would be canceled." I can't really say I blame them; if you ever do actually get a doctor to take the stand and testify against another doctor's flagrant and perhaps tragic malpractice, he's regarded as a "stoolie" and will be ostracized for life. Score another victory for the conspiracy. This is the sort of thing I'm trying to fight. Is it any wonder my name is anathema to these people?

But you know, I take pride in the fact that there's an instructor in one San Francisco medical school who asks his students, "What man has done the most for medicine in the past century?" They name Pasteur, Lister. He says, "No—Melvin Belli, because the son of a bitch has made medical men conscientious about their courtroom testimony, and has made lawyers learn medicine."

HALEY: Is a background in medicine essential for a lawyer?

BELLI: Absolutely. In our courts today, three fourths of the criminal and civil cases involve some understanding of some aspect of medicine and medical practice. If a general trial lawyer doesn't cultivate for himself something beyond a layman's knowledge of medical fields, he cuts himself off from essential information, and he deprives his client of an essential service. Every law student I meet, if he indicates to me that he wants to do something more worthwhile with himself than to be a jockstrap for some insurance company, or to keep some corporation's legal skirts clean, I advise him to arrange not only to see a complete autopsy but to learn firsthand about surgical procedures of every sort, to sit in on skin grafts, bone grafts, plastic surgery. I advise him to learn the functions of surgical instruments, to familiarize himself with hospital paraphernalia and procedures.

Let me tell you a very simple case of where medical knowledge paid off for *me,* among the hundreds and hundreds of times that it has. This was as simple as merely knowing a word, a medical term, when I heard it. I was cross-examining a doctor who contemptuously attributed several of my plaintiff's complaints to "amenorrhea." When I got up to present my argument to the jury, I had a medical dictionary in my hand. I read aloud the meaning of that word; it wasn't something with which my male client was likely to be afflicted. It means "irregular menstruation." My client won a handsome award. By now I probably know as much medicine as I do law. Here in my office I've collected a bigger medical library than is owned by probably any doctor in San Francisco. It rivals my law library—in which 29 of the books are my own, by the way.

HALEY: How do you find the time to study medicine, write books, give lectures, teach law courses—and still maintain your overflowing calendar of personal-injury cases?

BELLI: Well, somehow you manage to get done what you feel *has* to be done—especially if you don't see anybody else doing it. And besides, I love my work. But I sometimes wish I could be a werewolf, with two lives—the life I have now and another life. I yearn for the quietude and the thoroughness of dealing with only a few cases. The way it is now, I have to budget my time like a whore when the fleet's in. This morning I've been on the telephone, about different cases, with Canada, New York City, Pittsburgh, The Virgin Islands, and I've exchanged some cables with Hong Kong. I need time to work on my autobiography. I've been collecting stuff for 15 years. It's going to be big. And it's really going to lay into all those bastards.

HALEY: Who do you mean by "all those bastards"?

BELLI: You know: Bobby Kennedy, J. Edgar, the A.M.A., the A.B.A., the insurance companies, ad infinitum.

HALEY: Don't you sometimes feel that you've earned a few more enemies than you can afford?

BELLI: Maybe so. Maybe I should have better sense than to take them all on headfirst and simultaneously. Because you know what I'm scared of in this office today? The big frame-up! I'm always telling myself I have to watch my tongue. My fault is that of Adlai Stevenson. He likes to make cracks, too. It cost him the Presidency. But whatever the cost, I've got to fight for what I think is right—and against what I think is desperately wrong—or I wouldn't think much of myself as a human being.

I've told you how in my early days I began to acquire my bitterness against the guy with a billy, the entrenched powers. We see injustices all around us, and we all want to cry out—but how many of us dare? We all see Big Brother's steady encroachment because we *don't*. I know we have to give up some freedom to have some safety, some order in society, but I simply cannot tolerate very much of Big Brother—those who claim to know what's better for you than you do.

I don't believe that the average person, *informed* people included, really realizes the swiftly increasing degree to which our country is being run and controlled by an *unseen* government—not only by the FBI and the CIA and the A.M.A. and the A.B.A.—but by foundations, banks, ad agencies, insurance companies, trust companies and their monolithic ilk. In insidious ways, they are prescribing our moral codes, limiting our freedoms. Their cold-blooded business ethics are becoming universally, and passively, accepted.

The A.B.A. is at war with me—like the A.M.A. and the insurance companies—because I'm at war with those who abet evil by keeping silent when they see wrongs being perpetrated and perpetuated by the greed, malice and deception of these self-seeking institutions. I'm under attack because I believe in *crying out* against injustice. God knows, I've endured more than my share of slings and arrows: "Belli's a nut, a charlatan, a publicity seeker, an egomaniac!" Sure I'm flamboyant. I can afford to be, because I'm a damn good lawyer. You've got to ring the bell to get the people into the temple. But my brand of nonconformism is so offbeat they don't know what to label it. About the only thing they haven't tagged me is "Communist." It's a wise thing they don't: I'd sue. This, mind you, after all I've done for the law. I've tried more cases, I've had more judgments affirmed on appeal, I've made more new law than probably any lawyer, group or firm in the past 15 or 20 years. After I'm gone, they'll be teaching courses about Belli. But the pack is out in full cry salivating over me. So be it. If I'm going to go down, I'm going to go down fighting.

HALEY: Is your plight as serious as all that?

BELLI: You bet it is. And things have been coming to a head since the end of the Ruby trial. I was absolutely awed by the speed and the ruthless efficiency with which Dallas' multimillionaires retaliated against me for my uncharitable remarks to the press about their fair city. You've heard that money talks? Listen, money *screams!* By the time I got back to San Francisco I found that insurance policies of mine had been canceled without explanation; a book publisher had backed out on publishing *Black Date: Dallas,* the title

I had planned for a book: mortgages had been foreclosed; my name had been withdrawn from official lists of lawyers; my credit was frozen; some TV appearances and lectures were canceled. I'm not being paranoid when I say that those bastards in Texas were behind the whole thing. Why, you wouldn't *believe* some of the mail I got postmarked Texas. Imagine opening a letter addressed to you as "Dear Rectum." Heart-warming!

The best part of it, though, is their campaign—with the cooperation of the heads of the A.B.A., who have been waiting for an excuse—to have me kicked out of the American Bar Association. After the Ruby trial, I was notified that *I'd* be given a "trial," investigating my "conduct of the case"—though publicly I'd already been convicted by the A.B.A. "grievance committee." I was notified that my trial would be held in the Statler Hotel in Dallas. I replied that I wasn't about to come to Dallas. Out of curiosity I asked them if they intended for it to be held on the hotel's top floor with my seat next to the open window.

I was next peremptorily notified that my trial will be held in San Francisco instead. That suited me fine. Then they announced they had decided to take depositions against me. I asked that the depositions be delayed until a date when I could be present. Denied. I asked by what "rules of evidence" was I to be tried. No reply. I asked for the privilege of taking depositions on my own behalf. Denied. Next came an indefinite postponement of my trial. So I not only don't know *how* I'll be tried, or for *what* I'll be tried; I don't know *when* I'll be tried either.

HALEY: Can you continue practicing if you're ejected from the A.B.A.?

BELLI: I don't have to belong to the American Bar Association to practice. I don't even have to belong to the A.B.A. to take books out of their library. To practice, I just have to belong to my own state bar. As Bob Considine said, "Being kicked out of the American Bar Association is like being drummed out of the Book-of-the-Month Club." I'd cry all the way to the bank.

HALEY: Suppose you were disbarred also by the California state bar.

BELLI: Well, I've always got my solid-gold Honorary Life Membership card in the Bartenders' Union. Or maybe I could get the Coast Guard to renew my able-bodied-seaman papers. I think I might write, too. Back when I first started, I might as easily have gone into steelworking, or teaching, or exploring, or doctoring, instead of law—and I bet there are a lot of people who wish I had. But you know, it's hard for me even to think about having any other career than law. The law is my muse. She has in her wooing been a jealous mistress, but my courting of her these 30 years has been an exhilarating time.

GEORGE LINCOLN ROCKWELL

A Candid Conversation with the Fanatical Führer of the American Nazi Party

VERNON L. SMITH

"Genocidal maniac!" "Barnum of the bigots!" These are among the more temperate epithets hurled regularly—along with eggs, paint, pop bottles, rocks and rotten vegetables— at George Lincoln Rockwell, self-appointed führer of the American Nazi Party and self-styled messiah of white supremacy and intransigent anti-Semitism. Reveling in his carefully cultivated role as a racist bogeyman, he has earned—and openly enjoys—the dubious distinction of being perhaps the most universally detested public figure in America today; even the Ku Klux Klan, which shares his

Jew-hating, segregationist convictions, has officially disowned and denounced him.

Until his rise to notoriety, however, like that of the pathological Austrian paper hanger whose nightmare dream of Aryan world conquest he still nurtures, Rockwell would have been first on anyone's list of those least likely to succeed as a racist demagogue—or even to become one. The older of two sons born to "Doc" Rockwell, an old-time vaudeville comic, he spent his childhood years being shuttled back and forth between his divorced parents' homes—his mother's place in rural Illinois and his father's summer cottage on the coast of Maine, where he was dandled and indulged by Doc's ever-present house guests (including such showbiz cronies as Fred Allen, Benny Goodman, Groucho Marx and Walter Winchell).

Rockwell entered Brown University in 1938 and quickly became known among the faculty as a practical-joking, insubordinate student of doubtful promise. Though he spent less time studying than drawing cartoons for the campus humor magazine, he managed somehow to get passing grades; and he began to court the coed who was to become his first wife. Dropping out of school at the end of his sophomore year to enlist in the Navy, Rockwell finally got married, in late 1941, after completing his training as a fighter pilot—just in time to get shipped overseas when the War broke out. Stationed in the South Pacific, he was commanding a Navy attack squadron at Pearl Harbor when the War ended. He mustered out in late 1945, returned to Maine and took up belated residence with his wife, eking by as a part-time sign painter and free-lance photographer while he cast about for a permanent profession. Tightening the family's belt still another notch, he finally decided to quit work for study toward a career in commercial art. He moved his family to New York and signed up at Brooklyn's Pratt Institute, where his considerable graphic gifts were officially *recognized in 1948, when a poster he'd drawn for the Ameri-can Cancer Society was awarded the annual $1000 prize of the National Society of Illustrators. Then, quixotically turn-ing his back on art, Rockwell returned to Maine a year later to join three friends in opening an ad agency; when it went bankrupt a few months later, he again found himself scuf-fling for pin money from one odd job to another.*

Still an officer in the Navy Reserve, Rockwell was re-called to active duty in 1950 and served throughout the Korean War at the naval base in San Diego, where he befriended a married couple who shared his passionate con-viction that General MacArthur ought to run for President in 1952. In the course of their conversations, the woman gave him what turned out to be a fateful handful of right-wing political pamphlets—for among them was a particu-larly gamy piece of anti-Semitic hate literature, the first he'd ever seen. Though he dismissed it at first as racist trash, he found it morbidly fascinating and read it from cover to cover—and then again; it was beginning to make sense to him. The seed was planted. Nurtured by more of the same— cheerfully supplied by his new-found friends—it began to germinate; and when Rockwell picked up a copy of "Mein Kampf" in a secondhand bookstore and began to read, it took root. "I was hypnotized, transfixed," he said later. "Within a year, I was an all-out Nazi, worshiping the greatest mind in two thousand years: Adolf Hitler."

Leaving his wife and three daughters behind in San Diego when he was transferred to Iceland in 1952 as a bomber-squad commander, Rockwell was divorced and remar-ried—to an Icelander—within a year. When his tour of duty was completed in 1954, he moved to Washington, D.C., and made still another ill-fated effort to become a breadwin-ner—this time as the publisher of U.S. Lady, a special-market women's magazine aimed at what he felt was an untapped readership of military wives; because of financial pressures, he was forced to sell out after the first few issues.

In desperation, after a futile campaign to persuade well-heeled right-wing businessmen to underwrite his burgeoning but undefined political ambitions, he packed his wife and their few belongings into a car-drawn trailer and hit the road as a traveling salesman. No great shakes at this kind of work, either, he left more than one town empty-handed and dead broke; but his wife managed somehow to keep food on the table.

Rockwell began to sit up nights mapping grandiose plans for the resurrection of National Socialism, with himself as the reincarnated führer; and during the day, between house calls, he roamed the country seeking fellow malcontents and proselytizing for fearless, dedicated cohorts to join him in his crusade to purify the land of "Reds and blacks." By the summer of 1958 he had collected enough cash (via mailed donations from secret admirers, mostly in the South) and mustered enough fellow fanatics (11 or 12) to give the group a name—the American Nazi Party—and to begin agitating for attention. They got it: Their first official act was to picket the White House carrying such signs as SAVE IKE FROM THE KIKES. *Brandishing Lugers, clicking their heels and "heiling" each other in brown shirts, boots and swastika arm bands, they swaggered about their new "National Headquarters"—a tumble-down shack in Arlington, Virginia, just across the Potomac from Washington.*

When an Atlanta synagogue was seriously damaged in a mysterious bombing late that summer, the public unleashed a storm of outrage against the Nazis (though none was ever indicted), and their little shack became a target for bricks and Molotov cocktails, police raids, snipers, abusive mail and telephoned death threats. Seeing the handwriting on the wall—not to mention a widening pattern of bullet holes—Rockwell's long-suffering wife quietly packed her bags and left for Iceland.

Her decision, as even Rockwell later admitted, could hardly have been a wiser one, for that first siege proved to be merely the opening skirmish in a continuing campaign of psychological and guerrilla warfare—punctuated periodically by ugly, often violent confrontations—between Rockwell and the public, the press, the law, the courts, the Government, the Church, the civil rights movement, the John Birch Society, the Anti-Defamation League, the A.D.A., the K.K.K., the FBI, and just about every known racial, religious and political minority group from Berkeley to Baltimore. In almost every contretemps, Rockwell has come out on the short end—winding up usually either in jail for inciting a riot or in the hospital for sticking around to see how it came out.

Often bloodied (once by an outraged viewer in the middle of a television speech), but still unbowed (even by his most recent and humiliating defeat—for the governorship of Virginia), the indomitable Nazi chieftain announced recently that he plans to stage a "back-to-Africa" hate rally this summer at the corner of Lenox Avenue and 125th Street in the heart of New York's Harlem. Few think he's crazy enough to go through with it, but even fewer would be willing to swear that he isn't. In the hope of finding out for sure, and of learning how he got that way, we decided to ask the neo-Nazi for an interview. Unlike controversial past interviewees Klan Wizard Robert Shelton and atheist Madalyn Murray, Rockwell could not be called a spokesman for any socially or politically significant minority; indeed, his fanatical following is both motley and minuscule (estimates of Nazi Party membership range from 25 to 100). But we felt that the very virulence of Rockwell's messianic master-racism could transform a really searching conversation with the 48-year-old führer into a revealing portrait of both rampant racism and the pathology of fascism. The results—obtained for us by interviewer Alex Haley— explosively exceeded our expectations. Of the experience, Haley writes:

"I called Rockwell at his Arlington, Virginia, headquar-

ters and relayed PLAYBOY's *request for an exclusive interview. After assuring himself that I wasn't Jewish, he guardedly agreed. I didn't tell him I was a Negro. Five days later, as my taxi pulled up in front of Rockwell's "International Headquarters," a nine-room white frame house in Arlington (since padlocked by the Internal Revenue Service, which is currently investigating the labyrinth of Nazi financial backing), I noticed a billboard-sized sign on the roof reading:* WHITE MAN FIGHT—SMASH THE BLACK REVOLUTION! *I couldn't help wondering what kind of welcome I'd receive when they got a look at my non-Aryan complexion. I didn't have long to wait; the khaki-clad duty guard at the door stiffened as I stepped out of the cab and up the front stairs. When I identified myself, he ushered me uncertainly inside and told me to wait nearby in what he called 'the shrine room,' a small, black-walled chamber dimly lit by flickering red candles and adorned with American and Nazi flags, adjoining portraits of Adolf Hitler and George Washington, and a slightly larger, rather idealized painting of Rockwell himself—a self-portrait. On the table beside my chair sat a crudely bound and printed copy of Rockwell's self-published autobiography, 'This Time the World'; I was leafing through it when a pair of uniformed 'storm troopers' loomed suddenly in the doorway, gave the Nazi salute and informed me coolly that Commander Rockwell had ordered them to take me in one of the Party staff cars to his nearby personal headquarters.*

"Fifteen minutes later, with me and my tape recorder in the back and my two chaperones in the front, the car turned into a narrow, tree-lined road, slowed down as it passed a NO TRESPASSING *sign (stamped with a skull and crossbones) and a leashed Doberman watchdog, and finally pulled up in front of a white, 16-room farmhouse emblazoned at floor- and second-story levels with four-foot-high red swastikas. About a dozen Nazis stared icily as the guards walked me past them and up the stairs to Rockwell's door, where a*

side-armed storm trooper frisked me expertly from head to toe. Within arm's reach, I noticed, was a wooden rack holding short combat lengths of sawed-off iron pipe. Finding me 'clean,' the guard ceremoniously opened the door, stepped inside, saluted, said, 'Sieg heil!'—echoed brusquely from within—then stood aside and nodded permission for me to come ahead. I did.

"As if for dramatic effect, Rockwell was standing across the room, corncob pipe in hand, beneath a portrait of Adolf Hitler. Warned about my Negritude, he registered no surprise nor did he smile, speak or offer to shake hands. Instead, after surveying me up and down for a long moment, he motioned me peremptorily to a seat, then sat down himself in a nearby easy chair and watched silently while I set up my tape machine. Rockwell already had one of his own, I noticed, spinning on a nearby table. Then, with the burly guard standing at attention about halfway between us, he took out a pearl-handled revolver, placed it pointedly on the arm of his chair, sat back and spoke for the first time: 'I'm ready if you are.' Without any further pleasantries, I turned on my machine."

HALEY: Before we begin, Commander, I wonder if you'd mind telling me why you're keeping that pistol there at your elbow, and this armed bodyguard between us.

ROCKWELL: Just a precaution. You may not be aware of the fact that I have received literally thousands of threats against my life. Most of them are from cranks, but some of them *haven't* been; there are bullet holes all over the outside of this building. Just last week, two gallon jugs of flaming gasoline were flung against the house right under my window. I keep this gun within reach and a guard beside me during interviews because I've been attacked too many times to take any chances. I haven't yet been jumped by an imposter, but it wasn't long ago that 17 guys claiming to be from a university came here to "interview" me; nothing untoward happened, but we later found out they were armed and planned to tear down the flag, burn the joint and beat me up. Only the fact that we were ready for that kind of rough stuff kept it from happening. We've never yet had to hurt anybody, but only because I think they all know we're ready to fight any time. If you're who you claim to be, you have nothing to fear.

HALEY: I don't.

ROCKWELL: Good. Just so we both know where we stand, I'd like to make something else crystal clear before we begin. I'm going to be honest and direct with you. You're here in your professional capacity; I'm here in *my* professional capacity. While here, you'll be treated well—but I see you're a black interviewer. It's nothing personal, but I want you to understand that I don't mix with your kind, and we call your race "niggers."

HALEY: I've been called "nigger" many times, Commander, but this is the first time I'm being *paid* for it. So you go right ahead. What have you got against us "niggers"?

ROCKWELL: I've got nothing against you. I just think you people would be happier back in Africa where you came from. When the pilgrims got pushed around in Europe, they didn't have any sit-ins or crawl-ins; they got out and went to a wilderness and built a great civilization.

HALEY: It was built with the help of Negroes.

ROCKWELL: Help or no, the white people in America simply aren't going to allow you to mix totally with them, whether you like it or not.

HALEY: The purpose of the civil rights movement is equality of rights and opportunity, Commander—not miscegenation, as you seem to be implying.

ROCKWELL: Equality may be the *stated* purpose, but race mixing is what it boils down to in practice; and the harder you people push for that, the madder white people are going to get.

HALEY: Do you think you're entitled to speak for white people?

ROCKWELL: Malcolm X said the same thing I'm saying.

HALEY: He certainly was in no position to speak for white people.

ROCKWELL: Well, I think I *am* speaking for the majority of whites when I say that race mixing just isn't going to work. I think, therefore, that we should take the billions of dollars now being wasted on foreign aid to Communist countries which hate us and give that money to our own niggers to build their own civilized nation in Africa.

HALEY: Apart from the fact that Africa is already spoken for territorially by sovereign nations, all but a few of the 20,000,000 Negroes in this country are native-born Americans who have just as much right to remain here as you do, Commander.

ROCKWELL: That's not my point. When two people prove incompatible in marriage and they can't live together, they separate; and the mass of average niggers simply don't "fit" in modern American society. A leopard doesn't change his spots just because you bring him in from the jungle and try to housebreak him and turn him into a pet. He may learn to sheathe his claws in order to beg a few scraps off the dinner table, and you may teach him to be a beast of burden, but it doesn't pay to forget that he'll always be what he was born: a wild animal.

HALEY: We're talking about human beings, not animals.

ROCKWELL: We're talking about niggers—and there's no doubt in my mind that they're basically animalistic.

HALEY: In what way?

ROCKWELL: Spiritually. Our white kids are being perverted, like Pavlov's dogs, by conditioned-reflex training. For instance, every time a white kid is getting a piece of ass, the car radio is blaring nigger bebop. Under such powerful stimuli, it's not long before a kid begins unconsciously to connect these savage sounds with intense pleasure and thus transfers his natural pleasurable reactions in sex to an unnatural love of the chaotic and animalistic nigger music, which destroys a love of order and real beauty among our kids. This is how you niggers corrupt our white kids— without even laying a dirty hand on them. Not that you wouldn't like to.

HALEY: It's sometimes the other way around, Commander.

ROCKWELL: Well, I'll have to admit one great failing of my own people: The white man is getting too soft. The niggers are forced to do hard manual labor, and as a result, most nigger bucks are healthy animals—rugged and tough, the way nature intended a male to be. When you take a look at how the average, bourgeois white man spends his time, though—hunched over a desk, going to the ballet, riding around on his electric lawn mower or squatting on his fur-lined toilet seat—you can't help but observe how soft and squishy a lot of white men allow themselves to become; especially some of the skinny, pasty-faced white peace creeps with their long hair, their fairy-looking clothes and the big yellow stripe up their spineless back. What normal woman would want one of *these* cruds? Unfortunately, some of our white women, especially in the crazy leftist environment on our college campuses, get carried away by Jewish propaganda into betraying their own instincts by choosing a healthy black buck instead of one of these skinny, pansified white peace creeps who swarm on our college campuses.

HALEY: Are you implying that the Negro male is sexually superior to the white man?

ROCKWELL: Certainly not. The average white working-man, the vast majority of white men, are just as tough and ballsy as any nigger who ever lived. It's the white *intellectuals* who have allowed themselves to be degenerate physically, mentally and especially spiritually, until I am forced to admit that a healthy nigger garbage man is certainly superior physically and sexually to a pasty-faced skinny white peace creep.

HALEY: Do you consider Negroes superior to white men in any other way?

ROCKWELL: On the contrary—I consider them *inferior* to the white man in *every* other way.

HALEY: That's a fairly sweeping generalization. Can you document it?

ROCKWELL: When I speak at colleges, they often ask me the same question. I always answer with a question of my own: How do colleges determine the superior and inferior students? By *performance*, that's how! Look at history: investigate the different races. The Chinese perform; they've created a great civilization. And the white races certainly perform. But the nigger race, until very recently, has done absolutely nothing.

HALEY: How recently?

ROCKWELL: The past 20 or 30 years.

HALEY: What about the contribution of those millions of African Negroes and their descendants—along with that of migrants of every color from all over the world—who helped found and build this country?

ROCKWELL: I don't dismiss it, but the fact is that any contribution of the niggers has been almost entirely manual and menial. *Horses* could have done most of it, or well-trained monkeys from the same trees *they* were flushed out of back in Africa. They've picked up a few more tricks since then—but only what they've learned from the white man.

HALEY: Recent archaeological findings have documented the existence of advanced black African civilizations centuries before the dawn of comparable cultures in Europe.

ROCKWELL: If they were so far ahead of us then, why are they still shooting blow darts at each other while we're launching rockets to the moon?

HALEY: The American space program isn't a segregated

project, Commander. There are many Negroes working for NASA and in the space industry.

ROCKWELL: This only proves my point. A few niggers, like trained chimpanzees, have been pushed and jammed into such things as the space program by our race-mixing Presidents and the Federal Government; but niggers didn't originate any of the ideas or develop the fantastic organizations capable of putting men into space. The niggers in NASA are like chimpanzees who have learned to ride bicycles. A few trained monkeys riding bicycles doesn't prove that chimpanzees could invent or build or even *think about* a bicycle. The fact is that the average nigger is not as intelligent as the average white man.

HALEY: There's no genetic or anthropological evidence to substantiate that.

ROCKWELL: I know you're going to say you can show me thousands of intelligent niggers and stupid white men. I'm well aware that there are exceptions on both sides. All I'm saying is that the *average* of your people is below the *average* of my people; and the pure-black ones are even *further* below us. I have living evidence of this sitting right in front of me.

HALEY: If you mean me, I'm far from pure black—as you can see.

ROCKWELL: That's just it: You're an intelligent person; I enjoy talking to you. But, you're not pure black like your ancestors in the Congo. Now, this may insult you, but we're not here to throw pansies at each other: There *had* to be some white people in your background somewhere, or you wouldn't be brown instead of black. Right?

HALEY: Right.

ROCKWELL: Well, I'm saying that your intelligence comes from the blood of my people. Whenever they trot out some smart nigger and say, "See? Look how brilliant niggers are," what they usually show you is a part-*white* man with some nigger blood in him. This doesn't prove that niggers are great. On the contrary; it proves that white blood can make a part-nigger more intelligent.

HALEY: That's not proof, Commander. Can you offer any authoritative documentation to support your view?

ROCKWELL: A psychologist named G. O. Ferguson made a definitive study of the connection between the amount of white blood and intelligence in niggers. He tested all the nigger school children in Virginia and proved that the pure-black niggers did only about 70 percent as well as the white children. Niggers with one white grandparent did about 75 percent as well as the white children. Niggers with two white grandparents did still better, and niggers with *three* white grandparents did almost as well as the white kids. Since all of these nigger children shared exactly the same environment as niggers, it's impossible to claim that environment produced these tremendous changes in performance. [Ferguson's study, conducted in 1916, we later learned, has since been discredited by every major authority on genetics and anthropology; they call it a pseudoscientific rationale for racism, based on an inadequate and unrepresentative sampling, predicated on erroneous assumptions, and statistically loaded to prove its point.—*Ed.*]

HALEY: In his book *A Profile of the Negro American,* the world-famed sociologist T. F. Pettigrew states flatly that the degree of white ancestry does not relate in any way to Negro I.Q. scores. According to Pettigrew, the brightest Negro yet reported—with a tested I.Q. of 200—had no traceable Caucasian heritage whatever.

ROCKWELL: The fact that you can show me one very black individual who is superior to me doesn't convince me that the *average* nigger is superior. The startling fact I see is that the lighter they are, the smarter they are, and the blacker they are, the dumber they are.

HALEY: That's an opinion, Commander, not a fact. Can you back it up with any concrete evidence?

ROCKWELL: The evidence of lifelong experience. I've never met a black nigger—I mean a real *black* one, so black he looks purple—that can talk, and think as, say, you can. When I do, then maybe I'll change my opinion. All the really black niggers are either what you call Uncle Toms, or they're revolutionists, or they just want to loaf, loot and rape.

HALEY: Most sociologists would agree that the vast majority of Negroes—dark-skinned or otherwise—don't fit into any of those categories.

ROCKWELL: Like I said, there are always exceptions—but everybody knows that they prove the rule. Evolution shows that in the long run, if the superior mixes with the inferior, the product is halfway between, and inferior to what you started with in the original superior group—in other words, mongrelized.

HALEY: The words superior and inferior have no meaning to geneticists, Commander—and neither does mongrelization. Every authority in the field has attested that the world's racial groups are genetically indistinguishable from one another. All men, in other words—including hybrids—are created equal.

ROCKWELL: You're bringing tears to my eyes. Don't you know that all this equality garbage was started by a Jew anthropologist named Franz Boas from Columbia University? Boas was followed by another Jew from Columbia named Gene Weltfish. And our present Jew expert preaching equality is another Jew named Ashley Montagu. Any anthropologist who dares to preach the facts known by any farmer in the barnyard—that breeds differ in quality—is simply not allowed to survive in the universities or in publishing, because he can't earn a living. You never hear from that side. But Carleton Putnam has written a wonderful book called *Race and Reason,* showing that there is plenty of scholarly evidence to back up my contention that the nigger race is inherently inferior to the white race intellectually. [Putnam, a former president of Delta Airlines, has no academic credentials in sociology, anthropology or genetics. Explaining its "Not Recommended" classification for his book—fully titled *Race and Reason: A Yankee View*—*Book Review Digest* writes: "At no time does the author show himself qualified to speak as a scientist."—*Ed.*] This equality garbage is straight Soviet, Lysenkian biology—direct from the Communist Lysenko, who preached that by changing the environment you could grow one plant from another plant's seeds. This is the doctrine that's destroying our society—because it's not true. You can't grow wheat from corn by changing the environment.

HALEY: You can't grow wheat from corn by changing *anything.* In any case, we're discussing human beings, not foodstuffs.

ROCKWELL: I don't feel like quibbling. What I'm saying is that I believe the Jews have consciously *perverted* the study of anthropology and biology and human genetics in order to reach this phony conclusion—and thus destroy the great white race.

HALEY: What phony conclusion?

ROCKWELL: The totally erroneous notion that heredity has nothing to do with why, for example, the niggers have lower scholastic averages and higher illegitimacy rates than whites.

HALEY: According to geneticists, it doesn't. In any case, how would acceptance of this notion lead to the destruction of the white race?

ROCKWELL: By deluding people into believing that the nigger is only "underprivileged" rather than inherently inferior; into believing, therefore, that he can be cleaned up and smartened up by letting him eat in our restaurants, study in our schools, move into our neighborhoods. The next inevitable step is to take him into our beds—and this would lead to the mongrelization, and hence the destruction, of the white race.

HALEY: You said that the Jews are behind this plot. Since they're whites themselves, how would they benefit from their own destruction?

ROCKWELL: They won't be mingling like the rest of us. They believe they're too pure to mix; they think they're "the chosen people"—chosen to rule the world. But the only world they could rule would be a world of inferior beings. And as long as the white man is pure, they cannot succeed. But when the white man permits himself to be mixed with black men, then the Jews can master him.

HALEY: How?

ROCKWELL: They *already* run the niggers. Except for the Black Muslims, the Jews run practically all the big civil rights organizations.

HALEY: You're misinformed, Commander. The key posts in all but one of the major civil rights groups—the NAACP—are held entirely by Negroes.

ROCKWELL: They're just the front men. The Jews operate behind the scenes, pulling the strings and holding the moneybags.

HALEY: The Jews who belong and contribute to these groups serve strictly in an advisory capacity.

ROCKWELL: *You're* misinformed. As I started to say, Jews want to run the white people just the way they run the niggers. Once they get the white people mixed with the black people, the white people will be just as easy to run as the niggers.

HALEY: Why?

ROCKWELL: Because when you mix superior and inferior, like I told you, the product is inferior—halfway between the two. The Jews would be able to outwit and outmaneuver and thus manipulate the mongrelized white man just the way he already does the niggers. That's what the whole so-called civil rights movement is all about; and they're just liable to get away with it if the good white Christians of this country don't wake up and get together before it's too late to restore the natural order of things.

HALEY: And what's that?

ROCKWELL: Separation. In nature, all things of a similar being tend to group together. Chimpanzees do not run with baboons; they run with chimpanzees. This is the natural order of people, too. Even in thoroughly integrated colleges, when I visit them, I notice that niggers usually sit and eat at tables with other niggers—even though they don't have to. And the white people sit with other white people. I think this is the natural tendency, and to attempt to pervert this is to fight nature.

HALEY: You fail to make an important moral and constitutional distinction between *choosing* to associate with one's own race and being *forced* to do so. Left to themselves, some people will mingle and some won't; and most Americans think this is just the way it ought to be.

ROCKWELL: That's all very noble-sounding; it brings a lump to my throat. But what does it boil down to in practice? Every time your people move into my neighborhood, the white people move out; and often there's violence—by peaceful, decent white men who never before committed any, but are outraged at the black invasion.

HALEY: That's an exaggeration, Commander. The record shows that fewer and fewer white people are moving out when Negroes move into white neighborhoods; and the fact is that violence very seldom occurs because of Negro "block-busting." In most instances, after an initial period of strain, the newcomers are being quietly accepted.

ROCKWELL: I don't know what neighborhoods you've been hanging around in, but my own experience has been that violence and animosity are the rule rather than the exception. And that goes double when one of *my* guys moves into a place like Watts. Your people don't just riot; they try to kill him. This is natural. Their instincts are coming out, and they always will. And any effort to override these instincts, or deny they exist, will inevitably be unsuccessful. Nature will prevail.

HALEY: Negro hostility toward Nazis could hardly be offered as proof that integration is unnatural. Nor is anti-Nazi violence confined to Negroes.

ROCKWELL: You're right—the Jews are even better at it.

HALEY: You've been quoted as saying that the Watts, Harlem and Rochester riots, among others, were actually instigated by Jews. Do you have any evidence to substantiate that charge?

ROCKWELL: I didn't say they started them; I said they *engineered* them. First of all, they tell the niggers, "You people don't have to obey the laws you don't like"—just like Martin Luther Coon preaches. If a cop arrests a nigger, it's "police brutality." And he's told he should fight back. Whenever a policeman tries to do his duty, the Jew-oriented niggers have been told to try and take the prisoner away from this brutal cop. The Jews turn him into a psychological bomb—so that when a cop comes along and does his duty it's just like touching a match to a fuse. *Boom*—up it goes! Like it did in Watts. Like they do in Harlem.

HALEY: In both the Watts and Harlem riots, the bulk of the property damage was suffered by Jewish-owned stores and businesses. Why would the Jews foment violence that's bound to result in the destruction of their own property?

ROCKWELL: It just happens that most of the businessmen making money off the niggers in the ghettos are Jews. The big Jews in charge are willing to sacrifice the little Jews just as a general sacrifices some troops to win a war.

HALEY: But what could *any* Jews possibly win by engineering riots?

ROCKWELL: They're just natural-born agitators. They just can't help coming in and getting everybody all stirred up—and they're always the ones to suffer for it. Every time! But they just can't quit. It's irrational as hell. With all their liberalism and their preaching about equal rights for niggers, they've promoted disorder and chaos that's eventually going to bury them. The liquor dealers are getting it now. Last summer, all those kike store owners in Watts kept screaming, "Oy! Stop! Listen! We're your friends!"—while the coons beat their brains out. And that's just the beginning, just a sample of things to come. This summer I predict that racial violence even more terrible than Watts will erupt—all because of these two troublemaking inferior races.

HALEY: In judging Negroes "inferior" to whites, you said a while ago that you made this appraisal on the basis of "performance." Do you find Jews inferior for the same reason?

ROCKWELL: I've never accused the Jews of being incapable of performing. As a matter of fact, I think there's a good chance they're *superior* to everybody else in terms of actual mental capabilities. I think the average Jew is probably sharper intellectually than the average gentile, because for years and years he's had to live by his wits. Consequently, there has evolved a race of Jews who are more agile mentally than the rest of us.

HALEY: In what way do you consider Jews inferior, then?

ROCKWELL: Spiritually. I believe that a human being, in order to be a successful person, in addition to performing—inventing a rocket or something—has got to have something he *believes* in, something more than his own survival, something that's a little bigger than himself. The Jews don't. They've even got a rabbi now who admits he's an atheist—Rabbi Sherwin Wine of Birmingham, Michigan.

HALEY: Perhaps you didn't know that the current Church movement toward disbelief in God originated among the Protestant clergy. In any case, Rabbi Wine's convictions are a minority voice and could not in any way be said to represent those of the Jewish faith in general. Most Jews continue to believe in God, as set down in the Torah.

ROCKWELL: Jews *talk* a lot about God. But actually their god, just like Marx said, is money. Cash! This is where the Jews fail—in their lack of idealism. Most of them are strictly materialists at heart. Wherever the Jews have gone, they've moved into a friendly, unsuspecting country and promptly started to glut on its people and resources. They think they're engaging in business, but actually what they're doing is eating the country up alive. And when people begin to resent their viciousness and greed, and either kick the Jews out or kill them, they always scream "Persecution!" That's not persecution. It's self-defense.

HALEY: Are you implying that Hitler was justified in exterminating 6,000,000 European Jews?

ROCKWELL: I don't believe for one minute that any 6,000,000 Jews *were* exterminated by Hitler. It never happened. You want me to prove it to you?

HALEY: Go ahead.

ROCKWELL: We have the figures for the number of Jews in the world in 1939, before World War Two: 15,688,259; and the figures for the number living after World War Two: 18,000,000. Now, if you take the number of Jews for after World War Two—and add the 6,000,000 you say were gassed, you get a total of 24,000,000—which means that there would have to have been a 50-percent increase in the Jewish population during a period of about five years. Even people as good at sex as the Jews couldn't possibly reproduce that fast. So you see, the Jews' own figures convict them as liars!

HALEY: What's your source for these statistics?

ROCKWELL: The pre-War figures came from the 1947 *World Almanac*, page 219; and the post-War figures from *The New York Times*, February 22, 1948, in an article by Hanson Baldwin. [Subsequent investigation revealed that the *World Almanac* figure of 15,688,259 is correct as claimed. The post-War figures cited by Hanson Baldwin in *The New York Times* were in the following context: "In these countries (Palestine and Egypt), the Jews are tied by bonds of religion to the rest of the 15 to 18 million Jews of the world." According to every official source, however, Baldwin's estimates are in error. The figures compiled by the Population Reference Bureau in Washington, D.C., show that the world's Jewish population declined from 16,600,000 to 11,400,000 between 1939 and 1945—while European Jewry decreased 6,000,000 during that same period, from 9,700,000 to 3,700,000.—*Ed.*]

HALEY: Population figures aside, do you deny the validity of documentary photographic evidence showing the gas chambers themselves, and the thousands of bodies piled up in concentration-camp trenches?

ROCKWELL: I emphatically deny that there is any valid proof that innocent Jews were systematically murdered by the Nazis. The photographs you've seen that have been passed off as pictures of dead Jews have been identified as pictures of the corpses of German civilians—mostly women and children and refugees—who were killed in the one-night Allied bombing of Dresden, which slaughtered 350,000 innocent people.

HALEY: By whom have these pictures been so identified?

ROCKWELL: By Matt Koehl, my research chief, who says that you can recognize the buildings in the background of these so-called Nazi atrocity photographs as buildings in Dresden.

HALEY: We don't accept the findings of your research chief as authoritative.

ROCKWELL: I have conclusive evidence to *prove* that some of these "documentary" photographs are frauds, pure and simple. In a magazine published by the Jews and sold all over America, they show a bottle supposedly containing soap made by the Germans out of the poor, dead, gassed Jews.

HALEY: What evidence do you have for claiming that it's fraudulent?

ROCKWELL: Common sense. That soap could have been made out of *anything;* it could have been melted down from a dozen bars of Lifebuoy. But here's my ultimate proof of just how utterly ridiculous all the anti-Nazi literature you've read really is: an article in *Sir* magazine, March 1958, on how the Nazis gassed and burned and murdered everybody. It's by "a former corporal of the SS" as told to an American Army master sergeant who signs himself "Lew Cor." Well, "Lew Cor" is simply Rockwell spelled backward. I wrote it *myself*—as a test. I wrote the vilest lies I could think of! And here they all are in print in this magazine. Look at the photographs! These are supposed to be actual shots of Nazi victims mentioned in the article— victims that I invented!

HALEY: Your own willingness to lie about Nazi atrocities doesn't prove that the Jews have done the same thing, Commander. Do you also dismiss the testimony of hundreds of prison-camp survivors who have given eyewitness testimony about Nazi atrocities?

ROCKWELL: I have an affidavit from a Jewish doctor, a prisoner at Auschwitz, who says there *were* no gas chambers.

HALEY: Do you have that affidavit?

ROCKWELL: I'll send you a photostat. [It has not arrived.—*Ed.*] I believe the gas chambers in these concentration camps were built *after* the War—by Jewish Army officers. We know this for sure: It was mostly Jewish Army officers who went in there to liberate these camps. And it was mostly Jewish Army CIC officers who were in charge of the Nuremberg trials. It was they who tortured innocent

Nazis, using any kind of vile method they could to cook up phony evidence.

HALEY: Can you prove these charges?

ROCKWELL: I know of several cases where American personnel resigned in disgust at the methods used.

HALEY: That doesn't prove that torture was used to extract false testimony. In any case, you still haven't said whether you dismiss eyewitness testimony of Nazi atrocities.

ROCKWELL: Certainly I do. I've lost count of the times I've been in court, after being assaulted and beaten by gangs of Jews, and seen these same Jews get up on the witness stand, with tears pouring down their faces, and tell how *I* attacked *them*! The Jews are the world's master liars! They are geniuses at it. Why, when a kike is up on a witness stand, he doesn't even need *onions* to start the tears pouring.

HALEY: It's said that you keep a model gas chamber here at your headquarters. Is that true?

ROCKWELL: No, but we have an electric chair at Sing Sing that's already done a great deed for America in frying the Rosenbergs; and there are hundreds of thousands *more* Rosenbergs running around America who need frying—or gassing.

HALEY: By "more Rosenbergs," do you mean more Jews or more Communist spies?

ROCKWELL: More Communist Jews. They're practically the same thing.

HALEY: Are you saying that many Jews are Communists, or that many Communists are Jewish?

ROCKWELL: I use the term "Communist Jews" in exactly the same sense that I would say "Italian gangsters." Most Italians are not gangsters, but everybody knows that the Mafia is mostly Italians. Well, my experience is that communism is as Jewish as the Mafia is Italian. It's a fact that almost all of the convicted spies for communism have been atheist Jews like the Rosenbergs. And international communism was invented by the Jew Karl Marx and has since been led mostly by Jews—like Trotsky.

HALEY: Stalin, Khrushchev, Brezhnev, Kosygin and Mao Tse-tung, among many others, certainly aren't Jews.

ROCKWELL: The Jews operate nowadays mostly as spies and agitators for the Reds. Mind you, I'm not saying that there aren't vast numbers of Jews who *despise* communism.

HALEY: Yet you say there are hundreds of thousands of Jewish Communists in America?

ROCKWELL: Perhaps more.

HALEY: What evidence do you have to back up that figure?

ROCKWELL: Plain statistics. Fourteen of the 16 Americans convicted in U.S. courts of treason as Communist spies have been racial Jews and one of them was a nigger. Of the 21 Communist leaders convicted in Judge Medina's court, 19 were racial Jews. Of the so-called "second-string Politburo" Communist leaders rounded up, more than 90 percent were racial Jews.

HALEY: The total number of convicted spies who you say are Jewish comes to 33. That's far from hundreds of thousands.

ROCKWELL: There's also evidence in black and white. Even in their own publications, the Jews do not hide from the Jewishness of communism. It's there for anybody to see. For instance, the largest-circulation Communist newspaper in America is not *The Worker*, but a paper published in Yiddish called *The Morning Freiheit.* Any American can get a copy of this Jewish Communist newspaper and read, in the English portions, the open Communist treason they're preaching.

HALEY: The views of *The Morning Freiheit* certainly can't be said to reflect those of most American Jews, Commander. Can you give a specific example of a pro-Marxist statement by any recognized spokesman for American Jewry?

ROCKWELL: Just one? That's easy. Let's take a statement made by Rabbi Stephen Wise; he's one of the leading spokesmen for American Jewry.

HALEY: He died in 1949.

ROCKWELL: Well, before he died, he wrote, "Some call it communism; I call it Judaism." That's a direct quote. I'd say that's putting it pretty unequivocally, wouldn't you?

HALEY: Can you produce proof of that statement?

ROCKWELL: Certainly. I'll send it to you. [The proof has not arrived, nor was Commander Rockwell able to tell us the name of the publication in which the alleged statement appeared. An official at Manhattan's Hebrew Union College, where Rabbi Wise's entire works are kept in archive, later said that no such statement appears anywhere in the late rabbi's writings. Rabbi Edward Kline, Wise's successor at New York's Free Synagogue, told us further that no such quote appears in any of Wise's speeches; nor could he, as a lifelong foe of communism, said Kline, have been capable of making such a remark. Confronted with this evidence, Rockwell later retracted the allegation.—*Ed.*]

HALEY: Do you have any tangible evidence to substantiate your charges?

ROCKWELL: Would you accept evidence based on a statistical sampling?

HALEY: Let's hear it.

ROCKWELL: Out of the number of Jews that I have known personally, a tremendous proportion—at least 50 percent, maybe as high as 85 or 90 percent—have been pro-Red; either card-carrying Communists or accessories before or after the fact, either openly and knowingly aiding and abetting communism and promoting the Communist overthrow of this Government, or assisting the Communist enemies who are killing Americans, or consciously suppressing legal evidence which would tend to convict such traitors.

HALEY: Your own conjectures about the political sympathies of Jews you've known personally, Commander, could hardly be accepted as evidence to support your allegations about them, let alone the "hundreds of thousands" you say are pro-Red. In any case, you say they "need frying—or gassing." On what grounds?

ROCKWELL: Treason. Everybody—not just Jews—with suspicious records of pro-communism, or treasonable Zionism, or any subversive attack on this country or its people, should be investigated and arrested and the evidence placed before a grand jury. If they're indicted, they should be tried for treason, and if they're convicted, they should be killed.

HALEY: How?

ROCKWELL: Well, there are going to be hundreds of thousands of Jewish traitors to execute, don't forget. I don't see how you can strap that many people in electric chairs and get the job done before they all die of old age; so it seems to me that mass gas chambers are going to be the only solution for the Communist traitor problem in America.

HALEY: Your suggestion of gas chambers as a "solution for the Communist traitor problem" is reminiscent of the "final solution for the Jewish problem" instituted by the Nazis in Germany. Are you planning to lead another anti-Semitic crusade along the lines laid down by Hitler?

ROCKWELL: The crusade I plan to lead will be much broader in scope than that. In Germany, Hitler produced a local "lab experiment"; he provided me with an ideology in the same way that Marx provided one for Lenin. My task is to turn this ideology into a *world* movement. And I'll never be able to accomplish that by preaching pure Aryanism as Hitler did—by glorifying the Nordic-Germanic people as a "master race." There *is* an easily identifiable master race, however: the *white* race. You can find it all over the world. This is what I'm fighting for—not Aryan-

ism, but white Christian solidarity. In the long run, I intend
to win over the people of Greece, of Germany, of Italy, of
England, of Canada, of France, of Spain, of Latin America,
of Rhodesia, of South Africa—the people of every white
Christian country in the world. All the white Christian
countries of the earth I would try to mold into one racial,
religious, political and military entity. I want them eventually to have hegemony.

HALEY: Over the nonwhite, non-Christian nations?

ROCKWELL: Over the Afro-Asian bloc, which is to me the
ultimate danger the earth faces. Worse than the bomb!
These people have something both communism and democracy have lost. They're fanatics! They're full of this
wild-eyed belief and vitality that the white man has gradually been losing. If they ever unite, there will be almost a
billion of them against the white man—a ratio of seven to
one. They're breeding so fast that the odds could easily be
ten or fifteen to one before too long. When these billions
of primitive colored people are able to control an atom or
an H-bomb, as Red China may soon be able to do, we could
wipe out a hundred million of them, and there would still
be plenty more who kept coming. The white race couldn't
take that kind of a blood-letting for long. We'd be wiped
out! The huge masses of semi-animal colored people would
simply sweep over us, and there'd be nothing we could do
about it. It would be the ultimate victory of quantity over
quality—unless the white people unite first. We're in real
trouble if *they* get together first. But make no mistake:
There's going to be a battle of Armageddon, and it's going
to be not between communism and democracy, but between the colored millions of the world and the small but
elite corps of white men; ideological, economic and philosophical issues will play little or no part in it. When the
time comes—and it's later than we think—I plan to be
ready not only to defend myself, but to lead the millions of

whites all over the world who today are foolishly pretending they don't know what's going on.

HALEY: Estimates of your nationwide membership range from 25 to 100. Do you propose to lead the white Christian nations with this handful of followers?

ROCKWELL: In the first place, we're a *world* movement, just as communism is a world movement rather than a local or a national organization. We've launched a world union of National Socialists, of which I am the international commander. In the second place, you've got those figures wrong. In this country alone, we've got about 500 storm troopers—that's men ready for street action—plus about 1500 Party members. Also about 15,000 correspondents— people sympathetic to our cause who write in and donate. And our membership abroad numbers in the thousands.

HALEY: Where abroad?

ROCKWELL: Let me name you countries. Argentina: Horst Eichmann, Adolf Eichmann's son, is our leader there; he's either in jail or disappeared, but our movement is growing there. In Australia, our movement is temporarily busted up, but my leader—an American—is running around under cover, trying to get his group back together again. In Spain, we've got a pretty good undercover movement, but Franco doesn't appreciate it, so we have to stay under cover. In England, Colin Jordan is operating wide open—and doing *very* well. In France, we've got a damned good group; they were all arrested just a while back. In Belgium, I've got an ex-SS paratrooper in charge, and he's doing very well. In Sweden, we've got a tremendous group; they were all just arrested. In Austria—our guy is in jail, so things are pretty well broken up there. In Canada, John Beattie is leading a tremendous and successful movement. Our leader in Chile is in jail. In Germany, we've gone under cover; our leader is going to jail shortly. In Holland, we're doing fine. In Ireland, they're coming along fast. In Italy, we've got a real

tremendous movement. In Japan, one of our guys stabbed
the Socialist deputy. Remember? New Zealand is coming
along fine. But Norway isn't doing too good. We've a fine
group in South Africa now, though, and we've got a group
in Rhodesia now, too.

So you see, we've got groups all over the world. They're
still little. But after all, it's only been 20 years since Hitler
died. Twenty years after Christ was crucified, there were
almost no Christians. Right now, the followers of the swastika are in the catacombs, like the original followers of the
cross were then. I can't say we're a Christian movement in
the ordinary sense; in fact, I personally am an agnostic. But
I deeply believe that there is a power greater than ours
that's helping us in our fight to keep the world natural and
racially pure—as opposed to perverted and mongrelized.
We've got an ideology, a dedication, a belief, a vitality to
match the zealotry of the fanatical Asian-African bloc.
That's why we're going to grow; that's why—eventually—
we're going to prevail.

HALEY: Can you tell us just how you plan to go about
fulfilling this destiny—with or without divine interven-
tion?

ROCKWELL: I have a four-phase plan. The first phase is to
reach the masses; you can do nothing until you've reached
the masses. In order to reach them—without money, without status, without a public platform—you have to
become a dramatic figure. Now in order to achieve that,
I've had to take a lot of garbage: being called a nut and a
monster and everything else. But by hanging up the swastika, I reach the masses. The second phase is to disabuse
them of the false picture they have gotten of me, to educate
them about what my real program is. The third phase will
be to organize the people I've educated into a political
entity. And the fourth phase will be to use that political
entity as a machine to win political power.

That's the plan. They all overlap, of course. Right now

we're about 50 percent involved in phase two; we're actually beginning to educate people—in interviews like this one, in speaking engagements at colleges and the like. The other 50 percent is still phase one—just raising hell to keep people aware that there's such a thing as the American Nazi Party, not caring what they call us, as long as they call us *something*.

HALEY: What kind of hell-raising?

ROCKWELL: Well, I haven't done it yet, but one of my ambitions is to rent me a plane and skywrite a big smoke swastika over New York City—on Hitler's birthday. That sort of thing. Or I might get one plane to do the Star of David, and I'll come in another plane and squat and do brown smoke all over it—on Ben-Gurion's birthday. I've checked Federal regulations, and they couldn't do a thing about it. All I need is the money to do it. But that's in the future. One of the biggest things we've already done to propagandize ourselves is our "Coon-ard Lines Boat Tickets to Africa." It's our most popular mail-order item; white high school students order them by the thousands. Would you like me to read you what a ticket entitles one nigger to?

HALEY: Go ahead.

ROCKWELL: Six things. One: a free trip to Africa on a Cadillac-shaped luxury liner. Two: choice cuts of all the bananas and missionaries desired en route, and a free jar of meat tenderizer. NAACP members may sit up front and twist to Martin Luther Coon's jazz band. Three: a barrel of hair-grease axle grease delicately scented with nigger sweat. Four: a framed picture of Eleanor Roosevelt and Harry Golden. Five: an unguarded chicken coop and watermelon patch on deck, plus fish and chips for breakfast. And six: plenty of wine, marijuana, heroin and other refreshments. And six: On the reverse side, we offer white liberal peace creeps a year's supply of "Instant Nigger." It's described as "Easy-mixing powder! Just sprinkle this dingy black dust on any sidewalk! Just make water on it, and presto! Hundreds of niggers spring up—little niggers, big niggers, fat niggers, skinny niggers, light niggers, midnight-black niggers, red niggers, even Jew niggers." It reads here, "Why wait? With this Instant Nigger Powder, any nigger-lover beatnik peace creep can have all the niggers he can stand!" Want one? Compliments of the house.

HALEY: Is mail-order hate literature your main source of income?

ROCKWELL: That, plus initiation fees from new members; plus small donations from those who believe in what we're trying to do; plus the proceeds from special events like one of our "hate-nannies."

HALEY: What are they?

ROCKWELL: Big musical jamborees. We hold them on patriotic holidays.

HALEY: Would you give an example of a hate-nanny lyric?

ROCKWELL: Sure. Remember, you asked for it: "Ring that bell, shout for joy / White man's day is here / Gather all those equals up / Herd them on the pier / America for whites / Africa for blacks / Send those apes back to the trees / Ship those niggers back / Twenty million ugly coons are ready on their pier / America for whites / Africa for blacks / Ring that bell, shout for joy / The white man's day is here / Hand that chimp his ugly stick / Hand that buck his spear . . ." That's just the first part of that song. Do you want to hear more of it?

HALEY: No, we get the general idea.

ROCKWELL: Well, I believe a man ought to hoist up his flag and tell you what he is. And that's just what we do here.

HALEY: Are there any anti-Jewish ballads in your hate-nanny song bag?

ROCKWELL: Oh, yes! One of our favorites is *The Jews Are Through in '72.* It goes to the tune of *Mademoiselle from Armentières.* Want to hear it?

HALEY: We'll listen.

ROCKWELL: "The Jews are through in '72, *parlez-vous* /

The Jews are through in '72, *parlez-vous* / We'll feed them bacon till they yell / And send them all to kosher hell / Hinky dinky, *parlez-vous* ..." The chorus repeats, and then comes the next verse: "We'll steal the rabbi's knife and sheath / And make him do it with his teeth / Hinky dinky, *parlez-vous*." The rest of it I don't remember.

HALEY: The song says the Jews will be "through in '72." Is that date significant in some way?

ROCKWELL: 1972 is the year I'm going to be elected President on the National Socialist ticket. Five years of the Johnson Administration will leave the country so torn with racial tensions that some Republican will be a cinch to win in 1968. Then, in 1969, a great economic catastrophe is going to hit this country.

HALEY: The nation's economy has never been healthier than it is today, and most economists predict that the end of the boom is not in sight.

ROCKWELL: Nevertheless, there *will* be an economic catastrophe, though of what nature I'm not sure. It could be an inflation. I say so because all this build-up is based on sand. America's so-called prosperity is based on debt, war and inflationary money which has no backing and is bound to collapse. Along about 1969, it's all going to come tumbling down like a house of cards, and the President is going to be blamed for it. In the ensuing economic chaos, plus all the racial warfare, the people will welcome a man who stands unequivocally for the white Christian majority.

HALEY: What makes you think so?

ROCKWELL: As I travel, I find that people everywhere, from the smallest towns to the biggest cities, are looking for what I offer. Most of them won't agree with me openly, but if you take them aside, ask them privately, they'd probably tell you "Rockwell has the right idea: White Christian people should dominate." By 1972, with the economy coming apart at the seams, with the niggers pushing, with the Communists agitating, with all of this spiritual emptiness, with all this cowardice and betrayal by our Government, the masses of common, ordinary white people will have had it up to *here*. They'll want a real *leader* in the White House—no more spineless jellyfish, no more oily, two-faced demagogs, no more queers in the White House like Walter Jenkins and his friends. They'll be looking for a white leader with the guts of a Malcolm X, with the guts to stand up and say, "I'm going to completely separate the black and white races and preserve white Christian domination in this country, and I'm going to have the Jew Communists and any other traitors gassed for treason. And if you don't like it, you know what you can do about it."

HALEY: Do you seriously think you can be elected on that platform?

ROCKWELL: I know so. Things are going to be so desperate by then that it won't matter whether I've got two horns and a tail; I'll be swept into office.

HALEY: If you *are* elected, who from among contemporary public figures would you appoint to your Cabinet?

ROCKWELL: If he were still alive, I'd have General Douglas MacArthur as Secretary of State. For Secretary of Defense, Retired General of the Marine Corps "Chesty" Puller. For Attorney General, J. Edgar Hoover. For Secretary of the Interior, Governor George Wallace of Alabama. Let me think, now, others: Senators William Jenner and Harry Byrd, Charles Lindbergh—and William Buckley; he won't appreciate that, but I think his brilliance could certainly be valuable. You'll have to agree that this is a Cabinet to give nightmares to any Jew alive. They'd start swimming for Israel even before I was sworn in. But I don't think there's a man in that Cabinet who is known as anti-Semitic.

HALEY: How about anti-Negro?

ROCKWELL: Well, I'd prefer to call them pro-white.

HALEY: If you had carte-blanche power to do so as the Chief Executive, would you create a dictatorship along the lines of Hitler's?

ROCKWELL: No, I'd reinstitute the American Constitutional Republic the way it was set up by our *authoritarian* forefathers—who were, in essence, nothing more than National Socialists just like me.

HALEY: In no way did the founding fathers attempt to abridge the democratic right to "liberty and justice for all." How can you call them Nazis?

ROCKWELL: In the first place, I don't believe in democracy. In the second place, neither did our white forefathers. I believe, as they did, in a republic—an authoritarian republic with a limited electorate—just like the one the writers of our Constitution meant this country to be. When these white Christian patriots sat down to write the Declaration of Independence, there were no black citizens for them to worry about. In those days, all the niggers were slaves; but today, thanks to several misguided amendments, our Constitution provides even the blackest of savages with the same rights as his former white masters.

HALEY: Then you advocate the disenfranchisement of Negroes?

ROCKWELL: And the revocation of their citizenship.

HALEY: And the restoration of slavery?

ROCKWELL: No, we have machines to do their work now. I would simply revoke their citizenship and then offer them the alternatives of either returning to Africa with our generous help and assistance in establishing a modern industrial nation, or being relocated on reservations like the Indians were when they became a problem to the survival of the white people. This will apply to *you*, too, by the way. Nothing personal, you understand; I *like* you, personally; but I can't make any exceptions.

HALEY: Of course not. What would you do with America's 6,000,000 Jews?

ROCKWELL: I think the Jews can be dealt with individually rather than as a group—like the niggers must be because of their race. As I said earlier, I think all Jews—

in fact, all those connected in any way with treason, whether Jews or not—should be investigated and their cases put before grand juries; if they're indicted, they should then be tried, and if convicted, they should be killed.

HALEY: Having disposed of Jews and Negroes, would that complete your list of those slotted for removal?

ROCKWELL: Not quite. I'd also purge the queers. I despise them worst of all. They're one of the ugliest problems of our society, and they must be removed—I don't know if with gas, or what, just so they don't poison society. If they insist on being queers, put them on some island, maybe— but certainly not around the rest of society. They're the ultimate symbol of a decaying civilization.

HALEY: Since you're concerned about the problem, Commander, would you like to reply to a frequent charge by psychiatrists that the womanless atmosphere of military asceticism and institutionalized hostility that characterize your "hate monastery," as you've called your headquarters here, make it an ideal sanctuary for those with repressed homosexual tendencies?

ROCKWELL: My reply is that this is the standard Jewish charge. The biggest charger that we are a bunch of homosexuals is Walter Winchell, whose real name is Isadore Israel Lipshitz, or something like that. [Winchell's real name is Walter Winchel.—*Ed.*] He's always calling me "George Lincoln Ratwell, Queen of the Nazis," saying I'm a fairy, and so forth. Universally, I have found that the Jews themselves, as Hitler said, are the greatest people in the world for accusing others of their own crimes.

HALEY: You haven't answered the charge that your Party is a haven for homosexuals.

ROCKWELL: Well, I do think there is a tendency for queers to come here, because to a queer, this place is as tempting as a girls' school would be to me. Whenever I catch any of them in here, I throw them out; and I *have* caught quite a few of them in here. We had one case where we had reason to believe that the police would catch two guys in the act. The two of them left here hand in hand. I tried to get them prosecuted. We won't tolerate that sort of thing.

HALEY: How about heterosexual relations? Are they *verboten,* too?

ROCKWELL: Absolutely not. Any man who didn't vigorously enjoy normal sex could never be a National Socialist. One of the best American Nazis I've ever known used to use a vulgar expression, "Those who won't fuck won't fight." I wouldn't put it so crudely myself, but I heartily subscribe to that doctrine. I never knew a good fighting man who didn't enjoy a lusty sex life.

HALEY: Are any of your men married?

ROCKWELL: A few, but most are either single or divorced, like myself. I believe very strongly in the importance of basic morals to protect civilization, but it's almost impossible for a guy in this kind of work to have a normal marriage and family; so most of us have no choice but to make other arrangements. And I might add, to paraphrase a French bon mot, *vive les arrangements.* But I must admit that it's damn difficult—especially for me—to have any sort of normal contacts with women, since I'm so often approached in this regard for political blackmail.

HALEY: Is it true that you require your Party members to swear an oath against drinking, smoking and cursing?

ROCKWELL: All my officers take an oath against drinking, including myself. Most have also taken an oath against smoking. I, myself, would not smoke except that the corncob pipe I've smoked for so long has become sort of a trademark. As for cursing, it's hard to stop cursing in the rough situations in which we live, just like in the Armed Services; but I do all I can to discourage it.

HALEY: You've used swearwords in this interview. Is this setting a good example for your men?

ROCKWELL: Well, I exempt myself from that oath for

professional appearances such as this. In talking to you, I've used words like "nigger" and "kike" because this is a big interview in a national magazine, and I want to attract attention—to shock people into listening to what I have to say. If I were discussing, say, the favorite word of niggers— "mother-fucker"—I'd say it strictly as a factual observation and to make a point. But in private conversation, neither I nor any of my members ever use that word—or any other foul language.

HALEY: Do you also forbid the use of drugs?

ROCKWELL: Certainly. I've had a few guys in here who I think were marijuana smokers, but I've thrown them out and turned them in. Addiction to any drug is degenerative mentally as well as physically, and we're dead serious about our dedication to the healthy-body-healthy-mind philosophy.

HALEY: Is karate or judo instruction part of your training program?

ROCKWELL: Not so much of that. I've found that unless you're a real expert at karate or judo, it doesn't help you much. Unless you use it instinctively, it's no use at all. So we concentrate on physical education, boxing and weapons training.

HALEY: What sort of weapons?

ROCKWELL: Rifles and pistols.

HALEY: For what purpose?

ROCKWELL: Self-defense. I believe the white people of America should learn methods of surviving in the event of racial anarchy and general bedlam in this country, which I think is likely.

HALEY: Do you share the belief of the Minutemen in the importance of being prepared for an armed Communist invasion of the U.S. mainland?

ROCKWELL: The Minutemen are kidding themselves. If there *is* a total Communist take-over, they haven't got a prayer in the world of *surviving* it, let alone stopping it—

running around in the weeds with a few guns like little boys playing cops and robbers. All they're doing is giving themselves an emotional catharsis. They're wasting millions of dollars, and in the process they're getting a lot of good kids sent to jail for illegal possession of weapons. I think it's like the Klan. Their aim, insofar as being ready is concerned, I'm for. I'm for the Klan's principles, ideas and so forth— except the anti-Catholicism—but from my point of view, their methods stink!

HALEY: What methods?

ROCKWELL: Their *partial* terrorism. I feel that terrorism is a valid weapon in guerrilla warfare, or any kind of warfare; and under the circumstances in which our country finds itself, I would *favor* terrorism if it could be *complete*—if it would *work.* A hundred years ago, I'd have been a Klansman with a rope and a gun and the whole business. I'd have really gone all out during the Reconstruction to save the white South. And make no mistake about the terrorism: It did the job. But today, it plays directly into the hands of Martin Luther Coon; it manufactures martyrs for the Northern press, for the liberals, and it doesn't scare the niggers out of hell-raising anymore.

HALEY: But apart from your belief that racial violence against Negroes has become self-defeating, you have no moral objection to it?

ROCKWELL: None at all. What I object to is wars among *white* men. This is what we've been doing for centuries— fighting among ourselves and wiping each other out. The North versus the South is a perfect example: the biggest bloodletting we've had, the cream of the white population wiped out, all because of the niggers. It solved nothing; it really changed nothing—except that a lot of good white kids got killed. I'm *agin* that! If we have any more wars, I want to fight the Red Chinese or the Jews, or go over to Africa and fight the niggers. This I can see some point to. As far as violence on an individual basis is concerned, well, when I come to power I plan to have dueling for officers in the Armed Forces. I'll have two purposes in that: first, to maintain a corps of officers unafraid to face death—not just in case of war; and second, to restore the concept of personal honor. I don't think going to court and suing somebody is really a deterrent to libelous, vicious talk. But people don't flap their mouths quite so freely when they're liable to have to back it up with a gun. Right now dueling isn't legal, but the moment it is, I would be eager to face Billy James Hargis and Robert "Rabbit" Welch on a field of honor for going around calling me a Communist.

HALEY: Have you considered the possibility that you might be killed in such a confrontation?

ROCKWELL: I've not only considered it; I expect it. And I'm ready for it. Being prepared to die is one of the great secrets of living. I know I'm going to go—probably in some violent manner; the only question is when and how. But I don't think that's going to happen to me until I complete my mission. I know this is irrational, but I believe that I was placed here for a purpose and I think God has something to do with it: Our country needs a leader. So I think I'll be spared. As Rommel said, "Stand next to me; I'm bulletproof."

HALEY: Do you think you're bulletproof, too?

ROCKWELL: Not literally, of course, but I firmly believe that the more arrogant and defiant you are of danger, the safer you are from harm. I think that's the reason I've survived so many times when people have shot at me. If you're fearless enough, it implants a certain psychology in the guy that's trying to shoot at you. It's almost as if he could *smell* your fearlessness, the way an animal smells fear. But the effect is the opposite: Instead of being emboldened to attack, he's so unsettled that his hand shakes when he goes to pull the trigger; and this makes it almost impossible for him to hit you. Either that, or he'll back down entirely. When I go out in the street and toughs come up threatening to whip me, I look them straight in the eye and say, "Go ahead. Start." Maybe they *could* whip me, but so far nobody's tried.

HALEY: What's the closest you've come to getting killed?

ROCKWELL: The closest, I guess—though I didn't get hurt—was the time we had scheduled a picket by 14 of us of the movie *Exodus* in Boston. The other men were in a truck, and I had registered in a nearby hotel as Nathan Ginsburg, where I waited until the scheduled picket time of two P.M. The newspapers and radio estimated that 10,000 or more Jews were packing the streets waiting for us, and my truck full of boys couldn't get through the crowd. Well, our picket had been the subject of headlines for days, so I couldn't possibly chicken out at that point. I had to get through the crowd somehow to picket in front of the theater; so I put on an overcoat, went through the crowd quietly, and when I got in front of the theater, I took off the overcoat in the middle of all those Jews and stood there in full-dress uniform. They were shocked into silence for a moment; their jaws dropped. Then somebody hollered, "It's Rockwell! Get him!" And the whole huge mob marched in on me with their clubs and baling hooks. If I hadn't been rescued by a flying wedge of tough Irish cops, I would certainly have been killed. I was taken into protective custody and put in a cell. I'll tell you, I was glad I was out of that; it could have ended horribly. But I had to show my men that I wouldn't ask them to do anything I wouldn't do myself. Another reason I did it is the effect the Nazi uniform has on Jews: It turns them into insane hatemongers—easy to beat, outmaneuver and outthink. The most dangerous man on the face of the earth is a rational, carefully planning Jew, but a raging, hate-filled Jew will act foolishly; you can whip him.

HALEY: How many times have you been jailed for this kind of agitation, Commander?

ROCKWELL: Up to now, 15 times. But never for very long;

two weeks was the longest—that was in New Orleans. We'd gone down there with our "Hate Bus" to make fun of nigger agitators who were calling their bus the "Love Bus." Without so much as a warrant or any real cause, the Jew-dominated officials of New Orleans had us all thrown in jail on phony charges that were later dropped. We finally got out by staging a hunger strike; eleven of us went eight days without a bite. On the fourth day, one of our men began to crack and said he was going to eat, so we had to let him know that if he did, it would be his last meal. He changed his mind. Another time in Virginia, they put me in jail, and I was facing ten years' possible imprisonment for "starting a war against the niggers." You've never seen a man act as guilty as the sheriff who arrested me.

HALEY: Guilty about what?

ROCKWELL: He felt he was doing the wrong thing. Here was a fellow white man fighting for the same things he believed in, and he was throwing me in jail. But this town is in the clutches of this Jew who owns two huge department stores and grocery stores there; so the sheriff was acting under leftist political pressure. But that leftist hotbed is a sanctuary of segregationist archconservatism compared with Philadelphia. Believe it or not, my men and I were jailed there for picketing a hotel where Gus Hall, the head of the American Communist Party, was speaking. As far as I'm concerned, Philadelphia is the enemy capital. They've practically got Jewish flags flying from the flagpoles. In most cities, though, I've found that they're only bluffing when they threaten me with jail. I tell them, "You'd better start arresting, 'cause I'm going to start speaking." Nine times out of ten they chicken out. They're used to nonviolent niggers being willing to go to jail—not white supremacists. Well, here's *one* white supremacist who ain't afraid to go to jail. And neither are my men. As a matter of fact, we've got at least two or three Party members in jail somewhere in the United States almost 365 days a year.

Every Sunday night we honor them in ceremonies that we hold on the parade grounds in front of this building. We also award special decorations for conspicuous achievement on behalf of the Party and for acts of heroism above and beyond the call of duty. Our top award is the Order of Adolf Hitler, then the Gold, the Silver and the Bronze awards. The highest award I've given yet was the Silver; that was to a man who couldn't contain himself in Birmingham and belted Martin Luther Coon on the head for calling that nigger Jew Sammy Davis, Jr. "an example of the finest type of American."

HALEY: You know, of course, that Dr. King is widely respected and admired by the majority of the American public, black and white—while you, a champion of white supremacy, are regarded by most people as a "nut" and a "hatemonger," abominated by almost everyone—including the John Birch Society.

ROCKWELL: Martin Luther Coon may go on pulling the wool over the public's eyes for a while longer, but sooner or later they're going to find him out for what he is—an 18-karat fake, a fraud on the Negro people. When the black revolution comes, I wouldn't be surprised to see *him* get it first—from his own people. As for my being a nut, that name has been applied to some of the greatest men the world has ever known, from Christ to the Wright Brothers. I say it's therefore one of the highest accolades I could be given. My father once told me that his Jewish friends ask him, "How could you spawn such a viper?" Well, I'm *proud* that Communist Jews think me a viper. As for the threats and the beatings and the investigations and the assassination attempts and all that, when I hung up the Nazi flag, I *counted* on being jailed and hated and hounded. If I hadn't been, I'd figure I was a flop. Harassment is par for the course in the embryonic stages of *any* new movement that's opposed by the established powers—especially one as revolutionary as mine. I wouldn't be surprised if the Anti-

Defamation League already has a cross built for me, with the nails ready. But I don't consider myself persecuted. Maturity is to accept the consequences of your own acts. I think it's a symptom of paranoia to feel that it's anyone's fault but your own if you fail to accomplish what you set out to.

HALEY: We read a newspaper interview a few years ago in which you claimed you were being "gagged and slandered by the Jewish press," sabotaged by a nationwide journalistic conspiracy in your fight to put your case before the nation. When "the Jewish press" wasn't pretending that you didn't exist, you said, it was either deliberately misquoting you or doctoring your public statements to remove the sense and retain the shock value—in order to make you sound simple-minded or to portray you as a racist monster. Only this conspiracy of silence and misrepresentation, you claimed, was preventing you from getting your revolutionary message across to the white, gentile masses and rallying them to your flag. To some people, Commander, these might sound like the remarks of a man who's trying to blame his failures on someone else.

ROCKWELL: You think I'm being paranoid, is that it?

HALEY: Some people might.

ROCKWELL: In the *Columbia Journalism Review* about three months ago, Ben Bagdikian, a frequent writer for the Anti-Defamation League, wrote an article called "The Gentle Suppression" which asked the question, "Is the news quarantine of Rockwell a good thing?" Bagdikian openly reveals that the press maintains as much silence as possible about our activities. So you see, the Jew blackout on us is as real as a hand over my mouth. They know we're too poor to buy air time or advertising space, so they ban our publications from all channels of distribution, and they refuse to report our activities in the daily press. I could run naked across the White House lawn and they wouldn't report it. I'm being facetious. But I'm dead serious when I say that the only kind of free speech left in this country is that speech that doesn't criticize the Jews. If you criticize the Jews, you're either smeared or silenced. They have that same kind of "free speech" in Cuba, Red China and Russia and every other Communist country: You can say anything you like as long as it doesn't criticize the dictator. The Jews are *never* going to let me reach the people with my message in the American press; they can't afford to.

HALEY: How do you reconcile that statement with the fact that you're being interviewed at this moment for a national magazine?

ROCKWELL: I've been interviewed, taped and photographed thousands of times for just such presentations as these, but they never appear. The fact that you come here and get this interview doesn't prove that you'll print it, or that if you do, you'll print it straight. After the editors read over the transcript, they'll decide it's too hot to handle, and they'll chicken out rather than risk getting bombed by the Jews and the niggers when it comes out.

HALEY: We'll take our chances, Commander—if you will.

ROCKWELL: I'll take *any* chances to get my message read. But it's never going to happen. We've been kept out of the news too many times before. I'll bet you a hundred dollars this whole thing has been nothing but a waste of my time, because it's never going to reach the people who read your magazine.

DECEMBER 1966

SAMMY DAVIS, JR.

*A Candid Conversation with the Kinetic
Singer, Dancer, Comedian, Musician,
Mimic, Actor and Best-selling Author*

GEORGE RHODES

---

*Whether Sammy Davis, Jr., as so often billed, is really "the
greatest entertainer in the world" may be open to debate, but
even his critics would admit that no one has worked
harder—nor overcome more hardships and handicaps—to
earn that appellation. Literally a child of show business (his
parents, Sammy and Elvera Davis, toured with a vaudeville
troupe headed by Will Mastin, whom he called his uncle).
Sammy made his stage debut at the age of one and became
a full-time professional when he was three. He had no opportunity for formal schooling and was forced to scuffle for pin
money with Mastin and his father during the Depression*

years. But the younger Davis proved a quick study as a song-and-dance man, and soon eclipsed his elders to become the star of their struggling little act in carnival side shows and those few small-town theaters and night clubs that would book Negro talent in that pre—civil rights era.

After an eight-month hitch in the Army's Special Services—a traumatic firsthand exposure to racial bigotry and brutality for the 18-year-old entertainer (his nose was broken twice in beatings administered by white GIs)—Sammy rejoined the Trio with redoubled determination to make the big time. It finally happened in 1951, when Sammy (still second-billed to Mastin) electrified audiences—and earned rave notices—during a triumphant first engagement at Ciro's in Hollywood. Suddenly in demand for solo recordings and movie roles (in "Anna Lucasta" and "Porgy and Bess"), and celebrated for his kinetic performance in the Broadway hit "Mr. Wonderful," Sammy found himself rich as well as famous almost overnight. Living his new part to the hilt, after "a lifetime of waiting and wanting," he plunged headlong into the maelstrom of Hollywood night life: punishing the bottle, plunging at the gaming tables, playing around with the chicks and tossing big money away with spectacular—and self-destructive—abandon. His income and his audiences continued to grow, but his performances began to suffer—along with his health—and Sammy was soon several hundred thousand dollars in debt. But his fortunes had not yet reached their lowest ebb: Late in 1954, while driving from Las Vegas to Hollywood for a recording date, he was seriously injured in the automobile accident that cost him his left eye. Although he was soon working again at Ciro's, and even joking about his misfortune, he was privately distraught and depressed, and one night tried unsuccessfully to drive his car off a cliff. His two brushes with death, however, shook him into a fateful decision: A few months later, seeking "a purpose bigger than myself," he converted to Judaism amid a storm of publicity assailing him for insincerity.

If Sammy was looking for peace of mind, he was not to find it yet. When the news leaked out that he was secretly dating Kim Novak late in 1957, despite warnings from Hollywood higher-ups, Sammy became a target for racist hate mail—undeterred even by his brief marriage to a Negro dancer—that reached flood proportions with the announcement of his engagement to Swedish actress May Britt in May of 1960. Defying a barrage of anonymous death threats, Sammy and May were married six months later, with friend Frank Sinatra as best man and fellow rat-pack chum Peter Lawford among the guests. May's movie career was over, but the marriage flourished and Sammy's own successes multiplied—along with his family (they now have three children, two of them adopted). In the years that followed, he continued to make movies ("Ocean's Eleven," "Threepenny Opera," "Robin and the Seven Hoods"), performed at more benefits than any other entertainer in history, simultaneously starred in a successful Broadway remake of Clifford Odets' "Golden Boy," and in his spare time, co-authored "Yes I Can," a painfully candid best-selling autobiography. Saturating television with specials and guest shots, he eventually earned his own weekly series, but low ratings and lukewarm reviews forced its cancellation early this year after 15 shows. Undaunted, Sammy went on to produce and star in his most recent film, "A Man Called Adam," but it, too, was indifferently received both by the critics and by the public. Not pausing long enough to regret his mistakes—and well enough established by now as a jack of all entertainment trades to withstand such setbacks without jeopardizing his success—Sammy set out last summer on a nationwide one-man concert tour; the crowds were S.R.O. in every city.

PLAYBOY interviewer Alex Haley caught up with the peripatetic star during an engagement at the Forrest Theater in Philadelphia (shortly before Sammy was hospitalized in Chicago with hepatitis). Haley tells of his experience: "I had been trying to get his ear, and his confidence, for two weeks, dogging his tracks from city to city, trying to penetrate both his shell of reticence and the cordon of cronies and co-workers with whom he surrounds himself, waiting in vain for Sammy to alight anywhere long enough to buttonhole him for anything more than a wave and a greeting. Genuinely apologetic, he finally took me aside and vowed that somehow he'd make time for me in Philadelphia. He was as good as his word; but it was still an uphill battle.

"Late every afternoon during the four-day engagement, whenever Sammy woke up, his close friend and secretary Murphy Bennett would telephone me to join them in Sammy's lavish suite at the Hotel Warwick. There, for the next two or three hours, we would try to talk, swimming upstream against a steady tide of bellboys bearing telegrams and delivering packages—mostly gifts from fans, which were added to the vocational and avocational miscellany already overflowing the suite: books, tape recorders, scripts, contracts, cameras, record players, movie projectors and the wardrobe of 50 suits Sammy takes on the road. Adding a note of shrill urgency to the melee, the phone rang incessantly and without mercy. Most of the calls were fielded by Bennett, but a few Sammy had to take himself—among them, one from Vice-President Humphrey, inviting Sammy to Washington to discuss a possible Vietnam tour; and several from Mrs. Davis in New York, requesting advice on wallpaper and bathroom towels for the family's new apartment on Manhattan's East Side.

"Each evening at eight, Sammy left for the theater in his $25,000 limousine, custom-fitted with intercom, bar, stereo, television and telephone. His stocky chauffeur, an ex-Marine named Joe Grant, denied that he functioned as a bodyguard: 'Just call me Sammy's right-hand man.' Be that as it may, Joe's own karate-trained right hand can split a cinder block. The marquee at the Forrest Theater—where Sammy had

won an amateur free-style dancing contest at the age of three—read, SAMMY DAVIS—THAT'S ALL. *Inside, Sammy sang, danced, did his impressions and his pistol-twirling act, imitated the walking styles of current Western stars, and followed up with a pantomime and an uninhibited drunk routine. Then his dancers took the stage as Sammy quick-changed to finish the show as a wistful clown. The audience gave him a standing ovation. Back in the hubbub of his dressing room, he acted out impromptu ideas for improving the show, accompanying himself with fiercely mouthed sound effects. Then, after several hours, 20 or 30 people set off in taxicabs, following Sammy to one of his almost-nightly private screenings of unreleased feature films. Later, though this relentless round-the-clock schedule was obviously draining his strength (he had been rubbing more and more at his plastic left eye—a sure sign, according to Murphy, that the 39-year-old star was really exhausted), he would talk with me back at the hotel—this time without interruptions and distractions. Often as not, the light of dawn would find us still immersed in conversation. We began with a question about a subject that preoccupies his profilers and perplexes even his closest friends: What makes Sammy run?"*

HALEY: Sammy, you seem to be in a permanent state of exhaustion—and perpetual motion—trying to keep up with your nonstop schedule of commitments. What makes you drive yourself so relentlessly?

DAVIS: If you want to be the best, baby, you've got to work harder than anybody else. I'm not in this business to be second-rate. If you've worked and waited for a lifetime, and finally your opportunity comes, do you swing at the ball or do you bunt? Well, I want to swing at it.

HALEY: Some might feel that you're trying to swing five or six bats at once.

DAVIS: So what if I am? I'm not trying to *hit* anybody with them. I'm not Sammy Glick, stepping on people, destroying people. Why should you be put down because you're ambitious, because you want to succeed—so long as you're not hurting anybody? Jesus! Is it criminal to have drive?

HALEY: Of course not. But why do you take on more commitments than you can fulfill?

DAVIS: Well, nobody starts out to do three or four major things at once. You start to do one thing, and suddenly a chance comes to do another. You're handling these two all right, then suddenly here comes another thing you can't refuse, and so on. After a while, it gets out of hand.

HALEY: During the run of *Golden Boy*, you ran yourself ragged doing free benefits between shows—more than any other performer ever has done in so short a time. Why?

DAVIS: Well, I wasn't thinking about setting some record. People just *asked* me. This one, that one, people I knew, people who knew somebody I knew: "Sammy, baby, just a little half hour for us." Another one: "You can't let *us* down." I'd say, "Yeah, yeah, OK—when?"—even when I knew I shouldn't. The dates always sounded a while off. Word filtered around I'd try to help good causes, and the promises started piling up on me. Man, sometimes in one day I'd be doing two, three benefits, then the show that night. If I tried to beg off because I was beat, they'd say, "Sammy, this organization helps your people: You've *got* to make it! We'll send a limousine." I *had* limousines: what I needed was *sleep*. But if I said no, they'd hate me—and I saw some of that, too. So I'd sleep on the way over in the car; chauffeur would wake me up to walk in the door and do the benefit. I got so run-down I *looked* it. And you know what I'd hear then? "Sammy, you're too tired! You got to quit doing so many benefits—just this one more for *us*." I knew something was going to give. I kept feeling it, different ways—warnings, you know. I kept saying to everybody, "Give me some time off. I've got to have some rest." But they never really listened, and I tried to keep going—until finally it happened. I collapsed and had to miss several shows. You can only do *so* much to yourself, then your body acts to save itself. I learned my lesson. I'm not going to let myself get that overburdened no more. I'll still help, but within reason. Anxiety to help anybody I can is the particular bag I happen to swing in as a human being. But there must be 5000 good causes: I learned I can't help *all* of them.

HALEY: Your nervous collapse was only one of many problems—bad reviews, script changes, firings, frictions, accidents, injuries—that seemed to plague the run of *Golden Boy.* Has that experience soured you on the theater?

DAVIS: No, I'm going to go back, and I'm going to *keep* going back until I learn it. Most people cannot understand, even to this day, why a guy who makes a million and a half or two million dollars a year would want to come back and do a Broadway show. Well, I can't say I need the theater to exist as a human being: but it's my *vitamins.* Legitimate theater is marvelous if you can find the right set of circumstances to work under. In *Golden Boy,* we just didn't have all the right circumstances. It became too hard to perform—physically and mentally. I got hurt too many times, and finally I got bored with it.

HALEY: To judge by its low ratings and lukewarm reviews, your recent television series was even less successful than *Golden Boy.* Why do you think it didn't click?

DAVIS: I've got no cop-out. It was nobody's fault but mine. I apologize especially for those first five shows. I'm being as honest as I know how to be. They were horrible. We never got over that bad beginning—even when we started to swing those last six or seven shows. But it was a ball to be on for the 16 weeks it ran.

HALEY: Do you plan to try again with another series?

DAVIS: Someday, sure. I don't know about this coming

season, though. If NBC doesn't pick me up, I've been offered other parts—like CBS wants me to be the CBS eye.

HALEY: That sounds like type-casting. Your latest film, *A Man Called Adam*, which you produced and starred in, didn't fare much better than your TV series, either critically or commercially. Were you satisfied with it?

DAVIS: Not completely, but I liked it. I think we said some things never said before in a picture. I don't think it's as strong, as powerful, as great a picture, as, say, *Champion* or *The Defiant Ones*, or any of the others with that kind of punch. But I think it's a good, entertaining picture, in its own way. And even if the critics didn't like it, I'm pleased that a lot of them, and other people, were pleasantly surprised by my performance in it. I never before had a chance to really *act* in a picture, and I tried to act my ass off in this one, pal. I really did.

HALEY: It's often said that everything you do as a performer is characterized by what one critic has called "a fanatical desire for approval." Is there any truth to that?

DAVIS: Maybe so. I know every time I walk on a stage, or do a television show, or act in a movie, I feel like the cat in the old West who walks into a saloon with the guns on his hips and says, "OK, who's the fastest gun here?" And the audience out there is the cat who stands up and says, "I am. Let's go outside. I'm going to take you." Every audience is like that. Every time I walk on, I'm thinking, "Oh, God, is this *it*? Is this the time I fail? Is this the time this other cat's going to be faster than me?" But if I win them over, see, it's another notch on my gun. I have said on a stage, when I haven't been able to move them, "Look, you people, I ain't leaving this stage until I find something you all like." And after doing a full show, I have gone on as much as another hour and a half, until I won them. It's like you've got these marvelous paints, and you want to get on that canvas *exactly* this beautiful thing you've got pictured in your mind, but you just can't seem to get that sun *bright* enough. I know the audience will courteously applaud just because I'm singing loud, but that's not what I want. I got to have them *pulling* for me: I want them feeling, "Oh, God, if he doesn't make it, he might run off and cut his wrists." They want me to climb that mountain. And then, "Oh, God—he *made* it!" That's how I've got to make them feel.

It's a constant challenge, because there's no sure-fire act, no sure-fire performer. You can be the world's biggest star, and any night that stage can fall from under you. The way this business is going today, it's getting to the point where you're really only as good as your last performance. I have to fight myself to put that foot across that magic dividing line between backstage and on stage—because I can never be certain what's going to happen out there. Take this show I'm doing right now. Opening night, the audience liked the show all right, but I knew something was wrong. I just sat and sat and sat in my hotel suite after the show and tried to figure what to do. It wasn't till the third or fourth night that it finally clicked. Now it's right. I got them turned on.

HALEY: Your night-club and theater audiences are predominantly white. Do you think there may be some element of race consciousness in your compulsion to win their approval?

DAVIS: No question about it. I always go on stage anticipating what people out there may be feeling against me emotionally. I want to rob them of what they're sitting there thinking: *Negro.* With all the accompanying clichés. Ever since I recognized what prejudice is, I've tried to fight it away, and the only weapon I could use was my talent. Away back, when I was learning the business, I had no education, no power, no influence; entertaining was the only way I had to change prejudiced thinking. I could see it happen every time Will Mastin, my dad and I did our act. For as long as we were on stage, our skin had no color: the people were just seeing us as entertainers. We didn't become Negroes again until we stepped *off* the stage. Again in the Army, especially the Army, where I met the most concentrated bunch of haters I ever experienced: On that stage, for the eight months I was in Special Services, that spotlight erased my color. It made the hate leave their faces temporarily. It was as if my talent gave me a pass from their prejudice, if only temporarily. And when I spotted haters in the audiences, I tried to give extra-good performances. I had to *get* to them, to neutralize them, to make them recognize me. It was in the Army that I got the conviction that I had to become a great enough entertainer that the hatred of prejudiced people couldn't touch me anymore. See?

HALEY: You said "the most concentrated bunch of haters" you ever met was in the Army. Was their hatred directed at Negroes in general or at you in particular?

DAVIS: We all got it, but being a performer and a little guy besides, I guess I was an especially tempting target.

HALEY: For what? Verbal or physical abuse?

DAVIS: I don't like talking about it—even thinking about it. It don't *bother* me; I don't mean that. I mean I don't want nobody thinking I'm whining about it. When it was *happening,* I didn't whine; I fought it. And now it's over; it's past.

HALEY: Will you give us some idea of what you went through?

DAVIS: I met some prejudiced cats—all right? I got pushed and banged around some, got my nose broken twice—all right? But the roughest part wasn't that: the *roughest* was the psychological. Like, you know, I'd been all my life in show business. I had never known one white agent, manager or anybody else in any of the acts my dad, Will Mastin and I had worked with who hadn't been friendly, see? I don't mean every time we met they hugged me; they didn't. My point is that until the Army, nobody white had ever just *looked* at me and *hated* me—and didn't even *know* me.

From the day I got into the basic-training center—it was Fort Francis E. Warren in Cheyenne, Wyoming—from the first *ten minutes,* I started hearing more "nigger" and seeing more sneers and hate looks than I'd ever known all my life. Walked inside the *gate,* asked a cat sitting on some barracks steps to show me how to get to where I had to go: "Excuse me, buddy, I'm a little lost—" Cat told me, "I'm not your buddy, you black bastard!" When I got assigned a barracks, cats in there—most of them from the South and Southwest—don't want to sleep *nowhere* next to me. And there was this one guy elected himself head of the haters. First move he made, he ground his boot heel down on the $150 chronometer watch my dad and Will had borrowed the money to give me as a present. I had treasured that watch. Man, they did all kinds of things, *sick* things. One time I remember, I had just done my first show there at the center, and I mean I had *entertained* them. Well, back in the barracks, suddenly they all acted friendly. Offered me this beer—but it *wasn't* beer, man, it was warm piss. Then a cat "accidentally" poured it on me. Well, I went for him, ready to kill. He was a big cat, and I didn't weigh but 115 pounds. He broke my nose the first punch, but, man, I fought him like a wildcat, and before he beat me unconscious, I broke *his* nose, too. From then on, nearly as long as I stayed there, maybe every other day I had some knockdown, drag-out fight, until I had scabs on my knuckles! Got my nose broken again. It got so everybody white I saw, I expected to hear "nigger." Somebody ask me if I want my coffee *black,* I was ready to fight.

HALEY: Were all the white soldiers that anti-Negro?

DAVIS: No, there was *good* cats there, too—don't get me wrong—at least some that didn't want to get involved, or who didn't hate Negroes that bad. And I had a sergeant who was one of the finest men I'll ever meet. Anyway, I met

George M. Cohan Jr., and we got an act going with this WAC captain in charge of us. Well, one time some cats from headquarters came and said the captain wanted to see me, and I went with them into a building where they said she was—but there were four other cats waiting instead. Pushed me into a latrine; some of them held me and the others beat me. They wrote "coon" in white paint across my forehead, and "I'm a nigger" across my chest. Then they ordered me to dance for them, "Dance, Sambo—fast!" Man, I fought to get at them, but they pinned me and punched me in the gut until it looked like I'd have to dance or die. Don't even like to think about it! *Sick* cats! I danced until I couldn't no more. Then—bam! In the gut again— and I had to dance some more, until finally they saw I was ready to pass out. Then they poured turpentine over me, and told me the reason they'd given me "this little lesson": They'd been watching me "making eyes" at the white WAC captain. She was my *boss,* man, my commanding officer— and that's the way I treated her. Didn't make no difference. Anyway, they finally left me there. I was so sick, I just wanted to crawl into the latrine walls and die, man; I just lay down and cried.

That was when, for the first time in my life, I didn't want to go out and do my act—go out there and smile at people who despised me. But I made myself do it anyhow. I was fighting myself so hard to stay out there that the fighting made me do maybe one of the best shows I ever did in my life. And I'm glad it did, because I discovered something. I saw some of those faces out there grudgingly take on different expressions. I don't mean for a minute that any- body suddenly started loving me—I didn't want that from them anyway—but they *respected* me. It taught me that the way for me to fight, better than with my fists, was with my talent. For the next eight months, going across the country doing my act, I nearly *killed* myself every show trying to make them respect me. Maybe I still am.

HALEY: Do you feel any bitterness toward whites because of your Army experiences?

DAVIS: No, I can't harbor that, based on one very simple fact. If I'm going to look at you with a jaundiced eye because you're white, then how are you going to look at me? Am I going to try to hide my bigotry, hoping that you'll show your tolerance? It makes no sense. I don't know how I can ask to be regarded as a fellow man, as I wish to be, without myself extending that same respect to you. I've met too many decent white people to hold the prejudices of other whites against them—even in the Army. Like that sergeant I told you about. He's the one who got me started reading something besides comic books.

HALEY: You were in your late teens then. Is it true, as some writers have claimed, that you could barely read and write, that you'd never even gone to kindergarten?

DAVIS: Yeah, it's true. What's more, I'll be turning 40 this year, and I *still* haven't gone to kindergarten. Haven't spent a single day in school my whole life. I say that with mixed emotions. I'm very proud in one sense; I'm very ashamed in another. For instance, you know I'm always being asked for autographs. Say a girl tells me, "My name is Rosemari, with an 'i.' " Well, I don't know how to spell the names. I can't hardly write anything but my *own* name. It's a constant, daily embarrassment. It's even more of an embarrassment because of my articulate façade. People think, "Why, he's *got* to have education." But I can't even write! Nothing but chicken scratches! That I'm not proud of. I'm proud that I've pulled myself up by my own bootstraps, with the help of some people who cared enough; but I'm not proud of having no education. What little I do have started on the road, when Will Mastin and my dad found someone around the theaters to tutor me to read and write. We'd work between shows in the dressing room—when there *was* a dressing room—until it was time for me to go on for the next show. Then in the Army, like I told you, this sergeant took a liking to me and started me reading books. Things like *The Picture of Dorian Gray* by Oscar Wilde, and some of Carl Sandburg's books about Lincoln; books by Dickens, Poe, Twain; and a history of the U.S. I would read every minute of the day I had free, then in my bunk until taps, then in the latrine until after midnight. At the PX I bought a pocket dictionary, and I would look up words in places where nobody would see me, then I'd read the books over again.

Imagine somebody 18 years old, grown, discovering the thrills of *Robinson Crusoe* for the first time—reading that kids of 10 take for granted. And a showbiz kid is already 10 years up on the average cat, in street-knowledge terms. Like, man, I'd had my first serious affair at 14, and at 18 I still didn't know what a serious *book* was. That's a sad paradox. I remember so well the first book I ever read about my own people, and the effect it had on me. It did something to me. That was *Native Son*, by Richard Wright. Then, later, I read *Black Boy*. They made me feel something about being black that I had never really felt before. It made me uncomfortable, made me feel trapped in black, you know, in a white society that had created you the way it wanted, and still hated you.

But to get back to your question. People hearing me today don't think I have no education. I've worked hard—*hard*, man, to be able to give this impression. Blood, sweat and tears went into every combination of words that I use now. I've read, and I've remembered. I've listened and recorded in my mind. Now, I'd be confident anywhere I was asked to speak. But I still make mistakes that infuriate me, especially when I'm corrected. People *very* close to me do that sometimes. Like Burt and Jane Boyar, who did *Yes I Can* with me; to this day, one of them will say, when we're alone, "You're pronouncing this word wrong." It *infuriates* me—but I know they're right. Say, I'll get up and extemporaneously make a speech that would put Burt to shame if he tried it. It'll just come off the top of my knot; it'll roll—brrrrr—and I'll look at Burt triumphantly. Then later on, he'll get me somewhere away from people and say, "You pronounced two words wrong," and that little comedown really kills me, because I've struggled so hard, you know? It took me five years, I guess, to quit saying "Ladies and gennermen—" It just hurts when I'm told I was making a mistake, particularly by someone very close to me, even though I know he only wants to help me. And I *want* them to help me, but I'm torn between "Help me" and "Geez, I thought I was doing good."

HALEY: A friend of yours told us it bothers you that without a day's education, you earn more than the nation's top dozen college presidents. Is that true?

DAVIS: Yes and no. On the one hand, I feel guilty about making all the money that I do. It's like, say, I talk to a cat, a policeman, that's exposed all the time to crime and corruption, and he's just saved someone's life, and what does *he* make? You know? But then I think that if I draw the people in, and they're willing to pay the tab, then I'm entitled to it. It's a mixed-up feeling.

HALEY: While we're on the subject, would you mind telling us just how much you earn?

DAVIS: Well, it fluctuates. This year, two million dollars. I know that sounds like an awful lot, but you have to consider that just yesterday my accountant told me that to keep my books even—understand me, just to break *even*, in terms of salaries, spending money and household things, plus taxes—I've got to make $17,000 a week. After all, I'm in the 90-percent tax bracket. Next year, I'll make less, about a million and a half, because of the six months in London with *Golden Boy* there. You make a lot less on the stage than in night clubs as a top act.

HALEY: How much of that two million did you earn as a performer?

DAVIS: I'm not sure of the exact amount, but as you

know, I got a couple of other things going for me, too. There's the royalties from my book, for one thing. And I'm now sincerely and honestly in the motion-picture business. *A Man Called Adam* is on the screens now, and I've bought future film properties, such as Irving Wallace's *The Man*, which Ossie Davis will star in. I've also got two music-publishing firms—rather, my musical director, George Rhodes, has one and I have one. And I've got a record company: It releases through Reprise Records, but it's my company. All of the masters come back to me. And I've got a personal-management company; they're all part of my overall enterprises.

If you count the household help, and the West Coast office, I've got about 30 people working for me. I don't really know what the weekly payroll amounts to, or what I average spending just myself a week, either. But I know I don't spend as much as I used to.

HALEY: During the first few years after you made it big, you spent several million dollars on custom-made suits and shoes by the dozen, expensive jewelry, limousines, parties, chartered planes, and enough photographic and recording equipment to fill a small warehouse. Why? What were you trying to prove?

DAVIS: Listen, baby, you ever had a *mustard* sandwich? Just mustard spread on bread—and then tried to dance on the nourishment from that? Will Mastin, my dad and me, we used to heat a can of pork and beans on the radiator, when they were nice enough to *have* heat in the radiator, and split it three ways, eating right from the can. There were times when for a meal we had a Mr. Goodbar apiece. Or a grape soda. I remember our filling our stomachs with nothing but water! I mean, I paid my *dues*, baby; don't you ever overlook that, and anybody who does can go jump in the lake! We got stranded more times than I can count! Our beds were *benches* in drink-water train depots. And once in the winter in Ohio, I remember, it was so bad we went to the *jail* and asked the man to let us sleep in there. In the Thirties, I remember, we lost the old $90 car we had, and we had to join Hank Keane's carnival. Eight, nine shows a day—and that bally, "Heyyy! Here they come! Three little hoofers, hot from Harlem!" There was no dignities then. Nobody was trooping around saying "Let's have our rights." You were alone out there—*every* Negro performer was. We danced so hard our feet scarcely touched the floor; but we kept saying inside, "It ain't gonna happen, ain't *never* gonna happen for us." Jesus, man! We starved. About literally starved. If we got two little one-nighters a week, we were lucky! Like all Negro performers, though, we put on the best front we could. But the insults. The indignities. You haven't *known* indignity until you have to dance, and have people throw money at you, and you take the money off the floor.

Anyway, we'd go wherever it was, and we'd work. And then we'd go back to my grandmother's little railroad flat and sit waiting for some call, frustrated to death, knowing all the entertainment we had in us to give to people. And I'd sit all day waiting to tune in on Jack Eigen's celebrity interview program from the Copacabana. He'd always say, "I'm at the Copa, where are you?" And I'd holler at the radio, "I'm up here in my goddamned hole in Harlem, that's where I am!" And meanwhile, my grandmother's on relief, and The Man is coming around, checking up. "I hear your son was working"—meaning my father. And she'd say, "But he didn't make anything." And he'd say, "Well, if he's working, you're not supposed to be on relief." That seemed to be the concept in those days—if you were on relief, you were just supposed to sit there, and not even *try* to work.

It was a frightening thing to think, "*Jesus,* I'm never going to live, live *big*! I'm never going to be able to walk in some place and buy something and not ask the price. Never!" Just work, kill myself working, and waiting, and praying. It was like that song from *Sweet Charity*: "There's got to be something better than this." You know the humiliation for a Negro to walk in a store? You got on your front, that one good suit. You got on your Sunday shoes, the ones you use on the stage—we always prided ourselves on being neat on the stage; you walk in the store, you say, "I'd like to get one of those shirts you've got there in the window." And the man says, "You know that shirt's seven ninety-five." And you want to say, "Then gimme the whole fuckin' store!" You know? Because you knew his thoughts: "Snap, bop, broke, Negro, no money—deadbeat." Man don't want your business! Negro ain't got no money to pay for it! Negro going to ask for credit. Man, you'd dream it in your mind whether that's what he thought or not. If he'd done the same thing to eight white customers, it didn't matter to you. You see what I mean? So suddenly it becomes a personal vendetta with this guy. One time I walked in, taking the last ten dollars I had, when I had nothing else to *eat* on, and the man tells me the price of the shirt and gives me the eye, and I said, "Well, then, give me *two* of them!" And I walked out with my little package, saying to myself, "Boy, I sure showed him!" Who the hell did I *show*? What the hell did I *prove*? Nothing! But, boy, what satisfaction! Except that now I didn't have nothing to eat.

Anyway, we worked, and we starved, and we kept hoping that somehow, someday, something would happen. Only it seemed like it never would. You know? And then—suddenly—*pfoom!* It starts to happen! And you're looking around, blinking like you're staring at the sun. And all of a sudden it's *your* world. You *run* into stores. You say, "Hey, man! Gimme twenty of them! And eight of *them*! And a thousand of those!" Man—you understand? You walk around with a thousand dollars in your pocket. Like, that had been a *year's* salary! Nobody else can *know* that goddamn thrill—nobody! To be able to give a waitress a hundred-dollar tip. *Nobody* knows that thrill who hasn't been at the bottom of the barrel—where, as the joke goes, the rent was a dollar a month, and you was still 12 months in the 'rears—'cause you couldn't pay even *that* rent! So when I spend money now, I guess it's because that's how it was for so long, man. It was so hard, baby, I really couldn't tell you.

HALEY: A few minutes ago you said you don't spend as much anymore as you used to. Yet you still have a reputation for extravagance. Is it unfounded?

DAVIS: Not entirely. I still live way beyond my means; I know that. By that I mean I'm living beyond the means that my accountants would *like* me to live. The difference is now I have the security of knowing my family is taken care of. My wife is taken care of so that she's in good shape if anything happened tomorrow, and so is the rest of my family. My children each have million-dollar insurance policies on me, and money in the bank besides that. And I'm paid up on my taxes. I've got my enterprises and corporations set up—legitimately. I don't want to try to gyp the Government out of a goddamned dime. Including back taxes, I was $300,000 in debt when I met May. But you know something? I don't really have any regrets. I had lived *good*, you can believe that! 'Cause when I did it, baby, I *did* it. Cats see me come in a town today, cats who knew me then, and say, "Here he comes! My man! My *main* man!" And I tell them, "Cool it, baby, I'm not doing it anymore." The way I feel about what I blew is that it's a whole lot better to be able to say "I was there," instead of "I never was." You know? A young cat suddenly makes $20,000 a week, he doesn't know how to protect himself. He doesn't know how to move. He's vulnerable to anything, everything. But now I've been there. I've made the mistakes. I've had the love affairs; I've had the controversy. What happened was I met May, and suddenly all the rest of it ceased to be attractive.

HALEY: But you said you still live beyond your means.

DAVIS: Well, I'm not on any austerity kick. I've worked hard, baby, and I still want to enjoy the pleasures and the luxuries of life. *Nobody* enjoys luxuries more than I do. I've got a limousine that costs $25,000 with all the fixtures. I sit there, I press that button, a television comes up. Ain't no other pleasure in the *world* like that for me. Press another button: The tape recorder plays. The bar—fix me a drink. It's right there! That's my *pleasure,* man! Do you understand what I mean? I *enjoy* opening my closet door and saying, "Oh, what suit should I wear?" So I have 20 suits too many! So I have too many tape recorders! And too many cars! I ain't *hurting* nobody! I didn't take a gun and stick somebody up and beat them over the head. I didn't rape nobody's daughter to get it! So I've got a lot of gold lighters; who did I *hurt* to get them? So I bought some gold watches at Cartier's; it gives me *pleasure,* is all.

Now, I wouldn't do this if it meant my family wouldn't eat, or I'd promised someone money and couldn't come up with it. I ain't taking no dope. If a lens comes out for one of my cameras, I'll *buy* it, and I don't care *what* it costs. Everybody has his *shtick,* that he enjoys doing, to give him personal pleasure. Mine is luxury. I *love* luxury! If I could wear cashmere underwear, I'd wear it. I love having my underwear made. I love having suits made, sending to Hong Kong for special-made shoes. I'm not going to cop out with "I never had it as a kid," because very few people ever had it as a kid. My point is that it's my *pleasure:* I love it, and I earn it, and nobody gives it to me, and nobody works any harder for his than I work for mine. That goes for a riveter on a bridge, for a ditchdigger: don't *nobody* work no harder than me, no matter what he works at. I'm out there sweating blood. So if I feel like having me a little Rolls-Royce, I buy one.

I used to gamble in Vegas—lost more money than I could make. Once I was 40-odd thousand dollars in debt, gambling. Blackjack, craps, anything I could get my hands on. But I don't owe it anymore. Now, I can afford to lose $10,000 at the tables in a six-week engagement in Vegas. I can't afford no *more* than that. The difference is my accountants would like for me not to play at all. They don't realize that $10,000 gives me some sort of adrenaline, gives me whatever psychological answers make it possible for me to earn all that *other* money. See? Ain't nothing going to happen on that stage if I'm bugged mentally. I'd be in a hospital someplace.

HALEY: Aside from the things you've mentioned, what do you spend your money on? Do you make any contributions to charity?

DAVIS: Last year I gave to various charities better than $100,000, and this year I'm going to give more. A man don't just lay around and not contribute something to the society he lives in.

HALEY: How much of that amount goes to civil rights groups?

DAVIS: I don't know—maybe half or more. The rest goes to other causes, right across the board.

HALEY: Apart from donations, what do you do for civil rights?

DAVIS: I give my time—a lot of my time—to benefits, personal appearances and such, as a professional entertainer. You ain't going to find nobody in show business—except for Dick Gregory—giving more of his time to civil rights than I do.

HALEY: How about Harry Belafonte and Sidney Poitier? Do you contribute more than they do to the cause?

DAVIS: *Nobody* could contribute more than they do. I could never match them based on their commitment. But I'll match them based on mine. We're *all* doing whatever we can, however we can, within our abilities to do. I can go to sleep at night knowing I'm contributing all it's possible for *me* to do, consistent with maintaining my business, which is being out there on somebody's stage about 300 nights of the year.

HALEY: Have you participated, like Gregory, Belafonte and Poitier, in many civil rights marches or demonstrations?

DAVIS: Yeah, I do that, too. I flew to Jackson, Mississippi, and I flew to Selma. I don't like talking about it, though, because I don't go for this "Where were you? I didn't see you in the march!" That bag that a lot of civil rights people are in. Because there are plenty of other contributions as important as marching. Like if you're privileged to be a personality, there's the responsibility of what new image of the Negro do you project when you're reaching all them mass audiences in movie theaters and on national television, and those big live audiences like I play to. The way I see it, my Broadway show fails for me, the movies I make fail for me, if they aren't presenting Negroes in an image that ain't never been seen before—an image of dignity and self-respect. Every night I do my act, I like to think I change at least a few more white people's way of thinking about Negro people. So—I give my money; I give my time. And I'm out there beating at prejudice night after night. What more have I got that I can give?

HALEY: Most people would say nothing more. But you didn't start participating actively in the civil rights movement until five or six years ago. Why not?

DAVIS: During my years of driving myself to get somewhere in this business, and then in the kind of personal reactions I had to making it finally, I wasn't thinking about nothing but *making* it, and then having a ball; wasn't thinking about *nothing* else. I didn't give a damn about no race cause. I knew about the problems, but I just didn't care. I didn't care about nobody but me. I can't tell you the truth no more honest than that.

But then different things started to happen. Some of

them had to do with me; most of them didn't, until finally I called up Harry and Sidney. I go to them when I'm bugged about something. Harry has been my friend for many years. And Sidney, I named my son after him, Mark Sidney Davis. They talked to me, and so did Ossie Davis. I was confused and angry, and maybe a little guilty.

HALEY: About what?

DAVIS: Well, for a long time I had thought that money, fame, popularity, people asking for your autograph, that was what it was all about; but it was beginning to gnaw at me. It's like a cat that's balling every chick he can meet. Then one day he finds out, floating in this marvelous dreamworld, that having sex per se is not the be-all and end-all of existence. There comes a time when he wants something else, something *more.* And the fast cars, the fancy clothes, the money, the chicks, all that jazz, they're not enough anymore. It's fun and games; it's adult Monopoly. But it's not enough to justify your life, and any cat that thinks it is had better wise up before it's too late. Well, I finally did—but I didn't know where to turn. I wanted to commit myself, but I didn't know how or to what. So I talked to Harry and Sidney and Ossie, and finally I knew: I wanted to help my people. When I said to them, "OK, where do I start?" they embraced me, they were so happy. Ever since then, I've been trying to make up for what I didn't do in the past. And it's been a gas! This is a glorious time to be alive.

HALEY: And to be a Negro?

DAVIS: Right! That's something I never felt before, that none of us ever felt before: pride in our color and in our cause. Jesus, I'm proud to be black when I can see the moves that I make and that others are making, and the opportunities that are opening up to my people. To me, that's where pride comes from—when it's possible for my people, like everybody else, to *accomplish* something. Ain't nobody going to feel much pride in being black as long as we let ourselves fall into all the cliché categories they use against us: "They don't want to help themselves, they just want to sit back, and whatever we hand out, they'll take." That shows no dignity, no purpose, no nothing. Why can't we all live in a society where it becomes every man's obligation, white or black, to extend his hand, to help—to do what we know in our hearts is the right thing? I'm proud to say that I'm Honorary Mayor of Harlem. I did a lot of work up there with HarYouAct [a Harlem civil rights youth group]. And the most recent thing, a marvelous position, very dear to me: I've been made the head of the life-membership department of the NAACP. It's not something you *are*; it's something you *do*. It's the first time the job ever was held by a performer.

HALEY: Honorary Mayor or not, weren't you heckled out of the pulpit in the middle of a speech for HarYouAct in a Harlem church a few years ago?

DAVIS: I was booed right out of the church—by black nationalist rabble-rousers shouting, "You're not for the black man!" "What about your white wife?" Well, I carry a gun, you know. They let me carry one in New York, the hardest state to get a gun permit in, because they realized that I get some kind of threat about every day of my life. I'm not a violent man, but *that* marvelous day, that *fun* afternoon, I never in my life felt so much like shooting someone. What's my *wife* got to do with it? *I* was there! *I'm* black!

HALEY: Despite your commitment to civil rights, many Negroes seem to feel that you're trying to disavow your race and your responsibilities as a Negro by "mixing" in the white world. What's your reply?

DAVIS: Baby, the best answer I can give you is the background of all this. Everything rotten about me that's said around, or that's been in the press, was started by a Negro photographer. You remember that picture of me and Ava Gardner that was in *Confidential*? I was playing the Apollo

Theater in Harlem. Ava was in New York publicizing *The Barefoot Contessa*. She did me a favor to come up to the Apollo and let me introduce her. William B. Williams was escorting her, and a guy from United Artists. Well, the four of us had one quick drink after the show, then later on at her hotel suite, two photographers took a cover shot of Ava and me for *Our World* magazine, with me in a Santa Claus suit. Then, when I got out of the costume, one photographer shot some pictures of me and Ava together, with the United Artists guy standing right with us. I told the photographer to give me the film, but he said he'd develop it for me. I told him to be very careful, because in the wrong hands the shots could make trouble for Ava. I felt embarrassed even saying that to another Negro, knowing he'd understand. Well, next thing I knew, that picture came out on the cover of *Confidential*, the United Artists guy cropped out of it entirely; and it had the headline blurb, "What Makes Ava Gardner Run for Sammy Davis Jr. cheek-to-cheeking it in her 16th floor suite at New York's Drake Hotel?" And in the story, the one quick drink the four of us had had together became, "Ava sat glassy-eyed through a gay tour of Harlem with Sammy"; and quotes Ava had made about my performance on the Apollo stage—"exciting, thrilling, masculine"—were slanted to make them sound like she meant in bed.

That's what really started my troubles, black and white, all over the country. Eating me up! I don't care what I did, it was wrong. That "Sammy Davis Jr. thinks he's white" bit. I'd take out beautiful Negro girls, like an old friend of mine, Ruth King, a top model, and the columns would have something like "The Negro girl with Sammy was only a cover-up for the white woman who was *really* his date." You know? In fact, I sometimes use a line in my act that I got from what I used to really feel during that time. I say, "I buy *Ebony, Jet*, the *Pittsburgh Courier* and the *Chicago Defender* because I can't *wait* to find out what I'm doing."

One day I'll be proud when I can see my kids not having to bear a stigma for being the children of an interracial marriage, not having to struggle for the rights that every white American takes for granted, and that'll make it all worthwhile. But in the meantime, it's a pain in the ass sometimes to be Sammy Davis Jr., because I just can't make a right move racewise. My mother was born in San Juan, you know; her name was Elvera Sanchez. So I'm Puerto Rican, Jewish, colored and married to a white woman. When I move into a neighborhood, people start running four ways at the same time. It defies explanation, what it's like. No matter what you do, no matter where you go, you ain't right, even with your own people. It used to be I'd go uptown to Harlem, and all I could feel around me was arms. I could take my wife; it'd be beautiful. It was just downtown I'd get the hissing sounds. Now, uptown, too. The color don't make no difference. Every day becomes a challenge, to keep yourself level, to keep yourself from becoming embittered. Mind you, I'm *proud* to be black, but I don't want my blackness to be a burden to me. I don't want to have to wake up every morning saying to myself, "What can I do today to prove to white people that I don't fit the racial stereotype? And at the same time, what can I do to prove to my black brothers and sisters that I'm black, and I love them, and I'll help any way I can?" This is what certain groups indicate they want to make you do. It's unfair.

HALEY: Have you ever wished that you weren't a Negro?

DAVIS: Well, not professionally, anyway. Earlier in my life—despite all the barriers—it proved advantageous to be a Negro, because they hadn't ever seen a Negro doing impressions of whites, and all that jazz. I've never wished, or felt, that I'd be making it better in show business if I were white. That's been written about me, but it's not true. On a personal level, though, maybe I really have at least subconsciously wished, like probably every other Negro, that there was *some* way I just wouldn't have to go *through* all of it, you know? Because it's all based purely upon the pigmentation of your skin, or the way your hair is. You might be the next Nobel Prize winner, but it don't matter: "If you're black, get back." You'd just like to look like everybody else so that people wouldn't automatically start hating you a block away. White cat sees you walking down the street, maybe from across the street, and he never saw you before in his life, and he's not even close enough to distinguish anything about you except that you're not his color—and just for that, right there, snap, bop, bap, he *hates* you! That's the injustice of it, that's what makes you cry out inside, sometimes, "Damn, I wish I wasn't black!"

HALEY: Some say that's why you wear your hair straight.

DAVIS: Well, years ago that might have been so, but the only reason I leave it this way is because it's become part of my image. A show-business personality, if he's created a successful image of one kind or another, has to keep that image. Like, I don't want to see Cab Calloway with a crewcut: He's a great performer, but at this late date he'd look pretty silly with kinky hair, and so would I. Am I supposed to cut it short and let it grow in natural just to prove I'm proud to be black? Even if I did, the Negroes who don't like me would find something else to knock me for.

I don't care whatever move I make, some of my own people won't like it. Maybe they'll like me when I die. But I can't die like normal; I got to be shot by some sheriff in Mississippi. Like Dick Gregory got shot at Watts. Shoot me—*bam!* Then they'll say, "I guess he really *was* on our side." I don't understand it. I would voluntarily *die* to have my own people love me as much as they love some of those goddamn phonies they think are doing so much fighting for civil rights! To me, the obligation of being a Negro is to carry the banner of being proud to be a Negro and helping in the areas you can best help in. In terms of the civil rights fighting front, if we're all picketing at Selma, or wherever else the particular locale is this month, then who's left to help put Negroes into motion pictures? Who puts the Negro into mainstream television? I've put dozens of Negro cats to work! I'm not bragging, but that's got to be recognized, too. We're all in the same battle; I'm just fighting it on another front.

HALEY: A moment ago, without naming any names, you referred to some civil rights leaders as "goddamn phonies." Would you care to tell us who they are?

DAVIS: I'd rather not.

HALEY: Well, do you number Martin Luther King among them?

DAVIS: I would give him my good eye. That's what I think of Dr. King. He's one of the great men of our time. They should retire the Nobel Peace Prize with his name on it.

HALEY: Despite his Peace Prize and his continuing dedication to nonviolence, Dr. King has been accused—most recently during last summer's Chicago riots—of fomenting violence. Do you think there's any substance in that charge?

DAVIS: Those who make such charges don't seem to realize that the Negro public's abiding faith in Dr. King's unflinching commitment to nonviolence—in the face of a rising tide of white violence against him and other Negro marchers—is just about the only thing that's kept the lid from blowing off the racial pressure cooker. Without his counsel of patience and brotherhood, the nonviolent Negro revolt could easily escalate into a bloody revolution.

HALEY: Among those advocating a revolutionary course are a number of racist groups dedicated to "getting Whitey" and sabotaging "the white power structure." How do you feel about their philosophy?

DAVIS: They're living in a dreamworld. They think they're going to "get Whitey" and take over the country. Well, I got news for them: They ain't going to get nobody or take over nothing! 'Cause whenever they get ready, right there is going to be the end of it. The Man will just open one eye and swat them like a gnat, and that will be that. They ain't made no razor *yet* that will stop an atomic bomb. You know what them cats should do that are so mad? Go down to Mississippi and kill them cats that killed them three civil rights workers. Everybody knows who did it. Find out who bombed that church in Alabama: Wipe them out. If you want to deal in justifiable violence, why kill the man who's trying to learn the right road to walk? Destroy the guy who has already proven to be your enemy. You know who it was that murdered Mrs. Liuzzo down in Alabama; they're out walking around. Go down there and wipe them out, you're so brave. When they bomb your church, bomb *their* church! 'Cause then that would prove, as it was proved in Africa, "Ten blacks may be killed for every white you kill, but you'll cause such an upheaval that every eye in the world will turn toward Africa. And the world will look and say, 'The sleeping giant is awakening.'"

HALEY: Are you serious about bombing white churches? Would two wrongs make a right? What if innocent children were killed, as they were in the Negro church bombing?

DAVIS: Of course, you're right. I don't mean literally bomb churches. I wouldn't literally bomb where even the most violent segregationists worship. Not for the segregationists as much as for the meaning of the institution. What I really mean is take care of the bombers themselves. I'm saying that if these extremist cats want to get Whitey, let them go take care of all those known murderers, the bombers and the others, who are walking around free because segregationist juries wouldn't convict.

HALEY: If they haven't been convicted in a court of law, how can you be sure they're guilty?

DAVIS: In practically every case I mentioned, the evidence was airtight: their guilt was established by the prosecution beyond a shadow of a doubt. The segregationist juries simply chose to ignore it.

HALEY: Then you'd feel justified in taking the law into your own hands?

DAVIS: Yes—just as long as the law permits whites to kill Negroes, or "white Negro" civil rights workers, and get away with it. I'm for any kind of protest—including retaliatory violence against known killers who get off—as long as Negroes are denied the full rights that any other American enjoys.

HALEY: Wouldn't such acts of vengeance—even if the victims were guilty—set back the Negro cause by alienating millions of whites, as well as Negroes, who deplore *all* lawless violence?

DAVIS: I imagine millions of whites *would* be alienated, the same way millions of Negroes were alienated when their church was bombed and their kids were blown to bits. I never will get out of my mind that famous *Time* cover showing that stained-glass face of Jesus shattered by the bomb that killed those little Negro girls sitting there in Sunday school hearing about peace on earth. That sticks in millions of Negroes' minds—same as that other famous picture printed around the world, of that Alabama white cop's heel on that Negro woman's neck. You see, baby, too many people don't want to face the terrible truth that violence *begets* violence. American Negroes have been on the receiving end of white violence for over 300 years; it would be a grievous error for anybody not to recognize that, if he wants to understand what's happening—and the consequences of doing nothing about it. Unless white society acts to end that violence by punishing those who commit it, Negroes may run out of patience and take care of the job themselves. And because violence begets more violence, it could spark a bloodbath in which the innocent on both sides would suffer along with the guilty. I'm not applauding it; I dread it. But I'm afraid that's what may happen if something isn't done—soon, and once and for all.

HALEY: Are you predicting more riots like the one in Watts?

DAVIS: I'm predicting riots that would make Watts look like a Sunday-school picnic—unless we get to work fixing what *causes* them. And you won't do that by blaming everything, like the FBI does, on black revolutionaries and Communist troublemakers. They don't start the fire; they just fan the flames. Put them all in jail, you'll still have riots. But the fact that riots are unplanned don't mean they're nothing but isolated outbursts of spontaneous hooliganism. Riots are simply *violent* manifestations of what Martin Luther King is protesting *nonviolently*, of what every black man in America is protesting, one way or another: the fact that our race has wrongly been denied that which is enjoyed and taken for granted by every other American. Rioters are people who have no stake in their country, no stake in their city, no stake in their homes, no stake even in their own survival. How much worse could death be than what they have to live with—and for? They feel they have nothing to lose—and they're probably right.

HALEY: Do you feel that enough is being done in Negro ghettos such as Watts, Harlem and Chicago's South Side to eliminate the conditions that breed riots?

DAVIS: Baby, you got to be putting me on! They ain't even scratched the surface in any of those places. You know what always seems to happen after every riot? Immediately, committees are formed to find out why it happened, and they investigate, and they study, and finally they turn in a fat, reassuring report—full of all the standard sociological platitudes—recommending *further* study and investigation and urging "better understanding between the white and black communities." The concrete results, if any, are way-out things like a new pocket park just about big enough to pitch pennies in, a front-page rat-extermination drive in one block where a baby was last bitten, a ceremonial street-cleaning campaign presided over by the mayor, and if we're really lucky, maybe a biracial civilian review board empowered to investigate police brutality and "make recommendations" for reform and discipline. Is it any wonder, when the *next* summer rolls around, that there's another riot? You can't bail out a sinking ship with a teaspoon.

You want to end riots? Fumigate their breeding grounds: Wipe out the black ghetto and the slums. It's a chain of cause and effect: Give the Negro the same chance whites have to get a decent education, so that he can qualify for a decent job, so that he can live in a decent home, so that he can lead a decent, self-respecting life—so that he can live in dignity as a human being, side by side with his white brothers.

HALEY: Many whites, particularly in Northern suburbs adjoining newly integrated neighborhoods, regard the Negro drive for equality of opportunity as a threat to their homes and jobs. Do you think there's any justification for that feeling?

DAVIS: Negroes don't want to take away nothing that belongs to white folks. White folks ain't giving up their own rights by giving the Negro his. There's enough human rights for *everybody*; don't need to fight over them. But you know, the real *gut* reason whites are afraid of us isn't a matter of job security and property values. It's because we're not the same *color*. Anything that's different they don't understand, and anything they don't understand they fear—and anything they fear they *hate*. Well, they're just going to have to get used to the idea of having us around as equal partners in this society. We share the same land, just as we share the same aspirations. We're stuck with each other, baby, so let's make the best of it. You accept our faults, we'll accept yours, and let bygones be bygones. 'Cause if we don't learn how to live together, we're sure as hell going to die together.

HALEY: How do you mean?

DAVIS: The Negro's destiny in America is America's destiny as a democracy. Malcolm X said it: "As the black man walks, so shall all men walk." Well, if the Negro falls, American democracy will fall, because all of the things it stands for will have been betrayed. But I don't think that's going to happen. It may sound hopelessly idealistic and unattainable, when you look around at all of the worsening racial strife we're confronted with today, but I honestly believe that the day is coming when the Ku Klux Klan and the White Citizen's Council will be relegated to the history books along with CORE and SNCC, when there'll be cobwebs not only on racist hate literature but on these NAACP life-membership cards that I try to get just about everybody I meet to sign up for. I may not be here to see it happen—even if I live to be 80—but I think my kids will be around to witness the birth of a truly color-blind society.

HALEY: As you know, extremist groups such as the Black Muslims share the view of the K.K.K. that American whites and Negroes will never be able to live together in peace and should therefore acknowledge the inevitability of racial separation. How do you feel about it?

DAVIS: I feel that the vast majority of Americans, white and black, want to get along with one another, and they're willing to do whatever they have to do to iron out their differences. That's what this country is all about. I think all those cats who don't believe in that, who don't think it'll work and don't want to try, who preach racial hatred and want to separate black and white, they should get the hell out of America and go to some desert island and live among their own sick kind. We don't need them.

It may sound hokey as hell, but I *love* my country. It's no paradise, God knows—and it never will be, color-blind or not—but it's *my* country, like the man said, right or wrong. If you're outraged by its racial injustices—and you ought to be—then fight to *do* something about them; don't be a defeatist and a dropout. If you don't like its foreign policy, then *bitch* about it as loud as you like, 'cause that's your privilege as a citizen; but don't put down the country that *allows* you that right.

HALEY: You sound like a patriot.

DAVIS: Maybe so. I'm a nut, I guess. I love America. It's given me opportunities that no other country in the world could've given me. If I had to go and fight, and lose my good eye, or die for this country, I would. Because there's no country better. I've traveled the world, and there ain't no place God ever created like America. Even with all the troubles we've still got to solve, if a guy doesn't want to let me into a hotel here, if I make enough money, I can *buy* the joint.

HALEY: As a major star, Sammy, you're not likely to be turned away by many hotels anymore, even in the South. In fact, you might be offered the red-carpet treatment at a hotel that refused patronage to other Negroes.

DAVIS: If I was, I'd tell them what they could do with the carpet. It's not any big, banner-waving thing with me; I just don't want to stay anyplace my people can't, and I don't care if they roll out an *ermine* carpet.

HALEY: Would you refuse, for the same reason, to perform in a white-only club?

DAVIS: Absolutely. I'd never even consider it. Even when I was poor and hungry, I didn't do it.

HALEY: In those early days with the Trio, were there many clubs that wouldn't book you because you were a Negro act?

DAVIS: I lost count of them. For years I remember telling Will and my dad that eventually we'd be able to make our way into clubs that had never booked Negro talent, if only we got good enough and pushed hard enough. But they kept telling me, "You can't. White folks ain't gonna let you get but so far." I been hearing that all my life. But I kept insisting, "Yes, I can!"—say, there's a good title for a book—and I kept believing that somehow, someday we'd be able to break down the wall of prejudice that was blocking us. Well, we finally did; but the battle still isn't won, because there are big clubs today—two of the biggest right in Las Vegas—that *still* won't book no Negroes on the stage; don't even want to see your black face inside the night club, star or no. And there are other clubs that wouldn't touch me with a ten-foot pole if I wasn't having the luck to be hot and swinging now and people weren't lining up to see me.

HALEY: On the whole, though, wouldn't you say that the opportunities open to the Negro performer today are considerably wider than when you were starting out?

DAVIS: Much wider, overall, and getting wider every year—in clubs, movies, television, theater, everywhere. But we're still on a trial basis, in terms of both the onstage and offstage attitude. They're still watching us. I know certain clubs that will book only Negroes who "behave themselves." That's such a *marvelous* line—"if they *behave* themselves." How about the drunken, loudmouthed bigtime Charlies in the audience? How about *their* behavior? I'm not knocking them for it, as long as they don't mess up my act. My point is that *we're* not allowed the luxury of getting as drunk as others can, the luxury of being as loud as others can get.

It wasn't long ago that you could make $20,000 a week in Las Vegas, but you couldn't live in a hotel on the Strip. I worked at one of them—packed in the people, could have rented a whole floor of the hotel with what I was making— and I wasn't allowed to go into the main room. You had to have your dinner served in your dressing room; and if you got a room to stay in, it was in the back. And you stayed there, you cooled it—no relationship with any of the people. It's not quite that bad anymore. But now there's kind of a gentleman's agreement going on. "Hey, baby, we love you, but do us a favor and stay in your suite as much as you can between shows, OK? It's nothing personal, you understand. It's the customers; we get a lot of them from the South." It's never "us"; it's always "them." At least they're *ashamed* of it now. That's some kind of progress. But we still got a long way to go.

HALEY: Do you think Negro entertainers have reached the point where they can succeed—or fail—on the strength of their talent alone?

DAVIS: Yes—most of the time. Only we're expected to have *more* than whites if we're going to make it—and I don't mean make it *big*; I mean just get by. Let's face it: Every Negro jazz group ain't Louis Jordan in his heyday; every Negro band's not Count Basie; every Negro singer ain't Nat Cole. We've got, proportionately, just as many bad bands and bad performers as the whites could ever boast of. Some of the saddest acts I've ever seen were colored—sad as McKinley's funeral, man. My point is that just as we've earned the right to be judged on our merits as entertainers, we've earned not only the right to stardom but the right to mediocrity, the right to be adequate, OK, unsensational—and still make a living in this business. At this point, though, Negro performers aren't allowed that luxury; if they're going to make the grade, they've got to have something going for them besides their good looks or their sex appeal.

HALEY: Shouldn't they?

DAVIS: Of course they should—but whites should have to meet the same requirements. And that brings up something else that bugs me about show business today. Young performers, black and white, are getting caught up in the overnight-star syndrome. Some electronically augmented rock-'n'-roll group makes it big with one hit record, and audiences go flocking to see them; yet they'll ignore 17 highly talented, maybe *more* talented performers who've been around for years refining their talent, getting better and better, turning out one great song after another—only nobody's listening! Somebody like Damita Jo. Marvelous!

One of the best voices in the business. Well, one night I went to catch her singing, and you could have shot deer in the place! There's no justice in it.

The kids breaking in today have plenty of ambition, and some of them even have talent, but they don't want to pay their dues; they don't want to *earn* their success. They're not interested in becoming *pros*—just stars. And they don't seem to have whatever it is that turned *my* motor on. You know, the all-consuming, almost disastrous desire to make it. I remember going into penny arcades and dropping a quarter into those Record Your Own Voice machines. I'd sing like Billy Eckstine, Louis Armstrong; I'd speak like Edward G. Robinson; I'd sing in my own voice; then I'd play the records over and over at home. And talk about *envy*: I'd go to the show at the Roxy and the Paramount, and all I could think about was, "Why ain't that *me* up there?" I'd go back home and dance before a mirror, copy a cat. And I wasn't afraid to ask for help. I'd go to Larry Storch and say, "Teach me how to do Jimmy Cagney, Cary Grant. I want to learn." And he taught me. Same with Mel Tormé, who taught me how to handle guns—which I've made a standard part of my act. Even when I had started making it, I was still asking, still listening, still watching, still learning, experimenting, accumulating, practicing, polishing. I learned, in time, something a lot of your young performers today don't appreciate, really—the importance of every single thing you do on that stage. Every gesture, every inflection, every tiny thing the audience sees, hears and senses about you makes a positive or a negative impression. Each one alone may seem insignificant, but cumulatively, they can make the difference between a good act and a great one.

HALEY: Other than your father and Will Mastin, who would you say has contributed the most to your success as a performer?

DAVIS: Frank Sinatra, Mickey Rooney and Jerry Lewis—

in terms of guys who really went out of their way, who did tangible things, who stood up and were counted where it needed to be done.

HALEY: You named Sinatra first. Why?

DAVIS: It would embarrass Frank if I told even half of the reasons why. I first met him in 1941 when he was singing with Tommy Dorsey in Detroit, when he was in his 20s. He just walked over, matter-of-factly, to Will, my dad and me, and stuck out his hand and introduced himself. That might sound like nothing much, but the average top vocalist in those days wouldn't give the time of day to a Negro supporting act. But every night, for the rest of that engagement, Frank would sit down on the dressing-room stairs with me, and we'd talk show business.

After that, every chance I could, I'd show up at his radio shows. He'd see me in the autograph line and invite me to his dressing room. I'm talking about when he was *big,* and I was a *nobody.* Then, months later, out of the blue, we were playing Portland when a wire came for us to open in the Capitol Theater in New York with the Frank Sinatra Show—and at $1250 per week! For us then, that wasn't just great money—it was incredible. Later I found out that Frank had insisted the management find us and book us with him. Introducing us to the audience, he'd say, "We've got three swinging cats here. Keep your eye on the little one in the middle; he's my boy!" After that show, Frank heard me do my impressions in his dressing room and gave me hell that I hadn't used them in the show. And he insisted that I needed to sing straight, using my own voice. I took his advice—and it seems to have paid off pretty good.

I guess a dozen times over the next several years, every contact I had with Frank, he went out of his way to do something for me, to help me up. That's the kind of guy he is: a sweet, outgoing, bighearted soft touch who'll do anything—literally *anything*—to help a friend. I don't know how many times—and he wouldn't want it known if I did—he has quietly picked up the tab for some friend in the hospital, or some other tight spot. But you don't hear many of these stories, and that's part of the reason Frank's such a misunderstood man. You don't hear about the *real* Sinatra, the father and the friend; you only hear about the legendary Sinatra, the swinger, the idol, the king, with guys supposedly standing around biting their nails to please him. You don't hear about what a kind, gentle guy he is; you hear about how he's supposed to be so *rude* to people. I can say, honest to God, I've never seen him say or do anything rude to anybody. If there are people asking for his autograph—and there always are—he signs, he's kind, he's courteous. Yet still he gets that bum rap. I've seen him order away guys trying to protect him from the autograph hounds and say, "Wait a minute, these are the people who make my career for me. Yes, of course, darling, it will be my pleasure." He ain't got to *take* no rudeness, though. He don't sit still for no stranger, drunk or not, coming up to him with a big "Hey, Frankie!" and a playful punch on the shoulder.

HALEY: With Sinatra's help, you were just beginning to make it really big when you had the accident that cost you your eye. How did it happen?

DAVIS: I was driving from Vegas to Los Angeles to do the sound track for *Six Bridges to Cross.* In Vegas, our act was playing the New Frontier—$7500 a week, the most we'd ever made—and to celebrate, my dad and Will had just given me my first Cadillac convertible. Charley Head, my valet, was with me. He'd been driving, then I'd taken over. We were keeping her under 50 that first 500 miles, taking it easy: I wanted to break her in nice, you know? When I took over the wheel, I remember I turned on the radio, and I heard myself singing *Hey, There.* Talk about a gas feeling, man! Then up ahead after a while was this green car— women in it; I could see their hats. The driver was pulling left, then right, then she'd straddle the lanes. I didn't dig what was happening with her for sure, so I stayed to the far right. Then suddenly she started into this wide U-turn—and stopped broadside across both lanes. No room for me to go right. My only move was to try swinging around her into the oncoming lane. Started around, saw cars coming at me, hit my brakes, cut hard right—but I knew I couldn't stop in time to miss her. I cut for her rear fender, trying to miss a broadside where the passengers were. Then, this *crash!* Never will forget that sound; you don't know what it's like unless you've been in a car crash. I saw her car spinning around, and then my forehead hit the steering wheel.

Man, the *pain!* But I saw my hand moving, so I knew I was still alive. Blood was running down my face. Charley was in the back seat moaning. I opened the door and got out to help him. I saw his jaw hanging all loose, blood running from his mouth. I had just gotten my arm around him, trying to help him out, when he looked up at my face, and he made this gargling sound. I reached up, feeling with my hand—and man, there was my eye, hanging by a string! I was trying to stuff it back in when I started sagging down, blacking out. I was on the ground praying. After all them hard years, our act was just starting to get somewhere. "God, please don't let me go blind. God, please don't take it all away now." And I heard a siren, and felt some movement; kept hearing the siren, and knew I was in an ambulance.

When I came to, I was in the hospital, and this doctor was standing beside my bed telling me very calmly that he'd removed my left eye. How do you take *that* news, baby? In that bed, my head wrapped up like a mummy, everything dark, I did a whole lot of thinking. I might have gone off the deep end if it hadn't been for that public. Stacks of letters! *Thousands* of them! So many flowers the florists ran out; couldn't even get them all in the hallway! The nurses were reading names off letters, and flowers, and Bibles, and all kinds of things—from everybody I ever knew in show business and out, and people I never heard of, white and black, all over America, even the deepest South. People sending me their prayers and best wishes. Man, that's one of the reasons you can't tell me the different races have to hate each other; I've seen too much of the *good* in people, white and black.

Then, finally, came the day when the doctor took off the bandages. When I saw that first gleam of light, baby, I was ready to jump up shouting! And then I saw the doctor and the nurse and my dad and Will Mastin all standing there at the foot of the bed, and I knew I wasn't finished. I had another chance.

HALEY: Did you have much difficulty adjusting to monocular vision?

DAVIS: It wasn't easy. For a while, right after the hospital, I'd reach for something and miss it by two, three inches. And the first time I tried dancing again, I kept kicking myself in the other leg and tripping. I knew I'd have to learn how to dance all over again. Wasn't nobody going to be saying, "He's *nearly* as good as before." I had to be *better*! But everything's pretty straight now. I'm still aware that I'm seeing with one eye; things look flatter to me than they do to you, and I've got a blind side that I have to keep aware of. But with this one eye, I see more now than you would if you closed one of your two good eyes. My field of vision has expanded to make up for the missing eye, like a wide-angle lens.

HALEY: For a year or so after the accident, you wore a black eye patch. What made you decide to take it off?

DAVIS: Humphrey Bogart convinced me to quit that. He asked me, "How long you gonna trade on that goddamn patch? How long are you gonna keep using it for a crutch? You want people calling you Sammy Davis or 'the kid with the eye patch'?" Well, you know, I'd had myself figured with a glamorous trademark, but what Bogart said kept on bugging me—especially knowing he was right—until one night in Vegas I took it off and threw the goddamn thing away. I don't need no pity, and I got nothing to hide.

HALEY: It wasn't long after the accident that you converted to Judaism. Did one have anything to do with the other?

DAVIS: In a strange way, yes. After one show I did with Eddie Cantor, he saw me looking at his mezuzah—that's a holy Hebrew charm for good luck, health and happiness—and he insisted on giving it to me. He told me that his religion had the basic belief that every man should have freedom to face God in his own way. Well, I wore that charm around my neck all the time from then on—until that day in my car, just before the accident, I missed it; I had left it in my hotel suite. If I had followed my impulse to go back and get it, I'd have both my eyes today—but I didn't.

Anyway, when the bandages were removed after my operation, I noticed a clear outline of the Star of David cut into the palm of my right hand. Then I remembered Tony Curtis and Janet Leigh walking alongside me as I was being wheeled to the operating room, and Janet pressing something into my hand, saying, "Hold tight, and pray, and everything will be all right." And I had clutched what she gave me so hard that it had cut into my flesh. It was kind of like a stigmata; it shook me.

Then one Christmas I read a history of the Jews, and it astonished me to see the affinity between Jews and the Negroes: their oppressions, their enslavements—despised, rejected, searching for a home, for equality and human dignity. For thousands of years, they had held onto their belief in themselves and in their right to a place in the sun. It got to me so much that I visited a rabbi, who gave me books to read. There were already a lot of Negroes converted to Judaism, but *my* talking about converting worried the rabbi, because it could so easily be taken by people as a publicity stunt. He insisted that I not rush into it just because I was filled up with what I'd read about Judaism. He told me that neither he nor anyone else could make me a Jew, that only I could do it.

Anyway, around this time, I was getting into deeper and deeper trouble—debts piling up into the hundreds of thousands; my performances weren't what they should have been, and all my high-lifing, until finally I tried suicide, as you know. I tried to race my car over a cliff, but right at the edge the drive shaft hit a rock and snapped, and the rear half of it jammed into the ground and held the car right there at the edge like an anchor. God had his arms around me. The hardest thinking session I've ever had was after that—until finally I said to God, as a Jew: "Here I am."

HALEY: Do you observe all the rituals and holy days of your new faith?

DAVIS: Well, in those orthodox terms, I couldn't rate myself the best Jew; but I'm certainly not the worst one, either. If it's possible, I'd say today I feel even more committed than when I converted. It took me a long time to really learn the truth about commitment, but finally I have, and it's one of the most beautiful things that ever happened to me.

HALEY: It was only a few months after your much-publicized conversion that your name hit the headlines again, this time linking you romantically with Kim Novak. Were they true?

DAVIS: Yeah, they were—but, ironically, not until *after* the first stories appeared about us, and maybe, in a sense, because of them. It all started so innocently. Tony Curtis asked me over to his house one night for a drink. He was having some people in. Kim Novak was there, and we were introduced. I doubt we exchanged 20 words. She was just one of the group. Well, the next day one of the columns carried an item: "Kim Novak's new sepia love interest will make her studio bosses turn lavender." I called Kim. She knew I'd had nothing to do with the item. She said, "Come on over and let's talk about it." She was cooking spaghetti and meatballs. I went over. She said her studio had called, wanting to know if she'd seen me, and when she said yes, they wanted to know how many times. When? Where? What was going on between us? It would have to stop! Well, like me, Kim just naturally rebelled against anybody making rules for her. And so we became conspirators, drawn together by defiance.

Well, from that point on, the press columns took it and ran. I mean, they made sure *everybody* found out about it—and they added a few trimmings of their own. Everybody I knew started advising me; and everybody *she* knew was telling her, "Don't wreck your career!" The scandal columns were running items that I'd been warned by Chicago gangsters if I ever saw "that blonde" again, both my legs would be broken and torn off at the knee. And the Negro press started riding me harder than ever. Stuff like: "Sammy Davis Jr., once a pride to all Negroes, has become a never-ending source of embarrassment. Mr. Davis has never been particularly race-conscious, but his recent scandal displays him as inexcusably unconscious of his responsibility as a Negro." That kind of thing.

Meanwhile, I rented a beach house at Malibu so we could meet secretly, and I had a guy drive me there incognito, like in the spy stories. The press was so hot on it, we didn't know if they wouldn't have movie cameras hidden on the road, so I got to hiding on the car floor while we drove there. Well, one night down on that car floor, it hit me in the face: What the hell was I doing there, sneaking around in the middle of the night? I was just confirming what they were saying: "You're not good enough to be seen with a white woman." I got up off the floor, told the driver to turn around, and that was that—the end of it. I never saw her again. If only I'd known my heart troubles were just beginning.

HALEY: You mean your first marriage?

DAVIS: If you want to call it that.

HALEY: Why didn't it work out?

DAVIS: It was doomed from the start. You got to understand the shape I was in. Deep in debt, from all my highlifing. Tax problems. Losing my eye. Then this Kim Novak thing down around my neck. For the first time in my life, I started drinking the hard stuff. I felt like a man being pulled down into quicksand, with mosquitoes buzzing around his head. I was taping my TV shows, and they were hollow. Then one night, after a show at the Sands, I got drunk in the lounge, then got in my car and drove over to the Silver Slipper. The show was letting out when I saw Loray White—a Negro girl, one of the dancers. Once we'd had a little thing going. We'd broken up when she couldn't play it for laughs. Well, I took another look at beautiful Loray, and the thought occurred to me that if I had a Negro wife, maybe the papers would get off my back. I was drunk, I proposed, and Loray accepted on the spot. It was unreal. Drunk, I pulled her up to the bandstand and I announced our engagement. The club's press agent brought a photographer. It was done. By morning, it was all over America. I wake up, my head's splitting, it's on the radio, front-paged in Vegas, long-distance calls from all over, telegrams pouring in. What had I done? But what could I *do*? All my career needed now—all Loray needed—was for me to back down.

Next time I saw her, she said, "You don't have to marry me, Sammy." "Yes, I do," I told her, and I explained why. She said OK. So we got married, and afterward there was a party in a West Side saloon. I drank like a fish. Finally we left in my car, a buddy of mine driving us. Well, something snapped inside me, and the next thing I know I've got my hands around Loray's neck trying to choke her—as if it was all her fault. When I realized what I was doing, I must have, like, gone into shock, 'cause my buddy had to carry me into the hotel, like a baby, up to the bridal suite. Loray was in hysterics; even *he* was crying. Man, it was a mess. Well, every paper in the country smelled it was phony, and all kinds of rumors started. I began to draw bigger crowds than ever—but for the wrong reasons. To the public, I wasn't a performer anymore; I was a geek, a side show. I was close to the bottom, professionally and emotionally. Well, of course, Loray and I got divorced. It's not a pretty story. I'm not proud of it.

HALEY: Two years later you met May Britt in Hollywood, and three months after that you announced your engagement, precipitating a storm of protest and hate mail from whites and Negroes throughout the country. Did you expect that kind of reaction?

DAVIS: Well, I didn't think it would win me any popularity contests, but I didn't expect such a flood of venom. As long as I've lived with prejudice, I'm incredulous every time it hits me in the face—and this time it just floored me. Threats. Obscenities. Ravings. I've never seen anything as sick, as vitriolic as some of the letters I received. Things like: "Dear Nigger Bastard, I see Frank Sinatra is going to be the best man at your abortion. Well, it's good to know the kind of people supporting Kennedy before it's too late." When I played the Geary Theater in San Francisco that month, there were threats to bomb it, and letters, including one with a bullet drawn on it and the heart-warming message: "Guess when I'm going to shoot you during your show?" Man, how would you like to perform, wondering which burst of audience applause will help to cover the sound of a gunshot? When I played the Lotus Club in Washington, the Nazis were picketing me—carrying signs like "Go back to the Congo, you kosher coon." And a black dog wearing a swastika, with a sign on his back, "I'm black, too, Sammy, but I'm not a Jew." It makes you ashamed that a country like America has to be tainted with people like these. But when I walked on stage in the club, the audience in a body stood up, calling to me, "The hell with 'em, Sammy. We're with you." The world is 98 percent filled with *nice* people, see? It's only the other two percent who are idiots.

HALEY: As you know, there was a widespread feeling among both whites and Negroes that you were marrying May in order to gain status in white society.

DAVIS: Yeah, I know. It's a sad commentary that so many people's minds would jump to that conclusion about me. Even if they think I'm low enough to do something like that, they should give me credit for not being stupid. If I had been thinking about improving my status in the white world, baby, the *last* thing I'd do is marry a white girl. Don't take no genius to figure that out. I stood to *lose* whatever status I had, not gain. I got a sneak preview of that right after we announced our engagement: Friends started dropping off rapidly, both hers and mine, and suddenly they were nowhere to be found—and we're not looking for them. That's why I feel bound by hoops of steel to those who proved tried and true when the chips were down, who were risking a lot themselves, in the convictions they exhibited. You know? Like Frank—standing up with me, being my best man. Pat Kennedy, coming to my party, and Peter Lawford, then the President's brother-in-law, and others that I haven't mentioned. They *knew,* and they risked a lot to prove their friendship.

For the information of those who may not have been able to figure out yet why I *did* marry May—despite everything we knew we were letting ourselves in for—it was love, sweet love, baby. How corny can you get, right? Well, I didn't care whether she was white, black, blue, green or polka dot—I *loved* her. And, miracle of miracles, she loved *me.* It was as simple as that. Well, maybe not quite that simple, because I kept asking myself *why* I loved her; I had to know, because it had to be for the right reasons. Well, I mulled it over a lot, and finally I realized it was because May, as my wife, in just being the kind of human being she is, would help me to make a better human being of myself; and that's just the way it's turned out. I'm not a new man or anything, but gradually, and in some ways rapidly, I'm getting to be a better person. She understands my drives, my needs, my frustrations, and she bends to them. She has been patient enough to let me develop in my own time and in my own way. And our love has been deepened and broadened by the things that we've had to face and to fight together—and I don't mean just the special problems of an interracial marriage.

HALEY: How have you faced the problem of adjusting your marriage to the demands of your work schedule? In the two weeks we've been following you around, you haven't had time even for a visit with your wife and children—except on the phone—let alone for a night at home. Certainly that's not a satisfactory arrangement.

DAVIS: Of course not. Even though May joins me on the road during the longer engagements, we're not together nearly enough, and I don't spend as much time at home as I wish I could. But at this point I've got no choice—and this is another area of her understanding. After the debts I piled up before my marriage, this is the first year I've been on my own financially. She understands that I need about two more years of this kind of working before I can *afford* to stay home more.

HALEY: You've already collapsed once because of the pace. How much longer do you think you can keep it up?

DAVIS: God willing, as long as I have to. I was told two years ago in this very room that I'd never sing again, that there were nodes at the bottom of my throat, and three specialists were going to strip my vocal cords, they were in such terrible shape from overwork. But I stuck by my guns, and I'm still singing today. So I think I'll be able to hold out long enough to get where I want to go professionally.

HALEY: Where *do* you want to go?

DAVIS: I'd like to work my way up to the class of the Duke, or Durante; they're so well established it doesn't matter whether they've got a show on or a movie running. They're liked, they're accepted, they're respected. But when you've devoted as many years to show business as I have, you know that it could all evaporate overnight, no matter how big you are. Things are really swinging for me now, but I can't help thinking that I might wake up some morning and find myself out of vogue, kaput, the way Frank did when the bobby-sox craze died out. He made a comeback; but I might not be so lucky.

You know what else haunts me? The thought of dying before I finish what I have to do. Like a few weeks ago: I'm in a plane, and Murphy is sitting next to me, and things have been going tremendously, and suddenly this cold feeling comes over me and I say to Murphy, "I'm going to die, because things are going too well. I'm going to die and I'll never finish it." If I can legitimately make the mark that I want to make as a human being and a performer, I'll be willing to go then. But I'm still hungry. I need more time. I need at least another good ten years in the business to try and create what I want to create.

HALEY: And what's that?

DAVIS: I want *two* kinds of success: One, I want to build—for myself and my family—an organization of enterprises and investments such as has made millionaires of some of my close friends. Like Frank. And to make all my own decisions. Frank don't let *nobody* tell him what to do. The other kind of success I want is as a human being. That don't have nothing to do with making money. Some friends I've got—visit their house, they ain't got this, ain't got that, have to borrow dishes, all that jazz, but I got to envy how successful they are as human beings. Before I die, I want to be able to know that I gave my full share of the blood, sweat and tears that millions of both white and black people have got to give to win freedom for their kids and mine. Whenever death comes, I'll consider my life's been full and fruitful if I can get these things accomplished.

HALEY: One more question, Sammy: If you could choose an epitaph for yourself, how would it read?

DAVIS: That's easy: "It's been a gas."

DECEMBER 1967

JOHNNY CARSON

A Candid Conversation
with Television's Foremost Host,
Clown Prince and Raconteur

JERRY YULSMAN

*There are few television personalities as engaging—and
none as paradoxical—as Johnny Carson, the suave, boyish, 42-year-old star of NBC's "Tonight Show." Five nights
a week, for 90 minutes—under the scrutiny of nearly
10,000,000 viewers and a studio audience of 234—Carson
wittily and assuredly converses with guests ranging from
Bobbie Gentry to Bobby Kennedy, in a style so ingratiating
that the average viewer, according to one psychologist, feels
he belongs to the "Tonight Show's" "family" and is taking
an active part in the proceedings. Out of the camera's range,
however, Carson maintains a passionately private life that*

has earned him an unenviable reputation as an uptight, lonely misanthrope. The puckish star, who often affects a whimsical naïveté while on the air, also proved himself to be an exceedingly tough hombre in his celebrated walkout last April: convinced that NBC had violated his contract by showing reruns during an AFTRA strike, Carson refused to go back to work when the strike ended and won a new contract that reportedly guaranteed him an income in excess of $4,000,000 for the following three years.

Despite occasional charges that the "Tonight Show" is "verbal Muzak" or that Carson deliberately skirts controversial subjects, the program attracts a hefty 40 percent of the late-evening audience. Recent challengers, such as Joey Bishop on ABC and Bill Dana on the short-lived United Network, have run far behind Carson not only in the Nielsen ratings but in the judgment of the critics. Time has called his show "the most consistently entertaining 90 minutes to be seen anywhere on television." The main drawing card of the program is Carson himself: a gracious, tolerant host and a quick-draw, sharpshooting ad-libber, he is able to eke laughs even out of mishap—as when a mechanical device refuses to work or when a guest fails to maintain the lively, cocktail-party repartee that is the "Tonight Show's" stock in trade.

Carson's mastery of his craft is the polished product of almost three decades as an entertainer. At the age of 14, as "The Great Carsoni," Johnny was earning three dollars an engagement for entertaining the Elks and Rotarians of Norfolk, Nebraska—his home town—with card tricks and other feats of magic; in high school, he was class historian—and an imaginative practical joker. After a two-year stint in the Navy (he once entertained Secretary of the Navy James Forrestal for several hours with his card tricks), Johnny entered the University of Nebraska, where he earned money off-campus as a comedian and radio announcer, met his first wife, Jody Wolcott, and wrote a thesis on comedy. Following a year in Omaha, where he acquired local renown as an offbeat radio personality, he moved to Hollywood and hosted a Sunday-afternoon television show called "Carson's Cellar." In 1954, while writing gags for Red Skelton, he got his first major break: Called upon to substitute for his boss after Skelton was injured in a rehearsal, he won plaudits for his performance—and his own nighttime-TV show on CBS; but "The Johnny Carson Show" lasted only 39 feverish weeks. The producer attributed its failure to Carson's lack of "power"; Johnny felt that too many people had been trying to give him advice.

After this setback, Carson acquired a manager, Al Bruno, and was promptly hustled off to New York. In the course of the next five years, as host of a daytime quiz show, "Who Do You Trust?," he learned to improvise risqué but socially acceptable double entendres and to coax humor out of lady wrestlers, snake charmers and the matrons who comprised the bulk of his viewers and guests. The rest of his time was filled with a heavy schedule of personal appearances on the Ed Sullivan, Perry Como and Dinah Shore shows, stints as a guest panelist on "What's My Line?" and "To Tell the Truth" and even feature acting roles on "Playhouse 90" and "The U.S. Steel Hour." When Jack Paar decided to step down as ringmaster of the grueling "Tonight Show" in 1962, he named Carson—who had successfully subbed for him on several occasions—as the only man who could fill his shoes. NBC agreed, but many observers wondered if the new man was really up to Paar. He was—and then some; since he took over "Tonight," Carson has eclipsed his predecessor's popularity; the show is the biggest money-maker on television, with both advertisers and studio tickets S.R.O.; and its host has become the biggest star in television.

In the opinion of many, however, Carson's success has made him cocky; and his reputed highhandedness has led colleagues to refer to their boss only half-humorously as "The

Prince." True to the image, when he secured his prodigious salary hike last April, he also demanded—and got—a free $1,000,000 insurance policy and more autonomy in the production of the show. One of his first acts after returning to work was to fire producer Art Stark, a friend for 11 years, whose ideas were reportedly too conservative for the star's taste.

Whatever else success has done to Johnny Carson, it has not made him sociable. In the past, he occasionally went out on the town and—according to some reports—showed up for work hung over from what an associate called "insecurity binges." Today, however, he and his petite second wife, Joanne, rarely leave their $173,000 duplex in the United Nations Plaza Tower—a posh co-op that also houses such public personalities as Robert Kennedy, David Susskind and Truman Capote. They dine out about twice a month, see an occasional play and attend Giants games during the pro-football season. Carson's remaining off-camera hours are spent in pursuit of a multitude of extracurricular interests— astronomy, archery, motion-picture photography, scuba diving and flying; he also plays guitar and drums. Recently, to acquire a short film clip for the "Tonight Show," he even spun around the track at Indianapolis in Andy Granatelli's turbine-powered racing car, allegedly banned from the "500" because it was too fast for the competition. On vacations—which add up to a quarter of the year—he plays to record night-club audiences at a reputed $40,000 a week.

Reporters, eager to capitalize on the irony that such a willing performer should be such a reluctant celebrity, have often characterized Carson as a withdrawn, unaffectionate, even hostile man. One "Tonight Show" guest has bluntly called him a "cold fish." Even his old friend announcer Ed McMahon has said that he "packs a tight suitcase." Though others have risen to his defense—notably, Mrs. Carson, who explained to a writer at some length that Johnny cares very *much about people but doesn't find it easy to verbalize his feelings—few succeed in glimpsing his private life, let alone in reaching him on a personal level.*

We decided to interview Carson early this fall, when he was riding high on the wave of public interest that followed his dispute with the network. Always wary of reporters, he regards the public's curiosity about him as a tiresome irritation that "just goes with the territory." But during his conversations with PLAYBOY *interviewer Alex Haley—which were conducted daily, over the course of a week, both at Carson's home and in his NBC office—he overcame his reticence and provided us with by far the most candid interview he has ever granted. "At first," Haley reported, "he was evasive, but by the end of our talks, I had come to like and respect him as a man with the guts to be stubborn about his convictions in a profession where the most common concern is to swing with the 'in' crowd, whatever the personal compromise." Haley opened the discussion by asking Carson about his offscreen image as a loner.*

HALEY: Recent newspaper and magazine articles about you have focused on the contrast between your affable television image and what they claim is your dour, antisocial personality in private life. Writing in *TV Guide,* Edith Efron even went so far as to say that "Johnny Carson is a dual personality; pure sweetness and light on the screen—and off-screen, plunged into some Dostoievskyan murk." How do you feel about this kind of armchair psychoanalysis?

CARSON: I couldn't care less what anybody says about me. I live my life, especially my personal life, strictly for myself. I feel that is my right, and anybody who disagrees with that, that's his business. Whatever you do, you're going to be criticized. I feel the one sensible thing you can do is try to live in a way that pleases *you.* If you don't hurt anybody else, what you do is your own business.

HALEY: Of course. But off the air—even to many of those who know you well—you seem withdrawn and even hostile. According to reports, longtime associates on the show say that you scarcely speak except as business demands, that you have almost no friends in or out of show business, that you hardly ever go out socially, that you shrink from your own public. Why?

CARSON: I think I owe one thing to my public—the best performance I can give. What else do they want from me? As for being sociable, I hate the phoniness in the showbiz world. I know this will be taken wrong, but I don't like clubs and organizations. I was never a joiner. I think most groups are hypocritical, restrictive and undemocratic. I don't run with anybody's herd. I don't like crowds. I don't like going to fancy places. I don't like the whole night-club scene. Cocktail parties drive me mad. So I do my job and I stay away from the rest of it. Isn't that my right? Am I not entitled to prefer the enjoyment of my home? Am I not entitled to a private life? I can't go anywhere without being bugged by somebody. I'd love to just hike out down the street, or drop in a restaurant, or wander in the park, or take my kids somewhere without collecting a trail of people. But I can't. When you get successful, you just have to quit going out in public as often as you used to. Wherever you go, some clown grabs you and demands an autograph; it's a pain in the butt. I've had a guy in a *urinal* ask me for an autograph!

HALEY: Don't all entertainers have to put up with that kind of thing?

CARSON: Of course. But it doesn't stop there. Everybody I meet in public seems to want to audition for me. If I ask a guy what time it is, he'll sing it to me. Everywhere I turn, there's somebody's niece who plays the kazoo or does ballet with skindiving flippers. I'll never forget coming out of a restaurant one night, when this hand reaches from an alley and literally turns me completely around. It was this woman. "I want you to hear my son sing," she says. And out she shoves this kid—"Sing, Albert!" And he did—right there in the street. I've had cab drivers pull over to the curb to tell me about some relative who ought to be on the show. That's why I've got cabophobia—the fear of being talked to death in an enclosed space. But you haven't heard the worst of it. One night, Ed McMahon and I dropped into a night club; we wanted to catch an act there. We had barely sat down when some drunken bruiser comes over and hauls me up by the arm. Right there, I was ready to rip into him; I didn't care how big he was—but I kept saying to myself: "Don't!" I could see the headlines if I did. He all but drags me to his table of maybe 15 or 20 friends and he yells to the band to stop so I can entertain them. I told him I was sorry, I was very busy. I had to get up early. Now he's insulted. "Come on—I promised my friends." Well, I walked away: Ed and I had to leave—and I'd made some enemies. You can't win. So you stay away from public situations.

HALEY: Have you changed since you became a star, or have you always felt this strongly about guarding your privacy?

CARSON: In other words, has success spoiled Johnny Carson? No. I don't think so. I don't think it's *you* that changes with success—it's the people around you who change. Because of your new status, they change in relation to you. Let me give you an example. I loved the towns I grew up in as a boy, and after I became a celebrity, I went back several times. I would have had the time of my life seeing the old places and the old faces again, but the attitude of those same people was, "I guess you're so big we bore you now." What was I supposed to say to that? Agree with them? They'd be furious. But if I said I was enjoying myself, they'd say I was being condescending. You see what I mean?

There was a "Johnny Carson Day" for me at the last Nebraska Centennial in Columbus, Nebraska. I went. I enjoyed most of it. It was a great honor, and I sincerely mean that. But I have since decided not to go back home again. It's just too much of a strain. My folks will have to come to New York to see me. I guess people will find all kinds of things wrong with my saying that: they'll say I'm conceited and egocentric—but I'm just being honest.

HALEY: To be honest, *are* you conceited and egocentric?

CARSON: Find me any performer anywhere who *isn't* egocentric. You'd better believe you're good, or you've got no business being out there. People are brought up to think, "It's nice to be modest. It's nice to hide your light under a bushel." Well, bullshit! I've never bought that. In my business, the only thing you've really got is your talent; it's the only thing you have to sell. If you want to call that conceit, go ahead. I don't know where you'll hear that word more than in show business—but it's often not conceit at all. Often it's a public compensation for shyness. That's certainly the case with me. From the time I was a little kid, I was always shy. Performing was when I was outgoing. So I guess I *am* a loner. I get claustrophobia if a lot of people are around. But there's a big difference between being a loner and being lonely. I'm far from lonely. My day is full of things I enjoy, starting with my show. Any time my work is going well and I have a relationship with a woman that's pretty solid, that does it for me.

HALEY: Last April, you won a healthy pay raise by going on strike against NBC. Is that one of the reasons you say your work is going well?

CARSON: Since when has it been wrong to ask for a pay raise? Have you seen carved in stone anywhere that it's unfair to bargain for a better deal for yourself? It was made to look as if I'm Jack the Ripper. Some of the columnists figured I was too greedy for a nice, small-town Nebraska boy. Like one letter asked, "How can you *do* that with people in the world starving?" What in the hell is the logic of that? I explained, time and again, carefully, why I stayed out—but nobody wants to believe you when you take a personal stand about something. The whole thing got written and talked far out of proportion. Look—the reason was simple; at least to me it was. *Tonight* was and is the biggest money-making show NBC has. It brings in $25,000,000 a year, cold cash; but NBC treated *Tonight* like some bastard stepchild. We had a ridiculous budget. I hadn't liked that setup long before the strike. But that still wasn't the specific issue with me. The specific issue was that NBC directly violated our contract during the strike: They used reruns of the *Tonight* show without any effort at all to negotiate. My contract stated clearly that any reruns would be negotiated in advance in good faith, to arrive at equitable fees. They knew why I stayed out. They sent me a check for the reruns and I sent the check right back. But finally, NBC and I came to terms. I'm satisfied. I think they are. The show's doing fine. That's that.

HALEY: Not quite—if you don't mind our pursuing the subject a bit further. It's been reported that your new contract will earn you more than $4,000,000 in the next three years. Is that true?

CARSON: I won't tell you—for two reasons. One is that a term in the new contract specifies that neither NBC nor I will make public the details of the contract; I intend to abide by that agreement. Another reason is that in Nebraska, I was raised to consider that it's not good manners to ask anyone, "How much money do you make?" All I will say is that the new contract calls for an increase in the monies that I receive for doing the show.

Look—do you know that Dean Martin makes a lot more, maybe half again, at least, than I do? But all that means nothing whatever to me. I have no use for 8 houses, 88 cars and 500 suits. I can't eat but one steak at a time. I don't want but one woman. It's silly to have as one's sole object in life just making money, accumulating wealth. I work because I *enjoy* what I'm doing, and the fact that I make money at it—big money—is a fine-and-dandy side fact. Money gives me just one big thing that's really important, and that's the freedom of not having to worry about money. I'm concerned about *values*—moral, ethical, human values—my own, other people's, the country's, the world's values. Having money now gives me the freedom to worry about the things that really matter.

But I wouldn't call myself a great deal happier now than when I was earning $47.50 a week in Omaha. You could live on that in 1949 in Omaha. The guys at the station and I used to sit around and yak about how great it would be if we could earn $150 a week. We couldn't have *believed* what I make now. We couldn't have believed where I live now, the job I have—none of it. But I'm still sleeping in a bed; it cost a lot more, but I don't sleep any better than I did then. And I still like hamburgers—but in all of New York City, you cannot buy one as great as I used to buy at the Hamburger Hut in Norfolk, Nebraska. You see what I mean? Believe me, it's all relative.

HALEY: During your year in Omaha, you often worked six and seven days a week almost around the clock. Doesn't it please you to be earning a great deal more than you did then, for a great deal less work?

CARSON: Maybe it looks easy to a lot of people, but sitting in that chair will take more out of you than if you were chopping down trees all day. I spend seven and a half hours on the air every week. I think anyone who does this show ought to get an Emmy just for showing up. I'm serious. It's not the physical strain; it's debilitating mentally. In fact, I'll tell you something: My biggest anxiety is about the day I'll know I've reached a point where I can't bring the show anything more that's new. I was 42 this October, see? Physically, I have no concerns; but mentally, it's one of those shows where you're working from wake-up in the morning until you go to bed, and then even in bed. The pressure is to keep it from getting dull. I believe we give more honest humor and entertainment in one week than most prime-time shows in a season. But think about trying to keep that up, five nights a week, and maybe you'll appreciate the strain. And that's just strain about the over-all planning; then you add the strain of each show when you're on the air. When that red light goes off at the end, I get up from that chair already planning the show for the next night. If it looks easy, I'm doing my job. It both bugs me and pleases me when people tell me how relaxed I make the show look. Great! Maybe the public figures I'm getting well paid for it, but it's the toughest job in television. Listen—understand that I'm not complaining. I love the show; otherwise, I wouldn't be there. I'm just saying it's tough.

HALEY: You said your workday begins when you wake up. Would you describe a typical day for us?

CARSON: Well, I get out of bed at nine or ten in the morning. And I'm not one of those who spring up yelling, "Yippee! Another day!" I'll grumble and sulk around a couple of hours, reading newspapers and trying to pick out an idea I might do something with on the show. But I don't really start functioning until noon or later; then about two I go to the studio and the pace begins to quicken. Planning the time slots for this guest, that guest, rehearsing the skits, trying to anticipate what could go wrong with some physical participation I want to do—like the time I dueled with a fencing master. Or the time I did a snake dance with Augie and Margo. Or when I try out gadgets or toys. Or the times I've done exercises with Debbie Drake. She's great fun. One of my good lines came with that. Debbie and I had just lain down on the exercise mats, side by side, and it popped into my head to ask her, "Would you like to leave a call?"

HALEY: Are all of your ad libs spontaneous and unrehearsed?

CARSON: Very few of them are. Ad-libbing isn't very often the instant creation of a good line. More often it's remembering something you've used before and maybe making a quick switch to fit a fresh situation. Once I had Red Buttons on and he was getting into an involved analysis of politics, so I told him finally, "You're kind of a redheaded Dr. Schweitzer tonight, aren't you?" and Red started being his funny self again. Now, that's a situation bit I've used many times. Every comedian has a bag full of them. I remember once a woman on *Who Do You Trust?* telling me at great length, *too* great length, about a pregnant armadillo. She was about to bore the audience, so I asked her, "How come you know these things if you're not an armadillo?" They're usually old bits, but they work like brand-new if people laugh. Like the time we had this Latin Quarter showgirl on the show. She walked on in one of those poured-in dresses, with her hair done up in some exotic style. I said, "I suppose you're on your way to a 4-H Club meeting," and the audience cracked up. That's the humor of the ludicrous, of extreme contrast. I've used it many times before and I know I will many times again.

HALEY: Apart from the skits and your participation bits and, in a sense, some of the ad libs, how much preparation is involved in each show?

CARSON: The minimum that's safely possible. That's part of the formula. I have little or no advance contact with guests, for instance, unless they're involved in some skit. And the writers prepare my opening bit—that first ten minutes after I walk on. But I edit what they give me until I'm entirely comfortable with it, using something topical I've found in the papers, if I can. Then the necessary staff people and I plan a run-down of the show. By the time all

this is done, it's six P.M., and we start taping the show at
6:30. Then I'm on my own. So the objective is spontaneity
within a planned framework: but for the most part, we're
wringing it. My job isn't to hog the show. Ideally, I'm the
audience-identification figure, the catalyst. When I've got a
guest who's going great on his own, I let him go. If he looks
good, I look good. Sometimes, of course, the chemistry isn't
right, or something will go wrong, and I'll have to change
the pace or pull a switch during a commercial or a station
break. Like one time Peter O'Toole came on. I think everyone was sure he was drunk. *I* thought he was, too. I'd ask
him a question and he'd reply something incoherent or
completely unrelated, as if he was off in some other world.
So I put on a commercial, and while it was running I asked
Peter if he was OK, and I found out the trouble. He had
just flown in from London to do the show and, because of
that long haul, he was just blind with exhaustion. So while
the commercial was still on, I said, "Well, Peter, why not
just cut?" He agreed and left without another word. When
I came back on, I explained it to the audience and everything was OK. But that sort of thing is a rarity, thank God.

All too often, though, a guest will either clam up or be
vapid and bland, and I'll have to cut it short and come on
next with a bullwhip demonstration, or some skit I can do
on a moment's notice, to wake us up—or wake up the
audience. Sometimes I can get us going again by coming up
with a good gag keyed to what a guest is talking about. Like
once during the New York World's Fair, I got off one that
the Moroccan Pavilion had a belly dancer, but the Fair's
business was so bad she had a cobweb in her navel. Another
time, Mr. Universe was on, explaining the importance of
keeping yourself fit and trim. That sort of thing can get
deadly dull, of course, and I was feeling for a good gag when
he told me something like, "Remember, Mr. Carson, your
body is the only home you will ever have." And I said,
"Yeah, my home is pretty messy. But I have a woman come

in once a week." Can you imagine the mail I got on that one? But nearly anything you say, you can't help offending somebody out there. If I say "naked," if I use the word "pregnant," I'll get probably 500 letters complaining that I'm hastening national immorality. A lot of them are from nuts—you can tell that—but many are from perfectly sincere people who happen to think that practically anything is immoral. Let me do a sketch about the President or about a rabbi and there'll be a storm of criticism.

HALEY: Do you let this kind of reaction affect your choice of material?

CARSON: You can't afford to. The only time I pay attention to audience mail is when it contains something I find possible to use for the show's benefit. You can't let an audience run your show for you. If you do, soon you won't have any audience.

HALEY: Do you feel the same way about television critics?

CARSON: I try never to let them bug me—but I'm not always successful. Nobody likes to be zinged; but whatever they say, I will continue to do what I think our show should do. I see little that I feel is constructive in what most TV critics write—about my show or anybody else's. One of the main reasons is that few television critics really know much about television. Too many of them are ex–sportswriters and ex–gardening columnists, completely unfamiliar with the medium. They haven't bothered to learn what makes it work. There are a few TV critics I respect: Jack Gould here in New York; and on the Coast, Hal Humphrey. But most of them are on a level with Sidney Skolsky, who once wrote that I wasn't Jack Paar. *I* could have told him that. I felt like wiring him that neither was he any H. L. Mencken. I often feel that I'd like to give all the critics just three hours a day of TV time and say, "All right, you're so bright, now you fill that three hours, every day." You'd hear less from them about what's wrong with television.

HALEY: What's your reaction to Newton Minow's celebrated indictment of television as a vast wasteland?

CARSON: Sure, there's a *lot* of chaff on television. No doubt of it. But let's not forget a fundamental fact about this medium. It starts in the morning, about six A.M., and goes off anywhere from one to three A.M. Where are you going to find the people to write consistently fine material 19 to 21 hours a day, 365 days a year? A Broadway play that's going to run for 90 minutes can take a year or more to get written, by the biggest playwrights in the business; then it can spend months and months on the road, being tested every night and changed daily; they can bring in the best script doctors in the country—and yet that play can still open on Broadway and bomb out the first night. How can you expect television to do any better—or even as well—when it's showing more in a week than appears on Broadway all year? I'm not defending the medium just because I'm in it: I'm just trying to explain that television has an impossible task. Why should it be the job of television to educate or edify or uplift people? This is an entertainment medium. I have never seen it chiseled in stone tablets that TV is philanthropic. Is it television's job to improve people's minds—when the libraries are full of empty seats? Are we supposed to provide instant education?

There are lots of things I'll knock the industry for—including the fact that there's too much junk on the air. But there are a lot of fine programs, too. And I think television is steadily working to improve its programing: the competition is so hot, it guarantees that. Another thing people so often entirely overlook when they're criticizing is that this still is a very young industry. My first TV broadcast was when I was at the University of Nebraska. I was playing a milkman in a documentary called, believe it or not, *The Story of Undulant Fever.* You know what the broadcast range of that show was? The cameras were in the university theater's basement and the screen was up in the auditorium—and that was the first television at the university. And that was in 1949: *that's* how young television is. So I don't go for this general rapping of the television industry. How long, how much longer, have the newspapers and the magazines and the movies been around? Does television offer any more junk than they do? Does television feed its viewers anything *like* as much rape and lurid details? Yet television is always being knocked in newspaper and magazine editorials. I'm not against the press, but that sort of attack is not only unfair but hypocritical.

HALEY: Do you share, at least, the general view of the press that television's *commercials* could stand both improvement and diminution in number?

CARSON: Well, I wouldn't say there are too many commercials. After all, the time has got to be paid for. The stations must make some money in order to continue programing, and the only way to do this is by selling products for sponsors. I think we have to recognize that and live with it. Every half hour we have just three one-minute network commercials; the others are within local station breaks. My gripe with commercials is that so many irritate me with their haranguing and shouting and overselling; and I think some commercials violate good taste. I go up the wall every time I catch that commercial with the kids bragging about "twenty-two-percent fewer cavities"! I happen to like and use the toothpaste, but I hate their commercial. And I'm sick, sick, sick of stomach acids going drip, drip, drip. Nor do I feel TV is the place to advertise relief for hemorrhoid sufferers. If I ran an agency that made commercials, my credo would be, "Be enthusiastic, but be quiet—and honest." I would love to see believable soap ads, like: "This soap won't get you a girlfriend, boyfriend, wife or husband—but it'll get you pretty clean!" I really think that would sell trainloads of soap. The advertising agencies should be called to task when they make phony claims and violate good taste and when they overemphasize sex and social-acceptance pitches, and status and snob pitches. Television advertising can't be avoided, but it could be a hell of a lot more honest—and more palatable.

HALEY: For most TV sponsors, the fate of a show is decided by its popularity rather than its quality, by means of rating systems that have been widely attacked not only for their life-or-death importance to network programers but for the inadequacy and inaccuracy of their audience samplings. How much stock do you place in them?

CARSON: I'm reminded of the story about this gambler in a small-town saloon who is taken aside and told that the wheel he's playing is crooked. He says, "I know, but it's the only wheel in town." The industry seems to want a yardstick, and I guess the ratings are the only one they can find. I don't know how accurate they are, but I'd hate to think that a random sampling of 1200 viewers gives a true national picture. I'm certain that people aren't watching what they tell the pollsters they watch. People often want to project themselves as some kind of intellectuals, so they'll say they watched the news, or some forum, or the National Educational Network show, when, in fact, they watched *Bonanza* or *The Flying Nun.* You know? One thing I'm sure of: Ratings certainly don't indicate if people are buying the sponsor's product. But I'm glad I have the ratings I get—accurate or not. Anybody would be. I don't concern myself too much about them, though, because one show will be up, another one down. If you start worrying about a particular show, chances are you'll do worse the next. What really counts is how your ratings average out over, say, six months. I never worry about an individual program after it's over. That was yesterday; what's tomorrow?

HALEY: *The Joey Bishop Show* went on opposite you several months ago. Do you feel that Bishop represents a threat to the *Tonight Show* popularity?

CARSON: To tell you the truth, I don't think anything

about it. I don't worry about what Joey Bishop is doing. When his show was ready to open, people asked me about it, and I told them I knew it would be the noble thing for me to say that I wished him much success; but honesty compelled me to admit that I hoped he would fall on his face. That's how *any* performer feels about his competition; and if you hear anybody say different, he's lying in his teeth. I think people will have much more respect for you if you're honest. But no competition is going to bother me in the sense that I'll lose any sleep over it. I look at it as professional golfers do. When he's out there in some tournament, Palmer isn't worrying about Nicklaus, or any of the rest. Any pro golfer will tell you that's the surest way to lose. I give all my concentration to what *I'm* doing. Some viewers will go for Mike Douglas, some for Merv Griffin, some for Bishop, some for me. Nobody is ever going to walk away with the whole television audience; there's plenty for everyone.

HALEY: In many cities, the *Tonight* show competes with one or more of the controversial new talk shows that are emceed by combative, opinionated moderators such as Tom Duggan, Alan Burke and Joe Pyne. Do you ever watch them?

CARSON: I am not a fan of those shows. I think their format, their whole approach, is a substitute for talent. They insult people. They're rude. It embarrasses me to watch that kind of prodding and goading. I don't think they'll last, because the public will get fed up with them. People will see the deliberate controversy for what it is.

HALEY: The *Tonight* show, under your control, has been criticized for deliberately *avoiding* controversy. Is there any truth to that?

CARSON: Well, bullshit! That's my answer. I just don't feel that Johnny Carson should become a social commentator. Jack Paar got into that, being an expert on everything happening. So did Dave Garroway and Steve Allen and

Godfrey. Who cares what entertainers on the air think about international affairs? Who would want to hear me about Vietnam? They can hear all they want from people with reason to be respected as knowledgeable. Controversy just isn't what this show is for. My number-one concern, and the concern of NBC, is a successful *Tonight* show. I'm not the host of *Meet the Press*. I think it would be a fatal mistake to use my show as a platform for controversial issues. I'm an entertainer, not a commentator. If you're a comedian, your job is to make people laugh. You cannot be both serious and funny. One negates the other. Personally, I want to be a successful comedian. Audiences have proved time and again that they don't want a steady diet of any entertainer airing his social views—especially if he's a comedian. When a comic becomes enamored with his own views and foists them off on the public in a polemic way, he loses not only his sense of humor but his value as a humorist. When the public starts classifying you as thoughtful, someone given to serious issues, you find your-self declassified as a humorist. That's what happened to Mort Sahl. He was one of the brightest when he began; then he began commenting humorlessly on the social scene in his shows. How many shows has Mort lost now? I think he realizes this now—and he's starting to get funny again. Like most people, of course, I have strong personal opin-ions. I might even be better informed than the average person, just because it's my business to keep up on what's happening. But that doesn't mean I should use the show to impose my personal views on millions of people. We *have* dealt with controversial subjects on the show—sex, reli-gion, Vietnam, narcotics. They've all been discussed, by qualified guests, and I've taken stands myself. But it's only when the subject rises naturally. I won't purposely inject controversy just for the sake of controversy. It would be easy, if that's what I wanted. I could get in the headlines any day by attacking a major public figure like Bobby Kennedy or by coming out in favor of birth control or abortion. But I just don't see it, and I don't play it that way. I won't make this show a forum for my own political views.

HALEY: Isn't it possible for you to air your social and political views without abandoning your role as a comedian? Can't you comment humorously and satirically rather than seriously on current issues?

CARSON: It should be—because that's the essence of comedy at its best—but that's not the way it works in practice, at least not on television. Americans, too many of them, take themselves too seriously. You're going to get rapped—by the viewers, by the sponsors and by the network brass—if you joke about doctors, lawyers, dentists, scientists, bus drivers, I don't care who. You can't make a joke about Catholics, Negroes, Jews, Italians, politicians, dogs or cats. In fact, politicians, dogs and cats are the most sacred institutions in America. I remember once somebody stole the car of Mickey Cohen, the racketeer, with Cohen's dog inside, and I said on Steve Allen's show that the police had recovered the dog while it was holding up a liquor store. Well, the next day this joker telephoned and said, "I don't want you should joke about Mickey Cohen," and I told him the joke was about his dog. "That compounds the felony," this character said. "You just better watch your step." Look—a comic has got to tread on some toes to be funny, but he's got to be careful how *many* toes he steps on, and who they belong to. I think the biggest rap mail I ever got was once when a girl said on the show that we should send Elvis Presley to Russia to improve our Soviet Union relations, and I said, "I don't know about Russia, but it might improve relations here." Presley fans tore me up. You can't say anything about practically anything that can be considered someone's vested interest. Once I planned to air a joke about how the Government ought to be run like Madison Avenue would run it. Write ads like, "You can be *sure* if it's the White House." But I was told,

"No, can't kid the Government." Well, why *not*? Another time I was intending to kid the phone company a bit, and I couldn't—because the *Bell Telephone Hour* was on the same network. If you plan to stay in television, you just have to adjust to these taboos, however ridiculous they are. But I must say that the timidity of the censors really floors me sometimes. For instance, it's touchy, touchy if you say "damn" on TV. Once, in 1964, somebody brought a dog on my show that actually said "Hello." It stunned me so that I blurted, "The damn thing talks!" Well, that word got blooped from the sound track before the show was aired. I say that any adult who gets offended at hearing "damn" or "hell" ought not to be watching television—or reading books. These same people, interestingly enough, seem to have no similar objection to the amount of violence on TV; otherwise, you wouldn't see so much of it. I've come to the conclusion that it's OK to kill somebody on television as long as you don't say "damn!" as you strike your victim down.

HALEY: In its recent cover story about you, *Time* magazine clucked editorially about what it felt was your taste for bathroom humor. Do you feel that's a justified criticism?

CARSON: That's one of the two things in that whole article that I resented. The other line I didn't like was that I had divorced my first wife. I didn't; she divorced me. I didn't initiate it. The way they put it made it sound like I was the kind of guy who made it big and then got rid of the one who had stuck with him all the way. Anyway, about that bathroom-humor bit. I think the writer didn't use the word he intended; I think he meant *double-entendre* jokes—because toilet humor I don't like at all, not from me or from my guests.

HALEY: Then you do indulge in *double entendres*?

CARSON: Occasionally, yes—but without striving for it and without violating what I consider good taste.

HALEY: The rap letters you've said you receive from viewers imply otherwise.

CARSON: There's a lot of hypocrisy in audiences. I'd never dream of telling even on a night-club stage, let alone my show, some of the jokes that are told in a lot of the living rooms from which we get those letters! If you can't talk about anything grown-up or sophisticated at midnight without being called immoral and dirty, then I think we're in trouble. After all, by the time we go on the air, the children are supposed to be in bed asleep. I can't just prattle about what I had for lunch and expect people to tune in every night. We'd be dead soon if we got dull enough *not* to get letters; we have to get in something now and then that's provocative. Take comics. You can't have Sam Levinson on all the time, talking about kids and school. You have to liven things up occasionally with somebody like Mel Brooks. Mel can get close to the line, on the line, or he'll edge beyond it; he may offend, but when he's going great, really winging, he's near a genius. There are some guests, of course, who make a fetish of blue material. But if I once feel that, you won't see them on my show again. Nor will I let a guest say something blue that I can sense in advance—especially if it's just to be blue. But I'm not going to worry about it if something happens to slip—and it can just as well be me as a guest. Even when no double meaning is intended, that pious bunch out there in the audience will make up its own and write in about it. That's more of a commentary about them, in my opinion, than it is about us.

HALEY: Many of those same people, and their journalistic spokesmen, seem to feel that the sexual suggestiveness—and overt erotica—they perceive on television, in movies, magazines and books is evidence of a moral decline in society at large. What's your reaction?

CARSON: Well, if you're talking about sexual morality, I wouldn't agree that it's declining; but it's certainly changing. Young and old, we are very much in the process of taking a fresh look at the whole issue of morality. The only decline that's taking place—and it's about time—is in the old puritanical concept that sex is equated with sin. You hear the word "permissiveness" being thrown around; right away, in so many people's minds, that translates to "promiscuity." But it just ain't so. You read about college administrators deploring the dangers of too much permissiveness on campus. The fact is that the biggest problems in this area are being experienced at colleges that are persisting in the old tight disciplines and trying to oversee every student activity that might hold any potential for sexual contact. It doesn't work, of course. At one school I know about, in the men's dorms, they're permitted to have female visitors only for one to two hours in the early evening. All that means is that if a couple wants to go to bed, they can't do it in the afternoon. On campuses with very little administrative supervision, there are no problems at all. Giving students latitude for personal freedom doesn't result in everybody jumping into the hay with everybody else. They're still just as selective about whom they have sex with. It's not promiscuity; it's just that private behavior is left up to the individual. I'm for that. Whether you agree or disagree with Madalyn Murray on the subject of atheism, you've got to admit she has a point when she said in her PLAYBOY interview, "Nobody's going to tell me I've got to get a license to screw." It's ludicrous to declare that it's wrong to have sex with anyone you're not married to. It's happening millions of times every day. If the laws against it were enforced, we'd have to build prisons to hold four fifths of the population.

HALEY: When you talk about the ludicrousness of laws and mores forbidding sex outside marriage, do you mean pre- or extramarital sex?

CARSON: Premarital. Some may consider it old-fashioned, but I feel that very few people can have sex elsewhere and still maintain a good marriage. It's tough enough to keep up a good, solid marital relationship even when both partners are completely faithful.

HALEY: How do you feel about such groups as the Sexual Freedom League?

CARSON: For some, they seem to work; but for me, I pass. I simply couldn't imagine engaging in anything like that. At the same time, I recognize there are all kinds of sexual deviations in this world; they are real *needs* for a lot of people, or they wouldn't be doing whatever they do. As long as it's this way, I think we ought to come to grips with the fact that there never can be any successful legislation against private, nonexploitive sex. I don't want to start sounding like some boy philosopher, but our sex laws seem to be predicated on the puritanical assumption that all sex—especially any variations from the marital norm—is dirty and should be suppressed. At the same time, our national obsession with sex seems to be predicated on the belief that sex constitutes the entire substance of the relationship between man and woman—and that's just as sick as feeling that it should have *no* part in human relationships. It's a damn healthy *part* of a good relationship, that's for sure. But it's just a part, and we seem bound and determined to make it unhealthy.

HALEY: How would you suggest we go about ridding society of these hang-ups?

CARSON: We need to start with the kids. We need to completely overhaul not only our own neurotic values but the abysmal sex education in our schools. When anthropologist Ashley Montagu was on my show not long ago, he said—and I couldn't have agreed with him more—that in any sexual relationship, adult or otherwise, married or unmarried, the key word is *responsibility*. We have to teach our young people to ask themselves, "Am I ready to assume the *responsibility* of a sexual relationship?" Even the clergy are openly saying this to youth now. They've quit, most of them, trying to sweep sex under the rug, as if it doesn't happen. Look at the high school girls who are getting pregnant. It's a little late to give them a good sex education. That's why I feel that it should start early, say in the fourth grade. I don't mean the whole clinical picture then, but a stress on the responsibility involved. When I was a kid, they called it "hygiene." They talked about sperm and vulva, and everybody giggled. No teacher ever said a word to us about the complex role of sex in our life with other people. Nobody told us it wasn't dirty, that it could be and should be pleasurable and that sex is a vital necessity to most people. It's the lack of this kind of open and honest education about sex that causes so many kids to grow up with sexual hang-ups. As it is, they're having to find things out by themselves—largely in rebellion against parental example. Kids are experimenting sexually and discovering that they don't wake up rotted or damned in the morning, like they've been told by their parents and their clergyman. Young people see adults wife-swapping and philandering, and yet piously maintaining that sex is sacred and counseling them hypocritically about the "sinfulness" or "immaturity" of intercourse outside marriage. Like their parents, kids flock to see James Bond and Derek Flint movies—outrageously antiheroic heroes who break all the taboos, making attractive the very things the kids are told they shouldn't do themselves. Well, they're figuring "Why *can't* I?" and they're not buying the adult advice anymore. Why should they? They're seeing a war that nobody wants, and the frightening prospect of a World War Three that would incinerate us all. If anybody is capable of doing that, it's the adults, not the young people. The vast majority of us don't want to face the fact that we're in the middle of a sweeping social revolution. In sex. In spiritual values. In opposition to wars no one wants. In opposition to Government big-brotherhood. In civil rights. In basic human goals. They're all facets of a general upheaval.

HALEY: One of the most conspicuous facets of that upheaval has been the exodus of thousands of young people out of society and into hippie communities. Do you feel they've chosen a viable alternative to the square society they find unlivable?

CARSON: No, I don't. They seem to be involved in some kind of search for identity, but I don't think they're going to find it—not in Haight-Asbury, anyway. Most of them, to me, seem lost and floundering. They've removed themselves from society, yet we see that they continue to expect society to provide them with necessities like medical help and food.

HALEY: Many of them are provided for by the Diggers. Don't you find that a reassuring evidence of self-reliance?

CARSON: How sustained do you think that will be? Aren't they doing it as a kind of kick? Let me see them continue looking after the hippies for a few *years*; then maybe I'll look at it differently.

HALEY: The hippie movement is linked in the public mind with usage of psychedelic drugs. How do you feel about this trend?

CARSON: I think it's one of the most frightening things youth, or anybody else, could possibly get involved in. We just don't have enough authoritative information yet about how dangerous it is to tamper with the mind—but even what little we do know should be enough to give them pause. Don't they know about the high ratio of genetic defects—known already, *this* early? These drugs are so new that research has just barely scratched the surface of the damages they can cause. Already, we know about chromosome debilitation. We see hospital emergency wards filling with young people, some not yet 20 years old, completely wigged out! Nobody ever tells them the facts. All they hear about is how they can take these chemicals and *expand* themselves, *find* themselves. Bullshit! Who have we yet seen emerge from the drug culture with any great new truths?

Timothy Leary? A brilliant man, obviously. But what's the philosophy he expounds? "Tune in, turn on, drop out." I wouldn't let him on my show. I wouldn't let him spout that nonsense.

HALEY: In condemning the use of chemical turn-ons, do you classify marijuana along with LSD and the other psychedelics?

CARSON: No, I don't put marijuana in the same bag with LSD or any of the hard narcotics. People are wrong when they say marijuana isn't addicting, though. I've known people who use it, known them all my adult life, and I know they are at least psychologically addicted. But it's just a mild stimulant, actually. And I think that the laws against its use are repressive out of all proportion. But that doesn't mean I'd want to try it myself—or any of the other hallucinogens: it's tough enough to navigate in this world *without* drugs. It may not seem like *much* of a world to the kids, but it's the only one we've got, and dropping out of it isn't going to solve anything.

HALEY: Many young people, of course, far from dropping out, have become activists in the student-protest movement, intent on changing society rather than abandoning it. How do you feel about this kind of rebellion?

CARSON: I feel that any of us has the right to dissent from what we don't like. But to what extreme do we wish to carry it? I think students ought to have the right to protest, but not to the point of anarchy—like that Berkeley situation. I got the impression that they often didn't know just what it was they were protesting against. Essentially, there was just a small, hard-core leadership throwing around words like "Freedom!" and "Rights!" What rights are they talking about? What about *other* people's rights? When they brandish four-letter placards and shout "Fuck!" at free-speech rallies, what the hell are they proving except how sophomoric they are? As for the burning of draft cards, I think it's stupid and pointless—though no more

stupid and pointless than the war itself. It's unlike any war
we were ever in. An undeclared war. An unpopular war.
And it keeps going on and on. I'm a father with a boy
coming out of high school next year, and I don't look
forward to his marching off over there. I don't think anybody dissenting against this war has any business being
called "un-American," but I still don't see burning draft
cards. I'm all for the right to dissent: lots of things need to
be changed. But I think we have to respect some boundaries, some limits, if we don't want to wreck the country. It
can happen a lot quicker than people think if too many
dissents and rebellions get out of perspective—and out of
hand.

HALEY: Do you think the Negro riots pose that kind of
danger?

CARSON: They certainly do—if we don't do something
to end them once and for all: and I don't mean with more
tanks. The big thing on television now is show after show,
special after special, about the reasons for the riots. Presidential commissions are formed, committees of mayors and
police chiefs convene, to investigate the causes and the
culprits. That's ridiculous. The *why* of the black revolution
is no great mystery. What's sparked it all, of course, is
desperation; and it's tragic that most whites can't seem to
grasp that simple fact. Negroes saw the Civil Rights Act
passed ten years ago—yet they haven't really seen much
since then in the way of enforcement. Why? Because too
many whites are in favor of integration and equality only
so long as it never touches them, only until some Negro
makes a move to buy into their block, until they find
themselves competing with Negroes for the same jobs. This
isn't to say that there hasn't been *some* progress in the past
decade; but it's been too little and too slow—just enough
to give Negroes a taste of freedom and equality, but not
enough to make either a reality. So the discontent and
frustration erupt into violence. It's understandable, but we

all know it's not going to solve anything. The exhortations of extremists like Rap Brown and Stokely Carmichael— urging Negroes to arm themselves and get Whitey—may not be designed to win friends and influence people, but they're not going to win freedom for the Negro, either. They're just going to result in massive retaliation by whites and ghastly carnage on both sides. So-called moderate leaders like Martin Luther King deplore these tactics, too—but what does he propose as an alternative? A guaranteed annual income of $3200 for all Negroes. He says it's a compensation, an overcompensation, to make up for what's been done to the Negro, for what the Negro has been deprived of, in this country. That's all well and good, but where's that money going to come from? If anybody is given any sum, somebody else has got to *provide* it. Black or white, if you're not working and I *am,* then if you receive $3200, *I'm* providing it. That's just replacing one injustice with another. Negro leaders call on the Government to appropriate 50 billion dollars to "erase the ghettos"—but that's not going to solve anything, either, not by itself. You could gut Harlem today and rebuild it tomorrow—but unless we do something to uproot the injustices that *created* the ghetto, all we'll have built, at a cost of billions, is a nicer cage. This obsessive emphasis on money, money, money—just money—simply isn't the answer. And neither is this pressure that's being applied by civil rights organizations, when a job is open for which a Negro and a white are equally qualified, to give that job automatically to the Negro, just *because* he's a Negro. Fundamentally, that's both condescending and subtly demeaning to that Negro. The problem isn't going to be solved by reverse favoritism any more than it is by giveaways. It comes down to just one basic word: *justice*—the same justice for *everyone*—in housing, in education, in employment and, most difficult of all, in human relations. And we're not going to accomplish that until all of us, black and white, begin to

temper our passion with compassion, until we stop thinking in terms of more guns and more money and start
listening to more realistic and responsible leaders—leaders
who will begin, however belatedly, to practice what they
preach: equality for all.

HALEY: Speaking of political leaders practicing what they
preach, what was your reaction to the widely publicized
transgressions of Congressman Adam Clayton Powell and
Senator Thomas Dodd?

CARSON: Well, whatever else they did, they became victims of an ethical double standard: the public's pious con-
demnation of its elected officials for conduct it condones in
private life. However unjustly and hypocritically, people
expect those in positions of public trust to be as spotless as
a minister. I certainly think we have the right to expect our
politicians to uphold their vow of office with honesty and
integrity—but only if we apply those same ethical standards to ourselves. As long as we shrug at the kind of
corporate espionage and financial hanky-panky that goes
on in business, as long as we take for granted the kind of
tax-loophole sleight of hand and expense-account padding
that goes on in everyday life, we'll get exactly the kind of
public officials we deserve.

HALEY: In the three years since President Johnson's re-
election, a great deal has been said and written about the
credibility gap—particularly in regard to the disparity between his professions of peaceful intentions in Vietnam
and his continued escalation of the war. How do you feel
about it?

CARSON: Well, I have to admit that at times I find myself
with the very uncomfortable feeling that the public isn't
getting all the information it ought to, that we're not being
told what's really happening—but not just in Vietnam. I'd
say it started, at least for me, with the U-2 incident. The
Government denied and denied and denied—and then the
truth came out. The most recent instance, of course, was

the revelation of CIA spying on college campuses by hiring students as undercover agents to report on so-called subversive activities. I get the feeling that George Orwell may have been right when he predicted that Big Brother might be watching all of us someday. It's not very reassuring about the ideals of those we entrust with the power to promote and protect the interests of this country.

HALEY: Let's talk about the *qualifications* of those who run for public office. How do you feel about the trend toward ex-show-business personalities in politics—men who, like George Murphy and Ronald Reagan, win elections almost entirely on the strength of their affable screen images?

CARSON: I couldn't care less about a candidate's previous occupation, as long as it was something respectable. I don't care if a hot-dog vendor gets to be President. He had to be voted in there by the people, who had other choices. We've had doctors, lawyers, automobile executives, even ex-haberdashers in public life and I haven't heard any complaints about *their* backgrounds. What makes them any more or less qualified than an actor? Why should a movie star be treated as if he's diseased or something just because he decides to run for office? He could have the *clap* and it wouldn't necessarily affect his abilities as a political leader. A politician should be judged by his performance in office, not by his former livelihood. If he does an incompetent job, the public can always throw him out. The night after Shirley Temple announced her candidacy for Congress, we did a skit on the show about "The Good Ship Lollipop" and had a little fun at her expense; but I certainly don't think the fact that she once played *Little Miss Marker* should disqualify her for office. Who knows? She might make a pretty good Congresswoman—certainly no worse than *some* we've seen.

HALEY: On your show a few months ago, New York's Governor Rockefeller suggested that you consider running

for Congress yourself—as a Republican candidate for the
Senate against Bobby Kennedy. What do you think of the
idea?

CARSON: No, thanks! Even if Governor Rockefeller
hadn't been saying that with tongue in cheek, I wouldn't
have the slightest interest in running for public office. I'd
rather make jokes about politicians than become one of
them. Once on the show, somebody asked me where tomorrow's *comedians* were coming from, and I told him,
based upon my recent observations, from the Democratic
and Republican parties.

HALEY: Your own origins as a comedian could hardly be
more unlike the familiar showbiz story that begins on the
Lower East Side and ends on the Great White Way, with
stop-offs en route on the vaudeville—burlesque—Borscht
Belt circuit. You've never talked much about your personal
background on the air or off, other than to say that you're
from the Midwest and that you were once an amateur
magician. Would you like to fill us in on the rest?

CARSON: Well—I was born in Corning, Iowa. No
cracks, please. I'm the product of a typical middle-class
upbringing. My father was then a lineman for the power
district; that means a guy who climbed up and down telephone poles. Later on, he became the power district's manager, and he has since retired. We moved around to
different small towns—places like Clarinda, Shenandoah,
Avoca. I started school in Avoca, Iowa. I think I was eight
when we moved to Norfolk, Nebraska, a town of about
10,000. I will never forget looking down on Main Street
from a fourth-floor hotel window there, thinking how high
up I was and marveling at so much traffic down in the
street.

I think it was that same year I first realized I could make
people laugh. I played Popeye in a school skit—you know,
imitating him, with that funny voice. My sister Catherine
and my brother Dick [now Carson's director] and I grew

on up through high school there in Norfolk. We had a big frame house in town. It was a typical small-town Midwestern boyhood. Dick and I fished and skinny-dipped in the Elkhorn river, and summers the family would vacation at a lake in Minnesota. I was at a friend's home one day when I picked up an old book I saw: *Hoffman's Book of Magic.* It described all the standard tricks and how to make some of the equipment yourself, and there was an ad for a kit of stuff from a mail-order place in Chicago. So I sent away for it, and the stuff came, and I couldn't think about anything else but making things and working with the magic. I ordered every catalog advertised and read them from cover to cover, and spent every quarter I could get for more stuff. Finally, one Christmas I got this magician's table with a black-velvet cover. I have never since seen anything more beautiful than that was to me. The next thing was ventriloquism. I bought a mail-order course, also from Chicago, for $15.

HALEY: When did you first realize you wanted to be an entertainer?

CARSON: I just can't say I ever *wanted* to become an entertainer; I already *was* one, sort of—around our house, at school, doing my magic tricks, throwing my voice and doing the Popeye impersonations. People thought I was funny; so I kind of took entertaining for granted. I was full of card tricks, too. Around the house, I was always telling anybody I saw, "Take a card—any card." It was inevitable that I'd start giving little performances. My first one was for my mother's bridge club. They thought I was great; and I *felt* great, making my mother so proud, you know? And after that I went on to give shows at Sunday-school parties, church socials, anywhere they'd have me. I was 14 when I earned my first fee for my act—three dollars from the Norfolk Rotary Club. Then I began to get a fee like that at picnics, county fairs, 4-H Clubs, service clubs, chambers of commerce. I was billed as "The Great Carsoni," wearing a cape my mother had sewed for me. In school, I was into every activity except sports. I went out for football, but the first time I ran with the ball and got tackled, the next thing I remember is the coach looking down in my face and asking if I was all right. He recommended that I give my full extracurricular time to other activities. I was in every school play, wrote a column for the school paper, everything. I got pretty good grades, but most of my effort was directed elsewhere.

By 1943, when I graduated from Norfolk High, I was making pretty fair pin money with my act. Funny thing, though, I still didn't have any intention of entertaining as a serious career. I was still very small town in my outlook. It would be another three or four years before I'd find out that the Catskills weren't a dance team. I was still playing with the idea of becoming a psychiatrist, an engineer or a journalist. And I had decided on engineering when I entered college. But the War was on, you know, and I was accepted for a V-12 program that would get me a Naval Air commission; but they sent me to Columbia University's midshipman school instead; there just weren't any flying training openings then. I got my ensign's commission and went to the Pacific on the battleship *Pennsylvania*. I had dragged a footlocker of gear for my act with me and I entertained the officers and men every chance I got. In the comedy bits, mostly, I'd knock officers; the enlisted men loved that. Later, when I was at Guam, I did the same thing there.

Finally, when I got out, I entered the University of Nebraska, this time trying journalism. I thought it would help me learn to write comedy. But that who-when-where-why-what bit couldn't have bored me more, so I switched to radio and speech. It was while I was at the university that I got my first radio job for ten dollars a week at the local station, WOW, for playing in a comedy Western called *Eddie Sosby and the Radio Rangers*. It came on three mornings a week and I had to get permission to be 15 minutes late those mornings for my Spanish class. Then, in my senior year, I did a thesis on comedy. I analyzed the best comics then performing and taped excerpts of their performances to illustrate things like timing and sequence, building punch lines, recognition devices and running gags, things like that. Comedians like Fibber McGee and Molly, Jack and Mary Benny, Rochester, Ozzie and Harriet, Milton Berle and Bob Hope. When I got my A.B. degree in 1949, I went straight to my first job, $50 a week for doing anything and everything at WOW. I did commercials, news, station breaks, weather reports, everything.

I guess the next thing was my first marriage—to Jody. We'd been going together several years. Soon my first son was born, Chris. Meanwhile, I got a radio show, *The Squirrel's Nest* I called it, and I picked up $25 on the side for magic acts I'd do anywhere I could. In Omaha, I remember, there was a group campaigning to get rid of pigeons, which were accused of defacing city hall. I came on my radio show with "Equal Time for Pigeons," imitating the birds cooing their side of the story and pleading for mercy; we won a reprieve: The campaigning was dropped. Doing just about anything a Jack-of-all-trades in radio could do, it was almost automatic that I would eventually go on WOW-TV.

All the time, I kept thinking in the back of my mind about where I was headed, in a career way. I was getting along well enough where I was, but at the same time, I knew that I could never go very far as long as I stayed in Nebraska. The action and the opportunities were all either in New York or California. So I got a cameraman friend to shoot a half-hour film of me doing a little bit of everything I could do. When a vacation came up, I packed the wife and kids in our beat-up Olds, with a U-Haul trailer, and we took off for California. When we arrived in San Francisco, I knocked at every radio and TV door; at most of them, I couldn't even get inside. They'd say, "No openings, sorry."

So we went on into Los Angeles—looking like something out of *Grapes of Wrath* driving down Sunset Boulevard. Same kind of hearty welcome.

But finally, a childhood family friend, Bill Brennan, who had gone into radio sales in L.A., successfully recommended me for a staff-announcer job that had opened at KNXT, a local station. I went there and did everything except sweep out the place. When I could find the time, like on nights when I was disc jockeying, while the record was playing, I was sitting there in the booth putting together an idea for a TV show. See, I had made an agreement with myself when I got to L.A.—that if I didn't have my own show after a year, I was going to move on to New York. I was never one who believed in "waiting for the breaks." I believe we make our own breaks. Well, the CBS people finally looked at my idea and gave me a spot they had open locally on Sunday afternoons. You won't believe the budget—for each show, $25! I wrote my own scripts, mimeographed them and acted in them—and got pretty fair newspaper notices. On one show, I had a friend rush past the camera on the air and I announced, "That was my guest today, Red Skelton." Well, Skelton heard about it and really did turn up for one of my shows. Then some others did, including Fred Allen. Skelton and I really got on well, and finally he offered me a job writing for his show. I grabbed it.

I guess you'd call it the proverbial big break when the telephone rang one day and somebody told me Skelton had been hurt in a rehearsal. He was supposed to walk through one of those breakaway doors, but the door hadn't broken and Red had been knocked cold about 90 minutes before showtime. I had always been doing bits and cracking gags around the office and they wanted to know if I could make it to the station and go on for Red. I don't know how I got there in time, but I did. And I made cracks about Red getting hurt and said, "The way I fell out here, I think Red's doctor ought to be doing this show." Well, it came off all

right. I got good notices. And that got me my next job—
The Johnny Carson Show. That was my first *big* lesson. It
ran out its contracted 39 weeks in 1955 and then folded.
That's where I learned that if you get too many cooks
involved, that if you don't keep control, you're going to
bomb out, and there's nobody to blame but yourself.

HALEY: Will you explain what you mean by that?

CARSON: I mean that it was primarily through my own
naïveté that the show failed. I had built the show initially
around a format of low-key skits and commentary on topical subjects—something rather like the *Tonight* show. We
got good reviews, but the network people felt the ratings
should have been higher, and I let them start telling me
what to do. "We've got to make the show *important,*" they
told me. How would they go about doing that? With
chorus girls! They were going to make me into Jackie
Gleason! I'd come rushing on in a shower of balloons, with
chorus girls yipping, "Here comes the *star* of the show,
Johnny Carson!" And the rest followed in that vein. I let
myself be a poor imitation, and that's sure, swift death for
any entertainer. But I think if nobody ever fails, he never
has successes. The show flopped—but to me only in the
sense that it went off the air after 39 weeks. I learned the
hard way that you have to go with your decisions.

HALEY: Do you consider that show your greatest failure?

CARSON: Professionally it was. Personally, no. That was
when I was divorced from my first wife. That's the lowest
I've ever felt, the worst personal experience of my life. We'd
been married ten years—since college, in fact. And children were involved—three sons. I think that's the worst
guilt hang-up you can have, when children are involved. But
divorce sometimes is the only answer. I think it's almost
immoral to keep on with a marriage that's really bad. It just
gets more and more rotten and vindictive and everybody
gets more and more hurt. There's not enough honesty
about marriage, I think. I wish more people would face the

truth about their marital situations. I get sick of that old rationalization, "We're staying together because of the children." Kids couldn't be more miserable living with parents who can't stand each other. They're far better off if there's an honest, clean divorce. I'm happy to notice that my boys don't seem to be negatively affected by mine. I think they're getting along fine. I've got a very good marriage now. For a long time, I went around feeling guilty about the failure of the first one—but you can't go on forever like that, just nursing your hurts. Some friends here in New York had been talking with me about Joanne before I ever saw her. Finally, I telephoned her and we made a date over the phone. I met her with her father at Eddie Condon's and we hit it off great, right away, and it went on from there.

HALEY: After the low point you described, when *The Johnny Carson Show* went off the air, did things begin to improve professionally?

CARSON: Not by a long shot. I still had a lot more to learn—this time about the people who are supposed to give a performer so much *help* in this business. There I was: My show was closed. I was out of work. That kind of news flies throughout the show-business world with the speed of light. You're out. You're dead. But I've got a family to keep eating and every day I'm expecting to hear something from the agency that handled me. But I hear nothing. So I go over there. "Look," I told them, "I can get myself some kind of an act together. Get a couple of writers to work with me." You know what they said? "Sorry, Johnny, we can't do that." So I went home and wrote the act myself, and I went out personally and peddled it and finally got myself a date in Bakersfield at a place called The Maison Jaussaud, making $400 a week. But I was still naïve. I was hoping that some of the top agency people would come to see me. They didn't. They sent two junior members who sat at a table, then left. Nothing. Zero.

This was about the time I dropped back financially until

I had to borrow from my father. I decided I had to go to New York. I couldn't do any worse there and I might do better. So I borrowed more, from a bank that was good enough to let me have it. And in New York, finally I got the chance to go on *Who Do You Trust?*. Now, do you want to guess what happened? When I get solid on that show, really doing all right, here come this agency's top guys. Big deal—old buddy-buddy, let bygones be bygones, no hard feelings, let's forget the past. "How about our representing you again? We've got it all figured out how to shoot you straight to the top." I listened until they finished their spiel and then I said, "Thank you, no, gentlemen. Where were you when I needed you?" Anyway, I finally went with another agency, MCA, one of the giants. I was doing fine now, getting the treatment they call "servicing the client." I remember one day I was getting ready to leave their office to do the show, and this agency man makes moves to go with me. I asked him, "What are you doing?" He said. "Don't you want me to go to the show with you?" I told him I thought I could make it alone. What I *felt* like telling him was, "You want to do something for me? Iron my shirts." I don't even like to think about it. But now, I don't even have an agency. MCA dissolved, you know. I've got a lawyer who handles most of my affairs. I've *learned.* Agencies play the percentages. You make it, they'll take ten percent. When I needed 'em, nobody was there. I'll never forget it. I'm just telling it the way it is. If somebody wants to call that being a loner, if somebody wants to call that being vindictive, then so be it!

HALEY: How did the break come from *Who Do You Trust?* to the *Tonight Show?*

CARSON: In my first four years on *Who Do You Trust?*. I'd been offered all kinds of situation-comedy shows, but I had turned them down for one or another reason. And I had been doing guest spots, and I had filled in for Paar on *Tonight,* and I had done pretty well as his replacement. It

was NBC that came up with the offer for me to replace
Paar permanently. I turned it down, cold; not many people
know that. I just wasn't sure I could cut it. I just didn't feel
I could make that jump from a half-hour daily quiz show
to doing an hour and 45 minutes every night. I was doing
fine in daytime TV; I was solid and secure. And I felt I'd
be stupid to try to replace Jack Paar. But I kept sitting in
for him. And then, some months later, NBC made their
offer again; Jack was nearer to leaving the show. Somebody
had to replace him. My manager got on me, insisting that
I owed myself the opportunity of reaching the big night
audience. And NBC said they would wait until I finished
my contract on *Who Do You Trust?*. While all this was
going on, I was gradually building more confidence in
myself—the more I thought about it. Nobody could tell
me; I had to tell myself I could do it. And finally I did; I
accepted the offer. Everyone I knew had some advice after
that. One group told me I was nuts to try replacing Paar,
but that made me all the more determined. Others became
instant producers and told me, "Here's how to handle that
show. . . ." That bugged me; I'd been through that in
California and lost a good show because of it. I had cab
drivers, waiters, everybody giving me advice.

Two things were in the back of my head: One was that
I wasn't going to be any imitation of Jack Paar; I was going
to be Johnny Carson. The other thing was that I wanted the
show to make the most of being the last area in television
that the medium originally was supposed to be—live, immediate entertainment. I knew it wasn't going to be any
sauntering in and sitting at a desk and that's all. The main
thing in my mind that I had going for me was that I'd done
nearly everything you could in the industry—but at the
same time I knew that thinking that way was a danger. If
I went out there with every critic waiting, and if I did
everything I knew how to do, it would look like deliberate
showing off, like trying to say, "Hey, look at me—I'm so

versatile!" I had to fight that natural temptation to go out there and make some big impression. Finally, I decided that the best thing I could do was forget trying to do a lot of preplanning. I didn't want to come out with something that smacked of a month's preparation, because I wasn't going to be able to keep that up every night. It all boiled down to just going out there and being my natural self and seeing what would happen.

HALEY: What happened, of course, was one of the most remarkable successes in television history. But you mentioned going out there and being your natural self. Do you, really?

CARSON: Are we back to that—my reputation for being cold and aloof, for being a loner and living in a shell and all that crap? Look, I'm an entertainer; I try to give the public what it wants while I'm on the screen, and I'm completely sincere about it. If I don't happen to be a laughing boy off the screen, that doesn't make me a hypocrite or a phony. In any case, what I am and what I do on my own, it seems to me, is nobody's business but mine. As long as I don't commit any crimes, you have no right to judge me except by my performance as a professional. On that level, you're welcome to think whatever you want about me. But there's only one critic whose opinion I really value, in the final analysis: Johnny Carson. I have never needed any entourage standing around bolstering my ego. I'm secure. I know exactly who and what I am. I don't need to be told. I make no apologies for being the way I am. I'm not going to run around crying that I'm misunderstood. I play my life straight—the way I see it. I'm grateful to audiences for watching me and for enjoying what I do— but I'm not one of those who believe that a successful entertainer is *made* by the public, as is so often said. You become successful, the way I see it, only if you're good enough to deliver what the public enjoys. If you're not, you won't have any audience; so the performer really has more to do with his success than the public does.

As for myself, I've worked ever since I was a kid with a two-bit kit of magic tricks trying to improve my skills at entertaining whatever public I had—and to make myself ready, whenever the breaks came, to entertain a wider and more demanding public. Entertainment is like any other major industry; it's cold, big business. The business end wants to know one thing: Can you do the job? If you can, you're in, you're *made*; if you can't, you're out.

I knock myself out for the public—five shows a week, 90 minutes a show; and most of every day goes to working on that 90 minutes. It takes more out of me than manual labor would, and I simply won't give any more of myself than that. I demand my right to a private life, just as I respect that right for everybody else. The *Tonight* staff knocks themselves out with me; then they go their way, I go mine, and we get along fine. I make the major decisions. That's my responsibility.

I'm doing the best I know how. I've put my whole life into whatever you see on that screen. But whenever the day comes that I think it's my time to go, I'll be the first to tell the network to get somebody else in that chair. And when I do, they'll be saying, "Who could follow Carson?"—just like they said, "Who could follow Paar?" Well, believe me, somebody can—and will. The public is fickle, and you can be replaced, no matter how good you are. Until that happens, I'm going to go on doing my best. I like my work and I hope you do, too—but if you don't, I really couldn't care less. Take me or leave me—but don't bug me. That's the way I am. That's me. That's it.

JIM BROWN

*A Candid Conversation
with the Football Superstar
Turned Actor and Civil Rights Activist*

ALEXIS URBA

*Among professional-football fullbacks, Jim Brown remains
the legendary standard by which all others are measured. At
six feet, two, and 230 pounds, Brown was the most powerful
and elusive running back ever to play the game. With a
massive neck, steely arms and thighs thicker than most
men's waists, he could drag tacklers with him as he ran, send
them flying with a straight-arm, sidestep them with his
misdirective footwork and outdistance them with his flash-
ing speed. During nine seasons with the Cleveland Browns,
this gut strength and incredible agility—combined with a
juggernaut determination to win—netted him 15 N.F.L.*

records that most sportswriters agree won't be topped easily
or soon. Before a budding alternate career as a movie actor
and militant involvement in the race struggle provoked his
abrupt resignation from pro ball in 1966, Brown had
crashed his way to a record lifetime total of 126 touchdowns
and led the league in yards gained for eight of his nine
seasons, piling up a whopping 12,312 yards in the process—
also an all-time record.

Because repeated and jarring contact with bone-crushing
opposing linemen is one of the position's occupational haz-
ards, injuries have sidelined every other notable running
back in pro-football history. But Brown's superb physical
condition and playing ability made him a unique exception
to that rule—despite many a lineman's rapacious attempt
to put him on the bench, if not in the hospital; and he gave
them plenty of opportunity to try, by carrying the ball in
roughly 60 percent of all offensive plays. An adept ball
carrier off the field, too, he led the 1962 revolt of Cleveland
players that successfully brought about the ouster of their
brilliant but inflexible head coach, Paul Brown. The following year, as if to vindicate the uprising, Jim Brown became
football's sole runner to pass the mile mark in a single
season—a feat veteran sportswriter Myron Cope called
"perhaps the most incredible sports statistic of our time."

Brown's phenomenal prowess led the editor of Sport magazine to label him the "Babe Ruth of football," who "sits
alone, indestructible, superhuman." It also gave him the
additional—and more tangible—honor of taking home the
biggest pay check in pro ball, an estimated $65,000 a year.
But the crown didn't rest easily on Brown's head. Despite
lavish kudos from the press and considerable nationwide
attention, his natural reserve remained undented; to the
public and most teammates alike, he remained icily aloof.
The first rumblings of his eventual abdication came as early
as 1964, with the publication of his autobiography, "Off My
Chest." In it, Brown demonstrated that his hard-driving,

no-nonsense brand of football was a graphic metaphor for his life style: He appraised various football personalities with a brutal candor that left many bruised and angry; and he revealed an attitude of racial militance—further explored here—that added a facet of passionate social commitment to his already complex image. Unwillingly and briefly, Brown adopted yet another persona in 1965. In the period of a few months, two girls accused him of molesting them. One refused to press charges, but the other took her case to court. After Brown was acquitted, she tried again with a paternity suit—and lost that, too.

Not surprisingly, today's controversial Jim Brown is the product of a diverse and paradoxical background. Born on an island off the Georgia coast, he spent his first years in the care of a great-grandmother. At the age of seven, he moved north to Long Island to live with his divorced mother, a domestic worker. Always big and strong for his age, Brown applied his talents more in the street than in school and soon fought his way to "war lord" status in the Gaylords, a teenage gang. If local officials hadn't quickly recognized his rare athletic abilities, the Jim Brown story might have been another "Rebel Without a Cause"; but they turned him on to sports, and by Brown's senior year, athletic events at Manhasset High School were drawing overflow crowds who came to see him in action—in football, basketball, baseball, track and lacrosse. Shattering records in nearly every sport he tried, Brown was graduated with full-scholarship bids from 42 colleges. Ironically, he selected Syracuse, where Brown claims he wasn't really wanted—for reasons that had more to do with race than with football. Still on the fifth-string team after his freshman season, he crashed the varsity ranks as a sophomore, went on to become a Syracuse legend—and began to be called the greatest all-round athlete since Jim Thorpe. Then, turning pro with the Cleveland Browns, he set—even in his rookie year—new professional records.

During the off seasons, Brown began to dabble in the myriad pursuits that finally lured him away from football. He tackled show business, first as host of a modest daily radio show in Cleveland, then as a Negro cavalry trooper in "Rio Conchos," a movie Western. He broke into the business world by traveling and interning as a marketing executive for the Pepsi-Cola company. And in a move coinciding with occasional outings as a commentator on closed-circuit theater telecasts of boxing matches, he allied himself with Main Bout, Inc., a sports-promotion agency. Main Bout eventually handled the fights of the controversial and racially militant Muhammad (Cassius Clay) Ali, and Brown's association with the firm gave further flower to his own growing image as a hard-line racial activist: Some of his colleagues at Main Bout were Black Muslims. Brown disclaimed membership in the sect but said that he felt its views voiced the true feelings of most Negroes.

Amid the national controversy in 1966 that saw a Muhammad Ali fight blocked out of arenas across the country, Brown quietly signed to play a role in his second motion picture, "The Dirty Dozen," to be filmed in England that summer. He planned to return in time for fall football practice; but in England, heavy rains kept delaying the filming. Soon the Cleveland Browns were at practice— without their star fullback. Pressed by sportswriters, team owner Art Modell announced a daily fine until Brown returned; but Brown finally flanked the penalty with the bombshell announcement that he was quitting the game. Fans refused to believe it, thinking he would join up again once the film was finished. Though Brown did come back to Cleveland after completing the movie, it was only to reaffirm his retirement and announce that he intended to spend his time helping his race—by heading the National Negro Industrial and Economic Union, an organization he had founded. More motion-picture offers were in the works as *well, he added. Jim Brown was done with football for good—but not with the limelight.*

In the following months, he enlisted nearly 100 famous Negro sports figures to help him with his fledgling N.N.I.E.U. and opened offices in several cities across the country. When "The Dirty Dozen" opened and Negroes in unprecedented numbers flocked to see him—aptly cast as a racially militant soldier—it became clear that Brown's burgeoning screen fame showed every promise of rivaling his legend on the gridiron. At this point in his new career, we sent Alex Haley to interview the many-sided athlete-actor. "When I met him in Cleveland," reports Haley about the first of their many encounters, stretching over several weeks, "I soon discovered that his life now is probably more strenuous than when he was playing football. Between movies, he hustles through a 16-hour day that includes time at home, in his N.N.I.E.U. office, at public appearances and on the golf course—where he chafes if his scores reach the upper 70s. To keep up the pace, he burns a tremendous amount of fuel: I saw him consume two pounds of barbecued ribs as an appetizer while a four-pound T-bone broiled. Dessert was a quart of ice cream topped by a can of peaches.

"Brown tried to concentrate on my questions, but his Cleveland schedule—and his characteristic initial wariness—made it impossible. We agreed to meet again later in California, where he would be filming his third picture, the $8,000,000 Cinerama production 'Ice Station Zebra,' in which he co-stars with Rock Hudson. During our meetings in his dressing room, he proved appreciably warmer and more candid. Returning from camera calls, he relaxed as easily as he once did upon leaving the field after a game. Dropping his well-known mask of impassivity, he became amiable and animated, especially when he was talking about football. When racial matters came up, however, he turned dead serious and often punctuated his pungent remarks with a baleful glare and a meaty forefinger jabbed in my direction.

"Despite the long shooting days, Brown rarely went out at night, choosing instead to stay in his room and study his script. On weekends, though, he roamed, visiting friends like Lee Marvin and Bill Cosby, going into Los Angeles ghetto areas to talk to the kids there and putting in as much time as possible at his Los Angeles N.N.I.E.U. office. One day we got to the office and found a small crowd there being regaled by Muhammad Ali. Ali playfully made a lightning feint as Brown entered; in mock seriousness, Brown—who had once turned down an offer of $150,000 to become a fighter— invited him out back. Muttering dire warnings, Ali followed Brown outside, where they touched fingertips and whirled into a flashing, furious, open-handed bout. Head down, Brown would probe for an opening, while Ali danced, dodged and swatted back. Then they stopped as suddenly as they had begun, both sweat-soaked and laughing. In spite of the schoolyard levity they maintained throughout, I couldn't help feeling they were testing each other, secretly wondering what might happen in a ring."

The interview ended when Brown left for San Diego to do scenes parachuting from a plane to rendezvous with an atomic submarine for his role in "Ice Station Zebra." He would fly next to Bombay to film "The Year of the Cricket." Beyond that lay a three-year contract with MGM that involved several more motion pictures. In one of them, "Dark of the Sun," which premiers next month, Brown co-stars with Rod Taylor as a black mercenary involved in the Congolese uprising. No other athlete in history had ever managed such a successful transition to show business. We began by asking him about it.

HALEY: What's your reaction to Lee Marvin's observation about your performance in *The Dirty Dozen*: "Well, Brown's a better actor than Sir Laurence Olivier would be as a member of the Cleveland Browns"?

BROWN: That's great! I never heard that one before. Lee's wild! I love him! But about what he said: Look, my parts so far haven't really demanded too much of me as an actor; I know that and I'm not trying to rush myself. What I feel I'm not ready for, I stay away from. At this point I'm relying upon my presence; I'm concentrating on acting *natural*; and I'm soaking up every technique I can handle from the pros. I think everyone I work with can see that I'm trying to apply myself, and they go out of their way to teach me new things. So you might call it on-the-job training. Of course, I've always tried to be good at anything I get involved in. That's another way of saying that eventually I hope to be regarded as a good professional actor—I mean by other actors. They're the best critics.

HALEY: As a longtime pro in another field, how did you feel about being the rookie of the cast in *The Dirty Dozen*?

BROWN: I felt that was to my advantage. Everybody knew I had everything to learn, and they knocked themselves out helping me; so I probably learned faster than most rookies in films. The role I played helped me, too. I was Robert Jefferson, a college-trained soldier condemned to death for murdering a white racist who had brutally assaulted me. I strongly identified with Jefferson. I could feel and understand why he did what he did. I just made myself Robert Jefferson in my mind. And Bob Aldrich, the director, gave me every break he could. He rarely talked with me, but when he saw me getting uptight, he would say things that were constructive and calming. Even so, the pressure would build in me—you know, the doubts about whether I was really good enough to be there with them. But when Kenny Hyman, our producer, brought me a script for another movie, offering me a part, that was a sign of approval that meant a lot.

HALEY: While the picture was being made, a rumor circulated that you weren't getting along with several members of the cast. Was there any truth to that?

BROWN: None. I got on with that cast as w̶
have with any group in my whole life. Went
with most of them; never any arguments at al
must have been manufactured by press agent
ning to find out that press agents are an ᴏᴄᴄᴜᴘ--
hazard in this business—their imaginations. This particular story got started in Leonard Lyons' column, that Lee
Marvin and I left a party at Sidney Lumet's and that we had
a bloody fight to the finish outside. It was completely
fabricated! In fact, Lee and I had a beautiful relationship.

HALEY: Marvin has said there is an acting void that you
can fill, especially among Negroes: "He's seemingly more
believable to the average Negro than guys like Poitier."
And director Robert Aldrich has said, "There isn't another
Negro actor around quite like Brown. Poitier, Belafonte or
Ossie Davis aren't Brown's style." Do you think they're
right?

BROWN: I don't know; maybe I *am* shaping a new movie
personality. I'm just being myself; that's all I know how to
do. I'm sure not taking anything away from any of those
you named—and others like James Earl Jones. But there's
a crying need for more Negro actors, because for so long,
ever since the silent screen, in fact, the whole world has
been exposed to Negroes in stereotype roles. Have you ever
been to any Negro theater with a movie going, with a
Negro in it? Well, you can just *feel* the tension of that
audience, pulling for this guy to do something good, something that will give them a little pride. That's why I feel so
good that Negroes are finally starting to play roles that
other Negroes, watching, will feel proud of, and respond to,
and identify with, and feel *real* about, instead of being
crushed by some Uncle Tom on the screen making a fool
of himself. You're not going to find any of us playing Uncle
Tom's anymore. In my first picture, *Rio Conchos,* I played
a cowboy who fought not only Indians but white guys, too.
And I played a realistic Negro in *The Dirty Dozen.* And in

this picture I'm shooting now, *Ice Station Zebra,* I play a
Marine captain on an atomic submarine. It's not a part
written for a Negro, or for any race in particular; it's a part
with no racial overtones whatever. That's why I can say,
before this picture is even released, that a lot of Negroes are
going to come to see it.

HALEY: How did you get the part?

BROWN: Robert O'Brien, MGM's president, was very
happy with my *Dirty Dozen* performance and he discovered that unprecedented Negro audiences were attending.
He said, "Hell, this is beautiful all around!" He called me
about five one morning and said if there was a part I could
play in *Ice Station Zebra,* he'd have me in Hollywood the
next day. A white actor had been tentatively slated for this
part, but he wasn't signed, because he was still negotiating
for something else; and the next day I was in wardrobe. In
fact, they went over the whole script to be certain that no
racial overtones would occur because a black man was in
the role. I dug the part not only for that reason but because,
again, I could personally identify. Marine Captain Anders
is my kind of officer—a *man,* self-sufficient as hell, bad,
uptight, ready to do a hell of a job. He doesn't care who
likes him or who doesn't, so he doesn't try to be liked. He's
a terrific soldier, very tough on his men, but fair, and
anything he asks them to do, he can do better.

HALEY: Have you gained any more confidence in yourself
as an actor since *Dirty Dozen?*

BROWN: I think so. It's just like football: I had to get that
first play under my belt before I'd stop trembling. I still get
keyed up, but I keep it under control. And when I'm called
to go before the cameras, like I used to do before a game,
I just cut off my emotions and go act out whatever the
script calls for me to do. The only difference is that in
football, we didn't have a specific script; the other side
wouldn't have followed it, anyway.

HALEY: What made you decide to quit football so

abruptly at the height of your career? Was it the movie offers?

BROWN: Look—I loved playing football. It did a lot for me; it changed my life. Otherwise, I could have been some kind of gangster today; I led a gang when I was a kid, you know. But, taking a realistic look at my life and my ambitions, at the things I wanted to achieve, it was time for a change, see? I find this new career just as satisfying, and even more rewarding financially, and something I can keep at far longer than I could have lasted in football. Besides that, my other activities are benefited, especially working to increase Negro participation in the country's economic life. That's very important to me. Sure, sometimes when the weather's crisp outside and I'm watching a game on television, it's hard not to be out there with the ball. But still, leaving the game when I did is probably as lucky as anything that ever happened to me. Of course, I had some concerns about giving up football's certainties for the movies' *un*certainties. But the hard fact is that I feel I quit just in time. I got out still in my prime and without any injuries. I got out before I ever had to do like I've seen so many guys—sitting hunched over on the bench, all scarred and banged up, watching some hot young kid out there in their place; and, worse than that, just wondering if they'd slowed down so badly they'd never be called to go into the game anymore. You see, I believe a man grows up. He discovers there are other worlds. Basically, I'm a guy who has to progress or I feel I'm stagnating—I don't mean just materially, but as a person. My interests have expanded in various areas—in racial relations, my various investments and, of course, my new movie career, but most of all in my sense of responsibility to my people. For the rest of my life I am committed to taking part in the black struggle that's going on in this country.

HALEY: Another of the factors involved in your decision to retire, according to reports, was a contractual dispute with Browns owner Art Modell. Four years before, he had supported you in yet another dispute—against Cleveland coach Paul Brown. Acceding to an ultimatum from you and several other players, Modell finally fired Brown at the end of the 1962 season. Why did you insist on his dismissal?

BROWN: Well, first of all, it wasn't any *vendetta,* at least no personal kind of thing against Brown. At one stage in his career, Paul Brown was a genius; he set new trends in the game. But the man's ego was such that when other coaches openly stole his ideas, and added new twists, Paul Brown simply could not, or would not, change and adapt to the new styles of playing. And we players increasingly saw this. Our professional lives, our careers, were involved. We happened not to be the brainless automatons he wanted his players to act like. So we did what we had to do—in what we saw as the best interests of the players, the owner and the fans. And later events proved us right. That's really all there was to it.

HALEY: What were some of the adjustments you felt Paul Brown should have made but didn't?

BROWN: Well, the major thing, we felt, was that Paul immensely favored a ground game, with intricately devised through-the-line plays. And in passing, he liked only short passes. That's just two major areas where his refusal to change cost us games we could have won. The game had accelerated very fast, see, until any coach not utilizing long passes or frequent touchdown-run threats was bound to become obsolete. Paul would only very rarely approve our trying the long-bomb pass, which other teams used often. And I was the Browns' main runner. Man, I *loved* to run— especially on those outside sweeps; that was my major touchdown potential. But Paul refused to give me enough wide-running sweep plays. When we saw ourselves continually losing when we *knew* we could have won, it just took heart out of us. We lost that burning desire to win that a team has to have if it's *going* to win. How do you think we felt coming off a field beaten, and all of us there in the locker room knowing that the tremendous power we represented simply wasn't being used to its capacity? I don't like to knock the man, but truth is truth, that's all. If he had just been willing to compromise, to adjust only a little, he could have remained the top coach in pro ball. Anyway, some other players and I finally told Art Modell that unless the coaching methods changed, we'd either insist on being traded or quit. Well, any owner of a team is first and foremost a businessman. That next January—this was 1963—Art announced that Blanton Collier was replacing Paul Brown as head coach. We went into the new season a thinking, working team again. I had my best year and we took second place in the Eastern Conference. Then, in 1964, we won the league championship.

HALEY: And you won the Hickok belt as the year's best professional athlete. In your entire pro career, you accumulated 126 touchdowns among your 15 all-time N.F.L. records. Do you think anyone ever will equal or better those records?

BROWN: I think every record I've ever made will get wiped out, ultimately. Once people declared that my Syracuse records would never be broken; then Ernie Davis— the late Ernie Davis—broke all but three of them; and then Floyd Little broke all but one of Ernie's records. Records are made to be broken. You remember the four-minute mile? The ten-second dash? The seven-foot high jump? Always, you're going to have young guys coming along and improving. That's great, the way it needs to be, because that's progress, that's advancement. My personal records were never that important to me, anyway. As a matter of fact, I almost hated to break a record when I was playing, because I always felt I was becoming more and more a statistic in people's minds than a human being. But I never dwell on what I did; it's history now. I have a lot of pleasant memories of a game that was a good part of my life.

HALEY: Among the records you set, none seems likely to last longer than the 12,312 yards you gained in nine pro seasons—a large proportion of which you amassed in the spectacular sweep runs you made famous. Was the sweep your favorite play?

BROWN: Well, like I said, I loved those long sweeps— but any play that gained yardage was a good play as far as I was concerned. Most plays, you understand, aren't for long runs; they're just after a crucial few yards, maybe one yard, maybe even *inches,* for a first down. That's your power plays, which can be just as important as some flashy run. But you say I made the sweep runs famous; that's very flattering, but the fact is that I never would have been able to make them without a lot of company—without guys like John Wooten and Gene Hickerson, the Browns' guards, to clear a path for me. Once they did, once I was through the hole and into the other team's secondary, that's when I was on my own. Then I had a man-to-man situation going—me against them; that's when I'd go into my bag of stuff. They're in trouble now—I'm in their territory; 55 things are happening at once; I'm moving, evaluating their possible moves, trying to outthink and outmaneuver them, using my speed, quickness and balance. I've always had very good balance. I'm ready to use a straight-arm, high knee-action or shoulder-dipping. There's the full or half straight-arm, or just the forearm, then the shoulder. In the leg maneuvers, I'd "limber-leg," offering one leg, then jerking it away when somebody grabbed. Or high-stepping would keep a pair of tacklers from getting both legs at once. In that secondary, it was just a step-by-step thing, using brain-work and instinct; but sometimes it got down to just out-and-out strength and brute force.

HALEY: The great linebacker Sam Huff was once asked how to stop you. He said: "All you can do is grab hold, hang on and wait for help." Detroit's tackle Alex Karras was even more graphic about it: "Give each guy in the line an ax." Why did they have so much trouble tackling you?

BROWN: I'm the one that had trouble getting past *them.* You just don't run over guys like them; I had to try and fake them some way, like maybe drop a shoulder and struggle to get by. Some guys, of course, if they were small enough, I'd just run over them. When we hit, I'd dip a shoulder, hitting his pads, and cross either with a straight-arm to the helmet or a clubbing forearm.

HALEY: Speaking of that forearm, Matt Hazeltine of the Forty Niners has said: "Brown really shivers you. I wonder how many KOs he would have scored when there were no face masks." Did opposing players ever try to retaliate for all the clubbings you dealt out on the field?

BROWN: Oh, sure. If you're a successful, aggressive back, a scoring danger, roughings are a routine part of the game. But it still got pretty hairy sometimes. The biggest thing I resented was guys going after my face—fingers under my mask, after my eyes. That's the only thing that ever brought me close to turning chicken. I would get up, not dizzy, but I still couldn't get my eyes clear. You know how you blink and your eyes still won't clear? One time I remember, a Philadelphia Eagles defense man jammed his hand up under my face mask; I felt him clawing for my eyes and I got my teeth in that hand. Man, I tried to eat it up! I'll bet it hasn't run under any more masks since then. Later, there was a protest about my biting him. I said, "Look, I can't bite anybody *through* a mask, can I? Any hand under there was under there for some purpose, right?" There was no fine.

HALEY: On two occasions, you became involved in fights on the field. What made you blow your usual cool?

BROWN: Well, once was when the Giants' Tom Scott and I punched it out that time in Cleveland Stadium; the reason, again, was my eyes. In a Giant game two weeks before, I'd been hit and gouged in the eye seven or eight times, until

I was half blinded for the next couple of weeks. I went to the eye doctor and got drops and stuff, and I made up my mind that if anybody ever again came deliberately close to my eyes, I would retaliate in spades. So when I felt Scott's fingers grabbing for me, I just swung on him and we had that little scuffle. It really wasn't much of a fight, but we both were put out of the game. The only other time I swung on anybody was with Joe Robb of the Cardinals. He hit me twice. I didn't mind being hit; that's part of the game—but he hit me for no reason, no reason at all, and that I *did* mind. So I hit him back. But generally, I felt that my best retaliation on some guy was to run over him on the next play and make him look bad. That could hurt him worse than a punch. Most things didn't upset me too much, though. It's natural for the players to get emotional and fired up in a game. In fact, sometimes funny things happened.

HALEY: Like what?

BROWN: Well, like sometimes guys would get all excited and call somebody a name. Once in 1963, we were playing a preseason exhibition game against the Pittsburgh Steelers. On a third-down play, I fell pretty heavily on Lou Michaels, who's now with Baltimore. He was real mad about it, and when I got up, I was moving off and I heard him holler, "Why don't you go back to the *Mafia,* Brown?" I stopped and hollered back, "Mafia? You're mixed up, you dumb chump!" Lou was all flustered for something to say, and he finally stuttered, "I mean the *niggers!*" Man, it was so funny, it cracked me up!

HALEY: In the course of your entire football career, despite all the fights and roughings, you were never sidelined by a major injury. Most sportswriters consider this almost miraculous. Did you really manage to avoid getting hurt or did you just avoid showing it?

BROWN: A little bit of both—plus a lot of pure luck. It's true that I was never hurt badly enough to miss a game, but

I did get a lot of what you might call small injuries at different times—cuts, bruises, sprains, and so forth. That's part of the game. Look at my hands; see those scars? I still can't shake hands with much grip; can't even get an ordinary grip on a doorknob. I got hit on a nerve once. And though most people never knew it, during the 1962 season I played all the way through with a badly sprained right wrist. It was tough for me to shift the ball from hand to hand in open field, as I liked to do when running. Of all the blows I got, though, there's one I'll never forget. It was either 1958 or 1959, against the Giants. I had to hit the line, just one yard, for a touchdown. The Giants did a lot of submarining; and whenever I met submarining lines, if the gain was vital, I'd try leaping over their line—which can get you hurt. Well, we *had* to have this touchdown, so I went up to the line, expecting to jump, but then I saw just this little sliver of daylight and I decided to go against all my principles of caution and just drop my head and take a chance of getting a hell of a headache and go through somebody's stomach. Well, I stuck my head in there, and *Vrooom!* It was like I'd been caught in a vise between their tackle and end; then a Mack truck crashed against my helmet. Sam Huff! I had made the touchdown, all right— but, man! Bells ringing, afraid somebody was going to have to help me up and all that. I finally got myself up, slow, the way I always did. But it was like, *Jesus!* I was addled, you know? Nobody's used to blows like that. I played it cool, though, walking off like I was all right, because I didn't want anybody to know. But I guess the worst one-game injury was later that same year, also against the Giants. I drove into a charging line and in the pile-up, I got kicked in the head. My memory was knocked out; I stayed in the game, but I couldn't remember anything—even having come into the stadium to play the game. Our quarterback, Milt Plum, explained my assignments in the huddle and I carried the ball by instinct. That was in the first half; but even in the second half, I was still dreamy. Nobody knew it, though, but my teammates. Every tackle, whether I'd just had a brush block or I'd really been clobbered—like this time—I always reacted the same way. I got up slowly and I went back to the huddle slowly, without expression. It kept people from knowing if I was hurt, because I never acted any different, see? Even if my head was ringing, I could make that slow rise and walk. That's the main reason I had that no-hurt reputation.

HALEY: Didn't your physical condition have anything to do with it? Dr. W. Montague Cobb, a Howard University anatomist, has said, "Jim Brown's bone structure must resemble forged vanadium steel—the hinging of ankles, knees, elbows; the 'crawl' of muscles, the dynamism of effort easily tapped are all in immediate evidence."

BROWN: He's looking at the wrong part of my anatomy. I've always made it a practice to use my *head* before I use my body. I looked upon playing football like a businessman might: The game was my business; my body and my mind were my assets, and injuries were liabilities. The *first* basic was to be in absolutely top-notch physical condition—even more than any coach would ask you to be in. I always tried to train harder than anybody else. I even developed my own set of extra calisthenics, things I could do in a hotel room if I had to. And over the years, I made for myself a careful study of what things usually cause injuries and, as much as I could, I avoided doing those things. For example, you'll see backs constantly jumping into the air, over a line; they think it looks so dramatic. Well, it *can* work—in fact, I did it myself, as I mentioned earlier, whenever I felt there was no other alternative—but sooner or later, somebody's bound to catch you up there in mid-air and break you in half. Another invitation to disaster is to use your head as a battering ram. If you do, pretty soon you're going to get it unhinged, like I did with Sam Huff. You'll also see some backs trying those fancy crossover step maneuvers—the left-leg-over-the-right-leg bit; I used to do that kind of thing at Syracuse; I was a regular fancy Dan. By pro-ball time, though—playing against guys who outweighed me by 60 or 70 pounds—I had learned better. I learned that if I was going to make it with the pros, I was going to have to develop something extra, something more than sheer muscle and flashy footwork. I was going to have to *outthink* the opposition. I would say that I credit 80 percent of the success I enjoyed to the fact that I played a *mental* game. The purely physical part—keeping in condition, running, passing, stuff like that—I'd credit with no more than 20 percent. It's just common sense: Physically, many guys in pro football are more than my equals—big, strong, fast son of a guns. But some simply don't get as much out of themselves as others. Why? Their mental game doesn't match their physical capacity. My game pivoted on having planned ahead of time every move I intended to make on the field. The nine years I was in pro ball, I never quit trying to make my mind an encyclopedia of every possible detail—about my teammates, about players on other teams, about the plays we used, about plays I knew *they* used and about both our and other teams' collective and individual tendencies.

I know you've heard that I was supposed to have a reputation for being distant, aloof and hard to get along with, especially in football seasons, most especially close to gametime. Well, maybe I was. Maybe I was rude to people and had very little to say to anybody. The reason is that I was focused mentally on that coming game. I was concentrating, visualizing things that I knew could happen and what I would do if it went this way or that way. I knew I had it working right when I started seeing plays in my mind almost like I was watching television. I'd see my own line in front of me, the guards, the halfbacks, the quarterback, and then the other team over there—especially big Roger Brown and Alex Karras, two of the best tackles in football.

Both of them are quick, agile, smart, fast and big, and they like to hit *hard.* Notice I don't just say they hit hard, but they *like* to hit hard—that's mental; that's positive thinking, see? I'd walk around in the locker room, seeing Roger Brown in my mind—for some reason, not his face or hands or shoulders, but those thighs of his. Massive thighs, like some huge frog. I always envision Roger hopping up in the air, jumping over blocks—all 300 pounds of him. And Alex Karras—in pro football, he's just a little cat, just 250 pounds, but he's built like a stump, with a boxer's sneering mouth. I hear him growling; he actually growls when he's charging. Positive thinking again, see? Anyway, I'd be watching them mentally across the line and sizing up the moves they might make against me. I'd see plays running and things happening—see myself starting a run and having to make spur-of-the-moment changes of strategy and direction. Every play I ever ran, I had already run a thousand in my mind. Right now, I can see a sweep run. I'm starting—my first three steps are very fast. Then I'm drifting, to let my guard in front of me get into position. There he is; now others are throwing their blocks; my guard is blocking their halfback to the outside. Now I accelerate and I shoot through the gap. That outside linebacker is my greatest danger now. I can see the order in which the tacklers are going to come. I'm looking for that end first, or maybe that outside linebacker, since no one could get to him right away. I see myself making all kinds of instantaneous adjustments, step by step, through their secondary—and then into the clear and all the way for a TD. Do you see what I mean? You get a jump on the game when you visualize beforehand not only the regular plays you run but also the hundred and one other things that might happen unexpectedly. So when you're in the actual game, whatever happens, you've already seen it in your mind and plotted your countermoves—instantly and instinctively.

HALEY: You've been talking only about plays on which

you were the ball carrier. One of the few things for which you were criticized as a ballplayer was your alleged refusal to block for your teammates when someone else was carrying the ball. How do you—

BROWN: Who said that about me?

HALEY: Washington Redskins coach Otto Graham, among others. He has also said that the Browns would have been a better team without you.

BROWN: Well, I never saw that quote, but I'll assume it's true, because Otto has made a lot of other comments disparaging my playing ability. I think maybe it's time I reveal something I haven't before that might cast a light on his real reason. See, Otto and I had always been good friends, and we were playing in a pro-am golf tournament at Beechmont Country Club in Cleveland, when Otto had a bad break. He drove a ball off the second tee and hit a man in the nose. Maybe two years later, this guy decided to sue Otto. I was busy practicing for a game when Otto's attorney came on the field asking me a lot of questions about the event. I told him I remembered the man was about 25 or 30 yards away when the golf ball hit him, and I didn't really remember too many other details. Evidently, the lawyer reported to Otto that I didn't wish to be cooperative. Well, shortly after that, I read the sports headline that Otto Graham said I couldn't or wouldn't block and the Browns would maybe do better without me. I've always refused to fire back at him, feeling that he said it in the mistaken belief that I didn't want to testify in his behalf.

HALEY: But many others—coaches, players and fans alike—have made the same charge about you.

BROWN: Look, in the Browns' system, I simply wasn't cast to do blocking; our offense was geared for me to run. I think I had only five or six blocking assignments in our whole repertoire of plays. I'd have been the league's best blocker if the Browns had another guy doing the major running. But there are many, many great blockers in pro football and relatively few very good runners. If I had started blocking like the best guard out there and doing less running, we'd probably have won considerably less and my salary would have gone down by around $25,000. In fact, since the team depended on me running, I could even have lost my position. I always tried to satisfy the coach I worked for, and running was what they always asked of me—even in college. I always took Glen Kelly's point of view: He said he wouldn't hitch a race horse to a milk truck.

HALEY: Throughout your first year at Syracuse, the coaches didn't even want you as a starting player on the freshman team, let alone as its star fullback. Until your sophomore season was well under way, in fact, you were relegated to the fourth or fifth string on the varsity team. Why?

BROWN: I was black, that's why. You see, before I went to Syracuse, a Negro named Avatus Stone had been a great ballplayer there—a quarterback, a great punter. They wanted him to play end, but he refused and finally left and went to Canada. But the *real* rub was that Stone had been very popular among white coeds—which made him very *unpopular* with white males. So when I arrived, the only black man on the team, the coaches had nothing to say to me except, "Don't be like Avatus Stone!" My whole freshman year, I heard so many sermons about what I should be like, I got so many hang-ups, that my attitude became as bad as theirs. In practice, I was snubbed and ignored until I got to where I'd just sprawl out on my back during drills and nobody said a word to me. I was as sullen as they were, and the freshman season ended and the sophomore season began with me on the fifth string. But I hustled like mad when sophomore training season opened; and when the games began, they had moved me up to second string. I got in a few games, but nothing spectacular happened until, finally, in the fourth game, against Illinois, we had a lot of injuries on the team and I started. We got badly beaten, but

I carried 13 times, averaging five yards, and the fans caught
that. When I was on the bench, they started hollering, "We
want Brown! Brown! Brown!" Man, that made me feel ten
feet tall! Then came my really big break—against Cornell.
We lost 14 to 6, but I made a long touchdown run, over 50
yards, as I remember; and altogether I gained about 150
yards. Then, in the next game, against Colgate, I made two
touchdowns. That did it; overnight, the fans made me a
campus celebrity and, man, did I love it! In my junior year,
I opened thinking I had it made and Pittsburgh bottled me
up for 28 yards in 12 carries and the coaches demoted me
to second team. That made me so mad I saw fire; and in the
next practice scrimmage, I left first-string tacklers lying out
all over the field and ran four touchdowns in five plays.
After that, they left me on the first string. That's how I got
accepted, you know? I mean accepted as Jim Brown, not
Avatus Stone. And I'm saying nothing against Stone, because he's a beautiful cat. I'm just saying my personality
was my own and I didn't happen to feel that white coeds
had any monopoly on desirability for me. Anyway, once
the coaches made up their minds, they were men enough to
realize they had been wrong and they became fair in dealing
with me, and then I gave them all I had. I think maybe
having to fight my way up the way I did taught *me* more
about being a man, too.

HALEY: Did you have to contend with race prejudice in
pro ball as well?

BROWN: Of course! *Every* Negro in this country, I don't
care *who* he is, is affected by racial prejudice in some of its
various forms. Athletes probably enjoy as much freedom as
any black men in this country—but they're by no means
exempt from discrimination. The relationship with white
players *is* much better now; they respect whoever can help
them win that championship bonus check. And the fan
reaction is greatly improved, because so many Negroes are
starring and there are now even black team captains. The

problems arise *off* the playing field—and I'd say that the major problem area is related, in some way, to white women. It's a major factor why black and white players don't socialize, because sooner or later they are going to be in some situation involving women. The black athlete who is desirable to white women is going to run into all kinds of trouble. If he gets anywhere around white men with her, fellow athletes or not, pretty soon that black man is going to get reminded that he is not free, that he's still black in white men's eyes, star on the field or not. It's one of the reasons black athletes no longer particularly try to socialize with, or even get along with, white teammates. When the game is over, the whites go their way and the blacks go theirs, with very few exceptions.

HALEY: According to the Cleveland press, that separatism didn't apply to white women, at least in your case.

BROWN: I see I've got to remind you I'm married— married to a *black* woman. I think I'm no different from the vast majority of black men: I'm not dying to have a white woman. Stokely Carmichael uses a good statement in this area when that subject comes up. He says, "The white woman can be *made!* OK, we've got that settled—so let's go on to something important!" When I was in college, I dated both black and white coeds. It didn't matter to me. I've never seen any difference in white or black women. It's a question of individual characteristics, personality, habits and tastes. All that mattered to me was *pretty* girls. I always went after the finest-looking, the real *foxes!* I have a nickname, "Hawk," which comes from having very good eyesight. Visually, I appreciate anything that I consider beautiful—if it's a car, if it's a suit, a painting, a woman or what have you. And the woman I appreciate most is my wife, Sue, who seems to be happy and very much in love with me. I have never denied her and I have never denied those three big babies we have at home in Cleveland. So I'm sure that I'm doing no big damage by looking.

HALEY: Speaking of babies, you were once the defendant in a paternity suit filed by an 18-year-old Cleveland girl. Though you were subsequently exonerated, it didn't exactly enhance your public image. What were the details of the case?

BROWN: Actually, I was sued for assault and battery. Then the same party sued me for paternity. I figured, hell, I'm strong enough to fight it out publicly, and that's what I did. I sat a week in that hot courtroom, missing a number of important commitments. It never would have gone to court if I had been guilty; I would have dealt with it the way a man *should* deal with a thing of that nature. Anybody who doubts that doesn't know me.

HALEY: Quite apart from paternity suits, it's fairly common knowledge that you've long been the target of demonstrative admiration by many female football fans. Is it just coincidence that most of them happen to be white?

BROWN: You're just tipping around the edges of the big question at the bottom of the mind of every white man in this country: "What about you blacks and white women?" Right? Well, OK, let's talk straight about that. I'll tell you the very first thing that always knocks me out about that question. Why is there always the implication that the white woman is just mesmerized, just helpless, if she's with a black man? Everybody knows the smart, hip, 20th Century white woman is in complete control of herself and does exactly what she damn well wants to do and nothing else. So what's the reason the white man has her pictured in his mind as hypnotized and helpless with a black man? The other thing that bugs me about that question is the assumption by the average white man that any black man he sees with any white woman has got to be sleeping with her. To me, that instant assumption tells me a lot more about that white man than it does about the black man— or the white woman. Let's assume he's right that a lot of white women are either openly or secretly attracted to black men. It happens to be true—but let's ask ourselves why. Well, the answer is that the white man himself has *made* his woman this attracted to us.

HALEY: How?

BROWN: For generations, he has painted the black man as such an animal that it's not only natural but inevitable that the white woman's mind occupies itself with this big, exciting *taboo.* And, yeah, a lot of them do more than *think* about it; they decide to find out. And when they do, they find that the black man isn't the gorilla the white man has painted; that he may be as much of a gentleman as any man she has known and may even pay her more respect than her own kind. You can't blame her for responding—and you can't blame him for responding to *her,* because he's the same man who for 300 years couldn't open his mouth or he would *die,* while he saw the white man having sex as he pleased with the black woman. Let me tell you something interesting to do. Every time you see a Negro from now on, just take note of his complexion. See how few are jet black and reflect how *all* the Africans brought over here were jet black. It might help you to do some thinking about who genetically changed the color of a whole *race* of people, diluted them from black Africans not into black *Americans* but into *Negroes;* even the word is a white man's creation, a stigma, a kind of proper form for "nigger." Historically, there's been about a thousand times more sex between white men and black women than between black men and white women—and a thousand times more black man— white woman sex goes on in white men's *minds* than ever does in fact. And I'm not in the least criticizing where it *is* fact. I believe that whatever any two consenting adults— black or white—do in their own privacy, without causing harm to any other party, is entirely their own business. The white man may consider it *his* business; in fact, most do; but I don't feel that it's *mine!*

I know, and I accept, that certain exposures to white

women will likely encourage and develop friendships. I use the expression "friendships" because I don't want to be guilty of doing the same thing that I accuse people of doing to me—just see me *talking* with some white woman and instantly they assume, "There goes sex." I can't tell you how many times that has made me sick in this country. I can't remember once when someone wasn't waiting to see me outside the stadium after a game—different friends, some of them from college days, some of them white women. Half the time, their husbands and children would be standing off to one side and they would run up and hug me. It was a very warm thing between the two of us; after all, we hadn't seen each other in years—at least it *should* have been warm. But I can't remember one single time when, before I got through the crowd, I didn't catch some white faces giving me that frowned-up, dirty look that was saying, "Him and white women again!" Something beautiful and completely platonic disrupted by somebody who didn't even *know* us. Hell, it didn't even have to be a *grown* white woman! I've known it to happen with little girls! The autograph crowd is around, say, everybody excited and happy—and all of a sudden there's this little girl, under ten, say, whose parent tells her, "Go tell Jim Brown hello." OK, I bend over and the little girl, with instinctive affection, starts to reach up to hug my neck and kiss my cheek. You know? But I've been that route before. I anticipate the impulsive intent of a sweet, innocent little child—and I have to maneuver somehow to prevent her acting natural. Because too many times before, see, I had straightened up from a child's embrace and caught the disapproving white facial expressions. Finally, I began to feel that I'd just rather not see my old friends in that kind of situation. Which meant that *I* was becoming prejudiced. Many a time since then, I have walked on through a crowd, not speaking to anybody, and it helped to build my "mean and evil" reputation. But this kind of bitter experience isn't unique with me, or even with black athletes; it happens to every black man and woman in America.

HALEY: Though you've certainly experienced many of the injustices familiar to all Negroes, isn't it also true that you enjoy, as a celebrity, certain privileges that are denied to the average Negro?

BROWN: Well, I do have some of what you might call "back-door advantages." Numerous doors and opportunities have opened for me personally, for the individual me. I've got a few dollars in the bank, and a home, and my family eats and dresses well and I drive a good car. When I consider that my forebears were slaves, I know I'm lucky to be where I am and have what I do. But, to me, these are always a reminder of the fact that the same doors are not open for *all* black people. Although I appreciate the advantages for selfish reasons, this constant awareness of inequity makes them mean less to me. And there's something else a lot of people don't realize—that the more successful a black person is, the harder it is for him to live with the things that still go with being black. Let me give you an example, just one of the common examples. You've earned the money to buy yourself a better home in a better residential area, and you haven't even signed the papers before the word leaks out and white people start *running* before they'd live near you. The poor, ignorant type? No! Your better-class white people. The people who in another setting would smile to see their kids rushing you for autographs. How is one supposed to feel about that? I never will forget being bluntly refused an apartment in Cleveland soon after I moved there. The landlady looked me in the face and said, "We only take whites." I wound up buying the home we have now, in a nice, modest, predominantly Negro neighborhood. At the other place, I hadn't been eager to live around white people; I had just wanted a place near the field where the Browns practiced, which would be more convenient for me. It wasn't integration I was after; I just was bitter about being *segregated,* you understand? **HALEY:** Have you encountered any other kind of overt discrimination since you became well known? **BROWN:** Are you kidding? I don't even like to think about it. But I'll give you just one example. There was nothing really uncommon about the incident itself in the average Negro's experience, particularly in the South. But it had me choked up and bitter for a long time after it happened. It was in 1957 and I was in Army training down in Alabama. Three buddies of mine and I were in my convertible, with the top down, driving to Tuskegee. We had just gone through this little town, enjoying ourselves, when all of a sudden this police car roared up behind and barreled past us, cut us off and stopped; and, baby, I'm looking at this cop getting out with a drawn gun. "Get out, niggers!" We got out. "What are you making dust all over white people for?" Just about then, another car pulled up and stopped and another white guy got out. The cop was saying, "You hear me, nigger?" Well, my emotions were such that I hardly trusted myself to speak. "I don't know what a nigger is!" I said. Then he jammed the pistol right in my stomach. "Nigger, don't you know how to talk to white folks?" One of the guys with me said, "He's not from down here; he's from up North." The cop said, "Nigger, I don't care where you're from. I'll blow you apart! Where did you get this car, anyway?" I said, "It was given to me." He said, "*Given* to you! Who gave you a *car?*" I said, "It was given to me at school." "*What* school?" I said, "Syracuse University." Just about then, the other white man came over closer and he said, "That's right. I recognize this boy. He plays football up there." That was my reprieve. The cop took the gun out of my belly and said, "I'm going to let you go, but you better drive slow and you better learn how to act down here, nigger!" So we got back in the car and drove on. I don't know why I even told you that; it's not good to dredge that stuff up in your mind again. But you see, you don't forget a thing like that, not if somebody handed you every trophy in football and 15 Academy Awards. That's why a black man, if he's got any sense at all, will never get swept away with special treatment if he happens to be famous, because he knows that the minute he isn't where somebody *recognizes* who he is, then he's just another *nigger*. That's what the Negro struggle is all about; that's why we black people have to keep fighting for freedom in this country. We demand only to live—and let live—like any ordinary American. We don't want to have to be somebody *special* to be treated with respect. I can't understand why white people find it so hard to understand that.

HALEY: If you feel as strongly as you say about winning equal rights for Negroes, why didn't you ever join the Negro celebrities who participated with Dr. King in such nonviolent demonstrations as the Selma march?

BROWN: I felt I could do more by giving my time to my own organization—the National Negro Industrial and Economic Union—than by flying to Alabama and marching three days, another celebrity in the pack, almost a picnic atmosphere, and then flying back home a so-called hero because I'd been so "brave." I'm not knocking those who did; I'm just saying I felt differently about it. That kind of demonstration served its purpose well; but it finally outlived its usefulness.

HALEY: In what way?

BROWN: I'd compare Dr. King's methods with Paul Brown's brand of football. Like King, Brown was a genius in his time, but he refused to change and finally he became outdated. I think the sit-ins, walk-ins, wade-ins, pray-ins and all those other -ins advanced the movement tremendously by awakening the nation's conscience—making millions of white people aware of and sympathetic to the wrongs suffered by black people. When the white population was at that point, I think the movement's direction should have been altered toward economic programing for Negro self-help, with white assistance. Think what could have been accomplished if the nation's black leaders, at that time, had actively mobilized the good will of all the millions of white people who were willing, even anxious, to help the Negro help himself. We could have had millions, white and black, working toward that goal, with tremendous results. That was what I felt and what I tried to do, in forming my National Negro Industrial and Economic Union. But no one listened—not in the movement and not in Washington. What happened, instead, was that the marching went on and on, getting more and more militant, until a lot of white people began to resent it—and to feel threatened. Whenever any human being feels threatened— it doesn't matter if he's right or wrong—he starts reacting defensively, negatively. We lost the white sympathy and support we'd fought so hard to win: Badly needed new civil rights legislation began to die on the vine; existing laws were loopholed, modified or ignored; poverty funds dried up. On the threshold of real progress, the door simply closed in our faces. The inevitable consequences of that frustration set fire to Watts, Detroit, Newark and two dozen other cities.

HALEY: Police authorities in several cities have claimed that the riots were fomented not by frustration but by "Communist agitators." Do you think there's any truth to that charge?

BROWN: If by "fomented" they mean planned, like some kind of revolutionary battle strategy, they just don't understand the explosive state of every ghetto in this country. The average ghetto Negro is so pent up and fed up with white lies, hostility, hypocrisy and neglect that riots don't *need* planning. All they need is a spark to set them off, and the cops usually provide that without any help from the Communists. Once a riot gets started, of course, the Communists, along with a lot of others, will be out there fanning the flames. Communist money and people are working in every ghetto, especially the major ones. It's no big secret that the Communists' main objective in this country is to attract a large following of Negroes. You'll hear black kids standing around on corners talking defiantly about "feudalism" and "capitalism" and "man's exploitation of man" and all that stuff; they don't even know what the words mean, but it sounds hip to them, you know? If there's anything the vast majority of Negroes in this country have proved, however, it's that they aren't Communist-inclined. They don't *need* Communist indoctrination to tell them that they're second-class citizens, and they don't need Communist help to become *first*-class citizens. They can—and will—do it on their own, no matter what it costs. Black people are demonstrating that they're willing to die for total freedom. There's not going to be any turning back now. It's going to be either total freedom or the concentration camps I hear they're getting ready for us. If there's anything the black man has learned thoroughly in his history in this country, it's that begging, appeasing, urging and imploring has gotten him nowhere. He just kept on getting slapped around, and only when he started to slap back did he begin to get any kind of respect.

HALEY: Are you an advocate of Negro violence?

BROWN: Don't talk to me about *Negro* violence. The greatest violence this country has ever known has been on behalf of the various vested interests of white people, demanding whatever they were convinced were their rights. You could start with the American Revolution. Then the Indian wars—outright criminal violence, depicted in the history books and on television as heroic! Then the Civil War, in which the black man wasn't really the true issue;

he was nothing but the excuse. And on down the line to the labor movement. Heads got split open, people shot down, property destroyed all over the country. If you want to talk about race riots, the Irish, not black people, fought the bloodiest riot ever seen in America; in the late 1800s, they went looting and burning and killing down Lexington Avenue, which was then the richest, most fashionable part of New York City. There's no point in dragging this out forever, if you see my point.

HALEY: You've strayed from our original question: Are you an advocate of black violence?

BROWN: I am a 100-percent advocate that if a man slaps you, you should slap him back. I know that if a man hits me, I'm going to try to hit him twice—harder—because I want him to do a lot of thinking before he ever hits me again. I am an advocate of freedom for everybody, freedom that isn't something handed out at one group's discretion and taken away if someone makes that group angry. The law is the law; that's what I believe, and I believe right is right. We're all supposed to abide by this country's so-called laws—not only the laws against civil disorder but the laws *for* civil *rights*. There's a very simply stated way to eliminate the race problem: Just enforce the same laws and the same standards for everybody, black and white alike. That's the only thing the black people are after. Am I personally an advocate of black violence? I'm an advocate of *stopping* black violence before it *starts*—by facing the facts, by curing the *reasons* black people engage in violence. I've gotten frantic calls from high places when riots were in progress, begging me to "do something," and my reaction has been, "Later for you! When I was trying to tell what our N.N.I.E.U. could do to *prevent* riots, you didn't want to listen. Well, now you've waited too late!" Whatever I think, or any other black personality thinks, isn't going to make any difference once riots get started.

HALEY: Can they be stopped, or do you think they'll escalate, as some predict, into a race war?

BROWN: If nothing is done to *prevent* riots—and I don't mean with more tanks—race war is a very real and immediate probability. Too many black people who have been kept methodically at the bottom of the ladder for centuries don't really care what happens. They figure, what have they got to lose? The building up of police forces, the various thinly veiled threats, like concentration camps, have no deterrent effect whatever. All it does is make the blacks madder, and that will send them out in the streets quicker than anything else. As of right now, only a very small percentage of Negroes have actually rioted, or even have thought about physically participating in rioting. But the number grows with every threat. And there's one thing in particular that I'd think about a long, long time if I were any city's police chief or mayor or a state governor—and that's the curfews that get slapped down whenever there's trouble. After the Watts trouble, which involved only a few of the Negroes in Los Angeles, suddenly a "riot area" curfew was declared that went far beyond the locale of the rioting—all the way to the borders of the total black community in Los Angeles, excepting only the handful of so-called upper-middle-class blacks who happened to be living in so-called integrated high-income areas. With that single act, hundreds of thousands of Negroes—be they criminals, hoodlums, preachers, doctors, lawyers, nurses, schoolteachers, firemen, policemen or politicians—discovered that it made no difference, that what really was being put down was *black people*! Nobody caught in that curfew net ever will think the same again. It was very obvious to them what was being said.

HALEY: You said the riots may escalate if nothing is done to prevent them. What do you think *can* be done?

BROWN: First of all, these mayors' and governors' offices have got to drop this implied revenge attitude I was talking about—building up police forces and beefing up the National Guard. That's just working toward the concentration camps. There's got to be, somehow, some truly sincere understanding achieved between Negro leaders and the concerned state and city administrations. And by Negro leaders, I don't mean the Martin Luther Kings and the Whitney Youngs; I mean the people who have followings in the ghettos. They've got to be listened to, and worked with, and given respect, and urged to help with programing where money and other aid will actually filter down to the lowest level of the ghetto, where you find the people most prone to riot—those who are most bitter and alienated and frustrated and suspicious. So much has been done *to* them, it's a pins-and-needles job to make them believe anybody actually will do anything *for* them. But if the city governments are willing to listen to and work with these *real* Negro leaders, I think there is a tremendous chance of quieting racial disorders. I say this because I head up an organization—the N.N.I.E.U.—that offers, free, some of the greatest black talent in this country, most of it never used before. I can call upon 50 or 60 of the top black athletes in this country to run summer programs and work directly in communities with these young kids. But when I can't get the Vice-President's committee to fund such a summer program, I think something is radically wrong.

HALEY: Considering the mood of Congress in the wake of the riots, isn't it unrealistic to expect the Federal Government to allocate funds for a program implemented by ghetto gang leaders who many whites feel were instrumental in starting the riots?

BROWN: It was unrealistic, it seems to me, to expect that the people sealed up in these ghettos would remain quiet in them forever. If you're trying to stop riots, I call *any* man qualified, street hoodlum or not, if he controls the people who riot. I know what I'm talking about; I've seen what can happen with these people. You've got to persuade the black men who are respected in their area to go in and crack the door, crack the ice. I've been able to do this myself a few times in a few places. The ghetto people know I'm straight, that I speak up and stand up and I wouldn't betray them. I've gone into ghettos and talked with the toughest cats. I've told them, "Now, look, I think you know I'm my own man. Now, here's what seems to me a hell of a program, but it needs your help to get wide community support behind it." In most cases, these guys will give 100-percent support. Give the toughest cats a certain respect, because *they* have respect from the people you're trying to reach with help, and they'll work with you. Sure, they're hostile and suspicious, but they'll talk sincerely with you if they figure you're *with* them. You find their greatest disappointment and bitterness come from promises, promises that proved later to be some political sham or that just weren't followed up. Whatever program there is has to be followed up, day to day. And the best people to monitor that is these tough guys: Give them jobs doing it. All they want is decent salaries; they have to eat, to live, just like anyone else. But I find that city administrations don't like this idea. They're still after political points. They want to dictate the terms, and the ghetto people resent anybody bringing them any program with white strings, so naturally it gets nowhere. And that's why we're likely to have more black uprisings, which lead to more white "revenge" talk and threats, and the vicious cycle continues. I hope that black freedom can be won peaceably. That's my *hope.* But things I keep seeing make me skeptical. Historically, great battles for freedom have seldom been won peaceably.

HALEY: Have you read the polls that show that a large majority of Negroes think the whites would lose in a race war?

BROWN: Yes, I have. That's emotionalism. Because, without a doubt, black people couldn't win any mass encounter. How could they? Outnumbered ten to one? With a handful of guns, some homemade Molotov cocktails, sticks, rocks and switchblades? Against the white man's jets, tanks, chemical warfare and H-bombs? That's just plain silly. I think anybody who doesn't realize this simply isn't being a realist. But this is just one of many facts of life about which black people, especially the extremists, aren't being realistic.

HALEY: You were affiliated, as an official of Main Bout, with the Black Muslims who ran the organization. Do you feel that the Muslims' extremist philosophy of separatism is realistic?

BROWN: No, I don't. Like many, many Negroes— maybe 90 percent of us privately—I agree with much of what they say, but I don't personally accept their separatist philosophy, and I'm not a member. My business relationship in Main Bout with Herbert Muhammad and John Ali was a very pleasant and compatible one, however, and I respect the organization for instilling black people with pride in their race and for teaching black people to pull themselves up by their own bootstraps and take care of their own. I also respect the Muslims' right to practice their own religion—a right legally recognized by the Government, if not by the white press, which I feel has grossly misrepresented them. The main reason they're so disliked by whites is that so much of what they say about the black condition is the truth, and white America doesn't like to hear the truth about its own bigotry and oppression.

HALEY: Do you feel the same way about such black-power firebrands as Stokely Carmichael and Rap Brown?

BROWN: I feel there is a need for them. Unfortunately, the average white seems to need a good scare from the Carmichaels and Rap Browns before he'll listen to less dramatic requests. Speaking for myself, I think it's too easy to just go out and threaten Whitey. What is that doing to help black people? At the same time, I've been turned down by so many Administration officials, seeking money and support for our self-help program—and not just turned down but suspected of being "subversive"—that I've been tempted to take the easy way, too, and start hollering against Whitey myself. As long as Administrations refuse to sponsor programs that give black people constructive alternatives to violence, I can't really blame these guys for their extremism. I think they symbolize a lot of those their age who are sick of passive resistance, who are really fighting for freedom—young Negroes with great pride in themselves and their race. They are not trying to be assimilated; but they believe there should be, and must be, equality. Like them or not, they are what the white man is going to have to deal with more and more. They're brash and fearless and they're going to fight in any and every way they feel necessary to be respected and to win their freedom in this country. Where I disagree with guys like Stokely and Rap is that it was a mistake for them to get identified with merely defining and defending black power. It has deflected their energies from effective programing into sloganeering.

HALEY: How would *you* define black power?

BROWN: First and foremost, I'd define it as a creation of the white press. From the moment Stokely Carmichael used the expression in a speech two years ago—though he quickly explained that he meant it in the sense of political and economic power—the press, and millions of white people, instantly interpreted those two words as an ominous threat of black mass uprising. It says more to me about the interpreters than about the two words. To me it says white fear, white guilt seeking a justification, a target. It was whites, not blacks, who turned it into a hate thing and used it to label exponents of black power as advocates of racial violence.

HALEY: Would you call yourself an exponent of black power?

BROWN: I'm for black power the same way I'm for Irish power, Jewish power, labor power, doctor power, farmer power, Catholic power, Protestant power. I'm for all the special vested-interest groups' using their economic and political strength to demand that others pay them respect and grant them equality. Only I call it *green* power. That's my idea of what needs to become the black people's special interest. I want to see black people pooling their monies, their skills, their brains and their political power to better themselves, to participate more fully in the mainstream of American life. And that requires white support. The black people simply don't have the money to support the programs needed to train them in what they can do for themselves.

HALEY: When you say you need white *financial* support to help Negroes help themselves, does that mean you share the deepening cynicism of such militant Negro groups as CORE and SNCC about the direct personal involvement of white volunteers, however sincere and committed, in the civil rights movement?

BROWN: Speaking for my own organization, the one I've founded—which is the only one I can really speak for— we know that there are many, many sincere and truly committed white people, and one of our major efforts is to get more and more of them to help us. But we no longer want or need the same kind of help they've offered in the past: We don't want them to march with us anymore, because marches are a thing of the past; and we don't want them to work with us in the ghetto anymore. We want their moral and financial support—as long as there are no strings attached to either—but we want them to work with their own kind and leave us alone to work with ours.

HALEY: Why?

BROWN: Simply because the people in the ghetto just don't trust whites, no matter how sincere or well intentioned they are; hell, they don't even trust the average so-called accepted black leaders—which is to say, the black leaders approved of by the white establishment. The suspicions and hostilities, born of 300 years of white bigotry and betrayal, run too deep. But that's where we can use all the help we can get from concerned whites: in uprooting racial prejudice where it originates—in the hearts of *other* whites.

What it comes down to is: Who can work best where? For the same reason a white man would last about five minutes preaching brotherhood on a Harlem street corner, black people can't run around in white communities trying to change white attitudes; they'd get arrested for "disturbing the peace." Sincere white people have got to go to work upstairs, downstairs, next door, down the block—talking, teaching, reasoning, organizing, whittling away at white prejudice wherever they find it; and they'll find it everywhere. Our job, the job of sincere and committed blacks such as the athletes in my N.N.I.E.U.—who may be the only kind of guys the toughest street cats will accept and listen to—is to work inside the ghetto to eliminate the *effects* of racial prejudice and discrimination by helping black people acquire the green power they need to make life, liberty and the pursuit of happiness a tangible reality rather than an empty catch phrase.

HALEY: How did you evolve this strategy of liberation through economic self-help?

BROWN: Well, when I was with the Cleveland Browns, as you know, for some time I had a summer-season job with Pepsi-Cola. I had access to much of their internal operational program, and they had me do a lot of traveling to various places, as a representative. In the process, I began to get a pretty good understanding, better than any I had before, of how economics is the very foundation of this country. When I say white people have got to face some hard truths, I also believe that black people have got to face some hard truths; and the most basic of these truths is that, for all the crimes committed against him, the black man in America still has not begun properly to take advantage of even the limited opportunities that he *has* had. We have become a consuming people and we have produced almost nothing. Therefore, automatically, what few dollars we make don't circulate among us, to help *us*; they go into other pockets instead. We've wasted too much time hollering and complaining that we don't have this, we can't do that, and so forth—all because of Whitey. We've squandered energies that should have been spent focusing upon what we *could* have and *could* do with what we *do* have! As a race, we suffer from a terrible mistrust not only of the white man but of each other. That's why we've never really been able to get together, why we haven't had more cooperative business ventures. For another thing, we're just not economically oriented by nature; we're too impulsive, impractical, unpragmatic and emotional about money. It's the sad truth that we continue to drink the best imported Scotch, to wear the finest shoes, to drive the biggest Cadillacs, and we don't own one single distillery, shoe factory or Cadillac agency—at least not to my knowledge we don't. Right now, for instance, there are thousands of jobs going begging that industries are offering to black youth. The message in that fact for black people, I think, is loud and clear: Get off the streets and into the schoolrooms and the colleges and the libraries.

Now, in saying all this, by no means am I letting the white man off the hook. He has sinned; he has held the black man down for centuries. I'm just saying that the black man, in hard fact, hasn't done enough to help himself. We've used our being a minority as a crutch. We're said to be ten percent of the population; but the Jews are only about three percent, fewer than 6,000,000, and they came here with far less than black people now have in resources and they met all kinds of prejudices. But they worked together; they used their brains and the law and money and business acumen, and by now you can't find any ethnic group in America commanding more respect. *Commanding* it! Do you know that once Jews weren't wanted in Miami? So they bought it. Same with the Catskills. I rarely give a speech today without suggesting the Jews as a model of what black people need to do with themselves economically.

Anyway, this was the trend of the private thinking I had been doing for a long time—about how the black people could truly become a part of American society and share in its good things. Well, the Pepsi-Cola experience gave me the insights and the know-how I needed to put that thinking into action—by getting others who feel as I do to help me form an organization to help black people help themselves economically. The first thing I needed was a staff to whom black people would listen, from whom they would take advice and guidance. And I knew of one ideal group— black athletes. It may sound immodest, but it's a fact that we tend to be heroes among black people, especially black youth. Something that's haunted me for years is that look I have seen so many times in some of those black teenagers' eyes looking at me up close: For just an instant, that animal hipness and suspicion leaves the face and you see a look in the eyes that seems to say, "For God's sake, for just a minute, will *somebody* care?" It gets to me, because *I* was that kid once, see? So it's one of those "There but for the grace of God" things with me—and it's the same for all the other athletes I know. So among my own teammates, and wherever we played, I filtered the idea around. And that's where I got my first major encouragement. They just snapped it up! It was funny, man! On the field, cats were trying to run over each other, break each other in half; then the evening after the game, we're all huddled together excitedly discussing this new project. Guys like John Wooten and Walter Beach of the Browns, Bernie Casey of the Atlanta Falcons, Brady Keys of the Pittsburgh Steelers, Bobby Mitchell of the Redskins, Leroy Kelly, Bill Russell, Curtis McClinton, Timmy Brown, lots of others. We

mapped out an organization that would sell memberships
to anybody and everybody for from $2 to $100, to raise
money to finance good ideas for small black businesses,
because so many good black ideas can't obtain financing.
And we decided to make use of black professional people—these "middle-class Negroes" we hear so much talk
about—to draw them in with us, to lend their talents to
young Negroes in all the various ways they could. And we
decided to use the image value of black athletes in personal-
contact programs with black youth, especially in the ghettos.

   We all put in some of our own money to get it started.
I personally donated more than $50,000. Then we hired a
secretary and rented an office in the ghetto area of Cleveland, where people wouldn't feel uncomfortable coming to
see us. Well, we've been almost two years now working,
researching, recruiting, opening another office in Los Angeles and operating limited programs in four other cities.
With more financing, I think we have the potential of being
one of the most meaningful and effective programs anywhere in this country.

HALEY: How many Negro athletes are involved now?

BROWN: About 100, at least, from stars to rookies, from
old-timers like me down to young kids like Lew Alcindor.
He works for us like a Trojan in his off time. Quite a few
white athletes have come in with us, too, as investors in
black business ideas. And you wouldn't *believe* some of the
*non*athletes who have volunteered to come and work with
us for nothing but subsistence! People like Spencer Jour-
dain, a Harvard graduate, who quit a great job at Corning
Glass to work full time for us, just for subsidy, because he's
so committed to our idea.

HALEY: With so little city, state or Federal support, financial or otherwise, how much have you been able to
achieve?

BROWN: Well, aside from a couple dozen new black

businesses now in operation, I think we could rightly claim some major credit for the fact that last year, Cleveland didn't prove to be the nation's number-one riot area, as had been predicted by the so-called experts. We got together with the city administration and with the Greater Cleveland Foundation and persuaded them to cooperate, through the N.N.I.E.U., with those who were truly in control of the ghetto—the kind of people who really control every ghetto, people your average sociologists couldn't even *talk* to, because they don't know their language, even. The really tough cats, you know? The kind who are the most dangerous people in any society. Like this young man called Ahmad, who has a very sizable following and influence in Cleveland's ghetto. We got together with him and we got him to agree to serve on a committee to discuss ghetto needs, to offer plans, and we saw in Ahmad a very changed attitude—because suddenly this guy was given some *respect,* see? Now *he* works to do constructive things for the area. We were also able to get the Greater Cleveland Foundation to fund a youth center for us. One of the first things we did was establish courses in black history, business administration, economics and many other such self-help subjects. We offer entertainment, too—dancing, theater, talent night; the kids love it. And we've developed a job-procurement program. We involved everybody we could get our hands on, with special emphasis on redirecting into constructive channels the energy of special groups who were capable of starting trouble. One young fellow, who had been viewed generally as a prime troublemaker, we were able to turn into a crackerjack director of our youth center; we have six Cleveland Browns athletes doing volunteer work *under* him. We're headed into the 1968 summer now. The popularity of our youth center has so overflowed it that we're asking the Greater Cleveland Foundation to fund five more of them for us. I truly think that if we can expand, we're capable of conducting special programs simultaneously in at least six major cities. We want to open formal offices also in Washington, New York, Boston and Chicago. Given more city-administration aid and cooperation, I know we can prove what we can do. If anybody else wants to help us, or just find out more about us, would you be good enough to print that our N.N.I.E.U. headquarters address is 105–15 Euclid Avenue, Cleveland, Ohio 44106?

HALEY: Gladly. On another front, how do you feel about the election of your former N.N.I.E.U. legal counsel, Carl Stokes, as mayor of Cleveland—and about the victories of several other Negro candidates for high city office throughout the country?

BROWN: Cleveland—and the country—will benefit. Carl won not because of—or despite—his being a Negro, but because he's a take-over guy who's going to produce a positive, dynamic administration for black and white alike. As for other Negro mayors and city officials in the North, like Hatcher in Gary, it simply had to happen, because otherwise, with the big Northern cities becoming more and more Negro-populated as white people rush to the suburbs, we wouldn't have representative city government. But the most heartening sign to me is the fact that Negroes are competing with—and winning against—white candidates on the basis of personal qualifications rather than skin color, and winning with white support.

HALEY: You seem to be much more optimistic about the racial situation than you were a few years ago—and much less cynical about the prospects of white cooperation. Why?

BROWN: The only change is that once I dealt with the negative aspects; now I deal with what I see as positives. I'm working now trying to do something about what ails us black people. Now I have an organization. I have responsibilities toward the people who believe in me. We've talked, talked, talked about discrimination for years. Now I'm trying to help get rid of it.

HALEY: With the kind of movie schedule you've been keeping, do you feel you're giving all the help you should?
BROWN: Not nearly as much as I'd like. But the other athletes carry on full time when I'm away, as their schedules permit. And whatever success I earn in the movies is going to be invested in building and promoting the N.N.I.E.U.; so I don't feel like I'm neglecting my duty. What bothers me more is that I haven't been able to be at home with Sue and the kids more than a few weeks at a time for about 18 months now. I don't think the kids will suffer too much because of it, thanks to the great job Sue is doing in keeping them well adjusted; but I'd like to be there more, all the same. I'm getting older, you know, and I want my family ties to be as strong as the ties to my people. The best way I can see to strengthen both of them, in the long run, is by doing what I'm doing: trying to become a good actor. I may not make myself any more popular by saying some of the things I've said to you today, but I'd lose respect for myself if I told anybody just what I felt they *wanted* to hear. Just about whenever I've stood up and spoken my mind about situations that bothered me as a black man, somebody I thought I trusted, somebody I thought knew and understood me, has advised and urged and all but begged me—with the best of intentions—not to express my objections publicly. "Jim," they tell me, "it'll hurt your image. It'll alienate the good will of your public"—meaning the *white* public. Well, I don't need that kind of concern for my welfare. I'm not going to be anybody's little boy. I'm a *man*, a *black* man, in a culture where black manhood has been kicked around and threatened for generations. So that's why I don't feel I need to take too much advice about how I'm supposed to think and act. And that's why I have to tell the truth like I see it. Maybe some people will holler; maybe they'll hate me for it. But I'll just stick it out, walk tall and wait for the truth to be vindicated.
HALEY: How long do you think that will take?

BROWN: I can't say how long; I can't worry about that. That doesn't even matter to me. All that matters is to see more and more black people mobilized and working toward constructive self-help goals. I want more black people to realize the hard fact that unless we do this, all the other gains aren't going to make any difference. If in my lifetime I can see that this idea really has taken hold, then I will have the satisfaction of knowing that true freedom—as black men and as black *Americans*—will finally be within our grasp.

ROOTS:
THE MIXING OF THE BLOOD

For 12 years, Alex Haley researched and wrote the story of the seven generations of his family that he would call "Roots." It began when Haley, a writer who conducted the first "Playboy Interview" and many others, was on a PLAYBOY assignment in England and first saw the Rosetta stone, the key to deciphering Egyptian hieroglyphics. He became curious about some African phrases he remembered hearing from his relatives as a boy in Tennessee and, in particular, the name Kunta Kinte, whom he believed was his African ancestor.

Poring over old records, consulting experts in linguistics, anthropology and genealogy, Haley tracked down every lead until his research finally led him to a village in Gambia. There, in a moment of high drama, the tribal historian, known as a griot, was retelling the story of the village through past generations and came to a day in 1767 when a 17-year-old boy was abducted by white men in the woods near the village and never heard from again. His name was Kunta Kinte.

Beginning with life in the village of Juffure, "Roots" describes Kunta Kinte's early years, his kidnaping, his trans-

portation in the filthy, hellish hold of a slave ship across the Atlantic and his sale to John Waller, a Virginia planter. Rebellious and fiercely independent, Kunta tried to escape so often that his pursuers chopped off part of his foot as punishment. He eventually married Bell, the plantation cook, who gave birth to a girl named Kizzy. Bell taught their daughter how to get along with whites and was delighted when, for instance, Kizzy became fast friends with the Waller niece, Missy Anne, who taught her to read and write. But Kunta remained stubbornly committed to passing along at least some of his African heritage, telling her about Juffure and relating old village customs—such as his method of keeping track of time by dropping pebbles into a gourd. By the early 1800s, the first of Kunta's descendants to be born in America had grown to be a pretty girl and was living a relatively sheltered life as a house slave.

"DO I GOT a gran'ma?" asked Kizzy.

"You got two—my mammy and yo' mammy's mammy."

"How come dey ain't wid us?"

"Dey don' know where we is," said Kunta. "Does you know where we is?" he asked her a moment later.

"We's in de buggy," Kizzy said.

"I means where does we live?"

"At Massa Waller's."

"An' where dat is?"

"Dat way," she said, pointing down the road. Uninterested in their subject, she said, "Tell me some more 'bout dem bugs an' things where you come from."

"Well, dey's big red ants knows how to cross rivers on leafs, dat fights wars an' marches like a army, an' builds hills dey lives in dat's taller dan a man."

"Dey soun' scary. You step on 'em?"

"Not less'n you has to. Every critter got a right to be

here, same as you. Even de grass is live an' got a soul, jes' like peoples does."

"Won't walk on de grass no mo', den. I stay in de buggy."

Kunta smiled. "Wasn't no buggies where I come from. Walked wherever we was goin'. One time I walked four days wid my pappy all de way from Juffure to my uncles' new village."

"What 'Joo-fah-ray'?"

"Done tol' you don' know how many times, dat where I come from."

"I thought you was from Africa. Dat Gambia you talks 'bout in Africa?"

"Gambia a country in Africa. Juffure a village in Gambia."

"Well, where dey at, Pappy?"

" 'Crost de big water."

"How big dat big water?"

"So big it take near 'bout four moons to get 'crost it."

"Four what?"

"Moons. Like you say 'months.' "

"How come *you* don' say months?"

" 'Cause moons my word fer it."

"What you call a 'year'?"

"A rain."

Kizzy mused briefly.

"How you get 'crost dat big water?"

"In a big boat."

"Bigger dan dat rowboat we seen dem fo' mens fishin' in?"

"Big 'nough to hol' a hunnud mens."

"How come it don' sink?"

"I use to wish it woulda."

"How come?"

" 'Cause we all so sick seem like we gon' die anyhow."

"How you get sick?"

"Got sick from layin' in our own mess prac'ly on top each other."

"Why'n't you go de toilet?"

"De toubob had us chained up."

"Who 'toubob'?"

"White folks."

"How come you chained up? You done sump'n wrong?"

"Was jes' out in de woods near where I live—Juffure—lookin' fer a piece o' wood to make a drum wid, an' dey grab me an' take me off."

"How ol' you was?"

"Sebenteen."

"Dey ask yo' mammy an' pappy if'n you could go?"

Kunta looked incredulously at her. "Woulda took *dem,* too, if'n dey could. To dis day, my fam'ly don' know where I is."

"You got brothers an' sisters?"

"Had three brothers. Maybe mo' by now. Anyways, dey's all growed up, prob'ly got chilluns like you."

"We go see dem someday?"

"We cain't go nowheres."

"We's gon' somewheres now."

"Jes' Massa John's. We don' show up, dey have de dogs out at us by sundown."

" 'Cause dey be worried 'bout us?"

" 'Cause we b'longs to dem, jes' like dese hosses pullin' us."

"Like I b'longs to you an' Mammy?"

"You's our young'un. Dat diff'rent."

"Missy Anne say she want me fo' her own."

"You ain't no doll for her to play wid."

"I plays wid her, too. She done tole me she my bes' frien'."

"You cain't be nobody's frien' an' slave both."

"How come, Pappy?"

" 'Cause frien's don' own one 'nother."

"Don' Mammy an' you b'long to one 'nother? Ain't y'all frien's?"

"Ain't de same. We b'longs to each other 'cause we *wants* to, 'cause we loves each other."

"Well. I loves Missy Anne, so I wants to b'long to her."

"Couldn't never work out."

"What you mean?"

"You couldn't be happy when y'all growed up."

"Would too. I bet you wouldn't be happy."

"You sho' right 'bout dat!"

"Aw, Pappy. I couldn't never leave you an' Mammy."

"An' chile, 'speck we couldn't never let you go, neither!"

For many years now, Kunta had gotten up every morning before dawn, earlier than anyone else on slave row—so early that some of the others were convinced that "dat African" could see in the dark like a cat. Whatever they wanted to think was fine with him, as long as he was left alone to slip away to the barn, where he would face the first faint streaking of the day prostrated between two large bundles of hay, offering up his daily Suba prayer to Allah. Afterward, by the time he had pitched some hay into the horses' feed trough, he knew that Bell and Kizzy would be washed, dressed and ready to get things under way in the big house, and the boss field hand, Cato, would be up and out with Ada's son Noah, who would soon be ringing the bell to wake the other slaves.

Almost every morning, Noah would nod and say "Mornin' " with such solemn reserve that he reminded Kunta of the Jaloff people in Africa, of whom it was said that if one greeted you in the morning, he had uttered his last good word for the day. But although they had said little to each other, he liked Noah, perhaps because he reminded Kunta of himself at about the same age—the serious manner, the way he went about his work and minded his own business, the way he spoke little but watched everything. He had often noticed Noah doing a thing that he also did—standing quietly somewhere with his eyes following the rompings of Kizzy and Missy Anne around the plantation. Once when Kunta had been watching from the barn door as they rolled a hoop across the back yard, giggling and screaming, he had been about to go back inside when he saw Noah standing over by Cato's cabin, also watching. Their eyes met and they looked at each other for a long moment before both turned away. Kunta wondered what Noah had been thinking—and had the feeling that, likewise, Noah was wondering what *he* was thinking. Kunta knew somehow that they were both thinking the same things.

At ten, Noah was two years older than Kizzy, but that difference wasn't great enough to explain why the two hadn't even become friends, let alone playmates, since they were the only slave children on the plantation. Kunta had noticed that whenever they passed near each other, each of them always acted as if he or she had not even seen the other, and he couldn't figure out why—unless it was because even at their age they had begun to sense the custom that house slaves and field slaves didn't mix with one another.

Whatever the reason, Noah spent his days out with others in the fields while Kizzy swept, dusted, polished the brass and tidied up the massa's bedroom every day—for Bell to inspect later with a hickory switch in her hand. On Saturdays, when Missy Anne usually came to call, Kizzy would somehow miraculously manage to finish her chores in half the time it took her every other day, and the two of them would spend the rest of the day playing—excepting at midday if the massa happened to be home for lunch. Then he and Missy Anne would eat in the dining room with Kizzy standing behind them, gently fanning a leafy branch to keep away flies, as Bell shuttled in and out, serving the food and keeping a sharp eye on both girls, having warned them beforehand, "Y'all lemme catch you even thinkin' 'bout gigglin' in dere wid Massa, I'll tan both yo' hides!"

Kunta by now was pretty much resigned to sharing his Kizzy with Massa Waller, Bell and Missy Anne. He tried not to think about what they must have her doing up there in the big house and he spent as much time as possible in the barn when Missy Anne was around. But it was all he could do to wait until each Sunday afternoon, when church would be over and Missy Anne would go back home with her parents. Later on these afternoons, usually Massa Waller would be either resting or passing the time with company in the parlor, Bell would be off with Aunt Sukey and Sister Mandy at their weekly "Jesus meetin's"—and Kunta would be free to spend another couple of treasured hours alone with his daughter.

When the weather was good, they'd go walking—usually along the vine-covered fence row where he had gone almost nine years before to think of the name Kizzy for his new girl-child. Out beyond where anyone would be likely to see them, Kunta would clasp Kizzy's soft little hand in his own as, feeling no need to speak, they would stroll down to a little stream and, sitting closely together beneath a shade tree, they would eat whatever Kizzy had brought along from the kitchen—usually cold buttered biscuits filled with his favorite blackberry preserves. Then they would begin talking.

Mostly he'd talk and she'd interrupt him constantly with questions, most of which would begin "How come...." But one day Kunta didn't get to open his mouth before she piped up eagerly, "You wanna hear what Missy Anne learned me yestiddy?"

He didn't care to hear of anything having to do with that giggling white creature, but not wishing to hurt his Kizzy's feelings, he said, "I'm listenin'."

" 'Peter, Peter, punkin eater,' " she recited, " 'had a wife

an' couldn' keep 'er; put 'er in a punkin shell, dere he kep'
'er very well. . . .' "

"Dat it?" he asked.

She nodded. "You like it?"

He thought it was just what he would have expected
from Missy Anne: completely asinine. "You says it real
good," he hedged.

"Bet you can't say it good as me," she said with a
twinkle.

"Ain't tryin' to!"

"Come on, Pappy, say it fo' me jes' once."

"Git 'way from me wid dat mess!" He sounded more
exasperated than he really was. But she kept insisting and
finally, feeling a bit foolish that his Kizzy was able to twine
him around her finger so easily, he made a stumbling effort
to repeat the ridiculous lines—just to make her leave him
alone, he told himself.

Before she could urge him to try the rhyme again, the
thought flashed to Kunta of reciting something else to
her—perhaps a few verses from the Koran, so that she
might know how beautiful they could sound—then he
realized such verses would make no more sense to her than
"Peter, Peter" had to him. So he decided to tell her a story.
She had already heard about the crocodile and the little
boy, so he tried the one about the lazy turtle that talked the
stupid leopard into giving him a ride by pleading that he
was too sick to walk.

"Where you hears all dem stories you tells?" Kizzy asked
when he was through.

"Heared 'em when I was yo' age—from a wise ol'
gran'mammy name Nyo Boto." Suddenly, Kunta laughed
with delight, remembering: "She was bald-headed as a egg!
Didn't have no teeth, neither, but dat sharp tongue o' her'n
sho' made up fer it! Loved us young'uns like her own,
though."

"She ain't had none of 'er own?"

"Had two when she was real young, long time 'fo' she come to Juffure. But dey got took away in a fight 'tween her village an' 'nother tribe. Reckon she never got over it."

Kunta fell silent, stunned with a thought that had never occurred to him before: The same thing had happened to Bell when she was young. He wished he could tell Kizzy about her two half sisters, but he knew it would only upset her—not to mention Bell, who hadn't spoken of it since she told him of her lost daughters on the night of Kizzy's birth. But hadn't he—hadn't all of those who had been chained beside him on the slave ship been torn away from their own mothers? Hadn't all the countless other thousands who had come before—and since?

"Dey brung us here naked!" he heard himself blurting. Kizzy jerked up her head, staring; but he couldn't stop. "Even took our names away. Dem like you gits borned here don' even know who dey is! But you jes' much Kinte as I is! Don' never fo'git dat! Us'n's fo'fathers was traders, travelers, holy men—all de way back hunnuds o' rains into dat lan' call Ol' Mali! You unnerstan' what I'm talkin' 'bout, chile?"

"Ycs, Pappy," she said obediently, but he knew she didn't. He had an idea. Picking up a stick, smoothing a place in the dirt between them, he scratched some characters in Arabic.

"Dat my name—Kun-ta Kin-te," he said, tracing the characters slowly with his finger.

She stared, fascinated. "Pappy, now do my name. He did. She laughed. "Dat say Kizzy?" He nodded. "Would you learn me to write like you does?" Kizzy asked.

"Wouldn't be fittin'," said Kunta sternly.

"Why not?" She sounded hurt.

"In Africa, only boys learns how to read an' write. Girls ain't got no use fer it—over here, neither."

"How come Mammy can read an' write, den?"

Sternly, he said, "Don' you be talkin' dat! You hear me? Ain't nobody's business! White folks don' like none us doin' no readin' or writin'!"

"How come?"

" 'Cause dey figgers less we knows, less trouble we makes."

"I wouldn't make no trouble," she said, pouting.

"If'n we don' hurry up an' git back to de cabin, yo' mammy gon' make trouble fer us both."

Kunta got up and started walking, then stopped and turned, realizing that Kizzy was not behind him. She was still by the bank of the stream, gazing at a pebble she had seen.

"Come on, now, it's time to go." She looked up at him and he walked over and reached out his hand. "Tell you what," he said. "You pick up dat pebble an' bring it 'long an' hide it somewheres safe, an' if'n you keeps yo' mouth shet 'bout it, nex' new-moon mornin' I let you drop it in my gourd."

"Oh, Pappy!" She was beaming.

Just after Christmas of 1803, the winds blew the snow into deep, feathery drifts until in places the roads were hidden and impassable for all but the biggest wagons. When the massa went out—in response to only the most desperate summons—he had to ride on one of the horses, and Kunta stayed behind, busily helping Cato, Noah and the fiddler keep the driveway clear and chop wood to keep all of the fireplaces steadily going.

Cut off as they were—even from Massa Waller's *Gazette,* which had stopped arriving about a month before with the first big snow—the slave-row people were still talking about the last bits of news that had gotten through to them: how pleased the white massas were with the way President Jefferson was "runnin' the gubmint," despite the massas' initial reservations toward his views regarding slaves. Since taking office, President Jefferson had reduced the size of the Army and Navy, lowered the public debt, even abolished the personal-property tax—that last act, the fiddler said, particularly having impressed those of the massa class with his greatness.

But Kunta said that when he had made his last trip to the county seat before they had gotten snowed in, white folks had seemed to him even more excited about President Jefferson's purchase of the huge Louisiana Territory for but three cents an acre. "What I likes 'bout it," he said, " 'cordin' to what I heared, dat Massa Napoleon had to sell it so cheap cause he in sich hot water in France over what it cost 'im in money, 'long wid fifty thousan' Frenchmans got killed or died 'fo' dey beat dat Toussaint in Haiti."

They were all still warming themselves in the glow of that thought a later afternoon when a black rider arrived amid a snowstorm with an urgently ill patient's message for the massa—and another of dismal news for the slave row: In a damp dungeon on a remote French mountain where Napoleon had sent him, Haiti's General Toussaint had died of cold and starvation.

Three days later, Kunta was still feeling stricken and depressed when he trudged back to the cabin for a mug of hot soup and, stamping snow from his shoes, then entering pulling off his gloves, he found Kizzy stretched out on her pallet in the front room, her face drawn and frightened. "She feelin' po'ly," was the explanation that Bell offered as she strained a cup of her herb tea and ordered Kizzy to sit up and drink it. Kunta sensed that something was being kept from him; then when he was a few more minutes there in the overwarm, tightly closed, mud-chinked cabin, his nostrils helped him guess that Kizzy was experiencing her first time of the bloodiness.

He had watched his Kizzy growing and maturing almost every day now for nearly 13 rains, and he had lately come to accept within himself that her ripening into womanhood would be only a matter of time: yet somehow he felt completely unprepared for this pungent evidence. After another day abed, though, the hardy Kizzy was back up and about in the cabin, then back at work in the big house— and it was as if overnight that Kunta actually noticed for the first time how his girl-child's previously narrow body had budded. With a kind of embarrassed awe, he saw that somehow she had gotten mango-sized breasts and that her buttocks had begun to swell and curve. She even seemed to be walking in a less girlish way. Now, whenever he went through the bedroom separator curtain into the front room, where Kizzy slept, he began to avert his eyes: and whenever Kizzy happened not to be clothed fully, he sensed that she felt the same.

In Africa now, he thought—Africa had sometimes seemed so distantly in the past—Bell would be instructing Kizzy in how to make her skin shine, using shea-tree butter, and how to fashionably, beautifully blacken her mouth, palms and soles, using the powdered crust from the bottoms of cooking pots. And Kizzy would at her present age already be starting to attract men who were seeking for themselves a finely raised, well-trained, virginal young wife. Kunta felt jolted even by the thought of some man's *foto* entering Kizzy's thighs; then he felt better after reassuring himself that this would happen only after a proper wedding. In his homeland at this time, as Kizzy's *fa*, he would be assuming his responsibility to appraise very closely the personal qualities as well as the family backgrounds of whatever men began to show marriageable interest in Kizzy—in order to select the most ideal of them for her; and he would also be deciding now what proper bride price would be asked for her hand.

But after a while, as he continued to shovel snow along with the fiddler, young Noah and Cato, Kunta found himself feeling increasingly ridiculous that he was even thinking about these African customs and traditions anymore:

for not only would they never be observed here, nor respected—indeed, he would also be hooted at if he so much as mentioned them, even to other blacks. And, anyway, he couldn't think of any likely, well-qualified suitor for Kizzy who was of proper marriageable age—between 30 and 35 rains—but there he was, doing it again! He was going to have to force himself to start thinking along lines of the marrying customs here in the toubob's country, where girls generally married—"jumpin' de broom," it was called—someone who was around their age.

Immediately, then, Kunta began thinking about Noah. He had always liked the boy. At 15, two years older than Kizzy, Noah seemed to be no less mature, serious and responsible than he was big and strong. The more Kunta thought about it, the only thing he could find lacking with Noah, in fact, was that he had never seemed to show the slightest personal interest in Kizzy—not to mention that Kizzy herself seemed to act as if Noah didn't exist. Kunta pondered: *Why* weren't they any more interested than that in each other, at the least in being friends? After all, Noah was very much as he himself had been as a young man, and therefore, he was highly worthy of Kizzy's attention, if not her admiration. He wondered: Wasn't there something he could do to influence them into each other's paths? But then Kunta sensed that probably would be the best way to ensure their never getting together. He decided, as usual, that it was wisest that he mind his own business—and, as he had heard Bell put it, with "de sap startin' to rise" within the young pair of them who were living right there in the same slave row, he privately would ask if Allah would consider helping nature take its course.

It was a week after Kizzy's 16th birthday, the early morning of the first Monday of October, when the slave-row field hands were gathering, as usual, to leave for their day's work, when someone asked curiously, "Where Noah at?"

Kunta, who happened to be standing nearby, talking to
Cato, knew immediately that he was gone. He saw heads
glancing around, Kizzy's among them, straining to maintain a mask of casual surprise. Their eyes met—she had to
look away.

"Thought he was out here early wid you," said Noah's
mother, Ada, to Cato.

"Naw, I was aimin' to give 'im de debbil fo' sleepin'
late," said Cato.

Cato went banging his fist on the closed door of the
cabin once occupied by the old gardener but which Noah
had inherited recently on his 18th birthday. Jerking the
door open, Cato charged inside, shouting angrily, *"Noah!"*
He came out looking worried. "Ain't like 'im," he said
quietly. Then he ordered them all to go quickly and search
their cabins, the toilet, the storerooms, the fields.

When they returned to their cabin, Kizzy burst into tears
the moment she got inside: Kunta felt helpless and tongue-
tied. But without a word, Bell went over to the table, put
her arms around her sobbing daughter and pulled her head
against her stomach.

Tuesday morning came, still with no sign of Noah, and
Massa Waller ordered Kunta to drive him to the county
seat, where he went directly to the Spotsylvania jailhouse.
After about half an hour, he came out with the sheriff,
ordering Kunta brusquely to tie the sheriff's horse behind
the buggy and then to drive them home. "We'll be dropping
the sheriff off at the Creek Road," said the massa.

"So many niggers runnin' these days, can't hardly keep
track—they'd ruther take their chances in the woods than
get sold down South." The sheriff was talking from when
the buggy started rolling.

"Since I've had a plantation," said Massa Waller, "I've
never sold one of mine unless my rules were broken, and
they know that well."

"But it's mighty rare niggers appreciate good masters,

doctor, you know that," said the sheriff. "You say this boy around eighteen? Well, I'd guess if he's like most field hands his age, there's fair odds he's tryin' to make it North." Kunta stiffened. "If he was a house nigger, they're generally slicker, faster talkers, they like to try passin' themselves off as free niggers or tell the road patrollers they're on their master's errands and lost their traveling passes, tryin' to make it to Richmond or some other big city, where they can easier hide among so many niggers and maybe find jobs." The sheriff paused. "Besides his mammy on your place, this boy of yours got any other kin livin' anywheres he might be tryin' to get to?"

"None that I know of."

"Well, would you happen to know if he's got some gal somewheres, because these young bucks get their sap risin', they'll leave your mule in the field and take off."

"Not to my knowledge," said the massa. "But there's a gal on my place, my cook's young'un, she's still fairly young, fifteen or sixteen, if I guess correctly. I don't know if they've been haystacking or not."

Kunta nearly quit breathing.

"I've known 'em to have pickaninnies at the age of twelve!" the sheriff chortled. "Plenty of these young nigger wenches even draw white men, and nigger boys'll do anything!"

Through churning outrage, Kunta heard Massa Waller's abrupt chilliness. "I have the least possible personal contact with my slaves and neither know nor concern myself regarding their personal affairs!"

"Yes, yes, of course," said the sheriff quickly.

Saturday morning after breakfast, Kunta was curry-combing a horse outside the barn when he thought he heard Cato's whippoorwill whistle. Cocking his head, he heard it again. He tied the horse quickly to a nearby post and cripped rapidly up the path to the cabin. From its front window he could see almost from where the main road intersected with the big-house driveway. He knew that Cato's call had also alerted Bell and Kizzy inside the big house.

Then he saw the wagon rolling down the driveway— and with surging alarm recognized the sheriff at the reins. Merciful Allah, had Noah been caught? As Kunta watched the sheriff dismount, his long-trained instincts tugged at him to hasten out and provide the visitor's winded horse with water and a rubdown; but it was as if he were paralyzed where he stood, staring from the cabin window, as the sheriff hurried up the big-house front steps two at a time.

Only a few minutes passed before Kunta saw Bell almost stumbling out the back door. She started running—and Kunta was seized with a horrible premonition the instant before she nearly snatched their cabin door off its hinges.

Her face was twisted, tear-streaked. "Sheriff an' Massa talkin' to Kizzy!" she squealed.

The words numbed him. For a moment, he just stared disbelievingly at her, but then, violently seizing and shaking her, he demanded, "What he want?"

Her voice rising, choking, breaking, she managed to tell him that the sheriff was scarcely in the house before the massa had yelled for Kizzy to come from tidying his room upstairs. "When I heard 'im holler at her from de kitchen, I flew to git in de drawin'-room hallway, where I always listens from, but I couldn't make out nothin' clear 'cept he was mighty mad"—Bell gasped and swallowed. "Den heard Massa ringin' my bell, an' I run back to look like I was comin' from de cookhouse. But Massa was awaitin' in de do'way, wid his han' holdin' de knob behin' 'im. Ain't never seed 'im look like he did at me. He tol' me col' as ice to git out'n de house an' stay out till I'm sent for!" Bell moved to the small window, staring at the big house, unable to believe that what she had just said had really happened. "Lawd Gawd, what in de worl' sheriff want wid my chile?" she asked incredulously.

Kunta's mind was clawing desperately for something to do. Could he rush out to the fields, at least to alert those who were chopping there? But his instincts said that anything could happen with him gone.

As Bell went through the curtain, into their bedroom, beseeching Jesus at the top of her lungs, Kunta could barely restrain himself from raging in and yelling that she must see now what he had been trying to tell her for nearly 40 rains about being so gullible, deluded and deceived about the goodness of the massa—or any other toubob.

"Gwine back in dere!" cried Bell suddenly. She came charging through the curtain and out the door.

Kunta watched as she disappeared inside the kitchen. What was she going to do? He ran out after her and peered in through the screen door. The kitchen was empty and the inside door was swinging shut. He went inside, silencing the screen door as it closed, and tiptoed across the kitchen. Standing there with one hand on the door, the other clenched, he strained his ears for the slightest sound—but all he could hear was his own labored breathing.

Then he heard: "Massa?" Bell had called softly. There was no answer.

"*Massa?*" she called again, louder, sharply.

He heard the drawing-room door open.

"Where my Kizzy, Massa?"

"She's in my safekeeping," he said stonily. "We're not having another one running off."

"I jes' don' understan' you, Massa." Bell spoke so softly that Kunta could hardly hear her. "De chile ain't been out'n yo' yard, hardly."

The massa started to say something, then stopped. "It's possible you really don't know what she's done," he said. "The boy Noah has been captured, but not before severely knifing the two road patrolmen who challenged a false traveling pass he was carrying. After being subdued by force, he finally confessed that the pass had been written not by me but by your daughter. She has admitted it to the sheriff."

There was silence for a long, agonizing moment, then Kunta heard a scream and running footsteps. As he whipped open the door, Bell came bolting past him— shoving him aside with the force of a man—and out the back door. The hall was empty, the drawing-room door shut. He ran out after her, catching up with her at the cabin door.

"Massa gon' sell Kizzy, I knows it!" Bell started screaming, and inside him something snapped.

"Gwine git her!" he choked out, cripping back toward the big house and into the kitchen as fast as he could go, with Bell not far behind. Wild with fury, he snatched open the inside door and went charging down the unspeakably forbidden hallway.

The massa and the sheriff spun with disbelieving faces as the drawing-room door came jerking open. Kunta halted there abruptly, his eyes burning with murder. Bell screamed from behind him, "Where our baby at? We come to git her!"

Kunta saw the sheriff's right hand sliding toward his holstered gun as the massa seethed. *"Get out!"*

"You niggers can't hear?" The sheriff's hand was withdrawing the pistol and Kunta was tensed to plunge for it— just as Bell's voice trembled behind him "Yassa"—and he felt her desperately pulling his arm. Then his feet were moving backward through the doorway—and suddenly the door was slammed behind them, a key clicking sharply in the lock.

As Kunta crouched with his wife in the hall, drowning in his shame, they heard some tense, muted conversation between the massa and the sheriff . . . then the sound of feet moving, scuffling faintly . . . then Kizzy's crying and the sound of the front door slamming shut.

"Kizzy! Kizzy chile! Lawd Gawd, don' let 'em sell my Kizzy!" As she burst out the back door with Kunta behind her, Bell's screams reached away out to where the field hands were, who came racing. Cato arrived in time to see Bell screeching insanely, springing up and down with Kunta bear-hugging her to the ground. Massa Waller was descending the front steps ahead of the sheriff, who was hauling Kizzy after him—weeping and jerking herself backward—at the end of a chain.

"*Mammy! Maaaaamy!*" Kizzy screamed.

Bell and Kunta leaped up from the ground and went raging around the side of the house like two charging lions. The sheriff drew his gun and pointed it straight at Bell: She stopped in her tracks. She stared at Kizzy. Bell tore the question from her throat: "You done dis thing deys says?" They all watched Kizzy's agony as her reddened, weeping eyes gave her answer in a mute way—darting imploringly from Bell and Kunta to the sheriff and the massa—but she said nothing.

"Oh, my Lawd Gawd!" Bell shrieked. "Massa, please have mercy! She ain't meant to do it! She ain't knowed what she was doin'! Missy Anne de one teached 'er to write!"

Massa Waller spoke glacially. "The law is the law. She's broken my rules. She's committed a felony. She may have aided in a murder. I'm told one of those white men may die."

"Ain't *her* cut de man, Massa! Massa, she worked for you ever since she big 'nough to carry yo' slop jar! An' I done cooked an' waited on you han' an' foot over forty years, an' he"—gesturing at Kunta, she stuttered—"he done drive you eve'ywhere you been for near 'bout dat long. Massa, don' all dat count for sump'n?"

Massa Waller would not look directly at her. "You were

doing your jobs. She's going to be sold—that's all there is to it."

"Jes' cheap, low-class white folks splits up families!" shouted Bell. "You ain't dat kine!"

Angrily, Massa Waller gestured to the sheriff, who began to wrench Kizzy roughly toward the wagon.

Bell blocked their path. "Den sell me an' 'er pappy wid 'er! Don' split us up!"

"Get out of the way!" barked the sheriff, roughly shoving her aside.

Bellowing, Kunta sprang forward like a leopard, pummeling the sheriff to the ground with his fists.

"Save me, *Fa!*" Kizzy screamed. He grabbed her around the waist and began pulling frantically at her chain.

When the sheriff's pistol butt crashed above his ear, Kunta's head seemed to explode as he crumpled to his knees. Bell lunged toward the sheriff, but his outflung arm threw her off balance and she fell heavily as he dumped Kizzy into the back of his wagon and snapped a lock on her chain. Leaping nimbly onto the seat, the sheriff lashed the horse, whose forward jerk sent the wagon lurching as Kunta clambered up. Dazed, head pounding, ignoring the pistol, he went scrambling after the wagon as it gathered speed.

"Missy Anne!... Missy Annnnnnne!" Kizzy was screeching it at the top of her voice. *"Missy Annnnnnnnnnnnnnnnnne!"* Again and again, the screams came: they seemed to hang in the air behind the wagon swiftly rolling toward the main road.

When Kunta began stumbling, gasping for breath, the wagon was a half mile away; when he halted, for a long time he stood looking after it, until the dust had settled and the road stretched empty as far as he could see.

The massa turned and walked very quickly with his head down back into the house, past Bell huddled sobbing by the bottom step. As if Kunta were sleepwalking, he came cripping slowly back up the driveway—when an African remembrance flashed into his mind and, near the front of the house, he bent down and started peering around. Determining the clearest prints that Kizzy's bare feet had left in the dust, scooping up the double handful containing those footprints, he went rushing toward the cabin: The ancient forefathers said that precious dust kept in some safe place would ensure Kizzy's return to where she had made the footprints. He burst through the cabin's open door, his eyes sweeping the room and falling upon his gourd containing his pebbles on a shelf. Springing over there, in the instant before opening his cupped hands to drop in the dirt, suddenly he knew the truth: His Kizzy was gone; she would not return. He would never see his Kizzy again.

His face contorting, Kunta flung his dust toward the cabin roof. Tears bursting from his eyes, snatching his heavy gourd up high over his head, his mouth wide in a soundless scream, he hurled the gourd down with all his strength and it shattered against the packed-earth floor, his 662 pebbles representing each month of his 55 rains flying out, ricocheting wildly in all directions.

Weak and dazed, Kizzy lay in the darkness, on some burlap sacks, in the cabin where she had been pushed when the mule cart arrived shortly after dusk. She wondered vaguely what time it was; it seemed that night had gone on forever. She began tossing and twisting, trying to force herself to think of something—anything—that didn't terrify her. Finally, for the 100th time, she tried to concentrate on figuring out how to get "up Nawth," where, she had heard so often, black people could find freedom if they escaped. If she went the wrong way, she might wind up "Deep Souf," where people said massas and overseers were even worse than Massa Waller. Which way was "nawth"? She didn't know. I'm going to escape, anyway, she swore bitterly.

It was as if a pin pricked her spine when she heard the first creaking of the cabin door. Springing upright and backward in the dark, she saw the figure entering furtively, with a cupped hand shielding a candle's flame. Above it she recognized the face of the white man who had purchased her, and she saw that his other hand was holding up a shorthandled whip, cocked ready for use. But it was the glazed leer on the white man's face that froze her where she stood.

"Rather not have to hurt you none," he said, the smell of his liquored breath nearly suffocating her. She sensed his intent. He wanted to do with her what Pappy did with Mammy when she heard strange sounds from their curtained-off room after they thought she was asleep. He wanted to do what Noah had urged her to do when they had gone walking down along the fence row, and which she almost had given in to, several times, especially the night before he had left, but he had frightened her too much when he exclaimed hoarsely, "I wants you wid my baby!" She thought that this white man must be insane to think that she was going to permit him to do that with her.

"Ain't got no time to play wit you now!" The white man's words were slurred. Kizzy's eyes were judging how to bolt past him to flee into the night—but he seemed to read that impulse, moving a little bit sideways, not taking his gaze off her as he leaned over and tilted the candle to drain its melted wax onto the seat of the cabin's single broken chair; then the small flame flickered upright. Inching slowly backward, Kizzy felt her shoulders brushing the cabin's wall. "Ain't you got sense enough to know I'm your new massa?" He watched her, grimacing some kind of a smile. "You a fair-lookin' wench. Might even set you free, if I like you enough—"

When he sprang, seizing Kizzy, she wrenched loose, shrieking, as with an angry curse he brought the whip cracking down across the back of her neck. "I'll take the hide off you!" Lunging like a wild woman, Kizzy clawed at his contorted face, but slowly he forced her roughly to the floor. Pushing back upward, she was shoved down again. Then the man was on his knees beside her, one of his hands choking back her screams—"Please, Massa, please!"—the other stuffing dirty burlap sacking into her mouth until she gagged. As she flailed her arms in agony and arched her back to shake him off, he banged her head against the floor, again, again, again, then began slapping her—more and more excitedly—until Kizzy felt her dress being snatched upward, her undergarments being ripped. Frantically thrashing, the sack in her mouth muffling her cries, she felt his hands fumbling upward between her thighs, finding, fingering her private parts, squeezing and spreading them. Striking her another numbing blow, the man jerked down his suspenders, made motions at his trousers' front. Then came the searing pain as he forced his way into her, and Kizzy's senses seemed to explode. On and on it went, until finally she lost consciousness.

In the early dawn, Kizzy blinked her eyes open. She was engulfed in shame to find a young black woman bending over her and sponging her private parts gently with a rag and warm, soapy water. When Kizzy's nose told her that she had also soiled herself, she shut her eyes in embarrassment, soon feeling the woman cleaning her there as well. When Kizzy slitted her eyes open again, she saw that the woman's face seemed as expressionless as if she were washing clothes, as if this were but another of the many tasks she had been called upon to perform in her life. Finally laying a clean towel over Kizzy's loins, she glanced up at Kizzy's face. "Reckon you ain't feel like talkin' none now," the woman said quietly, gathering up the dirty rags and her water pail, preparing to leave. Clutching these things in the crook of one arm, she bent again and used her free hand to draw up a burlap sack to cover most of Kizzy's body. " 'Fo' long, I bring you sump'n to eat," she said, and went on out the cabin door.

Kizzy lay there feeling as if she were suspended in mid-air. She tried to deny to herself that the unspeakable, unthinkable thing had really happened, but the lancing pains of her torn privates reminded her that it had. She felt a deep uncleanness, a disgrace that could never be erased. She tried shifting her position, but the pains seemed to spread. Holding her body still, she clutched the sack tightly about her, as if somehow to cocoon herself against any more outrage, but the pains grew worse.

Kizzy's mind raced back across the past four days and nights. She could still see her parents' terrified faces, still hear their helpless cries as she was rushed away. She could still feel herself struggling to escape from the white trader whom the Spotsylvania County sheriff had turned her over to; she had nearly slipped free after pleading that she had to relieve herself. Finally, they had reached some small town where—after long, bitterly angry haggling—the trader at least had sold her to this new massa, who had awaited the nightfall to violate her. Mammy! Pappy! If only screaming for them could reach them—but they didn't even know where she was. And who knows what might have happened to them? She knew that Massa Waller would never sell anyone he owned *"less'n dey breaks his rules."* But in trying to stop the massa from selling *her,* they must have broken a dozen of those rules.

And Noah, what of Noah? Somewhere beaten to death? Again, it came back to Kizzy vividly. Noah demanding angrily that to prove her love, she must use her writing ability to forge a traveling pass for him to show if he should be seen, stopped and questioned by patrollers or any other suspicious whites. She remembered the grim determination etched on his face as he pledged to her that once he got up

North, with just a little money saved from a job he would quickly find, "Gwine steal back here an' slip you Nawth, too, fo' de res' our days togedder." She sobbed anew. She knew she would never see him again. Or her parents. Unless—

Her thoughts leaped with a sudden hope! Missy Anne had sworn since girlhood that when she married some handsome, rich young massa, Kizzy alone must be her personal maid, later to care for the houseful of children. Was it *possible* that when she found out Kizzy was gone, she had gone screaming, ranting, pleading to Massa Waller? Missy Anne could sway him more than anyone else on earth! Could the massa have sent out some men searching for the slave dealer, to learn where he had sold her, to buy her back?

But soon now a new freshet of grief poured from Kizzy. She realized that the sheriff knew exactly who the slave dealer was; they would certainly have traced her by now! She felt even more desperately lost, even more totally abandoned. Later, when she had no more tears left to shed, she lay imploring God to destroy her, if He felt she deserved all this, just because she loved Noah. Feeling some slickness seeping between her upper legs, Kizzy knew that she was continuing to bleed. But the pain had subsided to a throbbing.

When the cabin door came creaking open again, Kizzy had sprung up and was rearing backward against the wall before she realized that it was the woman. She was carrying a steaming small pot, with a bowl and spoon, and Kizzy slumped back down onto the dirt floor as the woman put the pot on the table, then spooned some food into the bowl, which she placed down alongside Kizzy. Kizzy acted as if she saw neither the food nor the woman, who squatted beside her and began talking as matter-of-factly as if they had known each other for years.

"I'se de big-house cook. My name Malizy. What you'n?"

Finally, Kizzy felt stupid not to answer. "It Kizzy, Miss Malizy."

The woman made an approving grunt. "You sounds well raised." She glanced at the untouched stew in the bowl. "I reckon you know you let vittles git cold dey don't do you no good." Miss Malizy sounded almost like Sister Mandy or Aunt Sukey.

Hesitantly picking up the spoon, Kizzy tasted the stew, then began to eat some of it, slowly.

"How ol' you is?" asked Miss Malizy.

"I'se sixteen, ma'am."

"Massa boun' for hell jes' sho's he born!" exclaimed Miss Malizy, half under her breath. Looking at Kizzy, she said, "Jes' well's to tell you Massa one dem what loves nigger womens, 'specially young'uns like you is. He use to mess wid me, I ain't but roun' nine years older'n you, but he quit after he brung Missy here an' made me de cook, workin' right dere in de house where she is, thanks be to Gawd!" Miss Malizy grimaced. "Speck you gwine be seein' 'im in here regular."

Seeing Kizzy's hand fly to her mouth, Miss Malizy said, "Honey, you jes' well's realize you's a nigger woman. De kind of white man Massa is, you either gives in or he gwine make you wish you had, one way or 'nother. An' lemme tell you, dis massa a mean thing if you cross 'im. Fact, ain't never knowed nobody git mad de way he do. Ever'thin' can be gwine 'long jes' fine, den let jes' anythin' happen dat rile 'im," Miss Malizy snapped her fingers, "quick as dat, he can fly red hot an' ack like he done gon' crazy!"

Kizzy's thoughts were racing. Once darkness fell, before he came again, she must escape. But it was as if Miss Malizy read her mind. "Don't you even start thinkin' 'bout runnin' nowhere, honey! He jes' have you hunted down wid dem blood dogs, an' you in a worser mess. Jes' calm yo'self. De next fo', five days he ain't gon' be here nohow. Him an' his ol' nigger chicken trainer already done left for one dem big chicken fights halfway 'crost de state." Miss Malizy paused. "Massa don't care 'bout nothin' much as dem fightin' chickens o' his'n."

She went on talking nonstop—about how the massa, who had grown to adulthood as a po' cracker, bought a 25-cent raffle ticket that won him a good fighting rooster, which got him started on the road to becoming one of the area's more successful gamecock owners.

Kizzy finally interrupted. "Don' he sleep wid his missis?"

"Sho' he do!" said Miss Malizy. "He jes' love womens. You won't never see much o' her, 'cause she scairt to death o' 'im, an' she keep real quiet an' stay close. She whole lot younger'n he is; she was jes' fo'teen, same kind of po' cracker he was, when he married her an' brung her here. But she done foun' out he don't care much for her as he do his chickens." As Miss Malizy continued talking about the massa, his wife and his chickens, Kizzy's thoughts drifted away once again to thoughts of escape.

"Gal! Is you payin' me 'tention?"

"Yes'm," she replied quickly.

Miss Malizy's frown eased. "Well, I specks you better, since I'se 'quaintin' you wid where you is!"

Briefly she studied Kizzy. "Where you come from, anyhow?" Kizzy said from Spotsylvania County, Virginia. "Ain't never heared of it! Anyhow, dis here's Caswell County in North Ca'liny." Kizzy's expression showed that she had no idea where that was, though she had often heard of North Carolina, and she had the impression that it was somewhere near Virginia.

"Look here, does you even know Massa's name?" asked Miss Malizy. Kizzy looked blank. "Him's Massa Tom Lea." She reflected a moment. "Reckon now dat make you Kizzy Lea."

"My name Kizzy Waller!" Kizzy exclaimed in protest.

Then, with a flash, she remembered that all of this had happened to her at the hands of Massa Waller, whose name she bore, and she began weeping.

"Don't take on so, honey!" exclaimed Miss Malizy. "You sho' knows niggers takes whoever's dey massa's name. Nigger names don't make no difference nohow, jes' sump'n to call 'em."

Kizzy said, "My pappy's real name Kunta Kinte. He a African."

"You don't say!" Miss Malizy appeared taken aback. "I'se heared my great-gran'daddy was one dem Africans, too! My mammy say her mammy told her he was blacker'n tar, wid scars zigzaggin' down both cheeks. But my mammy never say his name." Miss Malizy paused. "You know yo' mammy, too?"

" 'Cose I does. My mammy name Bell. She a big-house cook like you is. An' my pappy drive de massa's buggy— leas' he did."

"You jes' come from bein' wid yo' mammy an' pappy both?" Miss Malizy couldn't believe it. "Lawd, ain't many us gits to know *both* our folks 'fo' somebody git sol' away!"

Sensing that Miss Malizy was preparing to leave, suddenly dreading being left alone again, Kizzy sought a way to extend the conversation. "You talks a whole lot like my mammy," she offered.

Miss Malizy seemed startled, then very pleased. "I specks she a good Christian woman like I is."

Hesitantly, Kizzy asked something that had crossed her mind. "What kine of work dey gwine have me doin' here, Miss Malizy?"

Miss Malizy seemed astounded at the question. "What you gon' *do*?" she demanded. "Massa ain't tol' you how many niggers here?" Kizzy shook her head. "Honeychile, you makin' zactly five! An' dat's countin' Mingo, de ol' nigger dat live down 'mongst de chickens. So it's me cook-in', washin' an' housekeepin', an' Sister Sarah an' Uncle Pompey workin' in de fiel', where you sho' gwine go, too—dat you is!"

Miss Malizy's brows lifted at the dismay on Kizzy's face. "What work you done where you was?"

"Cleanin' in de big house an' helpin' my mammy in de kitchen," Kizzy answered in a faltering voice.

"Figgered sump'n like dat when I seen dem soft hands of your'n! Well, you sho' better git ready for some calluses an' corns soon's Massa git back!" Miss Malizy then seemed to feel that she should soften a bit. "Po' thing! Listen here to me, you been used to one dem rich massa's places. But dis here one dem po' crackers what scrabbled an' scraped till he got holt a li'l lan' an' built a house dat ain't nothin' but a big front to make 'em look better off dan dey is. Plenty crackers like dat roun' here. Dey got a sayin', 'Farm a hundred acres wid fo' niggers.' Well, he too tight to buy even dat many. But he finally had to see wasn't no way jes' Uncle Pompey an' Sister Sarah could farm much as he like to plant, an' he *had* to git somebody else. Dat's how come he bought you." Miss Malizy paused. "You know how much you cost?"

Kizzy said weakly. "No'm."

"Well, I reckon six to seb'n hundred dollars, considerin' de prices I'se heared him say niggers costin' nowdays, an' you bein' strong an' young, lookin' like a good breeder, too, dat'll bring him free pickaninnies."

With Kizzy again speechless, Miss Malizy moved closer to the door and stopped. "Fact, I wouldn't o' been surprised if Massa stuck you in wid one dem stud niggers some rich massas keeps on dey places an' hires out. But it look like to me he figgerin' on breedin' you hisself."

The conversation was short.

"Massa, I gwine have a baby."

"Well, what you expectin' me to do about it? I know you

better not start playin' sick, tryin' to get out of workin'!"

But he did start coming to Kizzy's cabin less often as her belly began to grow. Slaving out under the hot sun, Kizzy went through dizzy spells as well as morning sickness in the course of her painful initiation to field work. Torturous blisters on both her palms would burst, fill with fluid again, then burst again from their steady friction against the rough, heavy handle of her hoe. Chopping along, trying to keep not too far behind the experienced, short, stout, black Uncle Pompey and the wiry, light-brown-skinned Sister Sarah—both of whom she felt were still deciding what to think of her—she would strain to recall everything she had ever heard her mammy say about the having of young'uns. She felt she'd give anything if Bell could be there beside her now. Despite her humiliation at being great with child and having to face her mammy—who had warned repeatedly of the disgrace that could befall her "if'n you keeps messin' roun' wid dat Noah an' winds up too close"—Kizzy knew she'd understand that it hadn't been her fault, and she'd let her know the things she needed to know.

She could almost hear Bell's voice telling her sadly, as she had so often, what she believed had caused the tragic deaths of both the wife and baby of Massa Waller: "Po' li'l thing was jes' built too small to birth dat great big baby!" Was she herself built big enough? Kizzy wondered frantically. Was there any way to tell? She remembered once when she and Missy Anne had stood goggle-eyed, watching a cow deliver a calf, then their whispering that despite what grownups told them about storks bringing babies, maybe mothers had to squeeze them out through their privates in the same gruesome way.

The older women, Miss Malizy and Sister Sarah, seemed to take hardly any notice of her steadily enlarging belly— and breasts—so Kizzy decided angrily that it would be as big a waste of time to confide her fears to them as it would to Massa Lea. Certainly, he couldn't have been less concerned as he rode around the plantation on his horse, yelling threats at anyone he felt wasn't working fast enough.

When the baby came—in the winter of 1806—Sister Sarah served as the midwife. After what seemed an eternity of moaning, screaming, feeling as if she were ripping apart, Kizzy lay bathed in sweat, staring in wonder at the wriggling infant grinning Sister Sarah was holding up. It was a boy—but his skin seemed to be almost high yaller.

Seeing Kizzy's alarm, Sister Sarah assured her, "New babies takes leas' a month to darken to dey full color, honey!" But Kizzy's apprehension deepened as she examined her baby several times every day; when a full month had passed, she knew that the child's permanent color was going to be, at best, a pecan-colored brown.

She remembered her mammy's proud boast, "Ain't nothin' but black niggers here on Massa's place." And she tried not to think about "sassaborro," the name her ebony-black father—his mouth curled in scorn—used to call those with mulatto skin. She was grateful that they weren't there to see—and share—her shame. But she knew that she'd never be able to hold her head up again even if they never saw the child, for all anyone had to do was compare her color with the baby's to know what had happened—and with whom. She thought of Noah and felt even more ashamed. "Dis our *las'* chance 'fo' I leaves, baby, how *come* you can't?" she heard him say again. She wished desperately that she had, that this was Noah's baby; at least it would be black.

"Gal, what's de *matter* you ain't happy, gret big ol' fine chile like dat!" said Miss Malizy one morning, noticing how sad Kizzy looked and how awkwardly she was holding the baby, almost at her side, as if she found it hard even to *look* at her child. In a rush of understanding, Miss Malizy blurted, "Honey, what you lettin' bother you ain't no need to worry 'bout. Don't make no difference, 'cause dese days an' times don't nobody care, ain't even pay no 'tention. It gittin' to be near 'bout as many mulattoes as it is black niggers like us. It's jes' de way things is, dat's all"—Miss Malizy's eyes were pleading with Kizzy. "An' you can be sho' Massa ain't never gwine claim de chile, not no way at all. He jes' see a young'un he glad he ain't had to pay for, dat he gwine stick out in de fiel's same as you is. So de only thing for you to feel is dat big, fine baby's *your'n*, honey— dat's all it is to it!"

That way of seeing things helped Kizzy to collect herself, at least somewhat. "But what gwine happen," she asked, "when sometime or 'nother Missis sho' catch sight dis chile, Miss Malizy?"

"She know he ain't no good! I wisht I had a penny for every white woman knows dey husbands got chilluns by niggers. Main thing, I speck Missis be jealous 'cause seem like *she* ain't able to have none."

The next night, Massa Lea came to the cabin—about a month after the baby was born—he bent over the bed and held his candle close to the face of the sleeping baby. "Hmmmm. Ain't bad-lookin'. Good-sized, too." With his forefinger, he jiggled one of the clenched tiny fists and said, turning to Kizzy, "All right. This weekend will make enough time off. Monday you go back to the field."

"But Massa, I ought to stay to nuss 'im!" she said fool-ishly.

His rage exploded in her ears. "Shut up and do as you're told! You're through being pampered by some fancy Vir-ginia blue blood! Take that pickaninny with you to the field, or I'll keep that baby and sell you out of here so quick your head swims!"

Scared silly, Kizzy burst into weeping at even the thought of being sold away from her child. "*Yassuh,* Massa!" she cried, cringing. Seeing her crushed submission, his anger quickly abated, but then Kizzy began to sense— with disbelief—that he had actually come intending to use her again, even now, with the baby sleeping right beside them.

"Massa, Massa, it too soon," she pleaded tearfully. "I ain't healed up right yet, Massa!" But when he simply ignored her, she struggled only long enough to put out the candle, after which she endured the ordeal quietly, terrified that the baby would awaken. She was relieved that he still seemed to be sleeping even when the massa spent himself, and then was clambering up, preparing to go. In the darkness, as he snapped his suspenders onto his shoulders, he said, "Well, got to call him somethin'." Kizzy lay with her breath sucked in. After another moment, he said, "Call him George—that's after the hardest-workin' nigger I ever saw." After another pause, the massa continued, as if talking to himself, "George. Yeah. Tomorrow I'll write it in my Bible. Yeah, that's a good name—George!" And he went on out.

Kizzy cleaned herself off and then lay back down, unsure which outrage to be most furious about. She had thought earlier of either Kunta or Kinte as an ideal name, though uncertain of what the massa's reaction might be to their uncommon sounds. But she dared not risk igniting his temper with any objection to the name he'd chosen. She thought with a new horror of what her African pappy would think of it, knowing what importance he attached to names. Kizzy remembered how her pappy had told her that in his homeland, the naming of sons was the most important thing of all, " 'cause de sons become dey fam'lies' mens!"

She lay thinking of how she had never understood why her pappy had always felt so bitter against the world of white people—toubob was his word for them. She thought of Bell's saying to her, "You's so lucky it scare me, chile, 'cause you don' really know what bein' a nigger is, an' I hopes to de good Lawd you don' never have to fin' out." Well, she had found out—and there seemed no limit to the

anguish whites were capable of wreaking upon black people. But the worst thing they did, Kunta had said, was to
keep them ignorant of who they are, to keep them from
being fully human.

"De reason yo' pappy took holt o' my feelin's from de
firs'," her mammy had told her, "was he de proudest black
man I ever seed!" Before she fell asleep Kizzy decided that
however base her baby's origins, however light his color,
whatever name the massa forced upon him, she would
never regard him as other than the grandson of an African.

ALEX HALEY

A Candid Conversation with the Author of the American Saga "Roots"

BRENT BEAR

If it weren't for the fact that it's a true story, "Roots" might well be the Great American Novel. In the months since its publication, it has been compared to both "Moby Dick" and "War and Peace," and at least one reviewer called it "among the most important books of the century." Double-day, its publisher, ordered the largest print run ever for a hardcover book (200,000), which sold out in a matter of weeks, and there are indications it may become the first book in history to sell over 1,000,000 copies in hardback—even before Dell brings out the paperback version.

Its author, Alex Haley, will undoubtedly become a house-

*hold name later this month, when ABC-TV broadcasts the
first episode of a 12-hour series based on "Roots," making it
the longest and most expensive ($6,000,000) dramatic televi-
sion production ever aired.*

We at PLAYBOY *take a special pleasure in featuring Haley
as our holiday interview subject. In 1962, when he was a
free-lance writer and journalist, we assigned him to conduct
a long question-and-answer session with Miles Davis, which
became the first "Playboy Interview." Besides interviewing
a number of personalities for* PLAYBOY, *ranging from American Nazi George Lincoln Rockwell to entertainer Johnny
Carson, Haley conducted our interviews with the two most
significant black leaders of the Sixties—Martin Luther
King, Jr., and Malcolm X. (One result of the "Playboy
Interview" with Malcolm X was the best-selling "Autobiography," which Haley wrote.) It seems especially fitting to us
that Haley be on the other side of the tape recorder this
month, since he seems destined to be one of the most significant black figures of the Seventies.*

*Now 55 and living modestly in West Los Angeles, Haley
is in the midst of a mammoth publicity tour for his book, but
in the past several months he found time for a series of
conversations with a man who also has a special place in
both* PLAYBOY's *and Haley's history. He is Murray Fisher,
former Assistant Managing Editor of this magazine, who
assigned Haley that first "Playboy Interview" and shaped
the format of the feature. It was both their professional
relationship and their personal friendship that led Haley to
ask Fisher to be his editor on "Roots," a task that has
occupied no small amount of Fisher's own time over the
12-year period it took Haley to write the book. Now a
Contributing Editor to* PLAYBOY, *Fisher conducted this interview with his old friend and colleague as "a labor of love."
It is Haley's story, but one that Fisher knows almost as well
as his own. His report:*

"In the 12 years since Alex had asked me to help him edit

'Roots,' we'd met to work on it in New York, Chicago, Los Angeles, Miami, San Francisco, New Orleans, the West Indies—just about everywhere but the place it all began: Henning, his home town in rural Tennessee, where he'd first heard the stories as a five-year-old on his grandmother's front porch. Now, at last, the book was published, and he had embarked on a promotion tour that included—among its 49 interviews and public appearances in 29 cities in 30 days— a half-day stop in Henning to film a television documentary of the prodigal son's return to his 'roots.' He invited me to join him there. 'Where will I find you?' I asked. 'We'll be moving around town. Just ask the first person you see.'

"He wasn't hard to find. On the lawn in front of a small white frame house were a crowd of people, cables, cameras and parked cars, and at the center stood Alex, surrounded by interviewers peppering him with questions while the camera crew prepared to shoot him walking up the path to the front door for the third time, each from a different angle. 'Some home-coming,' I said when we were out of earshot. 'I know,' he said. 'It's been just Grandma's house all my life, and now with all those lights and those reporters, suddenly it's a media event. But I guess I'll have to get used to that kind of thing. Now that the book is out, I'm beginning to realize that the stories I heard from Grandma—sitting in that very rocker right up there on the porch—don't really belong to me anymore. So I've decided to keep that chair; next time you come to my house, it'll be on my front porch.'

"In 1873, soon after Alex' ancestors had arrived in Henning by wagon train from the plantation in North Carolina where they had lived as slaves, most of them had become founders of the New Hope Colored Methodist Episcopal Church—where the documentary's final scene was shot that night at a special service held in honor of the town's most celebrated citizen.

"It was recently rebuilt in the gleaming white architectural style of a suburban corporate headquarters, and, waiting for him inside the new church, dressed in its Sunday best, bathed in the brilliance of quartz movie lights, sat the entire congregation, filling every pew.

"Glad to be there, but feeling a little out of place — though perhaps less so than the jeaned and bearded film crew from L.A.—I slipped in and found a seat in the back. A moment later, the doors opened and Alex started walking down the aisle toward the pulpit, followed by his younger brothers George and Julius, who had been invited by the TV people to make it a 'family reunion.'

"A black boy of about ten in the row ahead, staring at Alex with shining eyes, asked, 'Is that him?' He didn't have to wait long for an answer; later, everyone in that church was giving him a standing ovation. The cameras, of course, were rolling. Looking a little sheepish, Alex sat down on a bench behind the pulpit beside his brothers, and Fred Montgomery, a deacon of the church, an alderman on the town council and a lifelong friend of Alex', led the purple-gowned choir and the congregation in a rousing spiritual. Then a white aide to Henning's mayor got up to say a few words about the pride everyone in the community took in its native son.

"Then, standing nervously with one arm on the piano for support, a teenage girl, obviously her high school's valedictorian, recited tremulously a short speech she had not only memorized but undoubtedly written herself. By the time she got to the end, she was looking at the audience rather than the floor, and she said loudly and firmly, 'What Mr. Haley has done for us—and for the world—will remain eternal.'

"The congregation was on its feet again, and it was Alex' turn to speak. In that deep, down-home baritone he can pour on like honey over biscuits, he told them about his search for roots, 'a story that began right here in Henning just two *blocks from where I stand.' It was a shorter, but more personal, version of the dramatic and deeply moving speech that's made him one of the most popular speakers on the lecture circuit for the past ten years—a speech he's made so often that passages from it have become almost a narrative litany of oral history. Parts of it even turned up in his answers to my questions. But there in that Henning pulpit, he added something new: an obviously heartfelt tribute to his home town.*

" 'It's not a pretty place,' he said. 'There's nothing very special about it. But to me it's a symbol of small-town America, the birthplace of those old-fashioned virtues that are our deepest-strengths as a nation—like compassion for your fellow man: Even to this day, there isn't a door in Henning where somebody cold or hungry would get turned away. Values like respect for your elders—needing them, caring for them, listening to them; they've got a lot to teach us all.'

"There's no question that Alex has missed his calling as a fundamentalist preacher; or maybe he hasn't. Every few sentences were interrupted with outcries of 'Say it!' and 'Amen.' And when he was finished, people were weeping, cheering, applauding, rushing up to touch him, shake his hand, gush out their thanks.

"He couldn't afford to be late for a speech to 5000 teachers later that night in Memphis. But he's constitutionally incapable of brushing people off, and it was half an hour before he could make it to the door. Dazed with exhaustion after two weeks in a different city every night, he lapsed into silence and sat with his eyes closed almost all the way to the Mid-South Coliseum. Arriving just in time to be rushed onstage, somehow he managed to crank himself up into delivering another rafter ringer; and the crowd went wild again.

"He couldn't get back to his hotel until three A.M.; his plane was leaving at 7:30. As he trudged with me down the

*hall to his room, he was nearly out on his feet. 'If only they
wouldn't come at me so,' he said. We went on to talk about
that for a few minutes more, while he sat on the edge of his
bed and pulled off his shoes and socks, and then I said
good-night. Though this conversation was the last in the 20
hours of taping sessions we'd recorded, I decided to make it
our first exchange in the interview—for it seemed to fore-
shadow a new life for Alex that promised not only wealth
and fame but elevation, in some mysterious way, to the
mythic stature of a spiritual leader.*

*"The following personal opinion may compromise my
credibility as a journalist, but frankly, I value more highly
my credibility as a friend of Alex Haley's for 15 years. And
the simple fact is that I consider him the finest and most
decent man I've ever known. If we have to have a spiritual
leader, we could do a whole lot worse."*

FISHER: The reaction you've evoked in public appearances
since the publication of *Roots* has often been almost worshipful. How does that make you feel?

HALEY: It disturbs me. My most devout hope was to write
a book that would move people, and apparently I've succeeded. But I truly feel that I was merely a conduit for a
story that was *intended* to be told, and I know that it's the
story I tell, not *me*, that they're responding to. If only that
response weren't so intense. A few weeks ago, I was talking
with friends at a small party in Los Angeles, when a young
black woman I'd never seen before came rushing up to me,
grabbed my hand and fell to her knees, bubbling her gratitude. All I could think of to do was tell her to *stop* it and
pull her to her feet. Things like that aren't just embarrassing; they're unsettling. She just didn't understand that what
Roots is saying—to black people, especially—is that once
you find out who you really are, you don't have to go down
on your knees to *anyone* anymore. If people are starting to

look at me like I'm some kind of Gandhi, all I can say is: I'm not qualified for the job; and even if I were, I wouldn't want it. All I did was write a book, and I'm the same guy now that I was before I wrote it.

FISHER: But that book has become a runaway best seller and on January 30, it will debut in an unprecedented 12-hour television adaptation for which a nightly audience of at least 50,000,000 is being predicted. You may be the same guy you were before, but don't you think all this is bound to change your *life*?

HALEY: It already *has*. Hell, I feel like I'm living somebody *else*'s life. After 15 years as a journalist, I'd gotten used to a certain lifestyle: hustling for a buck, waiting for the phone to ring with an assignment, wangling my way past secretaries to interview their bosses. Now, all of a sudden, I'm going to be paying someone as much to handle my finances as I used to *make* in a year. The phone is ringing off the wall with invitations, such as to join assorted dignitaries for lunch at the State Department and dinner at the White House, queries from writers for magazines that used to reject my stuff, wanting to do stories on *me*; and now PLAYBOY is making me its first interviewer ever to *be* interviewed by the magazine. And, just to wrap up the irony, I'm being interviewed by you, the guy who used to be my editor at the magazine.

FISHER: Does that bother you?

HALEY: After all those years at the mercy of your blue pencil, I'm looking *forward* to it. The only trouble is, by this time we know each other so well that I know what you're going to ask before you open your mouth, and you know what I'm going to say before I open mine. So why don't we save ourselves the trouble of talking? I'll write your questions, you write my answers and we'll just *mail* it in.

FISHER: Good idea. But just for the sake of appearances, why don't we go through the motions of taping an actual conversation?

HALEY: Just as long as you promise not to ask leading questions. I've *heard* about you PLAYBOY interviewers.

FISHER: We'll give you the same consideration you always offered people when *you* were doing interviews.

HALEY: In that case, forget the whole thing.

FISHER: Fine, just as soon as we finish the interview. You were talking about what success has done to your life.

HALEY: Well, I'm being inundated with requests to appear on television shows hosted by stars whose *publicists* never used to return my calls, with letters from universities asking me to accept honorary degrees and address their graduating classes. I find myself being eased into plush leather armchairs and offered cigars in executive sanctum sanctorums that I couldn't have broken into with TNT a few years ago. My daily calendar, where I used to scrawl my grocery lists, is blocked out from breakfast to bedtime for meetings with people who want my name, my permission, my support, my endorsement, my commitment, my involvement and especially *money* — to underwrite everything from stuff like *Roots* T-shirts and Afro-American tour groups to worthwhile social causes and promising television and movie projects, some of which I plan to pursue as head of my own production company later this year.

FISHER: You're not complaining, are you?

HALEY: I'm having the time of my life. I've never felt happier, younger, stronger, more energetic and alive than I do today — because I set for myself a task that seemed impossible, and yet somehow I completed it. It took 12 years, but I feel it was worth every moment of it, because *Roots* tells a story that's needed to be told for 200 years. That was reward enough for undertaking it, but I'm happy to say that *Roots* is going to earn me something far more tangible, as well as precious: financial independence.

After being harassed by debt for more years than I care to remember, I now feel beyond a reasonable doubt that I will never have to waste another moment worrying about rent, taxes, alimony, the lot of it. I mean, it's funny that at this very moment, while I'm here talking to you, I'm sitting and folding my own laundry. But by the time this interview appears, I'll finally be in a position to buy what I've always longed for—the *time* to spend on things I care about that I used to have to spend on things I *didn't* care about.

FISHER: Do you think success may spoil—or stifle—Alex Haley?

HALEY: I pray not. Not as long as I remember who I am and where I came from. Every time I catch myself getting annoyed when I have to wait outside some studio for a while because the limousine is late, every time I pick up the phone in some fancy hotel to order a steak from room service rather than run down to the coffee shop for a hamburger, which I'd actually enjoy just as much, I think about Miss Scrap Green and Fred Montgomery and all the other good people I grew up with back in Henning, Tennessee, and I wonder what they'd say if they could see me now. And I'm glad they can't. Because their values are still my values, and they always will be. No matter where I go or what I do with my life, no matter how many books I write or movies I produce, I'll always be "Miz Haley's boy" to them, and that's the way it ought to be.

A while ago, just after I had been interviewed by a television host who introduced me as "the author of one of the great literary works of our time," I went home to visit the family and as I was walking down the street one morning, I met this old man—the ageless kind every small town has—going the other way. "Mornin', sir," I said. You just don't pass anyone in a small town without saying hello. "How do," he replied, stopping and squinting at me. "Ain't you Miz Haley's boy?" "Yes, sir," I said. "Ain't seen you aroun' for a while," he said. "What you doin' with yourself

nowadays?" "I'm a writer." "What you write?" "Books."
"How you do that?" "Well, it's kind of hard to explain."
"Write somethin' for me, then." "I'm afraid it doesn't work
quite that way." He considered that for a while, and then
he said, "Well, if you was to tell me you was a lightnin' bug,
I'd 'spect you to light up."

Ever since then, whenever I've been tempted to feel
important—and there've been a few times—I just remember that old man. Henning is what keeps me honest. It's my
roots, and those roots run deep—from my Grandma
Cynthia's porch all the way back to Africa.

FISHER: Wasn't that the porch where your grandmother
told you the stories about your family that led to the
writing of your book?

HALEY: Yes, it was. Whenever I go home to visit Henning,
I always go over to the old house and sit on that porch for
a while. The new owners don't seem to mind. Grandma's
long gone, of course, but while I'm sitting there—in the
same white-wicker chair she used to rock on while she
talked—I remember all the stories she told as if it were
yesterday.

FISHER: How long ago *was* it?

HALEY: About half a century now. The earliest I can
remember hearing them was a year or so after my grandfather Will Palmer died, when I was around five. Grandma
had lived for that man ever since the day they'd met 38
years before, and when he died, something inside her went
along with him. She'd always been a lively woman, but
from then on, she took to sitting out on the front porch and
just rocking for hours at a time. Since my mother was off
teaching school and my father had taken over Grandpa's
lumber mill, I spent most of my time alone at home with
Grandma.

But after a few months, she began inviting various sisters, nieces and cousins around her age—Aunt Plus, Aunt
Viney, Aunt Liz, Aunt Till, Cousin Georgia and a few

others—to come and keep her company. They'd arrive from exotic places like Dyersburg, which was all of 25 miles away; Inkster, Michigan; St. Louis; even Kansas City; and they'd stay for a few weeks, sometimes the whole summer, often five or six of them at a time, cooking, knitting, talking and puttering their way through the day. Every night, after the supper dishes had been washed, just around dusk, as the lightning bugs were beginning to flick on and off above the honeysuckle vines, they'd all drift out to the porch and settle down in their favorite rockers—with me scrunched up on the floor behind Grandma's—and they'd pick up where they left off the night before, with her taking the lead, telling stories about the family.

FISHER: Tell *us* a few.

HALEY: They were just bits and pieces, weaving back and forth through the years. Some were from Grandma's own life and Grandpa Will's—how the leading white businessmen of Henning, in a historic decision, had turned ownership of the town's only lumber company over to him when its drunken white owner had brought it to the brink of bankruptcy, and how he had gone on to become one of the town's most respected citizens. Only a generation before, they recalled, the same town's white business community had forbidden Grandma's father, Tom Murray, to open a blacksmith shop, so he'd built up a thriving trade with a rolling shop—an anvil and a forge on a wagon—which he drove from farm to farm.

After emancipation, it had been Tom who led the family—his half-Cherokee wife, Irene, and their eight children, his seven brothers and sisters and *their* children—across the Appalachians in a wagon train from "the Murray plantation" in Alamance County, North Carolina, all the way to Henning. They'd been lured to this backwoods settlement in western Tennessee, Tom had said, by his father, George, who'd returned from his travels as a freedman with tales of a "promised land" with soil so rich that "if you plant a pig's tail, a hog'll grow." Proud of his ancestry, George had kept alive the stories of the family he'd heard from his mother, Kizzy, by repeating them as a ritual at the birth of each new child by his wife, Matilda. But he was hardly a dutiful father and he earned a justified reputation as a ladies' man—and as a highrolling gambler on the fighting cocks he had trained since boyhood for his massa, Tom Lea.

FISHER: Hence his nickname, "Chicken George"?

HALEY: Which he carried with him proudly to his death, along with a derby hat and a rakish green scarf, which he wore like a trademark. Time and again there on the porch, I heard how Massa Lea had finally lost almost everything he owned in a wager to an English nobleman, who took Chicken George off to England as his gamecock trainer for three years. When he left, it seems that Massa Lea lost more than a cockfighter. When George was a boy, Kizzy had told him that he'd been sired by Massa Lea, who had raped her on the night of her arrival at the Lea plantation. At 16, she'd been sold away from her parents for helping a boy escape from the plantation of Dr. William Waller in Spotsylvania County, Virginia, where she had been born and raised. Her mother, Kizzy told young George, was the big-house cook, Bell. And her father—the furthest-back person anyone in the family ever spoke of—was a man they called the African.

FISHER: Did they know any more than that about him?

HALEY: They said he had been brought across the ocean to a place they called "Naplis," that he had tried four times to escape from the plantation of his first owner, "Massa John Waller," and that after his fourth attempt, he was offered the choice of castration or having a foot cut off. Because he chose the foot, said Grandma, "I'm here to tell about it." The African told Kizzy that the massa's brother, Dr. William Waller, had bought him, nursed him back to health, put him to work in his garden and later had him serve as his buggy driver. Though John Waller had named him Toby, the women said the African had always angrily insisted that the other slaves call him by his real name, which they pronounced "Kin-tay."

As Kizzy grew up, according to the old ladies on the porch, Kin-tay taught her words from his own language. He called a guitar a *ko*, for example, and as they rode in the buggy past the Mattaponi River near the plantation, he'd point and say something that sounded like *Kamby Bolongo*. The thing Kizzy remembered most vividly—and passed on to Chicken George, who later told *his* children, and so on down to me—was that when Kin-tay was a boy of about 17 "rains"—his word for years—he had been out in the forest, not far from his village in Africa, chopping wood to make a drum, when four men had set upon him, beaten him senseless and marched him in chains to the ship in which he was taken to America and sold into slavery.

FISHER: Did those stories make much of an impression on you at the time?

HALEY: I loved them, but I didn't *live* them, as Grandma did. With Grandpa gone, those stories were the most important thing in her life and she told and retold them—to the point where she and my mother actually had words about it. "I'm sick of all that old-timy stuff!" Momma would exclaim. "Why don't you quit talking about it all the time?" And Grandma would say, "Well, if you don't care where you come from, *I* do!" And they might not speak for two or three days.

FISHER: Why didn't your mother want to hear the stories?

HALEY: She was the first person in our family who ever went to college. You see it in every poor immigrant group that's come to this country; the first thing its members want to do as they begin to make it is to forget their homeland—its traditions and its culture—and to fit in with the new one. Momma wanted nothin' to do with no Africans, and even less with slaves; she was embarrassed by all that. But to a little boy like me, it was just a bunch of stories, like the Biblical parables I heard every week in Sunday school at the New Hope Methodist Church. They were more exciting, of course, because some of the people in them were sitting right there on the porch. But most of the family they talked about—Tom Murray, Chicken George, Kizzy, the African—were just characters to me, like Jonah, Pharoah, David and Goliath, Adam and Eve.

FISHER: When did the stories begin to mean something more to you?

HALEY: It took about 30 years. I had grown up and gone to college for two years and then joined the Coast Guard as a mess boy not long before World War Two broke out. During the long months at sea, I passed the time by writing letters to everyone I knew—maybe 40 a week—and after a while, I caught the bug, and started writing for *publication*; or tried to. I spent eight years writing some part of every single day before making my first sale to a magazine. When I finally retired—as Chief Journalist—after 20 years, at 37, I moved to Greenwich Village, where I planned to make it as a free-lance journalist; I guess I thought I'd pick it up by osmosis, simply by *living* in that writers' colony. But it didn't come quite that easy. One day, I was down to exactly 18 cents and two cans of sardines when a friend called me with the offer of a modest but steady job in the civil service. I took a deep breath and turned him down. The very next day, a small check arrived in the mail from some magazine, and I managed to hang on long enough to begin selling regularly. Those two sardine cans and that 18 cents, by the way, are framed and hanging on my wall even to this day, as a reminder of how close I came to the end of the line. Anyway, it was around that time that you assigned me to conduct an interview for PLAYBOY.

FISHER: That was the very first interview we published, in September of 1962.

HALEY: With Miles Davis. Which taught me a little bit

about jazz as well as journalism. But my association with Malcolm X, the second interview you assigned to me, led to my collaboration with him on my first book, *The Autobiography of Malcolm X*. I remember his telling me very calmly, as he read the finished manuscript two years later, that he'd never live to see it published—and he was right.

In a way, I have PLAYBOY to thank for setting my second book, *Roots*, into motion, too. It was soon after the Malcolm book came out, and you asked me to interview Julie Christie, who was making a movie in London. While I was there, waiting for an appointment—which never came about, as you know—I kept myself busy taking guided tours of the city. One of them stopped at the British Museum, where I found something I'd heard about only vaguely but which now entranced me: the Rosetta stone. I immediately read up on it and learned that it had been found in the Nile delta in 1799, inscribed with three texts: one in Greek, the second in a then-unknown set of characters, the third in ancient Egyptian hieroglyphics, which it had been assumed no one would ever be able to decipher. But in a superhuman feat of scholarship, a Frenchman named Jean Champollion had matched the two unknown texts, character for character, with the Greek text and proved that all three were the same, thus cracking the code and opening up to the world much of mankind's earliest history, which had been recorded in—and hidden behind—the mystery of those hieroglyphics.

FISHER: Why did all that fascinate you so?

HALEY: I wasn't sure. I felt that key which had unlocked a door to the past had some special significance for me, but I didn't realize what it was until I was on the plane returning to the U.S. In the stories Grandma and the others had told me, there were fragments of words from an unknown tongue spoken by the African who said his name was Kin-tay, called a guitar a *ko* and a river *Kamby Bolongo*. They were mostly sharp, angular sounds with K predominating. Undoubtedly, they had undergone some changes in pronunciation as they had been passed down across the generations, but it seemed to me that they had to be phonetic snatches of the actual language spoken by my ancestor and that if I could find out what that language was, I might be able to unlock the door to my *own* past.

When I got home, I knew there was somebody I had to see. Of all the old ladies from the porch in Henning, only one was still alive: Cousin Georgia, who had been 20-odd years younger than the others. She was in her 80s now and living with her son, Floyd, and daughter, Bea, in Kansas City, Kansas. I hadn't seen her in several years and she was ailing and bedridden, but the moment I mentioned my interest in the family stories, she jerked upright and started prattling away: "Yeah, boy, dat African say a guitar a *ko* and he call a river de *Kamby Bolongo* an' he was out choppin' wood, intendin' to make hisself a drum when dey cotched 'im." It was like echoes of the stories I'd heard during my boyhood.

When I told her that I wanted to see if I could find out where Kin-tay came from, which might reveal the identity of our ancestral tribe, she became so excited that Floyd, Bea and I had trouble calming her down. And as I left, she told me something that galvanized me—something that has driven and sustained me ever since: "Boy, yo' sweet granma and all of 'em—dey up dere, watchin'. So you go do what you got to do."

FISHER: What *did* you do?

HALEY: I soon discovered what I already feared: that because there was little tradition of family continuity among blacks, there were very sparse genealogical records of black families—certainly none of the kind that can enable some white families to trace their ancestors as far back as the Mayflower and across the Atlantic to wherever they came from. In the first place, newly arrived Africans were divested of their born names and given slave names—as

Kin-tay had been renamed Toby. Thus were they robbed of their past, beginning a process of psychic dehumanization that was compounded with the frequent breeding of slaves like livestock and the sale of their offspring—often before birth. It was not uncommon for a slave to grow up without knowing his own father. Not many got to know their grandparents. For family stories to go back, as ours did, to great-great-great-great-grandparents was almost unheard of. But because there were no established avenues for corroborating those stories, I had to kind of start from scratch.

FISHER: Which was where?

HALEY: Well, one day, while I was in Washington, D.C., on a magazine assignment, I went to the National Archives. Remembering that Grandma had said she was born on the Murray plantation in Alamance County, North Carolina, and figuring that the family had to have lived there around the time of the Civil War, I asked a black attendant for the census records of that county for the year 1870. They were on microfilm, and I threaded the first roll through the machine and began to turn the handle. There before me were columns of names in old-fashioned script, where the Ss look like Fs, and those people—head of household, wife, children, grandparents—began to parade past. The lists seemed endless, and by the end of the second roll, my curiosity was rapidly diminishing. The thought that I'd ever run across a familiar name among so many countless thousands seemed hopeless and I got up to leave. It gives me the quivers to think how, if I *had* left, none of this would ever have happened.

But as I was walking out, I passed through the genealogical-search room and I happened to notice that, unlike the reading rooms of most libraries, where people are sitting back relaxed and comfortable, everyone there was bent intently over old documents, some with magnifying glasses. And the thought came into my head: *These* people are all

here trying to find out who they *are*. I turned around and
went back to the microfilm room and picked up where I
had left off. Some rolls later, as I was slowly turning the
crank, I suddenly found myself looking down at the name
"Murray, Tom, Blacksmith, Black," and beneath that the
name "Murray, Irene, Housewife, Black," and beneath
them the names of their children, Maria Jane, Ellen, Viney,
Matilda and Elizabeth. Matilda was Aunt Till from Dyersburg. Elizabeth was Aunt Liz; I'd eaten her biscuits for
years. They were Grandma's older sisters; she hadn't been
born yet. I was staggered. To see those names right there in
an official document in the same building that houses the
U.S. Constitution somehow made it very real—and made
it *matter* in a way it never had before. That thought gripped
me—and still does. I had stumbled upon incontrovertible
evidence that I, my family, we black people, indeed, did
have a past, a heritage; it just wasn't very well documented.

FISHER: So that challenged you to keep going?

HALEY: It surely did. Between magazine assignments, I
spent the next few months commuting to Washington from
New York, searching in the National Archives and the
Library of Congress for further confirmation of the family
story, and slowly I found it. In bits and pieces. In time, I
discovered that those old ladies on the porch had been
incredibly accurate; they hadn't known it, but they were
oral historians of the highest order. Piece by piece, I began
to fit it all together about everyone in the family—except
for the African. There was simply nothing to be found
anywhere about a slave named Kin-tay, and even if I could
find some record of him under the name Toby, that
wouldn't help me find out where he came from. Slave
traders were interested in the value of their property, not
in its origin. I knew that those shreds of African words
passed down by the African would have to be the key. If I
had known then what I know now—that maybe *1000*

tribal tongues are spoken in Africa—I would have given up on the spot. But since I didn't know the odds against me, I forged blindly on.

FISHER: In what direction?

HALEY: Well, it seemed logical to seek help from as wide a range of Africans as I could find, so I began to hang around the lobby of the UN Building in New York around quitting time. It wasn't hard to spot the Africans. In the course of two weeks, I managed to buttonhole maybe two dozen of them. Everyone listened to me for a moment—and then took off. I couldn't blame them much; what kind of impression could I make trying to blurt out some alleged African sounds in a Tennessee accent—sounds that very possibly might have been distorted beyond recognition across the 200 years they had taken to reach me?

Finally, I told my problem to a lifelong friend from Henning, George Sims, who happens to be a master researcher. He promptly went into the Library of Congress and shortly brought to me a list of people recognized for their knowledge of African linguistics. The credentials of one of them, a Belgian Ph.D. named Jan Vansina, impressed me so much that I called him for an appointment at the University of Wisconsin, where he was teaching. He had written a book, *La Tradition Orale*, based on research conducted while he was living in African villages. I thought he might be just the man to help me, if anyone could. And he gave me an appointment to meet with him in Madison.

Dr. Vansina listened intently as I told him my story—every syllable of the sounds, everything else I could remember, buttressed by what Cousin Georgia had recently told me. He was particularly interested in how the sounds were passed along from one generation to the next. I told him there had always been one person in each generation who was keeper of the story: First it was Kin-tay, then Kizzy, then George, then Tom, then my grandma Cynthia and, finally, me. When I was through talking, he said he wanted to sleep on it and invited me to spend the night.

FISHER: Did you get any sleep?

HALEY: Not much. I didn't think he would have asked me to stay unless he felt some good reason for it. The next morning at the breakfast table, he said to me, with a very serious expression on his face: "The ramifications of the phonetic sounds preserved down across your family's generations could be immense." My heart all but stopped. He said he had consulted by telephone with one of his colleagues, an eminent Africanist, Dr. Philip Curtin, who concurred with him that the sounds I'd conveyed were in the tongue spoken by the Mandinka, or Mandingo, people. The word *ko*, for example, he said, probably referred to the *kora*, one of the Mandinkas' oldest stringed instruments. But the phrase *Kamby Bolongo* was what clinched it. Without question, he said, in Mandinka, the word *bolongo* meant a large, moving stream, such as a river, and preceded by *Kamby*, it probably referred to the Gambia River. Almost certainly, my African ancestor had been from the Gambia. I'd never heard of it.

FISHER: Did you say so?

HALEY: I was too excited to hide my ignorance; so I asked and he showed it to me on a map—a small, narrow country about midway on the west coast of Africa, bordered on three sides by Senegal and bisected by the Gambia River. I was determined to go there, preferably on the next plane; but I couldn't just pop up in Africa! I wouldn't know where to go, whom to talk to or how to ask. I knew I had to find someone who knew more than I did about the Gambia, which was almost literally nothing.

FISHER: Another research job for Sims?

HALEY: I didn't have to ask him. As fate would have it, only a week or so later, I was asked to speak about my Malcolm X book at Utica College in Upstate New York;

it was my first paid lecture. I got $100 for it, which would be about one tenth of my round-trip air fare to the Gambia. Afterward, talking with the professor who'd invited me to speak, I told him about my quest—and my plight—and he said he'd heard there was an outstanding student over at Hamilton College, about half an hour's drive away, who came from the Gambia. I drove up there and fairly snatched him from a class in economics. His name was Ebou Manga and he was the *blackest* human being I had ever seen. He seemed reservedly amused as I poured out my story in a rush of words, but when I asked him to accompany me to the Gambia—at my expense—his face lit up and he said yes on the spot.

FISHER: How did you intend to finance that expedition?

HALEY: I had no idea where I'd get the money for my *own* ticket, let alone his. But it fell into my lap like manna from heaven two weeks later, when you paid me for an interview. I'd already obtained a visa and the very next day, Ebou and I were off to Dakar, where we changed to a lighter plane and flew on to a small airfield in the Gambia. From there, we drove in a van the rest of the way along a rutted two-lane highway to the capital city of Banjul, which was then called Bathurst.

Ebou's father, Alhaji Malik Manga—they are a Moslem family—soon arranged for me to meet with a group of men who were knowledgeable about their country's history. So once again, I told my story. When I had finished, they seemed most interested in the name Kin-tay. "Our country's oldest villages," they told me, "tend to be named for the families that settled them centuries ago." And on a map, they pointed out a village called Kinte-Kundah and, nearby, another called Kinte-Kundah Janneh-Ya. The Kinte clan—of which my ancestor was undoubtedly a member, they said—was an old and well-known family in the Gambia, and they promised to do what they could to find a *griot* to help me with my search.

FISHER: A *griot*?

HALEY: I cocked my ear at that one, too. They said *griots* were oral historians, almost living archives, men trained from boyhood to memorize, preserve and recite—on ceremonial occasions—the centuries-old histories of villages, of clans, of families, of great kings, holy men and heroes. Some, they said, were the keepers of certain family stories so long that they could talk for three days without ever repeating themselves. When I expressed astonishment, they reminded me that every living person goes back ancestrally to some time when there was no writing, when the only way that human knowledge got passed from one generation to the next had been from the mouths of the elders to the ears of the young. We in the West, they said, had become so dependent on "the crutch of print" that we had forgotten what the memory of man was capable of.

FISHER: Did they find a *griot* for you?

HALEY: Yes, but it took months. I returned home to await developments—and to devour everything I could find to read about Africa. It embarrasses me to think how ignorant I was about the people and the culture of the earth's second-largest continent. Like most of us, black and white, I formed my impressions of Africa and of Africans mostly from *Tarzan* movies, *Jungle Jim* comics and occasional gleanings through old copies of *National Geographic*. So from morning till evening, I pored over book after book about African history and culture, and every night, before I turned out the light, I studied a map of Africa I'd put beside my bed, memorizing the location of each country, its rivers and major cities.

Finally, a letter arrived from the Gambia, which I almost tore open. My contacts there had found a *griot* who might be able to help me, and they'd put me in touch with him if I would return at my earliest convenience. Man, I went nearly wild with excitement—and then frustration. Where would I find the money? I was ready to work my way across as a cook on a freighter—that had been my job for several years on U.S. Coast Guard cutters—when a last resort occurred to me. I wrote to Mrs. DeWitt Wallace, cofounder with her husband of *Reader's Digest*. I had met her at a party several years before and she had said very kind things about an article I'd written for them. Told me to get in touch with her if I ever needed help. I figured she was just being polite, but I had nothing to lose, so I wrote her a letter. To my astonishment, Mrs. Wallace arranged for me to meet with a group of *Digest* editors to see what they felt about my project. I talked passionately and nonstop for about three hours, as if my life depended on it, and in some strange way, I felt it did. They came through—with a $300 monthly stipend and "reasonable necessary travel expenses."

FISHER: Sounds like a dangerously ambiguous phrase. They didn't know you very well, did they?

HALEY: I guess not. But they do now—and I think they've forgiven me. Anyway, two days later, I was back in Banjul, tape recorder and notebook in hand, chafing to get to the *griot* they'd found for me. "His name," they said, "is Kebba Kanji Fofana, and he is a *griot* of the Kinte clan." I was ready to have a fit. "Where is he?" I asked, I suppose expecting to find him waiting somewhere nearby, flanked by a PR man and an interpreter. They looked at me quizzically. "He's in Juffure, his village in the back country upriver," they replied. If I intended to see him, it soon became clear, I'd have to do something I'd never dreamed I'd be doing: organize a kind of modified *safari*!

FISHER: The great black hunter?

HALEY: You go straight to hell. This was totally serious business! It took me three days of bargaining and endless African palaver to assemble everything and everyone I was assured I couldn't do without for the journey. By the time I'd hired a launch for the trip upriver, a lorry and a Land Rover to make the journey overland with provisions and a total of 14 companions, including three interpreters and four musicians—

FISHER: Musicians?

HALEY: I was told the old *griots* didn't like to talk without musicians playing in the background. Anyway, by the time I got all that together, I felt like Stanley setting out in search of Livingstone. I tried to imagine the reaction back at the *Digest* accounting department in Pleasantville when they saw *this* item on my expense account.

FISHER: What did you find when you reached your destination?

HALEY: You've heard of the expression peak experience? That's what I had in Juffure. We put ashore at a little village called Albreda and set out across hot, lush savanna country, and finally we were approaching Juffure's bamboo fence, beyond a grove of trees. Little children playing outside ran in to announce our arrival, and by the time we entered the gate, everyone in the village—about 70 people, plus maybe half as many goats—had converged on us from mud huts. Among them was a small, wizened man in an off-white robe and a pillbox hat; somehow he looked important and I knew he was the *griot* we had come to see and hear.

The interpreters left our group to talk with him and the other villagers swarmed around me, three and four deep all around, and began to stare. For the first time in my life, every face I saw was *jet-black*. And the eyes of everyone were raking me from head to toe. As my own eyes dropped in embarrassment, my glance happened to fall on my hands. I felt ashamed.

FISHER: Why?

HALEY: It was the color of my skin—because I wasn't black. I was brown, the product of forced interbreeding under slavery; I felt impure among the pure. Finally, one of the interpreters came over and whispered in my ear, "They stare at you because they have never here seen a black American." They had been looking at me not as me, Alex

Haley, an individual, but as a symbol for them of a people—25,000,000 of us black people—whom they had never seen, a people who lived in a land beyond the ocean, as unknown to them as they were to us.

Just then, the old *griot* turned from the other interpreters, strode through the crowd and stopped in front of me, his eyes piercing into mine. Seeming to feel that I would understand his Mandinka, he looked straight at me as he spoke, then fell silent while the translation came: "We have been told by the forefathers that there are many of us from this place who are in exile in that place called America. . . ." With that, he sat down on a stool across from me, the people gathered round and he began to recite the ancestral history of the Kinte clan. This was a state occasion, an extremely formal and stylized ritual that dated back unchanged far into antiquity. As he spoke, he leaned forward, his body rigid, and the words would issue from deep within him, like a solid thing, as if carved in stone. After two or three sentences, he would stop, sit back—his eyes seeming opaque, his expression unreadable—and wait for the translation. Then, as if summoning all his strength, he'd lean forward and begin again.

FISHER: Were you tape-recording all this?

HALEY: Indeed, I was, along with the background chatter of monkeys, parrots, goats, chickens, children, and the like. But you could hear him droning through it all. Even in translation, it sounded much like Biblical recitation: So-and-so took unto himself the wife So-and-so and by her he begat . . . and begat. . . . He was talking about people and events 150 or 200 years ago—who married whom, their children in their order of birth, then whom those children married and *their* children, and so on.

FISHER: How long did that go on?

HALEY: For about two hours, there under a broiling sun, bathed in sweat, buzzing with flies. I'll just sum his story up as briefly as I can. The Kinte clan, the *griot* said, began back in the 1500s in a land called Old Mali. After many years, a branch of the clan moved to Mauretania and, from there, one son, Kairaba Kunte Kinte, a Marabout—or holy man of the Moslem faith—traveled south to the Gambia, where he eventually settled in the village of Juffure. There he took his first wife, a Mandinka maiden named Sireng, by whom he begat two sons, Janneh and Saloum. He then took a second wife, Yaisa, by whom he begat a third son, Omoro. When Omoro had 30 rains, he took a wife named Binta Kebba, by whom he begat four sons, named Kunta, Lamin, Suwadu and Madi. Here the *griot* added one of the many time-fixing references in the narrative that is how they identify the date of events: "It was about the time the king's soldiers came. . . ." Then, as he had done perhaps 50 times earlier in the course of his monolog, he added a salient biographical detail about one of the people he was discussing: "The eldest of these four sons, Kunta, went away from this village to chop wood—and he was never seen again."

Well, I sat there feeling as if I were carved of rock. What that old man in back-country Africa had just uttered dovetailed with the very words my grandmother had always spoken during my boyhood on a porch in Tennessee, telling a story she had heard from her father, Tom, who had heard it from his father, George, who had heard it from his mother, Kizzy, who had been told by her father, the man who called himself Kin-tay: that he had been out, not far from his village, chopping wood, intending to make himself a drum, when he had been set upon by four men and kidnaped into slavery.

FISHER: How did you respond?

HALEY: I must have looked as if lightning had struck me, because the *griot* stopped midsentence and leaned toward me with concern and bewilderment. Somehow, from my duffel bag, I managed to pull out the notebook in which I had recorded that very passage of the family story, as

Cousin Georgia had retold it to me at her bedside in Kansas City. When the interpreter read what was written there, it was all he could do to control himself sufficiently to translate it. The *griot*'s eyes shot wide and he leaped up, exclaiming loudly to the others while jabbing at my notebook with his forefinger. A shock wave seemed to go through the crowd, and without an order being given, every one of those 70 people—man, woman and child—formed a giant human ring around me and began chanting rhythmically, moving counterclockwise, lifting their knees high, stamping up reddish puffs of dust. Then a woman holding a baby to her breast burst from the circle and came charging toward me, scowling fiercely, and thrust her child toward me almost roughly in a gesture that said, "Take it!" No sooner had I clasped it to my chest than she snatched it away and another woman was pushing *her* baby into my arms, followed by another and another—until, in a couple of minutes, I'd say I had embraced a dozen babies.

FISHER: What did all that mean?

HALEY: I had no idea. I was too dazed to do anything but stand there. It wasn't until a year later that I was told by Dr. Jerome Bruner at Harvard, ironically enough, that I had been participating in one of the oldest ceremonies of humankind, the laying on of hands. They were telling me in their way, he said, "Through this flesh, which is us, we are you and you are us."

I don't remember much of what happened after that—except for a photo that was taken of me standing with several of my sixth cousins, direct lineal descendants of Kunta Kinte's younger brothers. And when we left a few hours later by Land Rover, my mind was still numb. As we careened down the pitted back-country road toward Banjul—dust pluming up behind us—I saw nothing, heard nothing, felt nothing around me. But in my mind's eye, from the journals I had been reading, I began to envision, almost as if it were a film, how my great-great-great-great-grandfather—and the ancestors of every single black alive—had been enslaved. I could hear their screams in the night, see the flames from torches licking at their thatch-roofed huts, hear their screams as they dashed outside into a rain of clubs and cutlasses wielded not only by white slave traders but also by traitorous fellow Africans who were in the hire of the whites. I could smell the blood and sweat as the survivors were linked neck to neck by thongs into processions—called coffles—which often were a mile in length before they reached the beach areas near where the slave ships waited.

I seemed to feel their horror as they were branded, greased, shaved, then lashed and dragged, screaming, claw-ing at the beach, biting up mouthfuls of sand, in their desperation for one last hold on the land that had been their home. I saw them thrown like firewood into long-boats and rowed out to the waiting slave ships, shoved and beaten down into stinking holds and chained onto rough wooden shelves. I heard their moans as the ships weighed anchor and they began to move down the river toward the sea.

My mind was still reeling with this nightmare vision when we came in sight of a village up ahead. The driver slowed down as we drew closer, for there were hundreds of people waiting, and every one of them waving and shouting.

FISHER: What was going on?

HALEY: Somehow, word had reached them of what had happened back in Juffure. As the Land Rover crept through the throng, their cacophony of shouting engulfed us. And the face of everyone—from robed elders to naked little boys to wrinkled old crones with toothless gums and breasts like belt straps—was wreathed in a smile. I found myself standing up and smiling and waving back; but it wasn't until we were about halfway through the village that I understood what it was they were all chanting: "Meester Kinte! Meester Kinte!"

Let me tell you something: I've never been considered overly emotional, but when I heard what those people were shouting, I threw my hands in front of my face and started to sob like I hadn't done since I was a baby.

I was weeping in grief—not only for the anguish of the ancestor I embodied for those cheering Africans but also for the suffering of his descendants down through the generations. But I was also weeping in joy, for I felt that through me, his great-great-great-great-grandson, Kunta Kinte had finally come home. And because of him—his courage, his pride, and the tenacity of his determination to keep alive the memory and the meaning of his roots as a free man in his own land—all of us who had come after him had finally rediscovered who we were.

FISHER: Seems like a good subject for a book.

HALEY: That's right, wise guy. When I arrived in New York, I went to Doubleday and told them that every black American goes back ancestrally to someone who was taken, as Kunta was, from some village, chained in the hold of some stinking ship, sold onto some plantation to live out his years in slavery—and had children whose children's children's children are still struggling for freedom. So the story of any one of us is really the saga of us all. I told them I wanted to write that story in a book called *Roots*. They told me to go ahead.

FISHER: Did you visit Cousin Georgia to tell her the news?

HALEY: Listen, let me tell you one of the major reasons why I feel that this book *Roots* was simply meant to be. Just before leaving on that second trip to Africa, I had visited old Cousin Georgia, who was in the hospital, recovering from a stroke, and in her dramatic, deeply religious way, she'd exclaimed to me as I prepared to leave: "Boy, I'm jes' a soldier on God's battlefield, an' I been *hit*! But you go on!" But now, when I came off the plane and telephoned my brother George, he interrupted my greeting to tell me that while I was gone, Cousin Georgia had died—at the age of 83. Later, after making time-zone calculations, I realized that she had passed away literally within the very *hour* of my arrival in Juffure. I truly believe that as the last survivor of those ladies who had told the family story on that porch in Henning, it had been Cousin Georgia's job to oversee me into our ancestral village—and then she'd joined the others up there watchin'.

FISHER: Did that inspire you to go on?

HALEY: That, combined with the mystical nature of my entire experience in the Gambia, filled me with a sense of mission and fired me with an obsessive passion I have felt ever since.

FISHER: Where did that passion drive you next?

HALEY: Before I knew where to go next, I had to piece together what I'd learned so far, like clues in a detective story. From what the old ladies on the porch had told me, the ship that brought the African across the ocean had landed at "Naplis," which had to be Annapolis, Maryland. And now I knew that the ship had to have sailed from the Gambia River. What I *didn't* know were the only things that really mattered. What ship? And what voyage?

FISHER: How did you manage to track them down?

HALEY: The *griot* had told me that Kunta had disappeared "about the time the king's soldiers came." Projecting backward six generations to Kunta, that must have been somewhere in the mid–18th Century. And since slavery was first and foremost a maritime industry conducted predominantly by England and her American colony, I figured there might be a record somewhere in London of a military expedition to the Gambia around that time. I was right. After weeks of digging among British parliamentary records, I discovered that a group called Colonel O'Hare's forces had been dispatched to protect Fort James on the Gambia River from attack by the French in the spring of 1767.

So now I knew approximately when Kunta's ship left. Somewhere among the many thousands of voyages logged in shipping records during the two centuries that the slave trade flourished, there must be the record of a voyage by some ship from the Gambia River to Annapolis in the spring of 1767.

FISHER: Where did you look?

HALEY: I soon discovered that various repositories here or there in London held a maze of old shipping records, some dating back to the 16th Century; and included were countless records of slave ships. Hardly pausing to eat or sleep, I breathed dust and squinted over yellowing records for nine hours a day every day for the next seven weeks. Finally, in the British Public Records Office one afternoon, I was about halfway down a list of 30-odd sailings in my 1023rd set of records when my finger traced a line that read: "*Lord Ligonier*, registered in London, Captain Davies, sailed from the Gambia River July 5, 1767, destination Annapolis"—with a cargo that included 140 Africans.

FISHER: What was your reaction?

HALEY: For some reason, it didn't seem to register right away. I jotted down the information, stuck it in my pocket and went next door for a cup of tea. I was just sort of sitting there, sipping away, when it hit me. I still owe the lady for that tea. Without even stopping off at my hotel to pick up my bag, I grabbed a taxi, told the driver, "Heathrow!" and got the last seat on that day's last flight to New York. All the way across the Atlantic, I could see it in my mind's eye—a book I'd come across several months before in the Library of Congress: *Shipping in the Port of Annapolis, 1748–1775.* Before I slept, I was going to have my hands on that book. And I did. Turning to ship arrivals starting in September 1767—allowing at least two months for the crossing—I found it in ten minutes: The *Lord Ligonier* had docked in the Port of Annapolis on September 29, 1767. In the Maryland Hall of Records, I looked up ship arrivals for that date, and there was the cargo manifest for the *Lord Ligonier.* On it were listed "3265 elephants' teeth, 3700 pounds of beeswax, 800 pounds of raw cotton, 32 ounces of gold and 98 Negro slaves." Forty-two had died en route.

FISHER: Almost a third. Wasn't that an incredibly high fatality rate?

HALEY: It was about average. The slaves on the *Lord Ligonier* were stowed "loose pack," as they called it, on their backs, shoulder to shoulder, on shelves. When they were shipped "tight pack"—on their sides, up against one another like spoons in a drawer—the death rate was even higher.

FISHER: Then why would they be shipped that way?

HALEY: The reasoning was that since more slaves could be fitted on board tight pack, the ship still might arrive with more salable merchandise alive.

FISHER: What was the cause of most of the deaths?

HALEY: Disease and debilitation, from being forced to lie in their own excrement and vomit, chained together at the wrists and ankles on shelves four or five deep for an average of two and a half months. After a few weeks—bitten by rats, infested with lice, often bloated with tapeworms ingested in tainted slop, rolling back and forth on the rough planks beneath them—they were a mass of ulcerated and often gangrenous wounds so deep, in some cases, that muscle and bone showed through. Some died of beatings; others were killed in insurrections; and a few threw themselves overboard to the sharks rather than wait to get eaten in *Toubabo-Koomi*, the land of white cannibals to which many thought they were being taken. What's surprising is not that so many died but that so many *survived* the nightmare.

It's ironic that, percentagewise, more whites than blacks died on the slave ships. The *Lord Ligonier* left Gravesend, England, with a full crew of 36 and arrived in Annapolis with 18. Whites were less resistant than blacks to many diseases, but most fell victim to the same afflictions that killed their captives; every week or so, the crew members had to scrub off the slaves and muck out the holds.

FISHER: Were they well paid for that kind of work?

HALEY: On the contrary, the crewmen earned around two or three shillings a day—if they lived to earn *anything*. The fewer of the crew to survive the journey, the fewer of them had to be paid. More crew members than slaves died from floggings by brutal captains and mates; they were re-cruited—in some cases, shanghaied—human dregs of the waterfront and were regarded as far less valuable than their black cargo.

Shipowners and the great insurance companies that bank-rolled the trade found it enormously profitable, how-ever. Nor did the slave-ship captains do badly, either. In fact, they earned far more doing that sort of dirty work than they ever could have done at the helm of a warship or a tea clipper. Most of them were castoffs from military service or trading lines, competent sailors who had been disgraced or dishonorably discharged for drunkenness, in-subordination, and so on. They had to earn a living at the only thing they knew—the sea—and it was a lucrative one. But many of them seemed to be ashamed of it. I learned in my research that some of our favorite hymns were written by retired slave-ship officers. *Amazing Grace,* for example, was written by an ex–first mate named John Newton. The familiar line "I once was lost but now am found" takes on a poignant new significance in that light.

FISHER: How did you find out about all this?

HALEY: By reading scores of slave journals, captains' memoirs and especially the records of the antislavery soci-ety. One of the most revealing tidbits I unearthed in this way was the fact that the surest mark of veteran slave-ship captains and mates was the number of human teethmark scars they carried on their lower legs—sustained while doing their job, which was to keep as many slaves as possible from dying, and to patch them up well enough to command a decent price on delivery.

FISHER: What sort of price would an average slave command?

HALEY: That would depend on the state of the market at the time, but the principal determining factors were obviously age, strength and health. The tribe a slave came from also sometimes made a difference to knowledgeable buyers. The Wolofs, who were quick, intelligent, natural leaders but proud and defiant, tended to sell for less than members of other tribes that were regarded as more tractable and hard-working. In 1767, an average field hand in prime shape was worth anywhere from $500 to $800. Though they weren't capable of the same kind of hard work, female slaves often commanded more than $1000, especially if they were young and attractive, because they could both provide pleasant diversion for their masters and increase their inventory of human livestock by breeding children.

FISHER: Were you able to discover Kunta Kinte's sale price?

HALEY: About $850 is my best guess, based upon then prevailing prices in the Maryland and Virginia area. But I found a specific record of when and where he was sold. In the microfilm records of the *Maryland Gazette* for October 1, 1767—two days after the *Lord Ligonier* docked—I found an advertisement in the far-left-hand column on page two, announcing its arrival and inviting interested parties to an auction in Annapolis three days thence of its cargo: "98 choice, healthy slaves."

FISHER: Was there any written record of those sold at the auction?

HALEY: Not that I could find. But I already knew who had bought Kunta, if the family story continued to prove as accurate as it had so far. Grandma had said Kunta had been sold to a "Massa John Waller," who named him Toby, and later, after his foot had been cut off, he had been sold to John's brother, Dr. William Waller, who put him to work in the garden at his plantation in Spotsylvania County, Virginia.

Since slaves were considered property, just like a horse or a plot of real estate, I reasoned that there might possibly be a record of Kunta's sale from one brother to the other somewhere among the state legal deeds on file in Richmond. So I began searching through those documents, starting a few months after his original purchase, to allow time for his four unsuccessful escape attempts. Finally, I found a deed—dated September 5, 1768—transferring 247 acres of land from John to William Waller. On the second page, like an afterthought, were the words: "And also one Negro slave named Toby." I sat staring at the document, unable to believe my eyes. It was impossible, but I'd done it: traced a man who had been dead for almost two centuries all the way from his home village in western Africa to a plantation in Spotsylvania County, Virginia. I felt like leaping up and shouting back across the years to Grandma and the rest of the ladies on that porch: "It's true! It's all true! Every word of it! It really happened just the way you said! We've found him!" One less detail in the family story, one missing document in my search to confirm it, and the trail could have petered out anywhere along the way. Somehow, just enough fragments had survived from what the African had told Kizzy, and what she and the others had passed on down through the generations, to lead me finally, there in that Virginia library, all the way back to my great-great-great-great-grandfather.

FISHER: Were you ready to begin writing the book?

HALEY: Hardly. I had traced my own ancestor all the way from freedom in the Gambia to slavery in Virginia, and I knew the outlines of the family story pretty well from that point on. But if *Roots* was going to stand a chance of transcending the story of one family and becoming the saga of an entire people, I knew I'd have to find out what it had been like not only for Kunta Kinte and his descendants but for millions like them on both continents from that time to this. I felt my job now was to immerse myself in research on two vast areas: tribal life in Africa and slave life in America. Since Africa's where the story began, I decided to study it first.

Most of what I'd read so far had been written by outsiders, predominantly white missionaries and anthropologists, and even among the most knowledgeable and well intentioned of them, the tone was somewhat paternal and condescending. Their insights and observations were inevitably limited by the cultural chasm separating them from their subjects. So I began going back to Africa, maybe 15 or 20 trips. Setting out with my interpreters into the back country, I'd arrive in a village with a gift of kola nuts or something and ask to speak with the most honored elders. And I'd sit for hours with three or four of those old men, asking them about their boyhoods—and about whatever they could recall their fathers telling them about *their* boyhoods. I was digging not only for firsthand cultural history but also for personal anecdotes that would illuminate the lifestyle and the character of these people; sensory impressions of taste, touch, smell and sight that would help me bring the story to life in a way that the reader could not only appreciate but at least vicariously *experience*.

FISHER: How much of what you learned conflicted with your preconceptions about Africa?

HALEY: Most of it. The worst misconception I had—in common with most Americans—was conditioned by the cartoon image of Africans as semisimians with bones through their noses, swinging from trees and dancing around fires over which missionaries were cooking in big pots. What I found out about my own ancestors, the Mandinkas—a fairly representative tribe among the thousands in Africa—was that they were a poor people, most of them simple farmers at the mercy of the harsh elements of western Africa, which range from flood to famine. They live in what we would consider primitive conditions, and during the hungry season they sometimes eat rodents and even insects to stay alive. But they are a highly civilized and sophisticated people who are brought up to be aware of, and proud of, a rich cultural heritage, and they have a deep respect for the value of all life. Most are devout Moslems, the men are literate in Arabic and not only conversant in their own language but schooled from childhood in Koranic recitation.

Conditioned as I was to think of Africans as savages, I was deeply moved when I learned about the age-old Mandinka ritual of child naming, which is still practiced in the back country. On the eighth day of his life, a newborn child is brought out before the people of his village in his mother's arms and held up before his father, who whispers three times into the infant's ear the name he has chosen; it's the first time that child's name has ever been spoken aloud, because the Mandinka people believe that *each human being should be the first to know who he is*. That night, the naming ritual is completed when the father takes his child out beyond the village gates and holds the infant above him with his little face turned toward the heavens. "Behold," says the father, "the only thing greater than yourself." As a black American, brought up to regard myself as second-class at best, my knowledge now of that simple ancestral declaration has profoundly changed the way I feel about my value as a human being.

FISHER: How long did it take you to collect that kind of firsthand research?

HALEY: Perhaps four years; then another six months organizing it into dozens of notebooks, including one for each year of Kunta's life in Africa, distributing every shred of information I'd been able to find on everything from weapons to kitchen utensils, from morning prayers to evening campfires, from birth to death, into what I feel is as comprehensive and authentic a profile of African cultural life as has ever been assembled.

FISHER: Were you as meticulous in researching the slave life in America?

HALEY: Maybe more so. It certainly *took* longer. There was hardly anybody to talk with who had direct experience of the period I was interested in, and the culture itself, unlike that of back-country Africa, had changed beyond recognition. So I had to rely almost entirely on reading. Digging long and deep in sources that had the ring of validity, finally, I unearthed solid material—out of antebellum memoirs, diaries, personal correspondence, and the like, by slavemasters and -mistresses; out of the Library of Congress, the Library of the D.A.R., the Widener Library at Harvard, the New York City Library's Schomberg Collection in Harlem, the Moreland Collection at Howard University, the Fisk University and Morehouse College libraries, and a good twoscore other specialized source places—my quest, my mission, being to get at the *truth* of slavery. I read the works of prominent ex-slaves such as Frederick Douglass, Sojourner Truth, Harriet Tubman and Phillis Wheatley, an African girl who grew up to become a celebrated poet. But the most invaluable—and heartbreaking—research I used in the book was gleaned from the transcripts of several hundred interviews with completely unknown ex-slaves that had been conducted by unemployed writers as a WPA project during the Thirties. Many of them are in a book titled *Lay My Burden Down*, which I recommend to anyone interested in the true and terrible story of slavery as told by its last survivors.

From all this reading, I finally amassed a staggering mound of research, which I then began to condense and classify into a second set of dawn-to-dusk, life-to-death, A-to-Z notebooks that constitutes, I think, a portrait of plantation America at least as exhaustive—and fully as authentic—as my research on tribal Africa.

FISHER: Did what you found out about slave life in the South force you to revise any more preconceptions?

HALEY: Many—but most of them, I'm happy to say, weren't my own. The worst of them, of course, was the popular white stereotype of slaves as ignorant woolly-heads who grinned and shuffled around the plantation with nothing on their minds but sex and watermelon: a lot of whites still think that way about us. But the *fact* is that most slaves were innately as smart as their masters, and not a few who got the chance at freedom and an education went on to excel in those fields they were allowed to enter.

But there wasn't a single slave who wasn't smart enough to lull white folks into thinking he was ignorant. As long as they were thought to be dumb, they'd pretty much be left alone. What whites seldom realized was that through a highly effective grapevine, nearly every slave out in the cotton fields learned in minutes just about everything that went on in the "big house," even behind closed doors. House slaves eavesdropped on most words their masters and mistresses spoke: they suckled babies, changed the bed sheets, fed their owners and then emptied their slop jars. Yet their masters knew next to nothing about *them*.

FISHER: What about the old stereotype that slaves were lazy and shiftless? Did your research shed any light on that?

HALEY: The facts are that they were worked *very* hard six days a week, usually from dawn till long after dark. House slaves, of course, didn't have the same kind of backbreaking responsibilities as those who worked in the fields; some of them, in fact, grew close to their white owners and enjoyed special privileges, rather like house pets. But field slaves were worked sometimes until they literally dropped dead. It's not surprising that they took every chance they could get to lighten up whenever they thought the overseer's back was turned; or that after emancipation, they tilled the same land with more dedication as sharecroppers than they had as slaves.

FISHER: Didn't the special treatment accorded to house slaves alienate them from field slaves?

HALEY: It didn't exactly create a bond between them, but more important than the fact that one group sweated in the fields while the other wore starched uniforms, fanned the "missy" with ostrich feathers and ate leftovers from the master's dinner table was the fact that they all recognized they were enslaved together. If any of them showed the slightest disrespect toward any white—or was even *suspected* of it—they'd all suffer the same consequences.

FISHER: What kind of consequences?

HALEY: Beatings were administered regularly by overseers, and often by white layabouts who happened onto slaves out alone on the road or in town. But all kinds of unimaginable cruelties were commonplace, for the most capricious pretexts. Ears were cut off for eavesdropping and hands for stealing, genitals for real or imagined evidence of any untoward interest in a white woman.

A particularly sadistic case among the hundreds I documented in my research was about an attractive young slave girl who had been raped by her master. When he died, his wife, who had been forced—like so many plantation wives—to endure in silence the humiliation of his infidelity, took a poker and beat the girl nearly to death: broke her jaw in several places, put out an eye, disfigured her for life.

But the atrocity I remember most vividly was the chopping off of Kunta Kinte's foot by those poor-white "pate-rollers" who caught him after his fourth attempt to escape. I found myself morbidly obsessed with it. Over and over in my mind's eye, I watched as Kunta, bound by his waist to a tree, struggled vainly to escape as his right foot was tied firmly across a stump. I saw the ax flash up, then down. I heard the thud, the horrible scream, saw his hands flail downward, as if to retrieve the front half of his foot as it fell forward, gouts of blood jetting from the stump. It was like a recurrent nightmare; I could see it, hear it. But I couldn't *feel* it. Finally, after studying the physiology of the foot, I began to internalize the agony he must have felt as the ax sliced through skin, tendons, muscles, blood vessels and bone and thudded finally onto the stump. Only then did I feel that I could write about it. And only when I did was I able to purge myself of the obsession.

FISHER: In *Roots*, you describe another attempt to empathize with the sufferings of your ancestor, when, boarding a freighter bound, as the *Lord Ligonier* had been, from western Africa to America, you spent every night of the crossing stripped to your shorts, lying on the rough planking of the dark hold. Did that help you lose yourself in the character—and his ordeal?

HALEY: I don't know. My discomfort, of course, was sheer luxury compared with what he went through. I felt I had to do *something* to make it more real for me, but lying there night after night seemed to drive me deep inside *myself* instead of him. I couldn't seem to get inside his skin so that he could cry out, through me, the agony he had endured. And that agonized *me*. But even beyond that, I felt myself sinking into despair over my inadequacy to the task I had undertaken, at my effrontery in taking it upon myself to tell the saga of an entire people. I had been working on the book for years. I was beginning to think I'd never finish. Finally, one night, I found myself standing at the aft rail of the ship, looking back at the waves behind us, and very slowly, not with despair but with a sense of exhilaration, it began to dawn on me that the solution to all my problems lay just one step before me. All I had to do was slip between the rails and drop into the sea that had been my home for 20 years; it would only be fitting that the birthplace of my career as a writer would be my burying place as well. It would all be over and I could join the others up there— Jesus!—*watching* me at that rail about to bury forever the past they had sent me out to find. So help me, God, I began to hear their voices talking to me—Grandma, Tom, Chicken George, Kizzy and Kunta Kinte—and they were all saying quietly, "Don't do it, son. Go on. Have faith. You're gonna make it." With all my strength, I pushed myself back from that rail and crawled on my hands and knees back across the deck to the companionway. And that night, in my cabin, I sobbed my guts out. After that, when I sat down at my typewriter and began to write, it flowed, it poured out of me like lava, the whole story of the slave-ship cruise, and I hope it hurts to read it as much as it did to write it.

FISHER: In your zeal to relive the story so totally, did it occur to you that you might be getting carried away by it?

HALEY: I *knew* I was getting carried away. I was lost in it, hopelessly in love with it. In the single-mindedness of my determination to track down every lead that might take me to something I thought I had to know or feel, I went days at a time without food, nights without sleep, months without touching a woman. Carrying every scrap of research I'd collected along with me in a pair of very heavy satchels that never left my side, I traveled maybe half a million miles, interviewed hundreds of people, read hundreds of books, pored over thousands of documents in more than 70 archives on three continents. I could have gone on that way forever, never satisfied that I'd learned quite enough, always hoping that tomorrow I'd stumble across one more piece of evidence that I couldn't do without.

FISHER: What stopped you?

HALEY: I simply ran out of two basic commodities: time and money. I was exactly four years behind my deadline for delivery of the manuscript, and though no one knew it, except you, I'd actually *written* only the African section and the slave-ship crossing. The eternal optimist, I would always convince myself that I'd be able to sit down and grind out the rest in six months of 18-hour days at the typewriter. But then I'd run out of money—I'd lost all of my credit cards and friends to borrow from—and I'd have to stop work on the book entirely for weeks at a time to go on the lecture circuit, *talking* about the book, to earn enough money to get back to it for a few more months. I must have spoken before more than a million people about "My Search for Roots" over a period of several years, and people were beginning to say that the book was just a shuck to get me lecture bookings. Even friends like you, who knew better, began to lose patience with me.

FISHER: But not faith.

HALEY: Well, yours lasted longer than mine. Finally, in exasperation, my attorney, Lou Blau, told me, in so many words, to just stop runnin' my mouth about it, take the research I had—which was enough for ten books by then—get off on some desert island somewhere and *write* the goddamn thing. I swore I would and promised—for the last time—to deliver it in six months; Doubleday gave me some money to live on until then. Squirreling myself away in a remote hilltop cottage in Jamaica, West Indies— beyond the reach of telephones—I sat down to do just that.

But as the months passed, I found that mail and telegrams were managing to find me—and nearly every one seemed to be an announcement from some collection agency that I'd better pay up or else; or a command from the IRS. It was hard to find a single creditor who was willing to accept my honest explanation that all those debts had accumulated—and couldn't be paid off yet—because of my desperate efforts to research and then write an important but seemingly interminable book. What with one thing or another, when I sat down and figured out what I owed various people and institutions, it was a total of around $100,000, including late charges, and just realizing that had what you might charitably call a deterrent effect on my creative output. If I didn't find a few bones to throw to the biggest and hungriest of those wolves howling at my door, I knew I wouldn't have a typewriter to finish the book on or a roof to do it under.

FISHER: Since you *did* finish, you must have found a few bones. Where?

HALEY: I did something I'm not proud of, but if it hadn't worked, I'd be even less proud of it. With just a few days left before my six months were up—knowing that I'd need at *least* another six months to finish—I wrote the first 20 pages of the next section of the book, polishing each and every word until it gleamed, and also the last few pages of the book, where I tell everybody what it all means. I didn't really have any *idea* what it all meant at that point, but I made up something that sounded good, and then I typed up about 750 pages of my research to the same margins, stuck them between the first 20 and the last few pages, numbered them all in sequence, put a big rubber band around the whole thing, stuck it in a satchel and took the next plane to New York, arriving in the office of my editor, Lisa Drew, exactly on deadline day.

Sitting at Lisa's desk, chitchatting for the first five or ten minutes, I could see her glance fastened hypnotically on that satchel at my side, so at the appropriate moment, I opened it up, pulled out this massive manuscript and set it before her on the desk. Her eyes narrowed warily as I explained that it was still just a rough draft but that I'd brought it along to reassure her that I was making progress. Then she began to read the first page, then the second and the third, and she began to smile, wider and wider. But when she kept on turning pages, I started talking and kept talking, faster and faster, asking so many questions that she finally began just skimming and then riffling around page 15. Then, as I knew she would from long acquaintance, she turned to the last page and read it carefully. I'd really poured it on at the end, and when she looked up, it was with moist eyes and a tremulous smile.

While she was still in a tender mood, I apologized abjectly for letting her down once again, after crying wolf so many times. All the more so because I would have to ask her one *last* time for another six-month extension—and another modest advance on my royalties, just enough to buy groceries, pay the electric bill and keep me in typing paper until I'd put the final polish on the manuscript. Flinching, sighing, but obviously impressed by the apparent existence of a rough draft for a book she had just about decided she'd never see, she authorized a check—for considerably less than I'd asked for, of course—and sincerely wished me good luck and Godspeed. And a warning that this was the last penny I'd see until the final draft was in her hands exactly six months from that day.

FISHER: Was it?

HALEY: Delivered on time or the last penny I saw?

FISHER: Either.

HALEY: Neither. One way or another, I managed to eke out enough of both time and money to finally finish the book—about a year later—but not without pulling one last shameless ruse. The last 100 pages of the manuscript, which I turned in to Doubleday as finished copy only five days after the final, final deadline—when I was told bricks would begin to tumble from the roof of the Doubleday building—were actually a kind of novelized synopsis of the actual copy I intended to write while the manuscript was being typeset. When I received the galleys for correction about a month later, I simply substituted my 200 new pages for the last 100 pages they had set in type. They fumed, of course, but it *was* incomparably better than the original version. I offered to pay for the cost of resetting—hoping they'd have the kindness to turn me down, which they did, since they knew I'd have to ask them for another advance to do it. But as things are turning out, it looks as if neither Doubleday nor I will have to hassle over the printing bills.

FISHER: Or any other bills, it would appear, since *Roots* seems destined to become the best seller of the season—

and perhaps, when the 12-hour television adaptation debuts at the end of this month, one of the best sellers of all time. After all those years of dodging creditors, how do you feel about the prospect of becoming a millionaire?

HALEY: Well, I still owe enough money that it'll be a while before I see a dollar without somebody else's fingers attached to it. But when it starts rolling in, I'm pretty sure I'll prefer it to poverty. The main thing I look forward to is being able to go to the mailbox and find a few checks in it instead of a pile of window envelopes with notes inside that begin: "Final notice: If you fail to call this number within 24 hours. . . ." Apart from that, and the creative independence it'll buy for me, the only reason I'm really excited about making some money is so I can fix up my back yard and maybe get me a nice stereo system for the living room. That's about it.

FISHER: Will you laugh all the way to the bank over some of the criticisms that have faulted *Roots* for having a "pulpy style that smacks of conventional romance"; for your reliance on the use of a slave dialect that becomes "wearing and ludicrous"; for devoting too much of the book to Kunta's "boring" life in Africa, which one reviewer found, "for all its troubles, a primal Eden"; and for glossing over the more recent generations of your family in "a hasty, sketchy, unsatisfactory way"?

HALEY: When almost all of the reviews received by a book are as admiring, and in some cases adulatory, as those written about *Roots*, you've got to expect your share of pot shots from some quarters. They roll off. But if you want me to comment on the specific criticisms you mentioned, I'll be glad to. As for my pulpy style, I'd rather describe it as I intended it to be: simple, direct, descriptive, dramatic— a style well suited to the story it tells, I think; and many other reviewers seem to feel as I do. The use of slave dialect, too, is not only intentional but authentic; some critics may find it ludicrous, but the fact is that that's the way those people talked. Should I have made them speak the king's English like their white owners? Differences in language were both symbolic and symptomatic of the vast gulf between slave and master. The reason I devoted the first 126 pages of the book to Kunta's life in Africa, which some critics found both long and boring, was that so little has been known up to now in the West, by white or black, about the depth and richness of African culture, which I happen to think we can all learn something from. I also wanted to plant Kunta's roots so deep, as I told the story of his life from birth to capture, that the wrench of his being torn from the soil of his homeland would be as heartbreaking for the reader as it was for me. As for depicting Juffure as a primal Eden, maybe it was, and still is, in many ways, compared with America's urban jungles; but I certainly made no attempt to romanticize the harsh realities of tribal life in western Africa.

FISHER: How about the criticism that the book glosses over the more recent generations of your family?

HALEY: I'd be inclined to agree with that one. I wish I'd had another year or even two to flesh out the lives and characters of Tom Murray and his family and all the others who came after them, all the way down to me, as I had been able to do with the rest of the book—from Kunta and Kizzy through Chicken George. The latter part of the story is just as rich as all that went before, and maybe someday I'll have the chance to go back and do it the justice it deserves. But the reason I didn't do it is that time, as I said earlier, simply ran out. Multimillion-dollar book-publication and TV-production plans had been set irreversibly into motion, and there was finally no way to resist them any longer. But the whole story is still there; I don't think the impact or the importance of the book has been diminished in any significant way.

FISHER: The final—and most frequent—charge is that, despite all your attempts to document the history of your family, *Roots* can't really be called nonfiction, because so few specific details could be corroborated that much of the book is a work of imagination.

HALEY: That's the one thing it's *not*. All the names and dates are real. All the major incidents are true, and the details are as accurate a depiction of what happened to my family, or to thousands of families like us, as years of research can achieve. When it comes to dialog, thoughts and emotions, of course, I had to make things up; but even those inventions are based as much as humanly possible on corroborated fact. Call it "faction," if you like, or heightened history, or fiction based on the lives of real people.

FISHER: However they choose to classify it, most reviewers have been ecstatic, hailing *Roots* as everything from "the epic of the black man in America" to "a book of such colossal scope that it arouses not only admiration but awe." Are you embarrassed by all that approbation?

HALEY: If I were, you couldn't tell whether I was blushing, anyway. But what can I say when I see words like colossal and epic applied to a book I spent 12 years of my life working on? That's the kind of thing any author would *dream* of having said about his or her book, and now that such a dream actually is coming true for me, it's a little hard to believe. But because *Roots* is more than just a book I happened to write, because it has come to represent far more than just the story of my family, I find myself able to step back and see it—above and beyond any personal considerations and whatever literary merit it may have— as something that really *is* an epic; the colossal epic of a people.

FISHER: Some readers feel the book isn't the story of the black man but of *man*. Was that your intention—and is that your hope?

HALEY: It was and is. On its most literal level, it is the story of both my family and my people, for the ancestors of all of us were brought over here in the same way. But as

I wrote it, another dimension began to emerge. Besides feeling that *Roots* might help restore to black people some sense of their identity and pride, I felt it might also help the descendants of their owners, and all peoples everywhere— Russian and Chinese, Catholic and Protestant, Arab and Jew—face the facts about the atrocities committed time and again, throughout history, in the name of everything from King Cotton to Almighty God. All of us, at one time or another, in one way or another, are both victim and oppressor, and fate seems to be rather capricious about who plays which role at any given time.

Black or white, for those of us here in America, this is our home. Except for the Indians, who already lived here when we arrived, the ancestors of all of us came across that same ocean on some ship. We must learn not only to live together but—by learning to see one another as *people* rather than as stereotypes—to love one another. That will happen when we face what we are and what we've done and then forgive one another—and ourselves—unconditionally, for everything.

FISHER: That's a beautiful speech. But do you really think that will ever happen?

HALEY: The truth? In the 55 years I've been around, I haven't run across any great signs of a new awakening. On an individual basis, yes; now and then, a spontaneous act of kindness and understanding, here and there heart-warming cases of genuine brotherhood—like our own 15-year friendship, if you'll allow me to get personal. But I can't say I feel too optimistic about the perfectibility of mankind. On the other hand, I'm encouraged by the tremendous upswelling of emotion that *Roots* seems to have set in motion, an emotion that—to judge from the outpourings of sometimes even tearful gratitude I'm encountering wherever I go these days—seems to be not only cathartic but, in some ways, *healing*. If people hadn't wanted and needed that, hadn't been ready for it, in some deep way, I don't think the book would be nearly as important as it seems to have become.

FISHER: Aren't people also responding to some pretty old-fashioned virtues in *Roots*? Whatever else it may be, isn't the book a kind of tribute to the family unit as a force of continuity in human society and the repository of its values?

HALEY: Say that again slow and let me write it down; I didn't know how profound I was. But, yes, to me the family has always been the source and heart of every culture. I didn't set out with that thought in mind as one of the messages of the book, but I guess it is. In the 40 or so years since I grew up in Henning, the family has been shrinking and drifting apart as America has moved from the country to the city, from huge, messy old homes echoing with the noise of three generations to closet-sized, $400-a-month apartments for swinging singles eating TV dinners alone in 600-unit high-rises; from sitting on front porches, listening to grandmothers tell family stories like the ones I heard, to sitting in suburban rec rooms with baby sitters while Mom and Dad go out; from screen doors left unlocked to steel doors triple-locked; from walking home after school by way of the fishing hole, the sand lot and Miss Scrap Green's house, where she'd always have a plateful of hot cookies waiting on Thursday afternoons, to riding home through cursing mobs behind the barred windows of school buses with armed drivers.

I don't mean to run down urban America; I live in Los Angeles and I drive a Mercedes. And I don't want to romanticize our past; when I was a boy, we did without a lot of conveniences—like electricity—that have made life easier for everyone, and I grew up in a segregated town. But there's no question that somewhere along the way between then and now, we've lost something very precious: a sense of community, which is nothing more than a congregation of *families*. Everybody in town knew everybody else in town; there wasn't much privacy and there weren't many secrets, but there was no such thing as loneliness, anonymity, psychiatry. People didn't think about "role models" or worry about losing their identities. They weren't so anxious to leave home and go "looking for themselves" in the big city when I was growing up. They usually wound up doing more or less what their fathers and mothers had done and spent their whole lives within a mile of where they were born. And felt good about it.

It was small-town America, and it was pretty much the same in Henning, Tennessee, as it was in Plains, Georgia, or Emporia, Kansas. I say *was* because the binding hardships that created them and the simple pleasures that held them together *are* slipping away, dying off even in the back country, along with all those square values like trust, decency, neighborliness, patriotism. Even those of us who never grew up there, as I was fortunate enough to do, feel a sense of loss and longing, as the media and the supermarkets and the exurban industrial complexes slowly homogenize the land from coast to coast.

FISHER: Do you think that process is inevitable—and irreversible?

HALEY: Probably, but I don't think it's inevitable that the moral and spiritual values that give meaning to our lives— that we most cherish in ourselves—have to disappear along with the rural America that nurtured them. This sense of self-worth can be revived and sustained—but only by restoring pride in who we are and what we mean to one another. We need, among other things, to start holding more family reunions; however sophisticated we become, that's where we all come from, and we can't afford to forget it. But my fondest hope is that *Roots* may start a ground swell of longing by black, white, brown, red, yellow people everywhere to go digging back for their own roots, to rediscover in their past a heritage to make them proud.

Man, that would make me feel 90 feet tall—to think I was the impetus for that!

FISHER: You don't expect people to go through the kind of ordeal you did, do you?

HALEY: No, just go rummaging through those old trunks up in the attic, in those old boxes under the bed; and don't throw anything old away if it has to do with the family. But the first thing they ought to do is simply open their ears. The richest source of family history you could find anywhere in the world is the memories of your parents and your grandparents—memories that will tell you things you never knew or have long since forgotten about yourself; but perhaps even more importantly, they will reveal to you, perhaps for the first time, the true identities of those who gave you life—and shared theirs with you for so many years. This will make them feel needed, relevant, *alive*—and that will bring out the same response in you. And almost certainly, this exchange of caring will deepen the blood bonds that can make a close-knit family the strongest social unit in the world. And in ways that will be understood best by those who belong to such families—the kind that eat together, stand up for one another, share births and deaths—it may leave you profoundly changed. The giving and getting, the sense of belonging and contributing to something larger than yourself, to something that began before you were born and will go on after you die, can make it possible for you to *accept* life in a way that makes you wish the whole world could realize how easy it is to feel as you do, and wonder why they don't. That's what having roots—and writing *Roots*—has done for me. I pray that *reading* it—and then reaching out for their families to join in a search for their own—will do the same for everyone.

FISHER: One last question: What do you think your ancestors would think about all the acclaim over *Roots*?

HALEY: I hope they would approve. I often think of the Mandinka belief that Kunta's father expresses in the book: that there are three kinds of people living in every village: those you can see, walking around; those who are waiting to be born; and those who have gone on to join the ancestors. That idea was brought alive for me again recently while I was on the set, watching them shoot the TV series based on *Roots*. I found myself wishing Grandma and the others could be there, too. I could almost *see* Grandma, wearing that hat she reserved for state occasions such as a revival meeting—the one with a feather like an apostrophe on it—and I could just *hear* her making her own private commentary on the film: Her father wasn't *that* fat, her grandfather wasn't *that* bald. And then I suddenly realized that she really *is* watching, along with Tom, Chicken George, Kizzy, Kunta and all the rest. *All* of them are up there watchin'—and not just over me now, but over all of *us*.

THERE ARE DAYS WHEN I WISH IT HADN'T HAPPENED

Nobody's Knocking Success, But It Sure Looks Different Once You've Seen Both Sides

Finally, after three A.M., practically out on my feet from exhaustion, I locked my hotel-room door behind me, pulled off my clothes down to my underwear and flopped onto the bed for whatever rest I could manage to get before running to catch the next plane at seven. A few hours before, I'd been among the 80,000,000 Americans who had watched the concluding eighth episode of the original *Roots* television miniseries, which had ended with me on camera speaking for several minutes to that unprecedented national audience. Of the earlier seven *Roots* episodes, I'd had to miss six. While they were on, I had been hurrying between airports, hotels and myriad other places in an effort to maintain a blurring schedule of back-to-back appointments in a grueling coast-to-coast promotional tour of interviews, speeches and personal appearances seven days a week, usually from before breakfast to midnight and frequently beyond.

But most assuredly, I wasn't—and still am not—complaining. After some 20 years of having crossed my fingers every time I mailed to editors something I had written, now

Roots, which represented 12 of those years of work, had already sold close to 1,000,000 hardcover copies, and the television miniseries had collectively attracted the largest audience in the history of the medium. I lay there on the hotel bed, thinking about how lucky I was, no matter what bone weariness it involved, and with those ambivalent thoughts I was drifting into sleep when the loud door buzzer jolted the silence. It couldn't be my wake-up call already! I peered at the night table clock's luminous dial: 3:30! Again the buzzer sounded.

Stumbling to the door in the darkness, I fumbled it open. A young blond-haired bellboy stood there stiffly, his hands at his sides, swallowing hard and looking very solemnly at me standing in the doorway in my underwear, blinking at him.

"Yes?" I managed.

He stuck out his hand. "Sir, I want to thank you for what you've done for America."

He couldn't have been more sincere. That's all he had to say. I wanted to hug him for feeling that way—and to punch him for getting me out of bed. I shook his hand, said I appreciated his saying that, and he marched away.

Then it hit me. So much for anonymity; I guess I'll be having experiences like that now and then for a while; of course, the TV exposure will cause more people to recognize me than did when it was just my picture on the back of the book jacket. . . .

In retrospect, that bellboy pushing the hotel door's buzzer was really kind of a signal that at least major aspects of my life were about to change abruptly, maybe forever. Let me tell you what happened: When I stepped out of my cab at Kennedy Airport later that morning, I got a passing glance from one of the busy skycaps, who practically whirled around, did a double take and exclaimed loudly, *"Alex Haley!"*

Within seconds, I was surrounded by people, jostling,

pushing, shoving so hard that I was separated from my bag. I think that skycap must have checked it in for me, for somehow it arrived on the same flight with me in Los Angeles. But right then, that missing bag was the last thing on my mind, amidst all those people yelling my name, shouting, "That's him! That's him!" I was confused, bewildered, I believe for the first time in my life actually afraid that I might be about to get hurt. The people, women especially, were grabbing whatever they could get hold of, tugging at my arms, pulling at my clothes. I felt someone's hand thrust down inside my collar, then I felt my shirt's top buttons pop off. It was about then that a man in a red American Airlines jacket pushed right alongside me; I heard him say in a low tone, "Stay next to me and follow me," and he began moving. It was like a football play in slow motion. I sensed with great relief that he knew what he was doing, which *I* sure didn't. He'd push with the weight of his body behind his shoulder and thus make a little space, and I'd squeeze into that space right behind him, while constantly exclaiming, "Thank you!" "Yes, ma'am!" "Yes, sir!" with a pen in one hand scribbling some semblance of my name on the pieces of paper that were being thrust at me from all directions. After about five minutes of this, we reached a wall and suddenly the man opened a door I hadn't noticed and we both sort of popped through it, rather like a champagne cork, and the man quickly shut the door behind us. I remember leaning up against the wall and taking a deep breath and demanding of him, "Man, what the hell's *happening?*"

He laughed and said I'd better get used to it, for I'd be seeing a lot more of it. Then he said I'd have to be "preboarded." I hadn't ever heard the expression before. After what had just happened, I followed him without a whimper through various doors and corridors, and suddenly there we were, on the plane, which was still empty. I handed him my ticket. "I'm sorry, Mr. Haley," he said, "but I'd really advise you to upgrade to first class." He saw my expression and began to explain, saying that in the experience of the airlines, VIPs couldn't expect much of a peaceful, relaxed flight if they were surrounded by a couple of hundred passengers. My hackles just rose at that; and I felt embarrassed. Wasn't I the same man I'd been for 50-odd years? I couldn't remember occasioning any public commotions in all that time. But when the fellow insisted, I gave him my credit card and he went to change my ticket.

I won't soon forget sitting alone in that first-class cabin, still needing sleep, astounded at the recent rush of events, my mind racing across the memories of all those years I'd lived alone in a little basement room on Grove Street in Greenwich Village, working through the nights, trying to finish magazine articles to pay the worst bills, taking long walks in the predawn hours and wondering if all of it ever would lead me anywhere. Well, it finally had—beyond my ability even to comprehend it—and I found myself wishing that I still had that little basement room, along with the quiet life that had accompanied it, because if that morning's airport arrival was any evidence, then, just for starters, when in the world was I ever going to be able to sit down again and practice the discipline of being a writer?

Two years later, the blessings have continued to come to me; mixed in among them, though, have been a great many rude awakenings to the hard realities of what fame also brings, including just a few bitter pills.

Through what I might call the early *Roots* days, I still clung hard to the idea that before long, all of the big to-do was going to calm down and I'd discover myself with the dream come true of having the time and the money to write at my own pace, freed forever of the terrible economic pressures I'd known for so many years. Keeping my heavy list of appointments around the country, I also kept it in my head—like a promised lollipop—that before long, just wait and see, I was again going to be able to enjoy good evenings of visiting and chitchat with close family and friends. I was going to have the leisure to take long trips, to investigate the world. I *love* to travel, and I had many journeys in mind. I was going to Egypt to see the Pyramids—and ride a camel. I was going to visit North and East Africa. I was going to get a Eurailpass and indulge myself in the beauty of the European countryside. After my 20-year career in the U.S. Coast Guard, the kind of travel I love most is on shipboard; I was going to sail the seven seas—on slow freighters.

But what happened? That first year, *Roots* continued rather like a roller-coaster ride of talk shows, press conferences, magazine profiles, critical accolades, a few critical attacks, autographing sessions attended by thousands, receiving keys to many cities and more than a dozen honorary doctoral degrees (each one a new thrill for someone who didn't even finish college); being embraced as a friend by celebrities I'd previously written about as a journalist; being a keynote speaker before august assemblies I never imagined would be interested in hearing what I had to say. My lifetime's most moving moments will have to include receiving special citations from the U.S. Senate, as well as from the House of Representatives, to both of which events I had the same internal reaction I've had so many times: wishing fervently that my momma and dad, my grandmas and grandpas—and all the others who came before them, *slaves* all, across the generations all the way back to Kunta Kinte—could have been with me, sharing such a moment. And then I'd realize that they *were*. Like my old cousin Georgia from Kansas City used to say, before she ascended to join them, "They all settin' right up there watchin' what you do, boy!"

In both a serious and a lighter vein, I've also been touched by how many relatives and friends *Roots* has surfaced for me, many of whom I never previously knew I had. As news of my good fortune began circulating, my inundation of mail, telegrams and phone calls included communications not only from dearly remembered old Service buddies but also from "shipmates" who named ships *I* never sailed on. Rather similarly, the relatives ranged from not a few with whom I'd long wanted to have direct contact, and just didn't know where they were, to others who fit best within the proverbial "16th-cousin" category. There is an almost infallibly repetitive pattern in my letters from no-ship shipmates and the 16th cousins: I am roundly congratulated upon my well-deserved success; they'd always known I'd make it one day—and they're certain I'll wish to manifest my appreciation of their deep faith in some financial manner. Some of them specifically state the appropriate sums, which have ranged to upwards of $100,000— to pay off their debts, to establish them in a business or some other endeavor, to cover medical treatments for themselves or members of their family or any number of other needs, desires or occasionally sheer fantasies.

I don't mean to make light of these requests. Most of them are heartfelt and legitimate. But the point is that I simply haven't the resources to become a charitable institution on a personal basis. And while I'm in this financial area, let me try to point out something very few petitioners ever seem to reflect upon. It's the case not only with me but with any others of us in the free-lance creative positions about whom one hears the great big dollar sums. In the first place, of whatever we may happen to earn through our efforts, a good *half* goes to Uncle Sam. Then come other deductions—substantial ones—of a professional nature. What's left after all that isn't nearly as impressive as it looked at first. I'm surely not crying poor—for, God knows, I never dreamed I'd ever gross what I now net. With it, I have established a foundation to help people to the degree I can afford, especially those in Africa who desperately need assistance of many sorts. Donations to the foundation, along with others last year, amounted to well into six figures. Beyond that, if I tried to supply even half of the funds for which people have asked, I'd very shortly be needing someone to help me. When my replies to money appeals have tried tactfully to explain this, as often as not a return letter merely requests a smaller amount, and when that isn't forthcoming, subsequent letters call me names among which "insensitive" and "stingy bastard" are not uncommon, until I have come to feel that by and large, no matter what you do, or what you try to give, you just can't win nohow.

On the other side of the ledger, I've received many *offers* of money—sometimes a great deal of money—for the use of my name on commercial endorsements, as a sponsor of this or that. Enterprising entrepreneurs have sought the rights to depict me, Kunta Kinte and other *Roots* figures on enough different kinds of products to fill a pretty thick catalog. When I've respectfully declined, they've expressed amazement that I'd have such bad judgment as to pass up profits they knew would exceed my wildest dreams. They ignore my own explanation that I'm proud of what *Roots* has come to mean for a very great many people, and not for any sum would I be likely to host commercial exploitations with their inevitably cheapening result.

If the mail I receive is any evidence, people *everywhere* have been reached by whatever it is that *Roots* has to say. After all this time since the book was published, I still get almost 500 letters a week from all over the world—in every one of the 24 languages in which translations have appeared—and most of them express variations of the same message: They want to tell me personally how *Roots* has changed their attitudes, even their lives, in a positive way.

Once in a while, of course, I'll get an anonymous letter—this kind always is—that lets me know how far we still have to go before the millennium finally arrives. A typical one, which I received the other day, read: "Dear Haley: Now that you have found out who your ancestors are, why don't you go back there and take the rest of your kind with you?" End of letter. That sort of thing would discourage me if there weren't so many more like the one that came in the same mail. It was a deeply touching note from a little boy in Nebraska. From his printing, I'd guess he was about ten years old. He wrote: "Dear Alex Haley, I am sending you some money to put on Kunta Kinte's grave. I'm sorry about what happened to him. Yours truly. . . ." And beneath that, there were 22 cents in coins he had Scotch-taped to the page. The contrast between those two letters was so diametrical, so emblematic, that I had them mounted side by side and hung them in my study, in case I need to be reminded, as I sometimes do, that neither good nor evil has quite triumphed in this world.

For me, though, it's still a problem to find the time and the place to buckle down to my craft. Once my phone had been changed the first few times, and my office was discovered, I finally had a friend rent for me—in his name—a little one-room efficiency studio clear across Los Angeles— to become my "hideaway." But I was soon spotted getting out of my car in the communal garage, whereupon the word circulated, and before long, I'd arrive to find sundry notes shoved under the door, usually asking for appointments to discuss writing or other problems, or large manila envelopes containing manuscripts, along with their authors' notes of confidence that if I'd spend only a little time in a reading, and perhaps some rewriting, then surely my contacts could get their work published and they'd share with me as much as half of the proceeds. I mean—you know? The hell of it is that those were genuinely nice people and I hated having to return the manuscripts untouched, especially since they did sorely need at the very least a radical rewriting—precisely as my own writing efforts once did. The trouble was, *is,* that I just haven't the *time* to give—even as I wish that I could to my own work. I've gotten another hideaway now, and this sounds awful—

it embarrasses me to admit it—but the garage is equipped with one of those electronic things that opens the garage door from down the street. I make certain when I arrive that no one's watching, circling the block, if necessary, then pressing the button. I drive in quickly and the garage door closes behind me. In the connected apartment, I will usually have written well into the wee hours, and often past dawn, before I leave.

One of the most unpleasant surprises about "success" is that time, whether spent at a typewriter or doing whatever else, *costs* so much more than it did before. The worth of an hour gets highly dramatized when you find yourself so pressured with work that you must decline invitations you'd give your eye teeth to accept, including some from the world's heads of state. At the moment, I've several state invitations as rain checks awaiting only when I can find the time clear to visit. Among the many lessons I've learned as a result of *Roots,* having to make choices like that has taught me how deep is my commitment to writing. I like to think it's unshakable.

But I badly miss just sitting and chitchatting with friends as I used to do, just running my mouth, or listening to them run theirs. It *hurts* to hear from friends and relatives whom I really love, who let me know that *they're* hurt, feeling that I've turned big-headed and cast them aside. I'll bet that last summer at least 50 old friends, new friends and relatives visited Los Angeles, rightfully expecting that we'd at least share one evening of dinner and reminiscing. But multiply one evening by 50! With me under the pressure of writing another book, assisting in the making of the *Roots: The Next Generations* 14-hour TV miniseries, not to mention all of the daily etc. of business, I just couldn't handle it. I spent as much of the summer as I possibly could working in seclusion at a friend's lodge at Lake Arrowhead. I just couldn't *afford* to stay home.

In another area, ironically, I've found I can't afford *not* to stay home. For years, during my *Roots* writing, I supported myself, and financed my continued writing on it, by lecturing all over the U.S. about "My Search for Roots." In fact, I did so much lecturing that many friends prophesied that I'd spend the rest of my life *talking* a book that I'd never finish writing, and I began to think they were right. I loved public speaking, and I still do—the travel, the contact with people, hearing their responses. But after *Roots* finally did get written and published, I simply had to quit lecturing, except in rare instances.

It bothered and embarrassed me to be surrounded by security guards as we'd move through crowds of people clamoring to say something or shake hands. I remember one night in Kansas City, a cluster of male fans accosted me standing at a urinal, demanding that I sign autographs for them right then and there. Another time, at a college in San Diego, I arrived so completely beat that I literally *fell asleep* standing before the microphone with a big audience sitting in front of me; wakening with a start, I wondered, What the hell did I just say? And how long ago did I say it? But they'd apparently thought I was just taking a long thought between sentences or something; at least I was jolted wide-awake in my embarrassment, so I managed to keep talking and finished the "speech."

But what actually precipitated my quitting the scheduled lectures was that one day my office received a bitter letter from someone saying that while I hadn't even bothered to acknowledge his group's request for me to lecture, I'd added insult to injury by turning up to speak recently at another place nearby. By that time, there were unopened canvas bags full of mail piled about the office; I'd never seen those folks' request, and neither had my cousin, Jennie Haley, who runs my office. Feeling terrible about hurting somebody's feelings in that way, and not wanting it to happen again if we could help it, I told Jennie and her assistant to drop everything for one day, go through all of those bags, sort out every lecture invitation and promptly answer them. And do you know what we discovered? By the end of that day, we'd stacked into piles atop desks 802 lecture requests—for projected dates roughly within the next six months. That was the day I knew I had to quit. There was no way even to *begin* to satisfy people's expectations. Even if out of the 802 I had selected a priority 365, to do one each day for a year, I'd have left those other hundreds of places calling me names, as often happens when requests simply can't be met. In any case, if I were to lecture for 365 consecutive days—even for the $5000 fee I'm offered now—the relentless traveling involved would sooner or later see me among some cemetery's more affluent remains.

I lecture now only once in a while, most often at high schools or grade schools; I love those kids. And now and then, when I can, I'll speak at a prison: Almost every time, I come away feeling very depressed that so many of our sharpest folk—minorities, in particular—are behind bars somewhere. Those, of course, are appearances I make without asking for a fee. I wouldn't ask for one even if I needed the money. And I don't.

You have to ask yourself, How much is enough? No matter how much you have, you can eat but one meal at a time, drive but one car at a time, live in but one house at a time, sleep in but one bed at a time, with but one woman—well, I've heard of multiple-bedmate situations, but one remains the limit of my own experience. Money cannot buy you one extra hour of life. Assuredly, no amount of money can buy you one single true friend. The primary worthwhile thing that it *can* buy you is the freedom to quit worrying about money any more—but you can be certain that it will also bring you brand-new money worries of sorts that you never dreamed about before.

I feel pretty well qualified on both sides of the subject by now. For many years, I was deeply in debt—hopelessly in hock to family, friends, banks, the "friendly loan" firms, the credit-card firms; in fact, anybody at all from whom I could borrow a few dollars to keep me going for a while longer. For long periods, the lack of money hounded me, haunted me, dogged my trail, seemed almost to paralyze me with guilt, frustration and a sense of hopelessness. On more than one occasion, I came close to despair—and once the depth of my debts was a factor in my literally contemplating doing myself in. But I hung in there, and finally, incredibly, the book was finished. And even more incredibly, it was a huge success. Was it *worth* the struggle? Absolutely. But not for the money.

All I'd ever previously dreamed for, materially, was to be comfortable. I'll change that: *really* comfortable, with some financial cushion available, should I ever need it. But I tell you the truth: If for some reason I needed to, I believe that I could return to my one room in a Greenwich Village basement tomorrow and be quite content. Most of the trappings of success available to me now, I find, not only hold no intrigue for me but often even embarrass me. When I must ride in a limousine someone has hired to get me around, I tend to sit way back; I wouldn't want anyone I'd known before all of this happened to maybe spot me in there. And I really prefer eating good home cooking, or in some small, quiet restaurant, to booth number one in some chic bistro with a maître d' whose instincts have told him even before I finish ordering that my discernment among wines is still not much past the muscadine and persimmon wines that Grandma used to make and bottle every fall.

It wasn't long ago that I was still considered a bit of a square—and rightly so—even in the way I dress. When all of this started happening, I always wore the corduroy suits I already had and liked so much because they seldom needed pressing, they just wore and wore. My friends began telling me tactfully that I needed new clothes, and I'd ask, "Why? What do you mean? These suits are fine. They're not shiny yet." Then, during an "Alex Haley Day" at Harvard University, I was walking along with a friend of mine, a beautiful dresser, and the television cameras were rolling. That night, I happened to see us on the evening news, me in my baggy corduroys and my friend looking as if he'd just stepped from a fashion magazine. The next morning, I called my office and said I needed some new suits. When I got back to Los Angeles, in my living room was this tailor waiting for me, practically bowing alongside this rack he'd brought with maybe 20 suits hanging on it. Right in my house! I'd never even imagined such a thing as that. But they were nice suits, so I decided to get a few. Suits I'd previously bought had ranged up to maybe $150, so I figured I could easily afford about six of them, for around $1000. I picked out six, the smiling tailor duly marked them and left, and by the next noon they were delivered—along with the bill. Well, my eyes just about fell out! The damned things had cost upwards of $600 *apiece*; and since they had been altered, I couldn't take them back. I've yet to wear one of them. Foolish I may be about it, but I just can't escape feeling that the suits symbolize something that makes me acutely uncomfortable; I guess my small-town upbringing is still a part of me; I still wear chinos and jeans whenever I can. For better or worse, I'm just more interested in what I *am* than in what I can put *on* me.

Much more recently, I was given as a present a truly beautiful Swiss wristwatch, described as "the ultimate in timepieces," thin as a silver dollar. I admire it, of course. I just don't *need* a wrist decoration that could easily pay someone's college tuition for a year.

There's one fringe benefit to success, however, that I cheerfully confess is an unmitigated joy. It has opened for me a magical door to a world of fascinating and powerful people I'd never dreamed I'd ever meet—except, perhaps, in my previous capacity as a journalist. It's a heady experience to enjoy luncheon or backstage chitchat with such personages as Henry Kissinger and President Carter. At one White House luncheon, Queen Farah of Iran invited me to Teheran: our next conversation was in her palace. In general, this aspect of experiencing success—particularly with the accompanying world-wide recognition that both the book and the television series have brought me—is rather like an *Arabian Nights* fantasy come true.

You want to try guessing how it feels to have ladies such as Lena Horne and Leontyne Price hug you and tell you that they love you for what you've written? You want to imagine being kissed on both cheeks by Elizabeth Taylor, and right in front of her husband, John Warner, the former Secretary of the Navy? You want to know how it felt having him say, "Can we have lunch?" to a former U.S. Coast Guard mess boy who used to deliver trays of coffee?

Speak of thrills: Dick Gregory telephoned me, saying that his friend Marlon Brando had asked for my home phone number. Then Brando did call, saying that he held such a high opinion of both *Roots* and my first book, *The Autobiography of Malcolm X*, that he wanted to ask, "Is it possible I could play some role in the new *Roots* series?" I mean, maybe the world's highest-paid actor *volunteering* his services? It practically put me on the floor; you can be sure we didn't waste any time offering him several parts to choose from.

One bond I've discovered I share with practically every other public figure is a feeling of kinship and compassion for anyone who finds himself or herself abruptly thrust into the harsh glare of the media spotlight. Celebrity status in this country, particularly in show business and the arts, renders one fair game for the press. But I have been luckier by far than a great many others I know of. The relatively few critical blasts of *Roots* didn't really bother me, except when I felt that a particular critic seemed to have gone out of his or her way to cut me unfairly. Some of my keenest critics, in fact, got longhand notes or telephone calls from me, thanking them for the caliber of their comments. The most that one can ask—even when criticized—is that the writer conduct himself with sincerity and with a sense of responsibility to portray his subject as fairly as he can.

I've had only a couple of really unfair media experiences, but they're the kind that give some credence to the old adage about the press putting people on pedestals so they can point out their clay feet. One popular national magazine's first major article about me was absolutely beautiful; but in the next piece, the editors seemed to feel that some "new" side of me should be presented, and the quotes attributed to me made me sound as if I were some jive-talking, finger-snapping pimp. In another case, a writer for the London *Times* published an article about *Roots* that was laced with inaccuracies, innuendoes and outright distortions. I was incensed that the article, which gained swift world-wide circulation, attempted to cast doubt on the authenticity of *all those years* of the most painstaking and meticulous research efforts. But what really upset me most was that, also, by implication, it clearly sought to impugn the dignity of black Americans' African heritage. But by now, I've come to view it philosophically, as a part of the rites of passage that *Roots* must endure if posterity is ever to declare it truly a literary landmark, which many are already saying that it is.

Far more troubling than any media brickbats has been the costliest product of success: Like so many who've made it big—financially as well as professionally—I've become a sitting duck for lawsuits. Six have been lodged against me since *Roots* came out. The week preceding this writing, three of the suits were dismissed by Federal judges. Two of those suits had alleged that I had copied major portions of *Roots* from another author's books. The complainant in the fourth lawsuit alleged that in *Roots* I wrote not my own story but *his* story, for which grievance he sought from me the sum of, I kid you not, $100,000,000! Two other suits, also alleging plagiarism on my part, are still awaiting resolution. No matter how unfounded, each and every lawsuit has to be fought—at an enormous cost, in money, in time and in psychic wear and tear. Believe me, there is something terribly hurtful about believing that you've tried your best to live your life as a reasonably decent person, working hard, trying to accomplish something worthwhile, and then finding yourself in a witness chair, being grilled day after day by a hostile lawyer with questions loaded with insinuations that at the very least you're some scheming thief.

I don't dwell on these unhappy incidents in order to ask for sympathy. No one who's been blessed with the incredible good fortune I've been lucky enough to enjoy has any right to bitch about what it cost. I just wanted to share with you a complex and extraordinary experience that has befallen few people in our time on such a scale. Perhaps it will serve as a reminder that our great god "success," with its omnipotent trinity of fame, wealth and power, is something we should learn to *respect* rather than to worship—lest it enslave us.

One moment in my life always comes back to me when I feel the pressures of my own success closing in on me, and it always makes them easier to bear. A friend of mine called me late one night and said he hated to wake me up, but he couldn't sleep and he had to tell me what he was thinking. He said, "I can't explain it, except that I just believe that when Kunta Kinte told his daughter Kizzy all about himself, he wasn't really talking to *her*, he was talking to *you*, across the centuries, so you could write what he had to say for all the world to share. And what he had to say was: I lived. And it mattered." That thought alone makes all the years I worked on *Roots,* and all of the difficulties I've encountered since, more than worth it.

A major apprehension among those who've known me for a long time, since before *Roots,* is: Have I changed? I don't think so. As I think I've shown you, my circum-

stances have certainly changed—in some ways for the
better, in some ways otherwise. But my friends tell me I'm
the same person I was before, and that makes me happy. It
feels like I've passed an examination. But the fact is that I
agree with them. I was at peace with myself before *Roots*,
and I'm at peace with myself now—even amidst the crush
of burdens and responsibilities that sometimes threatens to
submerge me.

Once that crush begins to lighten—after *Roots: The
Next Generations* is aired, after I've finished writing *Search*,
my journal of the 12 years that went into the making of
Roots—my life is going to change again. I'm going to start
accepting some of those invitations I've held in abeyance,
and catch up with my old friends, and live at a more
leisurely pace. I may even allow myself the luxury of sleeping as much as six or seven hours every night.

But I guess my great dream is still that down the line, not
too far in the future, I ought to have the things I've got to
do pretty well in hand, and finally be free to enjoy the rest
of my years doing the things I *love* to do. Like see the
world. And with time to do it right. I want to see the
Yangtze River. I want to see Morocco. I want to see Kili-
manjaro. I still want to see the Pyramids. And, come hell
or high water, someday I'm going to ride that camel.

QUINCY JONES

A Candid Conversation with Pop's Master Builder about Rock, Rap, Racism and His Thriller of a Career

ARNY FREYTAG

"Back on the Block," the latest hit album from Quincy Jones, may not sell as many copies as "Thriller," the all-time record-setting megahit he produced with Michael Jackson in 1982. It may not have the global impact of "We Are the World," his superstar-studded 1985 musical event, which raised $50,000,000 to fight hunger. It may not earn him another Grammy award, though he has won 20 of them since 1963. But "Back on the Block" is certainly the most historic achievement of Jones's extraordinary career. It's also the story of his life.

A virtuoso blending of bebop, soul, Gospel, rhythm-and-

blues, Brazilian and African music, rap and fusion, it's what one critic called "a virtual crash course in black popular music of the 20th Century." In his liner notes for the album, Jones wrote that his intention was "to bridge generations and traverse musical boundaries." Actually, that's what he has been doing ever since he broke into show business at the age of 15 as a trumpet player and arranger for Lionel Hampton.

In the 42 years since then, he has composed, arranged or produced hits for almost every major name in the music business, from such big-band greats as Count Basie and Dizzy Gillespie to modern-day superstars such as Frank Sinatra. He is also credited with helping catalyze the phenomenon of "crossover" by bringing black music across the color line into the musical mainstream. As a vice-president of Mercury Records in the early Sixties, Jones was the first black executive at a major label, and in 1963, he began a second career in Hollywood, where he became the first black to reach the top rank of film composers, with 38 pictures to his credit.

His biggest professional setback came in 1978, when he served as musical director of "The Wiz," a multimillion-dollar flop—but the project solidified a friendship with 20-year-old Michael Jackson (who starred as the Scarecrow) and launched a series of creative collaborations that culminated in "Thriller" and "We Are the World." His first excursion as a movie producer, in 1985, elevated him into the big leagues almost overnight. He persuaded Steven Spielberg to coproduce and direct "The Color Purple," cast Oprah Winfrey and Whoopi Goldberg in the roles that won them Oscar nominations, then supervised the entire production—and, for good measure, wrote the score.

But the strain of living in all those fast lanes, along with the disintegration of his third marriage, to actress Peggy Lipton, drove Jones into a nervous collapse that stirred memories of the near-fatal aneurysm—a hemorrhaging ar-

*tery in the brain—that had stricken him in 1974 after a
similar bout of overwork. This time, he took a month-long
"spiritual leave of absence" in Tahiti and returned "in
control of my life for the first time."*

*His eclectic album "Back on the Block" is the harvest of
that sabbatical. So is his new company, an entertainment
conglomerate partnering Jones and his chief executive, Kevin
Wendle, in a co-venture with Time Warner's Bob Pittman,
a former MTV executive. And so is the list of honors that
have come his way since then—among them this year's Soul
Train Heritage Award, which turned into a star-studded
57th-birthday tribute to "Q," as he's known to his hundreds
of friends and admirers in the business; a Man of the Year
citation at the annual conference of the international music-
business association MIDEM; and, most recently, a prestigi-
ous Legion of Honor award from the government of France,
where he is considered an American national treasure.*

*Paris was one of the settings for this conversation with
Alex Haley, whom he met in 1975 while the author was
writing "Roots." Jones was enthralled by the stories Haley
told him about his ancestors, and when David Wolper asked
Jones to score the first 12 hours of the television miniseries,
he and Haley became collaborators as well as friends. When
we called Haley with this assignment, he was in the final
stages of completing his long-awaited book "Henning," but
it's a measure of their friendship that he agreed to take time
out for this very special "Playboy Interview." He reports:*

*"On a desk in Quincy Jones's business office in Los An-
geles sits the biggest Rolodex I've ever seen. It contains, I'm
told, the names of more than 5000 friends and associates in
the entertainment industry. I believe it. There probably isn't
a heavier hitter in the business, or one more universally
admired.*

*"Whatever Quincy's doing, whether it's work or play, he
does it with his whole being. And he seems to keep busy
pursuing one or the other, in grand style, just about 24 hours*

a day. My interview with him, appropriately, began on a private jet en route to Manzanillo, Mexico, and continued beside his pool at the spectacular Las Hadas resort hotel, between takes for a feature-length documentary of his life, 'Back on the Block with Quincy Jones,' scheduled for theatrical release in September. Our next session followed a memorable dinner prepared by Quincy's French-Brazilian chef at his showplace Bel Air home, a stone's throw from the Reagans.

"A third session took place last summer in Paris during the bicentennial Bastille Day extravaganza, the orchestral highlight of which Quincy had been imported to conduct. The mayor of Paris headed a parade of Quincy's old friends, who visited him in his flower-banked suite at the Ritz. And after the festivities, before returning home, he and his traveling companions—Time Warner co-C.E.O. Steve Ross and his wife, Courtney, who was producer of the documentary—decided to stop off in London for dinner with Quincy's pal Dustin Hoffman. As we say in Tennessee, that's tall cotton. But somehow, through it all, success hasn't spoiled Quincy Jones. I wanted to know why. So that's where we began."

HALEY: "Lifestyles of the rich and famous" is a phrase that could have been coined to describe the way you live, Quincy—but you don't seem to have lost your humility. Why not?

JONES: I never forget where I came from, man. When I was seven, I remember my brother Lloyd and I went to spend the summer with my grandmother in Louisville, Kentucky. She was an ex-slave, but she'd moved up in the world since then. The lock on the back door of her little house was a bent nail, and she had a coal stove and kerosene lamps for light, and she used to tell us to go down to the river in the evening and catch us a rat, and we'd take that sucker home in a bag and she'd cook it up for supper. She fried it with onions, and it tasted *good*, man. When you're seven years old and you don't know any better, everything tastes good to you. That kind of memory makes you appreciate everything that much more, because from then on, no matter how good it gets, you never take anything for granted. I've had the whole range of experiences, from rats to *pâté*, and I feel lucky just to be *alive*.

HALEY: Why do you say that?

JONES: In the neighborhood where I was born, on the South Side of Chicago—the biggest ghetto in the world—we used to watch teachers getting killed and policemen shooting black teenagers in the back. Every street was like a territory, and every territory was run by a gang, and everybody used to carry a little switchblade. If I'd stayed there, I'd have been *gone* by now. Because nobody gets out, hardly.

HALEY: But when you were ten, your family moved to Bremerton, Washington, near Seattle. What was it like there?

JONES: The opposite end of the spectrum. My father and my mother had split up back in Chicago, and we moved in with my new stepmother and her three kids in a decent neighborhood in this nice little town where he'd gotten a job as a carpenter down at the naval shipyards. It took me a few months before I realized I didn't have to carry my switchblade anymore. The school I went to was like a model of multi-racial integration, and the kids got along together about as well as they do anywhere in the world. But it's not like we moved to Disneyland. There's no way you're going to live anywhere in America and not feel the pangs of racial prejudice. You still get that *hate* stare from certain kinds of white people, but that's a daily experience from the time you're two years old, and you learn to deal with it.

HALEY: When did you start getting interested in music?

JONES: When I was five or six, back in Chicago. There

was this lady named Lucy Jackson who used to play stride piano in the apartment next door, and I listened to her all the time right through the walls. And we used to listen to the songs my other grandmother in St. Louis would play on her old windup Victrola—Fats Waller, Duke Ellington, Billy Eckstine, all the greats. In Bremerton, I joined the school choir and the school band and learned how to play drums, tuba, B-flat baritone horn, French horn, E-flat alto horn, sousaphone and piano. I really wanted to learn trombone, so I could march right behind the drum majorettes. Then my father gave me a trumpet of my own, and soon I was wearing one of those red-and-white derbies and doo-wopping with my plunger mute in the National Guard band. In between the band concerts and singing in a Gospel group, me and my friends would be out playing gigs just about all the time, because this was during World War Two and Seattle had all these Army bases that were the last stop-off before getting shipped out to the Pacific, and that town was *jumpin'*, man.

HALEY: Where did you play those gigs?

JONES: A typical night for us would be from seven to ten at the Seattle Tennis Club in our white tuxedos, playing *Room Full of Roses* and all that hotsy-totsy stuff for a totally white audience. Then, at ten-thirty, we'd make the rounds of all the black get-down clubs, like the Reverend Silas Groves's Washington Social and Education Club, which was nothing but a juke joint with strippers. Or to the Black and Tan, where we played R&B for an incredible character named Bumps Blackwell, who owned a meat market and a jewelry store and a chain of taxicabs in addition to heading up a band. He's the guy who discovered Sam Cooke and Little Richard. Bumps's band even played for Billie Holiday when she came to town. And we didn't just play *horn* for Bumps. We danced, we sang, we did everything. We had two girl singers, a stripper, four horns, a rhythm section, a male singer and two comedians—that was me and a friend of mine. We doubled as the comedy team of Methedrine and Benzedrine. We put on a *hell* of a show. Anyway, around two A.M., after blowing with Bumps for a few hours, we'd wind up down at the Elks Club playing bebop for ourselves till five or six.

HALEY: Didn't you meet Count Basie around that time?

JONES: I met Basie when I was thirteen years old, when he was playing at the Palomar Theater in Seattle. At that time, he was the biggest and the best big-band leader in the world, but he took me under his wing, and we formed a relationship that lasted the rest of his life. He was my uncle, my father, my mentor, my friend—the dearest man in the world. And his trumpet man, Clark Terry, practically adopted me. He taught me and talked to me and gave me the confidence to get out there and see what I could do on my own. These are the guys who really trained me. They were my idols as musicians, but even more important, they were my role models as human beings. They were more concerned about getting better than about getting over.

HALEY: You've said that Ray Charles was another big early influence on you. When did you meet him?

JONES: When I was about fourteen, I went over to Bumps's house one night, and there he was—this sixteen-year-old blind kid playing the piano and singing *Blowin' the Blues Away*. He was so good he gave me goose bumps. He already had his own apartment, he had all these women, he owned four or five suits. He was doing better than me, and he was *blind*, man. So I just attached myself to him, and he became like a big brother to me. Taught me how to read and write music in Braille and how to voice horns and how to deal with polytonality, and that opened up a golden door for me, because I was fascinated with how all those instruments I'd learned how to play in the band, each of them with its own distinctive sound, could play their own individual variations on the tune and yet interweave them all into the fabric of a song. And from then on, I was hooked on the idea of orchestration and arranging.

HALEY: But it was Lionel Hampton who gave you your first big break. How did that happen?

JONES: I kept hanging out with his band whenever it was in town, until finally, when I was fifteen, he gave me the chance to blow trumpet and write some arrangements for the band. Well, that's all the encouragement I needed to pack up and get on the bus. Only, before we could pull out, his wife, Gladys, caught me on board and yanked me back onto the street. "That boy's gonna finish his schooling before he gets back on this bus," she told Hamp.

So I was *highly* motivated to finish school so I could go join that band. And the moment I graduated from high school—and completed one-semester musical scholarships at Seattle University and Berklee College of Music in Boston—that's exactly what I did. Because Lionel Hampton was a superstar back then. He had the first rock-and-roll band in America—I'm talking about that big-beat sound with the honking tenor sax and the screaming high-note trumpet. Hamp was a *showman*. He even had us wearing these outlandish purple outfits—matching coats and shorts and socks and shoes and Tyrolean hats.

HALEY: Weren't you embarrassed?

JONES: Mortified. But I didn't care, man, because I got to go to New York with the band. I was eighteen, and it was like going to heaven for me, because that's where all my idols were. Oscar Pettiford was like my big brother, and he introduced me to all of them: Miles, Dizzy, Ray Brown, Charlie Parker, Thelonious Monk, Charlie Mingus, all the bebop dudes. They were the new generation of jazz musicians, and they thought it was unhip to be too successful. They said, "We don't want to be entertainers. We want to be artists. We want to explore." But when they went into bebop, we lost some of our greatest warriors, because the public rejected them and they didn't make a dime, not a dime. I mean, they lived from day to day. And they went into this little cocoon and we ended up with a lot of casualties—a lot of people in the gutter, dying from heroin.

HALEY: What was it like touring with Hampton's band?

JONES: It was an education, and not just about music. After we left New York, Map's band went on a long tour through the South, 79 one-nighters in a row in the Carolinas alone. It was a grind. And every night was like going into a battle zone. About two thirds of the way through the show, somebody out on the dance floor would start a fight, and before the evening was over, there'd be two or three stabbings. You got used to that kind of thing.

What I didn't get used to was the discrimination. It was on that trip that I got my first real exposure to segregation in the raw, and it just about blew my head apart. Every day and every night, it kept hitting us in the face like a fist. It was like being in enemy territory. The older guys had been on the road for 30 years, and they'd seen it all. They knew just what to say and what not to say around white people down there, where you could stay and where you couldn't stay, where you could eat and where you couldn't eat. We'd show up in some towns and our white bus driver would have to go get us sandwiches and bring them back aboard, because there was no place we could eat. And once, in Texas, we pulled into this little town around five in the morning and there was an effigy of a black person with a rope around his neck hanging from the steeple of the biggest church in town. Man, that just fucked my mind up. I didn't know how to handle it.

But whenever it got to be too much for me, the older guys would say, "Don't feel so bad. It's no different for Lena Horne or Sammy Davis or Harry Belafonte. They may be big stars, but when they play Vegas, they still got to eat in the kitchen, they can't stay in the hotel where they're working, they can't even mingle out front with the

people who just paid to see them on the stage." Well, that didn't make me feel any better. But that's the way it was in those days. We've come a long way since then, but back in the Fifties, if you wanted to be treated like a person and appreciated for your musical talent, the older guys said Europe was the place to go.

HALEY: Was there less prejudice there?

JONES: Let's not get carried away, now. You'll run into the same attitudes in Europe as you'll find anywhere else in the world. But in this country, jazz and blues had always been looked down on as the music of the brothel. In Europe, they were mature enough to understand it from the beginning for what it was: one of the true original art forms ever to come from America.

HALEY: You toured Europe with Hampton's band in 1953. How did you go over?

JONES: We were a smash everywhere we went, and while we were in Stockholm, I also got the chance to compose, arrange and conduct four songs in a landmark recording session for Art Farmer, Clifford Brown and the Swedish All-Stars. After it came out, the word about us spread like wildfire all over Europe, and when we got to Paris, they wanted us to record some more albums. We were in Paris, I remember, when I got word from Jeri, my high school sweetheart, that she'd given birth to a little girl named Jolie. We'd gotten married before I left the States, and I didn't get to see either one of them till I got back home to New York. I quit the band to work in the city as a free-lance arranger, so I wouldn't be on the road so much. But we were too young to be married, let alone raising kids, and so it never worked out.

HALEY: Did you make it as an arranger in New York?

JONES: Scuffled around awhile, arranging for James Moody's band, but then Dinah Washington grabbed ahold of me and asked me to start writing arrangements for her. Dinah's material could get pretty raunchy sometimes. One of the songs I arranged for her, I remember, was called *I Love My Trombone Playing Daddy with His Big Long Sliding Thing*. I was ready to move on in 1956 when George Avakian of Columbia Records asked me to write arrangements for the first album by a 20-year-old San Francisco track star named Johnny Mathis. I told him yes, but before I had the chance to do it, Dizzy Gillespie called and asked me to do all the arrangements for a band that the State Department wanted him to take on a good-will tour of the Middle East.

As it turned out, America needed all the good will it could get just then because of the political situation in that part of the world. We arrived in Turkey in the middle of a crisis, and the same people who were stoning the American embassy came to our concert at night. And after the concert, they went rushing up to the stage and grabbed Dizzy, and we were scared to death about what they were gonna do. But they just picked him up on their shoulders and cheered, man, like he was a hero.

When we showed up in Pakistan, they'd never even seen a trumpet or a trombone, but they responded to our music like it was their own. We communicated with them on a level that transcended language and politics and cultural differences. It was on that trip that I felt for the first time the real power and universality of music as a bond among people everywhere.

HALEY: You've said that your next European tours, in 1957 and 1958, were major turning points in your life. In what way?

JONES: The first one was a gas, the second a disaster. In 1957, I was asked to be the musical director of Barclay Records, a very innovative company in Paris that was run by Eddie Barclay and Nadia Boulanger. Before she went into the record business, Nadia had been the musical mentor to some of the greatest composers in the world—guys like Aaron Copland and Igor Stravinsky—and I can't begin to tell you the lessons she taught *me*, not only about music but about living. It was through her that I got to meet incredible people such as James Baldwin, Richard Wright, Françoise Sagan, Josephine Baker, Pablo Picasso, even Porfirio Rubirosa. That year was wonderful.

HALEY: And the next was a bummer?

JONES: They say you learn more from your setbacks than you do from your successes, so I guess I should consider it a triumph. I was asked to become musical director for a Harold Arlen–Johnny Mercer musical called *Free and Easy*, and we took it on the road to Europe with my band. The plan was to tour the Continent for a few months and then pick up Sammy Davis on the way home to star in the show on Broadway. But when we got to Paris, the Algerian crisis had practically paralyzed the country, and the show folded, and we got stranded in Europe for the next 10 months. Every week, I had to scuffle to cover the $5000 payroll, and I wound up hocking all my publishing companies to cover the nut. The pressure of trying to keep everybody afloat finally got so bad that one night, I seriously considered grabbing a handful of pills and just checking out. But that very night, Irving Green of Mercury Records, who was a dear friend of mine, telephoned and gave me the faith and courage I needed to hang in there, and I did, until we finally scraped together enough to get home on.

HALEY: How long did it take you to get back on your feet?

JONES: It was almost seven years before I bought myself out of hock. But I went back to work from the day I got off the boat in New York. Started composing and arranging again for Dinah, who told me to keep an eye on the Reverend C. L. Franklin's young daughter, Aretha. "She's the one, I promise you," Dinah told me. And she was. I organized my own band to play with Billy Eckstine, Johnny Ray and Peggy Lee at Basin Street East, and we went to the Monterey Jazz Festival. By this time, I was beginning to get noticed. In 1961, I won *Jet* magazine's award for best arranger and composer—and my first Grammy nomination, for arranging *Let the Good Times Roll* for Ray Charles.

That's when I got an offer from Irving Green at Mercury to join him as an A&R man. A&R stands for Artists and Repertoire—which means you're in charge of the people you pick and what they sing. So I had to put on a suit and go in to work every day at nine, but I got to do what I love, and I learned a lot about the business side of the music industry, because Irving Green took me to *school*, man. I was producing people like Dizzy, Sarah Vaughan, Art Blakey, and they were getting great records. I was also starting to make good money—but I didn't realize at first that other people who did what I did were getting a percentage of the royalties on top of their salaries, and that's where the real money was. But I found out real fast, and that's when I decided to get into pop music, because I was tired of producing jazz music that got great reviews, only nobody was buying it. So I produced a song—*It's My Party*—for Lesley Gore and it went up to number one on the charts. I did lots of others with her, and they were all hits. Then I started to conduct for Sinatra, and we made a record together, and we worked the Sands in Vegas.

HALEY: Didn't you get married again around that time—in 1965?

JONES: That's right—to a beautiful Swedish model named Ulla. I met her on a business trip to Stockholm. She was only 19, so I don't know why I thought it would work out. But I was 32—old enough to think I was finally ready to settle down—and I was determined to be a real husband this time. So after knowing her for three weeks, I married Ulla. Three weeks later, I knew we'd made a mistake, but I didn't want to fail at marriage a second time, and I wanted desperately to have a real home and a mother for my kids—something I'd never really known when I was growing up. So we had two children and stayed together for seven years, but finally, we both felt so trapped that each of us was blaming the other for why we weren't happy together, and it was tearing both of us to pieces—and the children, too. So one Christmas, she went home to Sweden with the kids, and she called to tell me, "I'm not coming back." Both kids came to live with me later, and we've got a fantastic relationship today, but that was one of the low points of my life, man.

HALEY: Ironically, it was during those years that you moved to Los Angeles and established yourself as one of the most successful film-score composers in the industry. What made you decide to quit the record business and try movies?

JONES: It had been a dream of mine since I was 15, and I finally got my chance. I had scored a film for the Swedish director Arne Sucksdorff, and then Sidney Lumet asked me to write the music for *The Pawnbroker*, which got me an offer to score *Mirage*, my first picture for a major Hollywood studio. So I came out to L.A., and the people at Universal freaked out when they got a look at me, because they didn't know I was black. I don't think they'd seen many blacks around there, except maybe in the kitchen, and they tried to bail out of it. But Henry Mancini—who was a friend of mine—told them, "Hey, fellas, this is the Twentieth Century. Don't be stupid. And don't strangle the baby in the crib—he can handle it." And I did. After that, it got easier, and I really started cranking them out, maybe seven or eight a year. Thanks to Benny Carter, who wrote the music for *M Squad*, I got to do the music for a few TV series—including *Ironside*—and that led to movies like *In the Heat of the Night* and *In Cold Blood* and Goldie Hawn's first picture, *Cactus Flower*. And all of Bill Cosby's early shows—56 episodes of a series starring him as a high school coach and 26 episodes of a variety show.

But by 1969, I wanted to go back in the studio and record something that was designed to be listened to as a piece of music, not as background for another medium—and the first album I produced, *Walking in Space*, won a Grammy. And two years later, I won another one.

HALEY: Wasn't it some time after that that you got married again?

JONES: Yes. My daughter Jolie introduced me at a party to a very elegant and attractive lady named Peggy Lipton, who happened to be an actress. She had been starring in *The Mod Squad* for several years, and she was fed up with the business, and that was very attractive to me, after having met every ambitious young starlet in Los Angeles. Peggy was very sensitive and intelligent, and she was from a very solid family background, with these wonderful parents who had been married for something like 37 years. Well, the idea of two people being together for 37 years was totally alien to my experience—and that was another attraction. Maybe it would rub off on us if *we* got married. So we did, and we had two children, and we stayed together for 12 years, and for a long time, it was everything I hoped it would be.

HALEY: Your three wives have been white. Have you taken any heat for that?

JONES: From both sides. But it was never a choice I made on account of color. You just never know who you're going to fall in love with. I love ice cream, man, and I don't care if it's French vanilla, chocolate chip, maple walnut, lemon sherbet or black cherry. When I look at a woman, race is the *last* thing I'm thinking about. It's the last thing I think about when I look at anybody, unless they're looking at *me* that way. And my kids are the same way about it. They're all of mixed blood, but they choose to think of themselves as black, and they're proud of it—not because they don't want to be white but because they relate most deeply to the rich heritage of black culture, with all the heartache and all the joy that go along with it.

HALEY: You were at the top of your profession in 1974

when you suffered a massive aneurysm that almost killed you. What do you think brought it on?

JONES: I was pushing myself too hard, as usual. I'd been up three days working, and I was at my home in Brentwood, in bed with my wife, when all of a sudden, I felt this blinding pain, like somebody had blown a shotgun through my brain. It was just the worst pain I'd ever felt in my whole life, and I was screaming, and I didn't know what was happening to me. Peggy called the paramedics, but by the time they got there, I had blacked out and gone into a coma. They thought it was a heart attack, and my wife said, "He's strong as a mule, that can't be it." And she called my doctor, Elsie Georgie, who said, "I think I know what it is, but I hope it's not too late," and she took me down to the hospital for a spinal tap and, sure enough, she was right: I'd had an aneurysm. The main artery to my brain had popped and blood was pouring into my brain, which had swollen up so big they had to wait eight days before they could operate on me. Finally, they did, and I woke up and I was still alive.

That was the moment I realized for the first time that I didn't have a three-pronged cord plugged into my body that I could turn on at any time, whenever I wanted. I'd never imagined that I could fall apart like that. And coming through all that—there were actually two aneurysms and two operations a month apart—being blessed enough to come through all that alive, it really was a miracle.

HALEY: You didn't go back to work for several months after the aneurysms. Had they affected your thought processes?

JONES: I was afraid to find out. So for a long time, I didn't even try to work. I was also very weak from the surgery. But finally, I was faced with a decision that would put my recovery and my courage to the test. I had a commitment to tour Japan with a small band and I wasn't sure I should risk it, but Elsie Georgie told me, "You're anemic, but if you baby yourself now, you'll never be OK. So go."

But the surgeon who operated on me warned me not to play the trumpet. He had put a clip on my artery to keep it closed, and he told me that I'd blow off that clip and kill myself if I tried to blow that horn. I didn't believe him, of course, and I decided to take the tour, and I started blowing the horn, and one night, I hit one of those high notes and I felt something crack inside, like my head was gonna break right open. I was scared to death, and I went to the doctor and, sure enough, I'd almost blown off the clip. Well, the doctor didn't have to warn me again. I stopped playing the trumpet and I had to leave the band.

HALEY: How long did it take you to go back to work as a producer?

JONES: Not long. Surviving a second time made me realize that I didn't have anything to be afraid of—except maybe giving up on myself. I got together with two of the guys who'd gone on the tour with me—the Johnson brothers, who had a great sound on guitar and bass—and produced a record with them. We wound up with four hits in a row, and there I was, smack dab back in the record business. It was in the middle of all this that I was at a party in L.A. and ran into this beautiful brother from San Francisco who was writing this book about the story of his family and the history of black people in America, all the way back through slavery to Africa. He called it *Roots,* and it was just about the most moving and powerful story I'd ever heard. Well, it so happened that at the time, I was on a journey of my own, doing research on the evolution of black music, so I felt like it was fated that you and I should meet, Alex.

HALEY: Is it fair to say that you were fanatic about historical authenticity in scoring *Roots* with your African collaborators?

JONES: Letta Mbulu and Caiphus Semenya, yes. Anybody else might say I was fanatical, but to me, it was just trying to tell it like it was, trying to rediscover a heritage that was taken away from us. African music had always been regarded in the West as primitive and savage, but when you take the time to really study it, you see that it's as structured and sophisticated as European classical music, with the same basic components as you'll find in a symphony orchestra—instruments that are plucked, instruments that are beaten and instruments that are blown with reeds. And it's music from the soil—powerful, elemental. Life-force music. Composers from Bizet to Stravinsky have drawn on African influences. And in slave-ship times, it started spreading into the New World, from Brazil all the way up through Haiti to Cuba, through the West Indies, until some of the ships started landing in Virginia and New Orleans. The original African influence had been watered down and assimilated with other sounds along the way, but it was still strong enough that in 1692, the Virginia colony decided to ban the drum, because the slaves used it as a means of communication, and that was threatening to the plantation owners. But that didn't stop the slaves: They started making music with hand claps and foot stomps, anything to keep that spirit alive. The slaves weren't allowed to practice their own religions, either, but the black Christian churches became the keepers of the flame for black music in America: From Gospel, blues, jazz, soul, R&B, rock and roll, all the way to rap, you can trace the roots straight back to Africa.

HALEY: During the five years after *Roots*, you produced a string of hits for Chaka Khan, George Benson, Lena Horne and Donna Summer. And you began a collaboration with Michael Jackson that culminated in 1982 with the production of the biggest album of all time, *Thriller*. Did you know it was going to be a hit?

JONES: I knew from the first time I heard it in the studio, because the hair stood straight up on my arms. That's a sure sign, and it's never once been wrong. All the brilliance that had been building inside Michael Jackson for 25 years just *erupted*. It's like he was suddenly transformed from this gifted young man into a dangerous, predatory *animal*. I'd known Michael since he was 12 years old, but it was like seeing and hearing him for the first time. I was *electrified*, and so was everybody else involved in the project.

That energy was contagious, and we had it cranked so high one night that the speakers in the studio actually overloaded and burst into flames. First time I ever saw anything like that in 40 years in the business. And that's just what the album did when it hit the charts. Biggest-selling album in the history of music hyped by the biggest-selling video of all time—a fourteen-minute film that had the impact of a hit movie. There's never been anything like it.

HALEY: Jackson has a reputation for eccentricity that rivals the brilliance of his creative talents. Are both justified?

JONES: There's no question that he's brilliant—the most gifted composer and performer in popular music today. But I think it trivializes Michael to call him eccentric. He's an incredibly rich and complex human being with both the wisdom of an eighty-five-year-old sage and the magical, childlike curiosity and wonder of a Peter Pan. And the intensity of his creative energy is awesome, like a force of nature.

HALEY: We've heard that you work yourself up into a kind of fever pitch when you're composing and producing.

JONES: Well, I do have a tendency to become obsessed. When I've got a creative mode going with my composing partners, Rod Temperton and Siedah Garrett—I don't want you to get the idea I do this all alone—my mind gets so fired up that I can't turn it off and go to sleep at night. I can actually hear a song in my mind, completely orchestrated from start to finish, before we even go into the studio with my sound engineer, Bruce Swedien, to record it. But I've got to wait until the last minute to be at my best. It's the fever of the recording session that gets my juices going, and I ride it straight through to the end.

HALEY: That's the way you recorded *We Are the World*, wasn't it—in one long marathon session?

JONES: We had to. With all those superstars involved, it was like organizing D Day to get them all in the same studio on the same day. We had only 10 hours to do the whole thing, and we had to get it right in one session, because there wasn't going to be a second one. Lionel [Richie] and Michael and I knew all the things that could go wrong, so we planned it right down to where everybody in the chorus would be standing and where every microphone would be positioned so that we'd pick up each voice distinctly. And we didn't know what to expect with all those egos in the same room together. But they must have checked them at the door, because the mood in the studio was like a living embodiment of the idea behind the song. As one after another showed up—Tina Turner, Bob Dylan, Bruce Springsteen, Stevie Wonder, Ray Charles, just about all the top people in the business—the voltage in that studio kept rising and rising. For the first hour, they were signing autographs for each other. And that spirit of brotherhood communicated itself very vividly on the sound track and in the video.

HALEY: What do you say to people who characterize *We Are the World* as corny and commercial?

JONES: I say it takes a strange kind of mind to find fault with a project that raised 50 million dollars to feed the hungry. Thanks to Harry Belafonte, who planted the seed for the whole project, and to Ken Kragen, who got it off the ground, *We Are the World* raised the public consciousness about world hunger, and that helped push the government into coming up with millions more. Bob Geldof's Live Aid show paved the way, but *We Are the World* helped trigger a whole series of fund-raising events, like Hands Across America and Farm Aid and Comic Relief, that woke the kids up from their I-me-mine Yuppie mentality and got them involved in caring about what happens to somebody else for a change. Anybody who wants to throw stones at that can get up off his ass and go do something better. There's still plenty of starving Africans.

HALEY: After such megahits as *Thriller* and *We Are the World*, do you feel any pressure to hit a home run with every record?

JONES: You can't do that, because the business we're in as human beings is the *efforts* business. God is the only one in the *results* business. All we can do is the best we can. If you start thinking about sales while you're making music, man, you'll short-circuit your brain and the music won't have a chance of being any good.

HALEY: You made a big reach when you took on the role of coproducer for *The Color Purple*. How did you come to head up that project?

JONES: When Peter Guber brought me Alice Walker's book to read, it was such a powerful experience for me that I could see it unfolding like a movie right inside my mind, and I knew that I had to bring that vision to reality. So I asked Steven Spielberg to direct it, because he's one of the finest film makers we've ever seen, and *The Color Purple* deserved the best there is. I knew there would be a certain blackness that would be missing, and I took a lot of flak from some people for picking a white director, but I think the results more than justified my faith in him.

But it was probably the most difficult and taxing project I've ever worked on. It should have taken about a year to produce the movie, but Steven's other commitments made it necessary to get the whole thing done in five months, and then I had to hole up with my crew to write an hour and 54 minutes of music for it in just six weeks. Well, somehow I got it all done, and the picture won 11 Oscar nominations that year. But the whole experience took a terrible toll on me. And there were a lot of other pressures going on in my personal life at the same time.

HALEY: Such as?

JONES: For a long time, Peggy and I had been drifting apart. With so much of her life going into my career and my family, I guess she kind of lost track of herself somewhere along the way, and I'm sure I could have been much more sensitive and attentive to her needs. But by the time I was ready to, it was too late.

HALEY: All this undoubtedly contributed to your collapse in 1986 with what the newspaper accounts called "adrenal syndrome." What were the symptoms?

JONES: Memory lapses, lack of concentration, irritability, sleeplessness, everything. And finally, I just caved in. Adrenal syndrome is what the doctor called it, but I think that was just kind of a fancy name for nervous breakdown. I asked him what to do, and he told me to pull the plug and get away, go straight back to nature. So Marlon Brando offered me his place in Tahiti, and I took him up on it. Alice Walker gave me some spiritual books—*Rays of the Dawn* and *The Essene Gospel of Peace*—to take along with me. I thought these introspective books would help me dig inside myself to see what was really going on. I wanted to have a long talk with myself and get it right this time, maybe even build a platform that I could grow on for the rest of my life.

HALEY: Did you find what you were looking for in Tahiti?

JONES: I think I did. But I got a lot of help, and I needed all I could get, because I was in such bad shape, I was as helpless as a baby. It was just me and 13 Tahitians on that island. They devoted themselves to making me better, and they knew just how to do it. They fed me what they ate themselves. They would pick a papaya right off the tree and cut it up and then serve it on a coconut shell, dressed just like a chef would do it. We'd eat it with our hands, and then drink the milk from the coconut. And we'd share raw fish right out of the ocean. And that's all I ate, or felt like eating, for the 31 days I was there.

All the beauty of Tahiti was right outside my door, but I would have stayed in my room all the time if they hadn't come and taken me outside. One of the cooks would take me on long walks with him and tell me about the spirits of the ancient Tahitians. He told me, "Don't you worry, everything's gonna be all right, because I've connected you to the coconut radio, and they all know you're here." And this very talented writer and sculptor who called himself Huihini Bobby came by and took me down to this natural pool that was filled with these huge moray eels—some of them big enough to take your head off—and we sat there and watched while this guy went in the water with them and fed them right out of his hand. Another time, Bobby helped his friend's wife deliver her baby right there at home, and they were such close, loving friends that she gave him the placenta and the umbilical cord as a gift for birthing the baby, and he planted them underneath his window.

What I'm trying to tell you is that this was a magical place. These people were *connected* to the natural world around them, and the world inside them, in a way I had never known was possible and can't explain even now, but I know that just being there with them began to *heal* me. Not physically but spiritually. Because whatever was wrong with me had just struck me down and left me for dead. I felt utterly drained, vacant, empty, like my soul had left my body. I stopped looking in the mirror, because it was like looking at somebody I didn't know—a zombie—and I was afraid to look at anybody else without my sunglasses on, because I didn't want them to see that I wasn't there.

Then, one night, this sweet, beautiful girl named Vaca— she was a painter—looked into my eyes and said, "Your *kundalini* is gone." I didn't know what she was talking about, so she explained that according to Eastern philosophy, your *kundalini* is the core of your sexual energy, the core of your whole being. And mine was gone. But she said there was an ancient cure, and two of her friends came to my bungalow with this paste that comes from the bark of a tree, and they made me lie down and they snatched off my clothes and put the salve all over my back. Then they laid leaves on top of it, wrapped me all up in gauze and sat me in this big tub on a wooden block. Beside the tub, they had this huge pot full of herbs that had been cooking in water for about three hours, and they put this big towel over my head so that it hung off me like a tent, and they began pouring this steaming-hot stuff over me right through the towel, just like a homemade sauna.

Well, I started to inhale, and I'm telling you, I never felt anything like that in my life. That vapor went cleansing and healing its way right through my body into my very soul, and by the time I came out of there, I felt like a brand-new person—like I'd been reborn. I was still fragile, and for a long time, I couldn't handle noise or traffic or crowds or even television, but I knew I was whole again. And that for the rest of my life, I would be heading down another path.

HALEY: In what direction?

JONES: Toward the center. When I was young, I lived on the run, trying to make sure I wasn't missing anything. But I kept running into myself coming from the opposite direction—and he didn't know where he was going, either. It took me a long time to learn that the only thing I was missing was a good night's sleep. That I couldn't keep living my life as if I were running out of time. Because no matter how much you manage to get done, you're not ever going to finish everything you set out to do.

Since I got back from Tahiti, I've learned that the only way to keep my flame bright is abandoning myself completely to every moment I'm alive. I don't know whether I'll be here for another thirty years or another thirty minutes, so I want to just *inhale* my life—smell the roses and the butter and the seashore and everything else on the planet that I dearly love. I want to share that love with my six beautiful children—Jolie, Rachel, Martina, Quincy the Third, Rashida and Kidada—and with my friends and the people who listen to my music, because what I'm trying to express in my work is how I feel about life.

HALEY: Your latest hit record, *Back on the Block,* has been praised by critics for its "ecumenical spirit." What inspired you to bring together all the styles and periods of black popular music in America and orchestrate them into a single album?

JONES: They belong together, man. It's our musical legacy, like I was saying earlier, like a mighty river flowing all the way from the cradle of civilization in Africa down through the centuries to the black church in America, which has been the mother ship of black culture, musically and spiritually, ever since we came off the slave ships. I want the kids to know where they came from, to be proud of what we've contributed to American music and American culture. I'm talking about heart and soul, man. What else is there?

HALEY: Rap is one of the sounds on your new album. Do you think it's a fad or an important new kind of music?

JONES: It's no fad, man. And it's not just a new kind of music. It's a whole new subculture that's been invented by the disenfranchised. When you have no place in society, you say, "Fuck it, we'll start our own." Everything from graffiti to break dancing to popping and locking, hip-hop and now rap—the voice that vocalizes hip-hop—they're all symbols of a new culture that comes directly from the street.

Rap is also a new kind of communication. The point is, what are you trying to communicate? The hard-ass groups say they're just telling it like it is, but any brother or sister can go out in the street in the ghetto and *see* how it is. But once somebody has put all that about what's happening to your ass into poetic terms, he's got to get some positive information going. We got the diagnosis, so where is the prescription? It's easy to say blow the cops away with an AK-47 and it's all about bitches and money and getting high, but that's just talkin' shit. It might be a popular stance for kids to take, but it's irresponsible and it's disrespectful to the men and women of the community for anybody to think that's the way to be, because it sucks, and it's destructive. We've got to find ways to give people hope, help them put a value on their own life.

Rap at its best does just that. It may be profane and abrasive, but I think it's a very powerful and positive force. And it's the freshest thing that's happened musically in 30 years. It's already popular in Holland and Sweden and Italy and Germany, even Tokyo, and I think it's just getting started. Black music has always been the prologue to social change. It was true in the Fifties with modern jazz and rock and roll, and I think rap is a sign of the kind of changes that are sweeping the world today. It's a forum to mobilize the people of the street in a new direction—toward pride and freedom and the elevation of the spirit—and that's happening everywhere.

HALEY: How do you feel about the rest of the Top Forty music today?

JONES: Well, we've had great seasons, and we've had drought seasons, and—apart from rap—I think we're in a drought season now. There are significant exceptions in the case of a few individual performers, of course, but I'm not stimulated by much of what's happening right now. Most of it sounds homogenized. The problem is that technology is driving a lot of the music that's being recorded now. I'm not knocking technology, mind you. It has opened up all kinds of new horizons in pop music since 1953, when I was involved in the very first recording session with a new instrument invented by a young guy named Leo Fender. It was the electric bass, which, along with the electric guitar, has become the motor of rock and roll in the years since then. And I remember one day in 1964, when I went to visit this eccentric inventor named Paul Beaver at his house in L.A., and he was sitting at this keyboard with all kinds of wires coming out of it, and he said, "Here, try this." It sounded like a piano on acid, man. It made sounds I'd never heard before, just totally blew me away, and I asked him what the hell it was. "I call it a synthesizer," he told me. Between then and now, it's had the same effect on music that the jet plane has had on air travel. And in my own work, it's been like enlarging the alphabet from 26 letters to 1300.

The trouble is that electronics has the music industry completely wired by now, to the point where musicians—and certainly musicianship—are starting to be considered obsolete.

Take the drum machine. Drum machines don't have any human faults and frailties—they *never* miss the beat—and they're so sophisticated that I swear you couldn't tell one from the real thing with your eyes closed. It's very seductive to just let the machine do it; you don't have to learn how to play. There's just one problem: The drum machine is totally predictable, totally incapable of originality. And technology has been developed, or is being developed, that will make it possible to do the same thing with most of the other instruments. And that scares me, man. Eventually, we're going to have to reconcile the relationship between humanity and technology—and not just in the world of music—because if we remove people from the process, if we replace musicians with technicians, if we can't tell anymore whether it's real or it's Memorex, we're going to lose the whole reason for making music in the first place, which is to celebrate life.

HALEY: Is that what you're going to keep doing with your music? Celebrating life?

JONES: As long as I've got breath in my body. But not just with my music. I'm always going to love making albums, for myself and the people I love, and I've been thinking about going on a tour. I'd like to direct for Bobby De Niro. And I'm also working on the book for a Broadway show—a musical about dealing with your dreams.

And that's just the tip of the iceberg. I'm in partnership now with a guy named Bob Pittman, who dreamed up the whole idea of MTV and got it launched. It cost about 20 million dollars to start it up, and four years later, when they sold it to Viacom, it was worth 580 million. They wanted Bob to stay with it, but he said no, he wanted to try something new, and here we are, working together.

A dear friend of mine, Steve Ross, the co-C.E.O. of Time Warner, who's been like the godfather of this whole venture, has helped us form a new company, Quincy Jones Entertainment. We'll be developing new musical talent, making records, producing TV shows and movies. We've already got a half-hour sitcom and a home-video show under consideration at the networks, and we're planning to film the life of the poet Alexander Pushkin—who was of Ethiopian descent—in a coproduction with the Russians. We've also bought a TV station, and we've got plans to buy ten or twenty more. I mean, this man Pittman is out for *action*. On Friday, he asks me what I think about a politically oriented one-hour television talk show for Jesse Jackson, and on Monday, we're meeting with Jesse about it, and we've got a deal.

HALEY: What *do* you think about a TV show for Jesse?

JONES: It's a very marketable idea and it's a showcase for an important voice who deserves a forum for his views. I've been a close friend and supporter of Jesse's ever since he started Operation PUSH back in the Seventies. Over the years, I think he has really grown in stature and maturity, and even though we can still disagree with each other sometimes, I don't think there's any doubt that he's a force for keeping hope alive. And let's face it, we just don't have anybody else at this point in our history. He spans the whole spectrum, from the streets all the way to the corridors of power all over the world. There just isn't anybody else who stands up for us and speaks for us like Jesse Jackson does.

HALEY: At this point in his evolution, what do you think Jesse stands for?

JONES: The same things he has always stood for. When Jesse started Operation PUSH, he and his brain trust came up with a slogan, a kind of logo, that still sums up the challenge black people face in getting themselves together. He said the components that make up a human being can be expressed in the letters M-A-M-A-P-C-V, almost like a chemical formula. M is for motor skills. A is for affective, which is our feelings. The next M is for morality, and the next A is for aesthetic. P is for perception, C for cognition, which is related to education, and V is for volition. And he said that many of our kids in the ghetto have all those components in abundance except two, like having vitamin deficiencies. One big problem we face as a people comes from deficiencies in morality and cognition, both of which come from deficiencies in the family unit. And those are the two areas he has addressed since the start of Operation PUSH: building up the family unit and building self-esteem, through education and by creating economic opportunities that give people a chance in life.

HALEY: There's a widely held perception that the cause of equality has actually deteriorated over the past 20 years, that the gulf between races has widened. Do you think that's true?

JONES: You'd have to be deaf, dumb, blind or just plain stupid to deny that we have a world of problems left to overcome. But we've got to take the long view. Two centuries of racism aren't going to be erased in 20 years, or probably even 50. So we've got to keep on keepin' on. But I think we've got plenty of reason to feel good about what we've managed to accomplish so far. Because we've taken enormous strides. I think people get a misleading impression of what's really going on, because negativity is what makes *news*. They don't hear about all the folks who are getting along fine together. They don't see the everyday progress that's going on all over the country, North and South. I speak at a lot of universities, and I see all these brothers and sisters out there getting it together and doing their thing, competing in the market place, building careers, living in nice homes, raising kids who go to good schools—building their own proud version of the American dream.

HALEY: That's all true, but we also seem to be experiencing a resurgence of racial violence—cross burnings, letter bombs, personal assaults. Why now?

JONES: It baffles me and it saddens me, because I see young people involved in it, and it's the younger generation we have to look to for hope. But some of these neo-Nazi skinheads are worse than their forebears. In the past, you could chalk up such incidents to ingrained attitudes passed down from one generation to the next. But I thought we were starting to move beyond the Neanderthal period in race relations. I don't understand how it's possible to hate yourself so much that you have to hate somebody else just to feel better. I don't understand how these sick, poisonous hatreds can be surfacing again after all we've gone through and triumphed over. But the roots of prejudice run deep, and I guess we're going to have to keep pulling them up with every generation until we've stamped it out forever.

HALEY: The drug problem is another battleground for society today. Do you agree with President Bush that it's the most urgent crisis we're facing as a nation?

JONES: Well, I'm glad he finally decided to get on the right side of the issue. But I'm not sure he fully understands what he's trying to deal with. Because we're not just talking about a threat to America. We're talking about an epidemic that has the potential to bring *civilization* to its knees and, frankly, I don't know how we're going to make it through, 'cause we're going to lose a whole generation of kids to drugs and drug dealing. How are you gonna save them when they're dangling $1800 a day in front of 13-year-olds to sell dope? You can't tempt them with the promise of a college degree when they see brothers with master's degrees carrying bags at the airport or pushing fries at the Burger King. And I'm not just talking about black kids, because it's not just a ghetto problem anymore. Just like heroin. Smack was a crime until it got to Westchester, and then it became a social problem. Harlem preachers were screaming for help when the foot cops still could have stopped it in the street, but nobody gave a damn till the white kids started mainlining out in the suburbs. Well, it's everybody's problem now, and we'd better do something about it before it's too late.

HALEY: No matter what we do, isn't there always going to be a demand for drugs?

JONES: I guess there's always been some kind of libation you could take to get away from reality, and I guess there always will be, because that seems to be a part of human nature. And reality seems to be getting more complicated all the time. But so are the drugs. We've got designer drugs now that are stronger than cocaine or heroin. They'll take you further, faster, cheaper than anything we've ever seen before. For seven or eight dollars, you can buzz your brain in seventeen seconds. The trouble is that whatever problems you took the stuff to get away from are still gonna be there when you come down, and you'll have a brand-new problem to deal with on top of the ones you've already got—finding the money to get another hit, and another one, until you've run out of shit or bread. Then you've got to steal or deal to keep going until somebody blows you away or you do it to yourself.

HALEY: Is there any way out?

JONES: I feel strongly that we've got to legalize drugs.

The only way we're going to get through this plague alive is to take away the profit motive. Eliminate the crime and you eliminate the criminals. Then you'll be left with the problem of addiction, but I think most of the people who'd even think about getting high are already doing it. That's not saying more people won't start once it's legal, but I think you'll also see a big drop-off as a lot of people lose interest, because it's not clandestine enough for them anymore.

But the government doesn't want to make drugs legal. For a long time, Nancy Reagan tried to tell kids "Just say no," but of course, anybody who was really into drugs just laughed at her, and the rest were too hip to listen to that kinda shit. So now Bush has decided to declare war on drugs, and that's not gonna make a damn bit of difference, either, because you kill one grower or one dealer, and ten more spring up to take his place.

HALEY: Legalization won't help those who are already strung out on drugs or who might try it if they were legalized. What's the hope for them?

JONES: On an individual basis, the cure is to go straight back to the basics. If you're drinking and using and you can't stop, you've got to undergo a spiritual rehabilitation. You've got to realize you can't do it alone and surrender yourself to a higher power, like they say in A.A. Then you've got to clean yourself out: You've got to sit down and talk about the people who've wronged you, and the people you've wronged, and forgive them and forgive yourself, and start making amends. And start helping other people straighten out their lives. And decide how you want to spend your own. There's a lot of steps on the road back, and they're heavy steps, but I've seen it work for hundreds of people I know, because whatever the program, it's about the basic ethics of living, about the essence of what it means to be alive.

HALEY: You said earlier that those are the themes you're trying to deal with in your work. Isn't it enough just to provide great entertainment?

JONES: Not for me. If you want to be a whole musician, I think you have to be a whole human being. That's why you've got to be concerned with what's going on in the world around you—not only in your work but outside your profession—and do whatever you can do to help fight the deadly enemies: racism, ignorance, disease, homelessness and hunger. If you've been fortunate in life, you're not really straight until you've done everything you can to see that everybody else gets at least as good a shot as you did. That's why I feel such a strong obligation to contribute to worthwhile causes, whether it's cancer or sickle-cell anemia or the Africans or the United Negro College Fund or Operation PUSH or the A.C.L.U. or the NAACP Legal Defense and Educational Fund or the environment or Save the Whales. But it gets to the point where they're *all* important and they're *all* urgent, so one time, I just saved all the requests I was receiving and put them in a big basket, and at the end of a week, I added up what it would cost me to make all the contributions they asked me for, and it came to about seven hundred thousand dollars just for that one week. So I have to pick and choose the ones that mean the most to me—and if the rest of them think I'm cheap or I don't care, there's nothing I can do about it, because there's just no way I can deal with all of it.

It's the same with all the requests I get from people asking me to chair a fund raiser or set up a show or host a tribute or sit on the dais with Mayor Bradley to welcome some African diplomat or conduct the Berlin Symphony or meet a preacher who's got some new program for stopping drugs in the streets. I've got to be even more selective about that kind of obligation, because what those people want from me is my *time*. That's more valuable than all the money in the world. It's the most precious commodity we have, and it's irreplaceable. I realize that most especially when I think about my children. I was an absentee father for a lot of years when they needed me to be there for them. I'm doing my best now to make up for all the love we missed out on together.

HALEY: If you could clone yourself into three people, what would you assign each of them to do?

JONES: A few years ago, I'd have jumped at the chance. I'd have had one man who dealt exclusively with creative things: He'd come up with all the ideas for new projects. The second man would carry out those concepts: He'd be the executive producer. The third man's job would be to have a ball twenty-four hours a day. I'd send him around to do all the things I don't have enough time for—going places I've never been, having a great meal, swimming in a tropical pool, seeing a nice lady, making the people I care about feel good. But I guess I'll have to do the best I can with only one of me to go around.

HALEY: You seem to be doing a better job of it now than when you were *trying* to be three people.

JONES: Yeah, I feel like I'm behind the wheel in my life now. I'm running it. It's not running me. I'm letting go and grooving with the current, wherever it takes me. I had big dreams when I was a little boy looking out a window in Bremerton. I went after all of them, and most of them have come true. But the way I went at it, like there was no tomorrow, almost guaranteed that I wouldn't be around to enjoy it. But now that I've stopped pushing, all the doors in my life have been opening by themselves. And I'm walking through those doors to new adventures, places I've never been, things I've never done.

I don't know what I'm going to be doing six months from now, and that's just the way I like it. I just *love* jumping out and not knowing where I'm going to land but knowing I'm going to land on my feet. And even if I don't sometimes, I know it's gonna be all right, because I've had some killer bumps in my life, and I've learned something from all of them that makes life even sweeter for me.

HALEY: Of course, you're secure enough financially to be able to take such chances.

JONES: Sure I am, and that makes it a lot easier. But nobody can afford to be afraid of taking chances in life. If you're afraid to go chasing after your dreams, they're going to shrivel up, and so will you. You've got to create in your mind an invisible net underneath you, and jump. If you expect pain, that's just what you're going to get.

HALEY: And sometimes even when you *don't* expect it.

JONES: Of course. No matter what you do, you're going to go through some suffering. That goes with the territory. But you don't have to let suffering become your experience of life, and you don't have to pass it along to other people just because it hurts. Learn from it. And grow from it. And teach your pain to *sing*. I always think about Ray Charles when I think about the joy and the pain in life. He and I used to talk about how closely related they are. How he learned that the heavier the pain is, the higher the joy. And nobody knows that better than Ray Charles. All I can say is, after living through the pain and sorrow in my own life, if that's the price I've had to pay for all the joy I've known, it's been worth every minute of it, man.

MALCOLM X REMEMBERED

As Rappers, Historians and Spike Lee Lay Claim to the Martyred Black Leader, His Late Friend and Biographer Recalls the Man

In the summer of 1991, PLAYBOY *commissioned Alex Haley to write a memoir about Malcolm X. Haley was the ideal candidate for the assignment. He had ghostwritten "The Autobiography of Malcolm X" and conducted* PLAYBOY's *historic 1963 interview with him.*

As always, Haley delivered his manuscript to us letter-perfect and on time. He died six months later. Here, then, is the Pulitzer Prize—winning author's final contribution to PLAYBOY, *a fitting remembrance both of the author and of his subject.*

It was a cold gray day in February 1965, and I was trudging along a grimy sidewalk in the heart of Harlem, one among 20,000 mourners who would pay their last respects to the man who lay in state on a flower-decked bier several blocks away inside the Faith Temple Church of God in Christ. The news of his assassination by at least three black gunmen during a speech at the Audubon Ballroom sent shock waves through black America, sparked threats of race rioting and rumors of conspiracy.

As I finally gazed inside the bronze coffin, I realized that I had never met anyone who had been quite so vividly alive as the man whose body now lay before me. I found myself reliving the unforgettable moment when we had met five years before.

The Lost-Found Nation of Islam, an extremist religious sect headed by Messenger Elijah Muhammad, had been winning converts in the black community for its militant embrace of racial separatism and self-reliance—and also alienating the white community with its confrontational hostility. The media had discovered the Black Muslims, and I was assigned by *Reader's Digest* to write an article about them. The man I would have to see was their fearsome chief of staff who called himself minister Malcolm X. I was told he didn't have an office or a listed telephone number, but that I'd probably find him at the Muslim restaurant next door to Harlem's Temple Seven.

When I walked into the restaurant and explained my business, I didn't have to wait long. Within a few moments, a tall, tightly coiled man with reddish-brown hair and skin loomed beside my table, his brown eyes skewering me from behind horn-rimmed glasses. "I am minister Malcolm X," he said coldly. "You say you are a journalist, but we both know you're nothing more than a tool for the white man, sent here to spy." It was pointless to protest, so I showed him my letter of assignment, assuring him that the piece I wrote would be balanced and objective. Laughing, he said, "No white man's promise is worth the paper it's printed on." He then told me that I would have to be personally approved by Elijah Muhammad at Muhammad's home in Chicago before he would consider extending his cooperation.

I went and apparently I passed muster, because approval was granted. My story was printed the way I wrote it, and Elijah Muhammad sent me a letter expressing his appreciation that I had kept my promise to be fair. I also received a call from Malcolm X, who seemed pleasantly surprised that I hadn't betrayed them. But when I called back several months later with a request from *Playboy* for an interview with him, Malcolm X was reluctant to take the spotlight. He consented only on the condition that the editors understand he would speak not as a so-called celebrity but simply as a humble witness to the wisdom of his spiritual leader. Malcolm also demanded that the magazine print whatever he said without expurgation. The editors' reply: Agreed, as long as Malcolm answered every question he was asked. Fair enough, Malcolm said, and we had a deal.

The interviews were conducted over a two-week period, mostly at a secluded table in the Muslim restaurant. Serious-looking black men with close-cropped hair and wearing white shirts and black bow ties sat at nearby tables listening intently to every word. Our talk sessions crackled like electricity as I picked my way through the minefield of Malcolm's mind, trying to ask tough questions without antagonizing him to the point of jeopardizing the interviews. I knew without asking that even the sight of a tape recorder would terminate the assignment, and the discovery of one on my person could terminate my career, so I copied down in longhand every word that Malcolm said—as fast as I could go, unable to believe what I was hearing or that *Playboy* would dare to print it. A typical excerpt from the transcript:

PLAYBOY: How do you justify the announcement you made last year that Allah had brought you "the good news" that 120 white Atlantans had just been killed in an air crash en route to America from Paris?

MALCOLM X: Sir, as I see the law of justice, it says as you sow, so shall you reap. The white man has reveled as the rope snapped black men's necks. He has reveled around the lynching fire. It's only right for the black man's true God,

Allah, to defend us—and for us to be joyous because our God manifests his ability to inflict pain on our enemy. We Muslims believe that the white race, which is guilty of having oppressed and exploited and enslaved our people here in America, should be and will be the victims of God's divine wrath.

PLAYBOY: Then you consider it impossible for the white man to be anything but an exploiter in his relations with the Negro?

MALCOLM X: White people are born devils by nature. They don't become so by deeds. If you never put popcorn in a skillet, it will still be popcorn. Put the heat to it, it will pop.

PLAYBOY: Do you believe white people are genetically inferior to black people?

MALCOLM X: Thoughtful white people know they are inferior to black people. Anyone who has studied the genetic phase of biology knows that white is considered recessive and black is considered dominant. When you want strong coffee, you ask for black coffee. If you want it light, you want it weak, integrated with white milk. Just like these Negroes who weaken themselves and their race by integrating and intermixing with whites. If you want bread with no nutritional value, you ask for white bread. All the good that was in it has been bleached out of it and it will constipate you. If you want pure flour, you ask for dark flour, whole-wheat flour. If you want pure sugar, you want dark sugar.

PLAYBOY: If all whites are devilish by nature, do you view all black men—with the exception of their non-Muslim leaders—as fundamentally angelic?

MALCOLM X: No, there is plenty wrong with Negroes. They have no society. They're robots, automatons. No minds of their own. I hate to say that, but it's the truth. They are a black body with a white brain. Like Franken-stein's monster. The top part is your bourgeois Negro. He's your integrator. He's not interested in his poor black brothers. This class to us are the fence sitters. They have one eye on the white man and the other eye on the Muslims. They'll jump whichever way they see the wind blowing.

Then there's the middle class of the Negro masses, the ones not in the ghetto, who realize that life is a struggle. They're ready to take some stand against everything that's against them.

At the bottom of the social heap is the black man in the big-city ghetto. He lives night and day with the rats and cockroaches and drowns himself with alcohol and anesthetizes himself with dope to try to forget where and what he is. That Negro has given up all hope. He's the hardest one for us to reach because he's deepest in the mud. But when you get him, you get the best kind of Muslim. Because he makes the most drastic change. He's the most fearless. He will stand the longest. He has nothing to lose, even his life, because he didn't have that in the first place. I look upon myself, sir, as a prime example of this category—and as graphic an example as you could find of the salvation of the black man.

PLAYBOY: Is there anything, in your opinion, that could be done to expedite the social and economic progress of the Negro?

MALCOLM X: First of all, the white man must finally realize that he's the one who has committed the crimes that have produced the miserable condition our people are in. Elijah Muhammad is warning this generation of white people that they, too, face a time of harvest in which they will have to pay for the crimes committed when their forefathers made slaves of us.

But there is something the white man can do to avert this fate. He must atone. This can only be done by allowing black men to leave this land of bondage and go to a land of their own. But if he doesn't want a mass movement of our people away from this house of bondage, then he should separate this country. He should give us several states here on American soil where we can set up our own government, our own economic system, our own civilization. Since we have given over 300 years of our slave labor to the white man's America, helped to build it up for him, it's only right that white America should give us everything we need in finance and materials for the next 25 years, until our own nation is able to stand on its feet. In the white world there has been nothing but slavery, suffering, death and colonialism. In the black world of tomorrow, there will be true freedom, justice and equality for all. And that day is coming, sooner than you think.

PLAYBOY: If Muslims ultimately gain control, as you predict, do you plan to bestow "true freedom" on white people?

MALCOLM X: It's not a case of what we would do, it's a case of what God would do with whites. What does a judge do with the guilty? Either the guilty atone, or God executes judgment.

The interview was incendiary stuff, but *Playboy* published it in May 1963, just the way Malcolm had given it to me. It was the most controversial interview that *Playboy* had run up to that time, and readers reacted with shock and outrage. Perhaps more importantly, the interview propelled Malcolm X—almost overnight—into the national limelight, where he proceeded to command the stage as if to the manor born.

Within months Malcolm had accepted an offer to tell his life story in a book—"to help people appreciate better how Mr. Muhammad salvages black people"—and he wanted *me* to help him write it. Me, not only a writer for the white press but also a practicing Christian—another Muslim anathema. Malcolm had never shown the slightest warmth toward me, nor had he volunteered a shred of information about his personal life. But perhaps after working together on a couple projects, he felt enough trust to begin telling the truth about himself.

No such luck. "I don't completely trust anyone, not even myself," he told me one night early on in the book collaboration. "You I trust about twenty-five percent." But that was before he passed a white friend of mine leaving my Greenwich Village apartment as he was coming in one evening for an interview session with me. From then on, the moment he arrived, Malcolm—convinced that the FBI was bugging us—would announce sarcastically: "Testing, one, two, three, four." He would then proceed to pace the room like a caged tiger, haranguing me nonstop for the next three or four hours while I filled my notebooks with scalding Muslim rhetoric and worshipful praise of "the Honorable Elijah Muhammad." This went on four nights a week for a month or more, with Malcolm addressing me as "Sir" and bristling with irritation whenever I tried to remind him that the book was supposed to be about him. I was almost ready to call the publisher to suggest that they either abandon the project or hire another writer, when the night arrived when we both became fed up at the same time. I had been pressing him particularly hard to open up about anything, when he threw on his coat, jerked open the front door and stormed out into the hall, his hand on the knob to slam the door shut, probably for the last time. I heard myself saying, mostly in desperation, "Mr. Malcolm, I wonder if you could tell me anything about your mother."

Malcolm stopped in his tracks and slowly came back inside. He began walking and talking almost dreamily. "It's funny you should ask me that," he said. "I remember the kind of dresses she used to wear. They were always old and gray and faded. I remember how she was always bent over the stove, trying to stretch what little we had. We stayed so hungry we were half dizzy all the time." Pure poetry. He went on that way until daybreak. I didn't have to say another word. From that night on, and for the next two years, it all came pouring out of him, the whole amazing story of his life.

In 1929, four years after Malcolm was born to Baptist minister Earl Little and his wife, Louise, the family's home in Lansing, Michigan, was burned to the ground by white racists in retaliation for Reverend Little's involvement in Marcus Garvey's pan-African black independence movement. Two years later, Malcolm told me, Reverend Little was run over and killed in a trolley-car "accident." Mrs. Little struggled for six years to fend for herself and her eight children but finally suffered a breakdown. When she was institutionalized, the family fell apart and the children were split up.

Twelve-year-old Malcolm, living with family friends, was elected class president of his predominantly white junior high school and graduated with highest honors. But when he told a teacher he wanted to be a lawyer, the man said, "You've got to be realistic about being a nigger," and Malcolm dropped out of school.

And into a life of crime. After drifting through a series of menial jobs, he emerged with a new persona as "Detroit Red," a street hustler in Boston's black Roxbury district. From Roxbury he graduated to pimp and drug dealer in Harlem. He had moved into the big time as head of his own buglary ring, when he was arrested and sent to prison in 1946. It was during his six-year sentence that he underwent a spiritual rebirth. He gave up "the evils of tobacco, liquor, drugs, crime and the flesh of the swine" and joined the Black Muslims, abandoning his "slave name" Little and adopting a new identity as Malcolm X, minister of Islam.

He had been preaching the gospel to a rapidly multiplying flock ever since. I didn't fully grasp how many were in the flock, or how deeply they cared about Malcolm, until he began to take me along on what he called his "daily rounds" of the Harlem streets. A matinee idol, a homeboy among his own people, Malcolm strode along the sidewalks greeting everyone he met, that angry glower he wore for the cameras softening into a boyish grin. "Brother," he told a wino amiably, "Whitey likes you drunk so he'll have an excuse to put a club upside your head." Or, "Sisters," he said with courtly charm to a group of ladies sitting on a stoop, "let me ask you something. Have you ever known one white man who didn't do something to you or take something from you?"

"I sure ain't!" one of the ladies replied, and the others burst out in laughter.

I also remember passing a raggedy street musician one night who was huddled on a side street strumming on his battered old guitar and singing to himself. Recognizing Malcolm, he leaped to his feet and snapped into a respectful mock salute. "Huh-ho!" he exclaimed. "My man!"

That's the way it was everywhere we went. The people loved Malcolm. And it was obvious that the feeling was mutual.

But no one loved him more than the young black men of Harlem, who held him in awe. One of my most indelible memories of the time I spent with Malcolm was the day I was riding with him in his car and there was a screeching of brakes. Malcolm was out the door, bounding to the curb. Before I could gather my wits, he was looming over three young men who were shooting craps on the steps of the city library. Inside that library, Malcolm told them sternly, people of other races and colors were studying the Schomberg Collection, the greatest archive of black literature in the world. "They are studying about your people," Malcolm admonished, "and the best you can do is sit out here shooting craps against the door. You should be *ashamed* of yourselves!"

What was so impressive to me about this—knowing

what I did about the Harlem street community—was that no one else could have spoken that way to those three young toughs without endangering his life. Yet they knew full well who was tongue-lashing them, and without a word they averted their eyes and slunk away as he stood glaring after them. I have often wished that more young black people would heed the message in that incident.

By this time, Malcolm had begun meeting me at J.F.K. Airport when I would arrive home from trips. He would drive me back into Manhattan, where we would continue our work on the book. Our interview sessions had reached a level of intimacy I would never have dreamed possible. There were moments of tenderness in many of the stories he told. I remember one night in particular when Malcolm laughingly recalled doing the lindy in Harlem ballrooms. He actually grabbed a wall pipe in the corner of my apartment and danced around it before regaining his composure. It was during this period that my phone rang one night at two or three A.M., and a familiar voice said, "I trust you seventy percent." And then he hung up.

Malcolm never breathed a word to me about the intense personal stress and hardships he was undergoing. Despite his passionate following in the ghetto— and perhaps because of it—Malcolm was making powerful enemies. Not just with Klansmen and neo-Nazis but with U.S. government officials who feared that his extremism might provoke the racial Armageddon he predicted would occur. But perhaps the most ominous threat of all came from those surrounding Elijah Muhammad. "Malcolm got to be a big man," Muhammad had said. "I made him big." Malcolm was not only beginning to eclipse his mentor but also to draw federal heat upon the Muslim organization. I would later find out that Muhammad had suspended Malcolm from his duties. The bitterness Malcolm felt over this rift precipitated him to question his commitment to the white-baiting separatism that made him and the Muslims a symbol of confrontational racism and hatred.

"The young whites, and blacks, too, are the only hope that America has," Malcolm said to me after an exhilarating evening of give-and-take before the white student body of a local college. Another day, in his car, we had stopped at a traffic light beside a car with a white driver who recognized Malcolm and called to him, "I don't blame your people for turning to you. If I were a Negro, I'd follow you, too. Keep up the fight!"

Malcolm called back sincerely, "I wish I could have a white chapter of people like you!" But as we drove away, Malcolm said to me, "Never repeat that. Mr. Muhammad would have a fit."

But the damage to their relationship was already done. Although Malcolm had avoided the press ever since his suspension, rankling with the frustration of enforced inactivity, his reputation had assumed a life of its own. I began to hear—never from him—about reports of threats on Malcolm's life.

Finally, Malcolm went to the press himself, telling the *Amsterdam News* that former close associates in his Harlem mosque had sent out "a special squad to try to kill me in cold blood." But he said he had learned of the plot in time and averted it by confronting his intended assassins and forcing them to back down. When I called to express my concern, Malcolm said, "I can take care of myself," explaining to me that he had a loaded rifle in his home. "Still, I'm a marked man, Haley. If I'm alive when this book comes out, it will be a miracle." Any money due him from the autobiography, he said, should go either to his wife, Betty, or to Muslim Mosque, Incorporated, a new organization he was forming. He told me he intended to waste no time drawing up a will.

Malcolm sent a note informing me that he was leaving the country for a while—"on a pilgrimage to the Holy

City of Mecca." A few weeks later, I received an astonishing letter from him: "I have eaten from the same plate, drunk from the same glass, prayed to the same God, with fellow Muslims whose eyes were the bluest of blue, whose hair was the blondest of blond, whose skin was the whitest of white, and truly we were all the same."

He returned from his journey a new man with a new name, El-Hajj Malik El-Shabazz. He had converted to true Islam and committed himself to a new cause, his nonsectarian, nonreligious Organization of Afro-American Unity. Disavowing the racism of the Nation of Islam, Malcolm embraced a deeply felt new belief in the possibility of mutual respect between blacks and whites. "My trip to Mecca opened my eyes," he told reporters at a crowded press conference. "I have adjusted my thinking to the point where I believe that whites are human beings, as long as this is borne out by their humane attitude toward Negroes." Could any whites join the OAAU? "If John Brown were alive, maybe him." But Malcolm certainly hadn't been transformed into a nonviolent moderate. Vowing to send armed guerrillas to Mississippi—or to any place where black people's lives were threatened by white bigots—he added, "As far as I'm concerned, Mississippi is anywhere south of the Canadian border."

After a second trip to Africa, Malcolm returned to announce, "I'm trying to internationalize our problem, to make the Africans feel their kinship with their blood brothers in America." I had also heard that Malcolm had urged several African heads of state to sanction the U.S. in the United Nations and to call for an international tribunal on human rights. That never came to pass, but it was becoming clear that the new Malcolm might be viewed by certain special interests as more militant and dangerous than the old one. Indeed, Malcolm thought so.

The death threats escalated into actual attempts on Malcolm's life, a succession of increasingly close calls that culminated in a high-speed chase by followers of Elijah Muhammad. According to a friend who was riding with him, Malcolm picked up his walking cane and stuck it out the car window as if it were a rifle, and the assailants fell back long enough for Malcolm to reach police protection.

Soon afterward, Malcolm and his family were asleep in their Long Island home when, at about three A.M., a Molotov cocktail was thrown through the front window and set fire to the house. He had been stalling eviction by the Muslims, who owned the house, but his pregnant wife and their three children now had to take refuge with family friends while Malcolm scrambled to cover a small down payment on another house. "All I've got is about a hundred and fifty dollars," he told me on the phone, asking if I could persuade the publisher to advance him the $4000 he needed from the projected profits from the book.

For several weeks, Malcolm had been pitching himself back into the book with a sense of urgency, reviewing the final draft of the manuscript in a race to see it finished— "before they finish me." He was tormented, but less by fear of death than by the pain of being rebuffed by his own people. "I'm still too militant for the moderates," he said, "but now I'm too moderate for the militants." He was groping for a positive new role for himself, yet he sensed he wouldn't live long enough to play it. A few days later, he told a friend, "It's a time for martyrs now. But if I'm to be one, it will be in the cause of brotherhood."

A week later, Malcolm called Betty at home to tell her that the phone in his New York hotel room had just rung, and a man he didn't know had said, "Wake up, brother," and then hung up.

"You'd better not bring the kids to that meeting today," Malcolm told his wife. He would be speaking that afternoon in the Audubon Ballroom in Harlem. Betty went anyway, taking the children along, and watched in horror while four men leaped to their feet and gunned down her husband.

Malcolm was reviled as a hate-mongering demagogue and revered as a martyr to the cause of freedom. Yet, in death he "cast a spell even more far-flung and more disturbing," wrote the NAACP's Roy Wilkins, "than any he cast in life." At his funeral, Malcolm was eulogized as "our great black shining prince," and pictures of "Saint Malcolm" began to appear in homes from Harlem to the mud-and-wattle huts of Africa.

Even now, a generation later, the legend he left behind remains larger than life. Black rap groups chant his words like a litany, black teenagers wear T-shirts emblazoned with his face and black mothers name their children after him. Streets and colleges have been named in his memory. The autobiography I helped him write has become required reading in many university curriculums, more widely read by black people than any work in history other than *Roots* and the Bible. Even now, 27 years after Malcolm's death, people ask me as many questions about Malcolm X as they do about Kunta Kinte. And that number has risen dramatically since Spike Lee started production on a controversial 30 million dollar motion picture based in part on my story of Malcolm's life. Just the announcement of Lee's plan to shoot the film triggered threats from militant black groups. Poet Imamu Amiri Baraka derided Lee as a "buppie" and vowed not to "let Malcolm X's life be trashed to make middle-class Negroes sleep easier." But I doubt that any moviemaker in the world could either script or direct a film biography of Malcolm that would satisfy all the diverse groups that consider themselves rightful keepers of the flame.

Providentially, Malcolm lived long enough to return from Mecca with a vision of peaceful coexistence between the races—a vision he shared, ultimately, with his nonviolent counterpart, Martin Luther King. It was a vision left unfulfilled. But the things Malcolm X and Martin Luther King stood for—fierce pride, unflinching courage, absolute determination to win freedom from injustice—are as potent today as they were when both men were alive.

And now, just as John F. Kennedy once said, the torch has been passed to a new generation. Malcolm's daughter Attallah has joined with King's daughter Yolanda to form an organization called Nucleus, which travels the country showcasing programs of unity within the black community. It is a symbolic and symbiotic partnership: Malcolm was a champion of defiance, King an apostle of peace. Both men were tragically struck down and now live on in the hearts of their people, intertwined, indivisible, immortal.